HISTORIC PHOTOS OF
QUEENS

TEXT AND CAPTIONS BY
KEVIN SEAN O'DONOGHUE

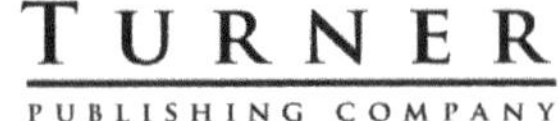

Along with Wainwright & Smith's pavilions, Playland once provided popular entertainment for the citizens of Queens. Here in 1906, throngs congregate on the beach with the amusement park and its roller coaster in the background.

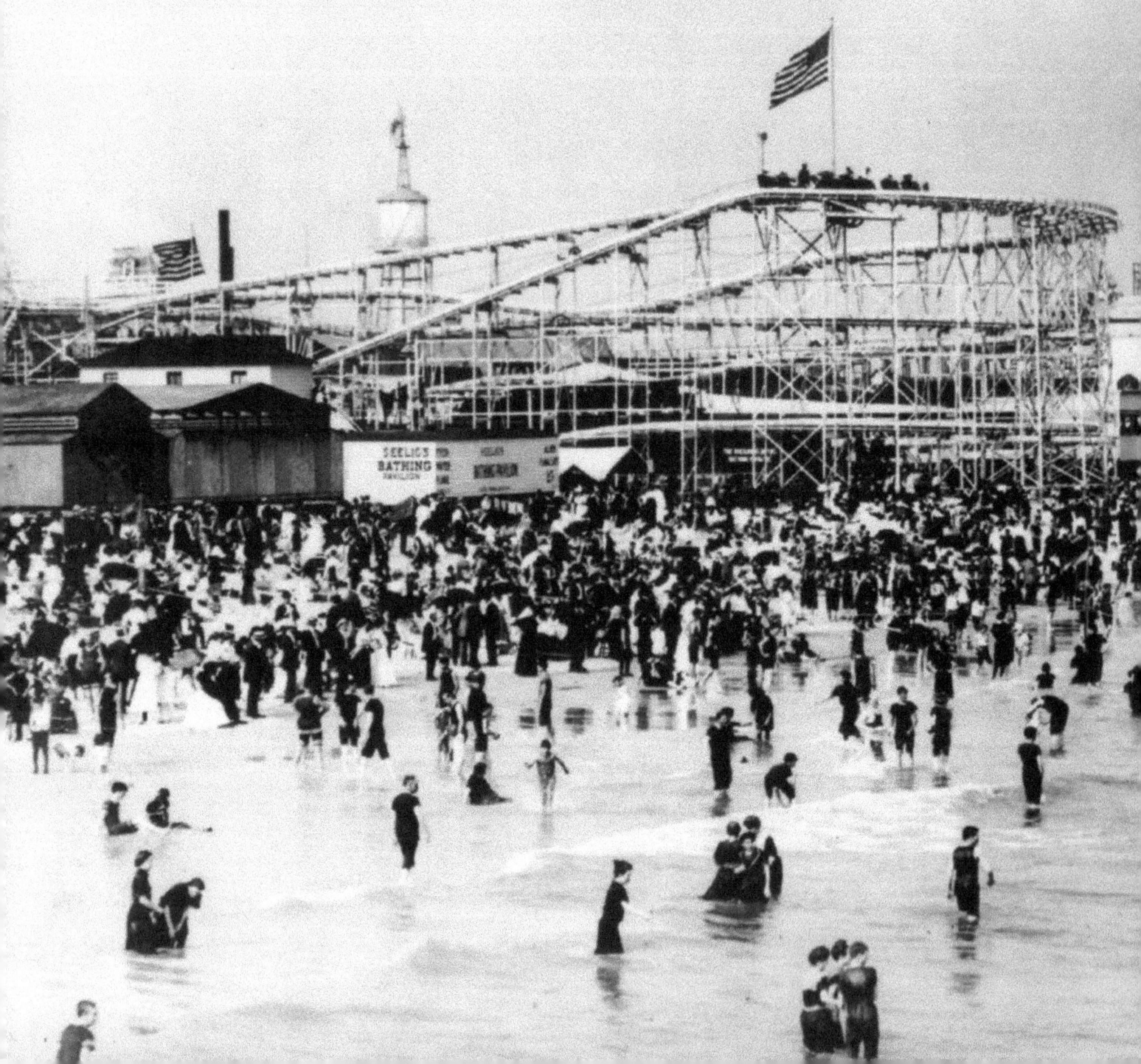

HISTORIC PHOTOS OF
QUEENS

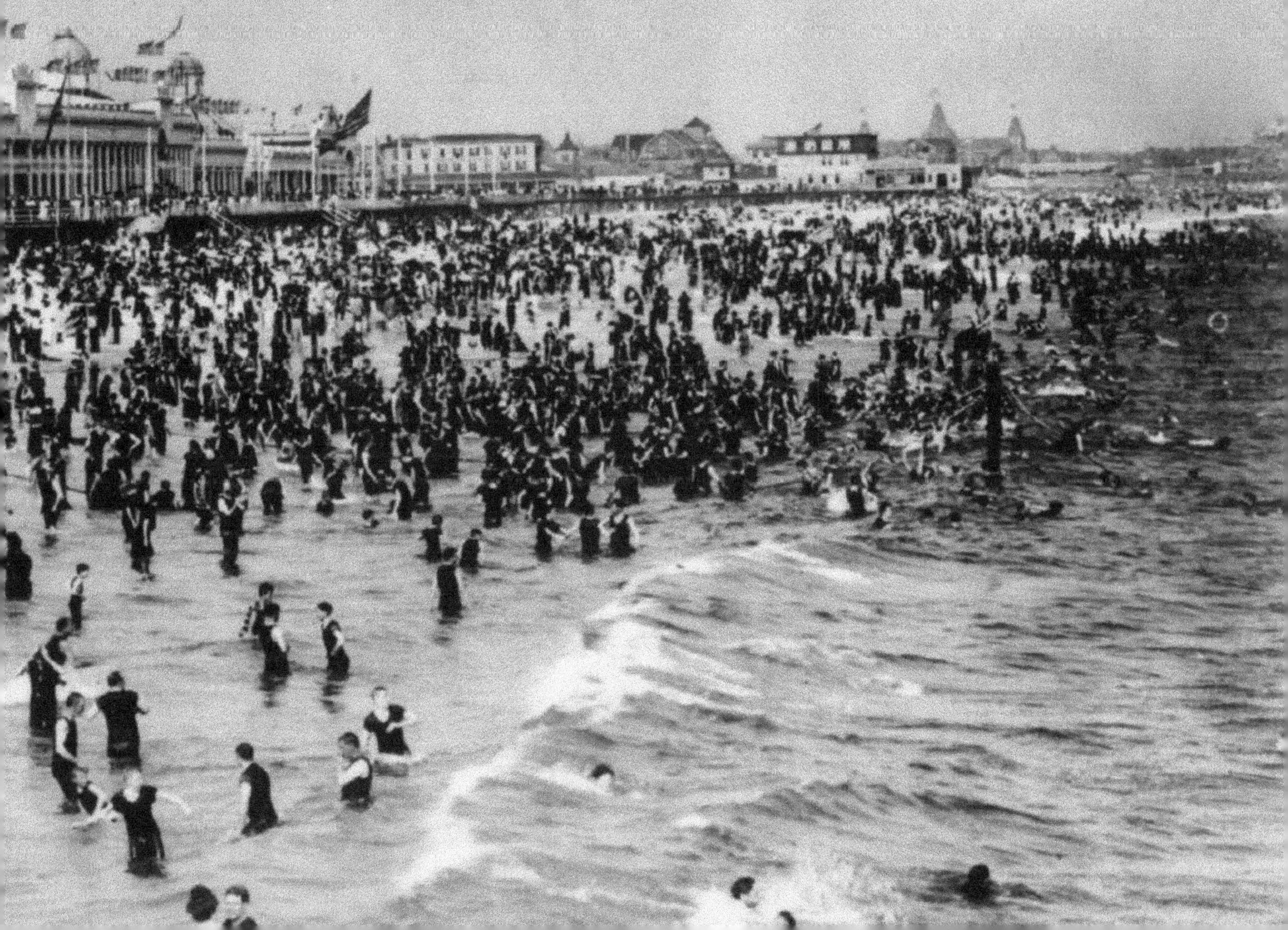

Turner Publishing Company
www.turnerpublishing.com

Historic Photos of Queens

Library of Congress Control Number: 2010921716

ISBN: 978-1-59652-573-3

Printed in the United States of America

ISBN 978-1-68442-051-3 (hc)

Contents

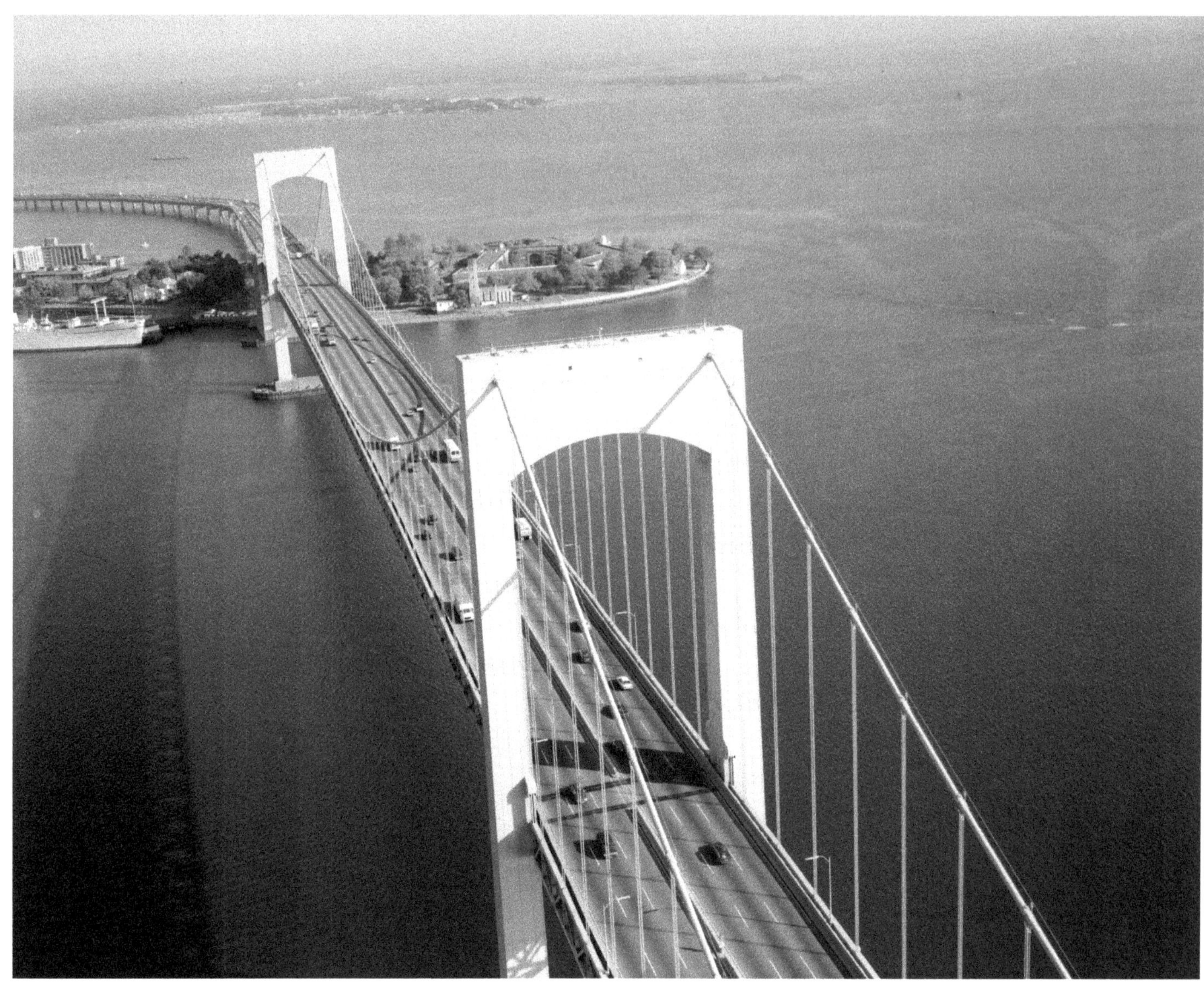

An aerial view of Queens' own "Golden Gate," the Throgs Neck Bridge, which connects the Bronx to Bayside. This view, looking south, shows Little Neck Bay with Queens stretched out in the mist in the far distance. Completed in 1961, the bridge is nearly 3,000 feet long and was designed by Othmann Amman, who was also responsible for the George Washington, Triborough, and Verrazano-Narrows suspension bridges. The Throgs Neck was built to relieve traffic build-up at the nearby Whitestone Bridge.

ACKNOWLEDGMENTS

This volume, *Historic Photos of Queens,* is the result of the cooperation and efforts of many individuals and organizations. It is with great thanks that we acknowledge the valuable contribution of the following for their generous support:

The Library of Congress
The New York State Library
The Queensboro Public Library

I would also like to thank my wife, professor Kate O'Donoghue, who patiently proofread all of my work and let me wake up late on Saturdays after I worked on the book.

Preface

Queens has thousands of historic photographs that reside in archives, both locally and nationally. This book began with the observation that, while those photographs are of great interest to many, they are not easily accessible. During a time when Queens is looking ahead and evaluating its future course, many people are asking, How do we treat the past? These decisions affect every aspect of the city—architecture, public spaces, commerce, infrastructure—and these, in turn, affect the way that people live their lives. This book seeks to provide easy access to a valuable, objective look into the history of Queens.

The power of photographs is that they are less subjective than words in their treatment of history. Although the photographer can make subjective decisions regarding subject matter and how to capture and present it, photographs seldom interpret the past to the extent textual histories can. For this reason, photography is uniquely positioned to offer an original, untainted look at the past, allowing the viewer to learn for himself what the world was like a century or more ago.

This project represents countless hours of review and research. The researchers and writer have reviewed thousands of photographs in numerous archives. We greatly appreciate the generous assistance of the individuals and organizations listed in the acknowledgments of this work, without whom this project could not have been completed.

The goal in publishing this work is to provide broader access to this set of extraordinary photographs that seek to inspire, provide perspective, and evoke insight that might assist people who are responsible for determining the future of Queens. In addition, the book seeks to preserve the past with adequate respect and reverence.

With the exception of touching up imperfections that have accrued with the passage of time and cropping where necessary, no changes have been made. The focus and clarity of many images are limited to the technology and the ability of the photographer at the time they were recorded.

The work is divided into eras. Beginning with some of the earliest known photographs of Queens, the first section takes a look at the closing decades of the nineteenth century. The second section spans the metamorphosis of Queens from a rural to an urban borough, from the beginning of the twentieth century to the eve of the Great Depression. Section Three takes focuses on the 1930s. The last section covers the World War II and postwar era to recent times. In each of these sections we have made an effort to capture various aspects of life through our selection of photographs. People, commerce, transportation, infrastructure, religious institutions, and educational institutions have been included to provide a broad perspective.

We encourage the citizens of and visitors to Queens to think about the city as they stroll its parks and move about its neighborhoods. It is the publisher's hope that in utilizing this work, longtime residents will learn something new and that new residents will gain a perspective on where Queens has been, so that each can contribute to its future.

—Todd Bottorff, Publisher

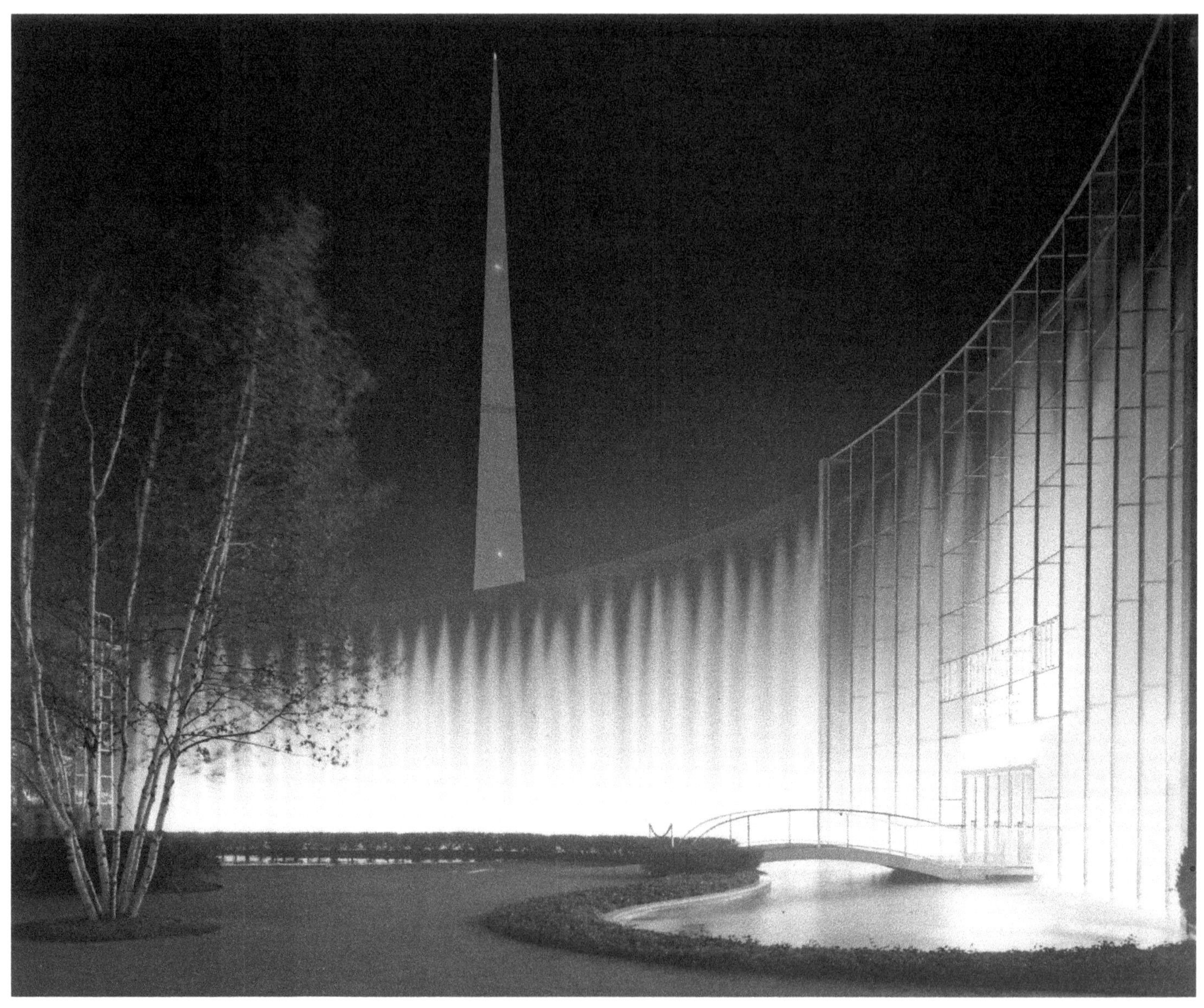

The 1939 New York World's Fair was held in Flushing Meadows and was one of the largest of all time. Shown here are the Consolidated Edison lighted fountains and the 700-foot-tall Trylon. New York would host another world's fair on the same site in 1964.

A Shrinking County, a Growing Borough

(1880s–1899)

It wasn't until 1897 that Queens County became the Borough of Queens. From its earliest history in the seventeenth century, when Queens encompassed most of Long Island as one of New York State's original counties, it has been uniquely situated—close to "the City" but not quite urban, with its broad expanses of greenery and waterfronts drawing vacationers and permanent residents for centuries.

By the late nineteenth century, the western parts of Queens—Long Island City, the Village of Astoria, Newton, and as far east as Flushing had been settled and partially developed. The Dutch still had a strong role in the area, as did many of the British who stayed around after the Revolution. But in the century since American independence, other immigrants had arrived as well and it had already become as diverse as it was large, at one point stretching into what is now Suffolk County.

Still, with incorporation into New York City, new alliances had to be made and old grudges set aside. The railroads were bringing more than vacationers out to the area—permanent residents were settling from Elmhurst in the north to Queens Village in the east to Rockaway in the south. This was a new beginning—this was the Borough of Queens.

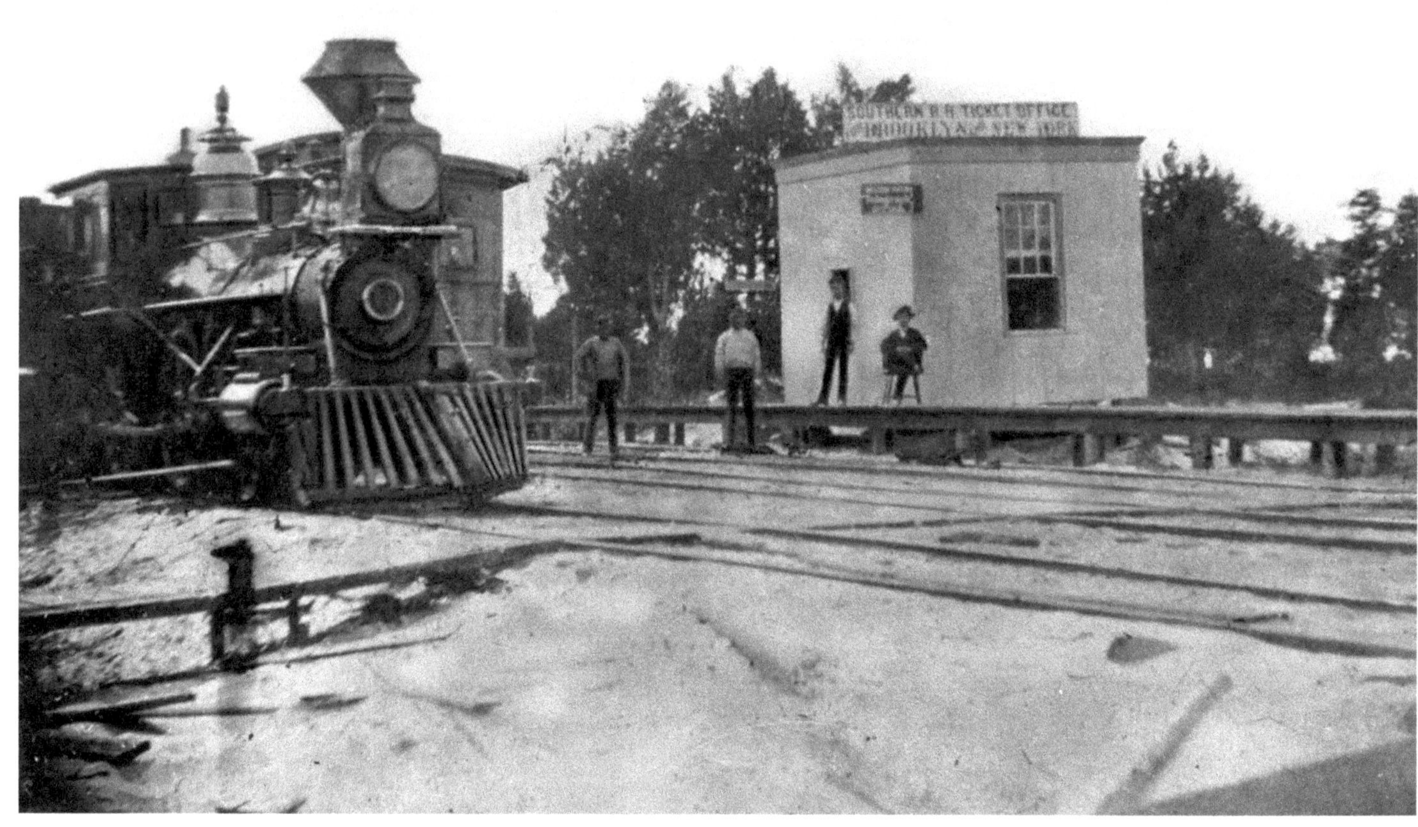

The Southern Railroad was an early competitor of the Long Island Railroad, running from Brooklyn to Montauk on part of what is now the LIRR's Main Line. The LIRR eventually assumed control of the Southern's lines, including this one in Far Rockaway, which brought early city dwellers to the Atlantic beaches.

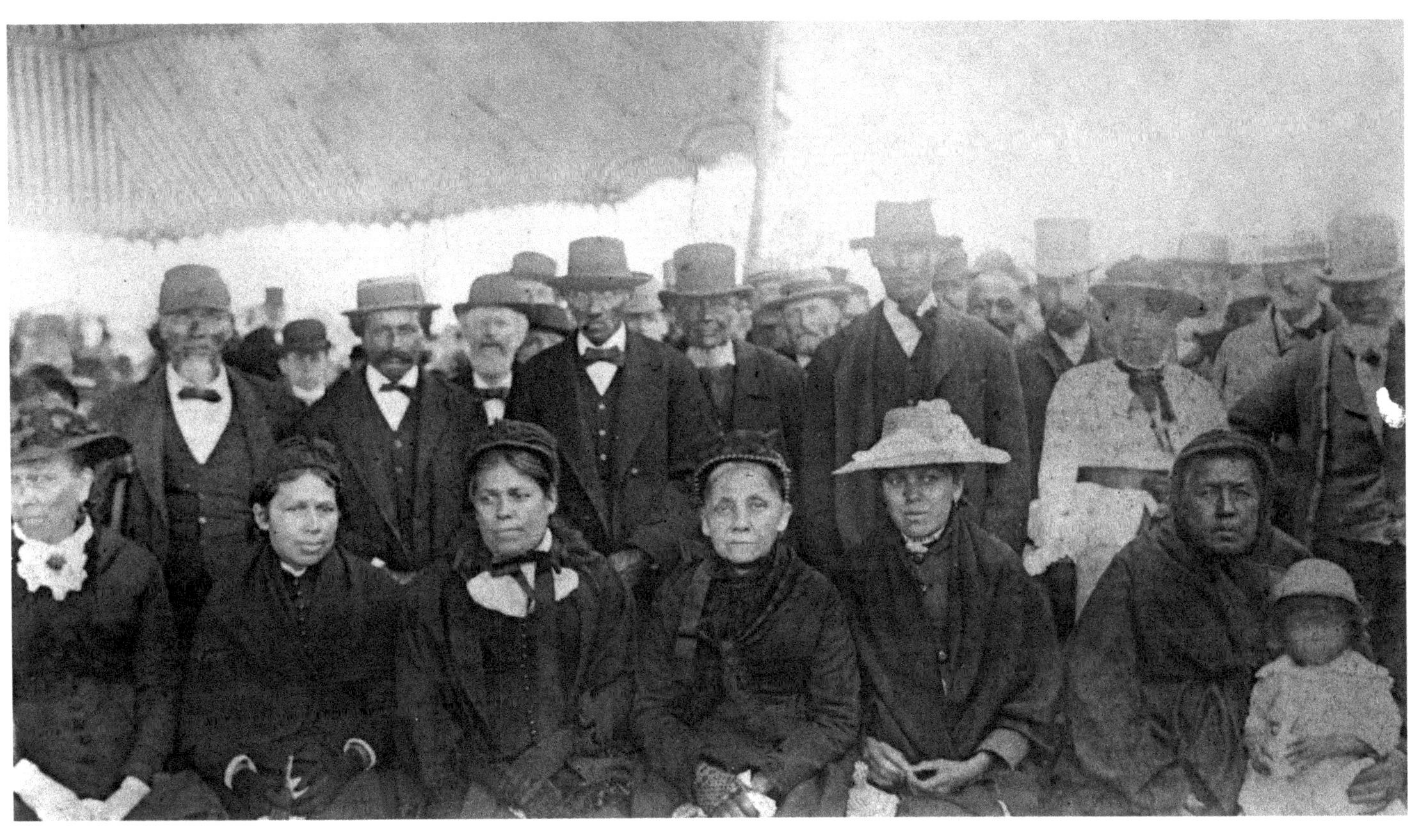

Disease reduced the Shinnecock Nation to about 200 members in the late nineteenth century. The tribe has faced multiple "extinction" rumors as demonstrated by the title "Last of the Shinnecock Indians" on this photograph taken in Flushing in 1884. However, the tribe continues to have a presence on eastern Long Island, including a reservation where 600 people reside, adjacent to the town of Southampton.

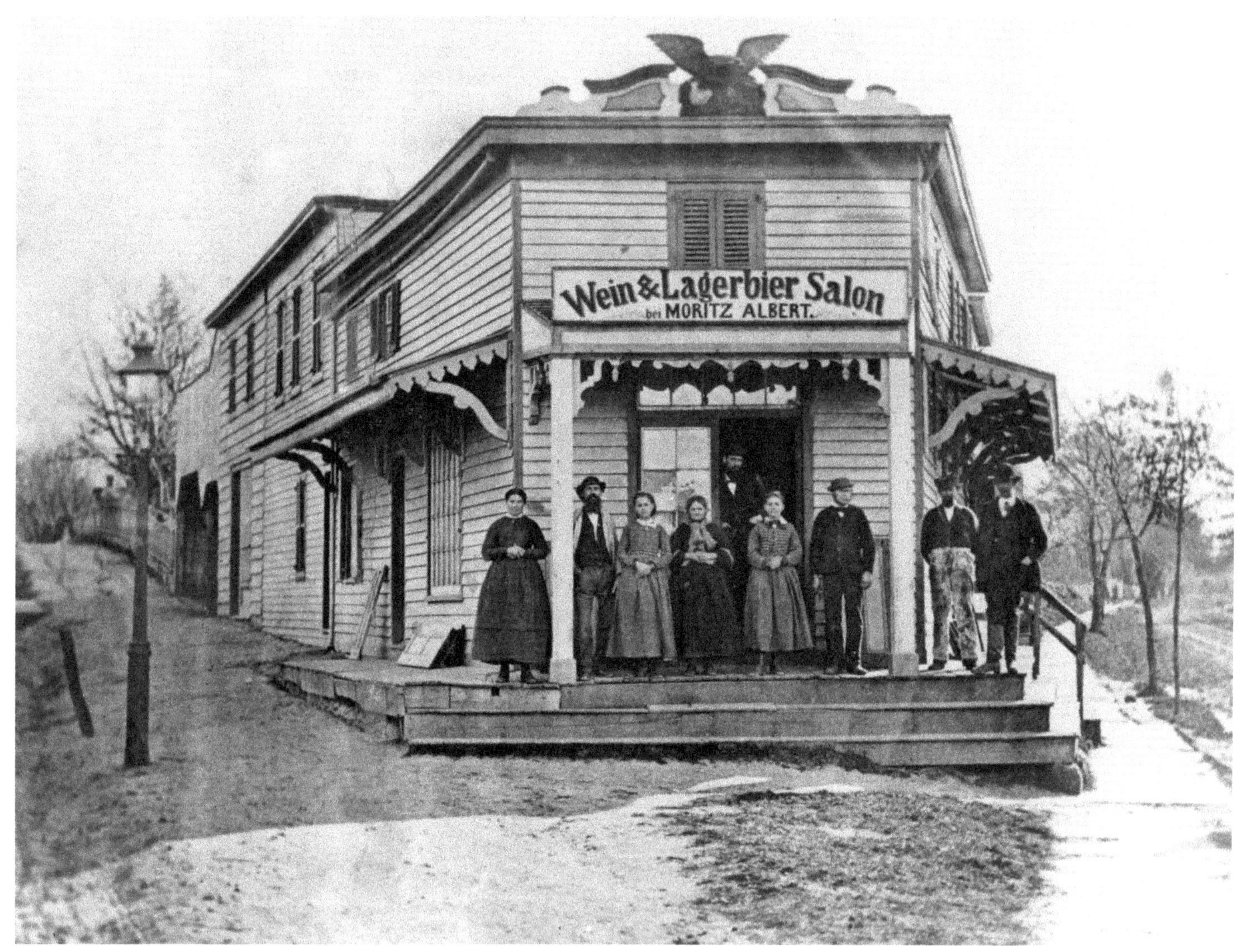

This photograph shows Albert Moritz's tavern at the intersection of Astoria Boulevard and Newtown Road, located in what had been the Village of Astoria. The village joined the newly incorporated Long Island City when it split from the town of Newton, one of the original towns composing Queens County.

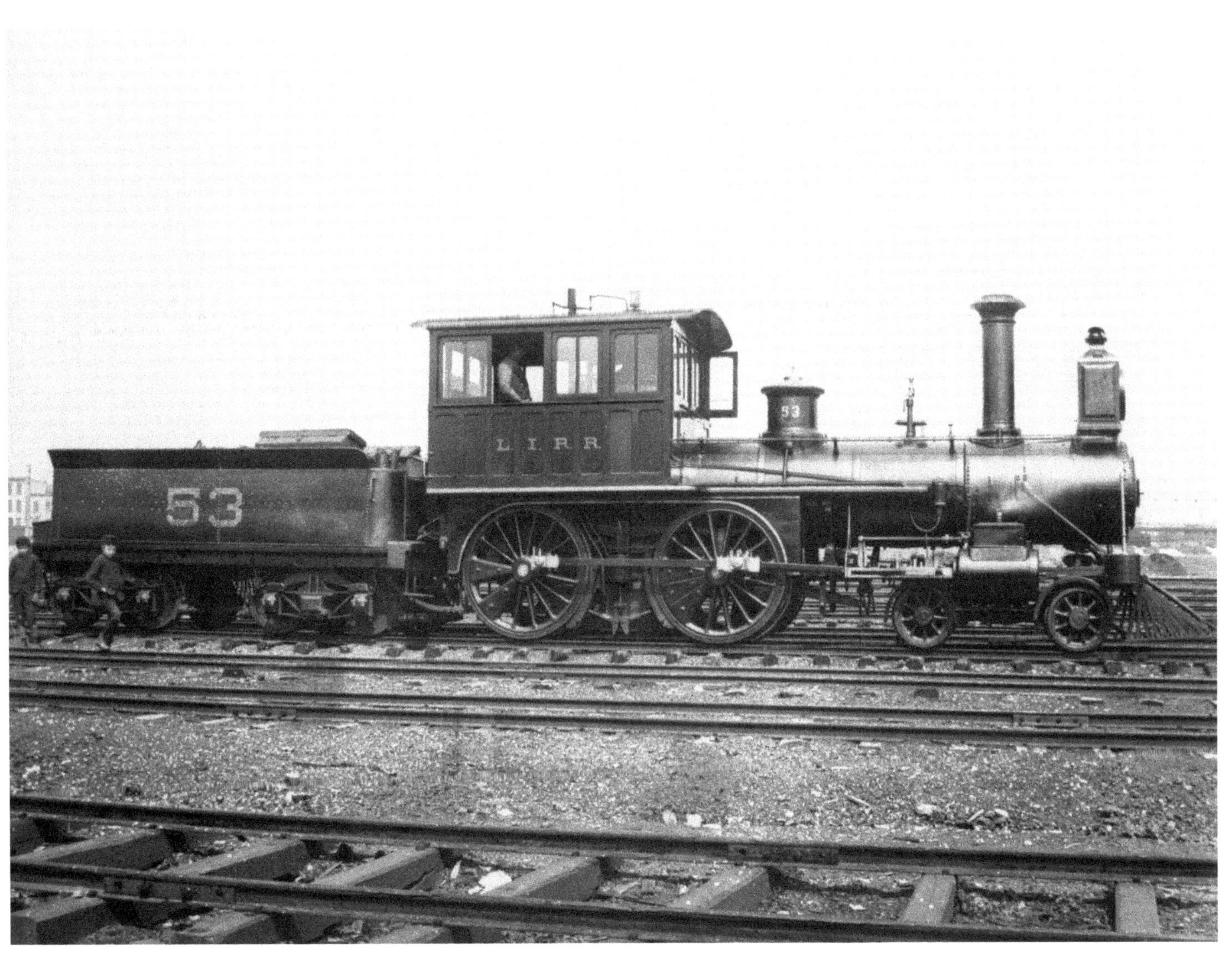

The venerable Long Island Railroad once transported more than just passengers along its lines and was a conduit both into and out of New York City. Its lines crossed the full length of Queens, which at the time stretched deep into what is now Suffolk County. Here the 4-4-0 Engine no. 53 is seen pulling freight through the Long Island City yards.

This mill, identified as "Wilson's Mill," stood in what would have been the Village of Astoria. At the time, Astoria was a recreational area for wealthy citizens, who built large vacation homes in the countryside just across the river from Manhattan.

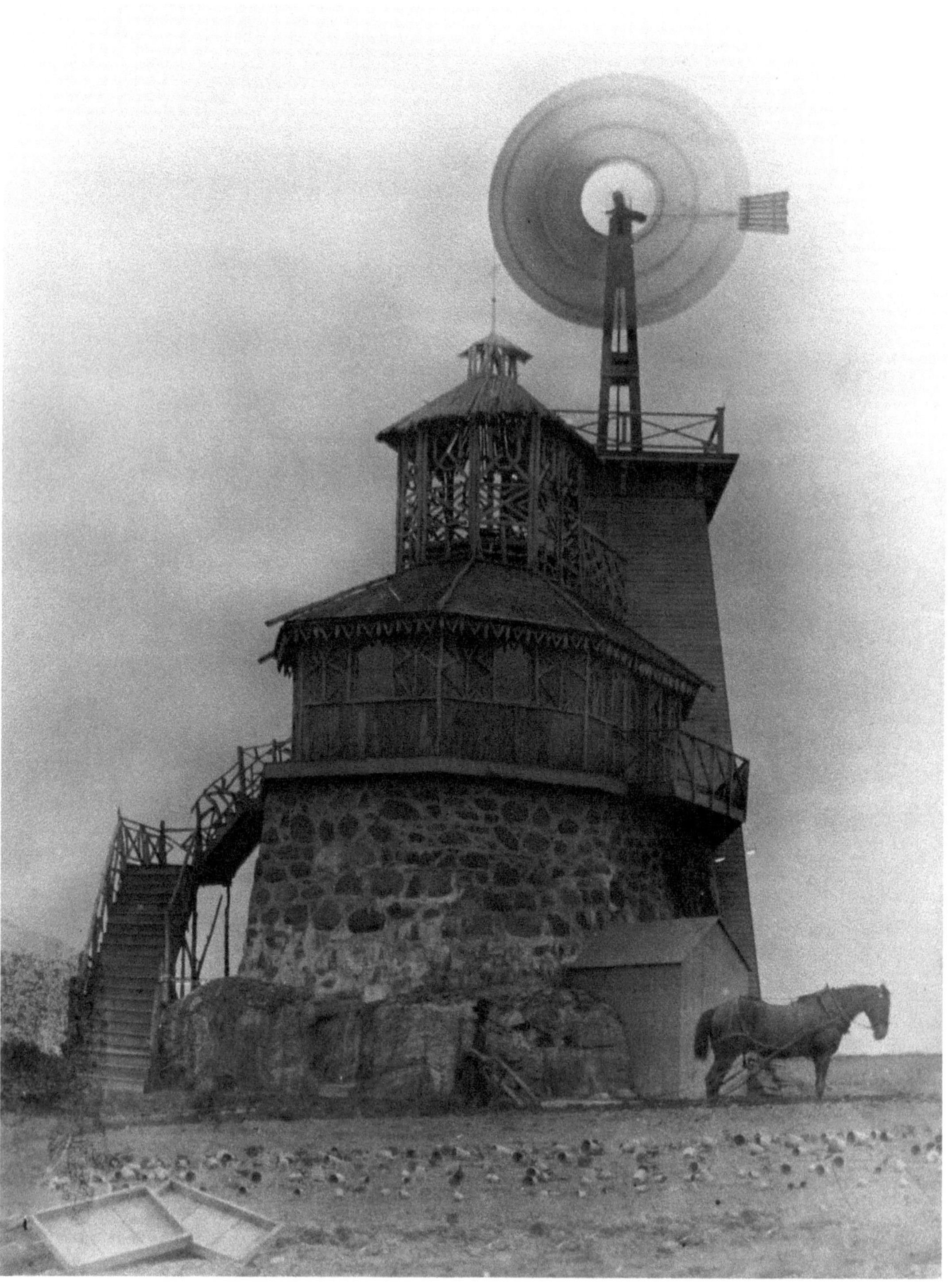

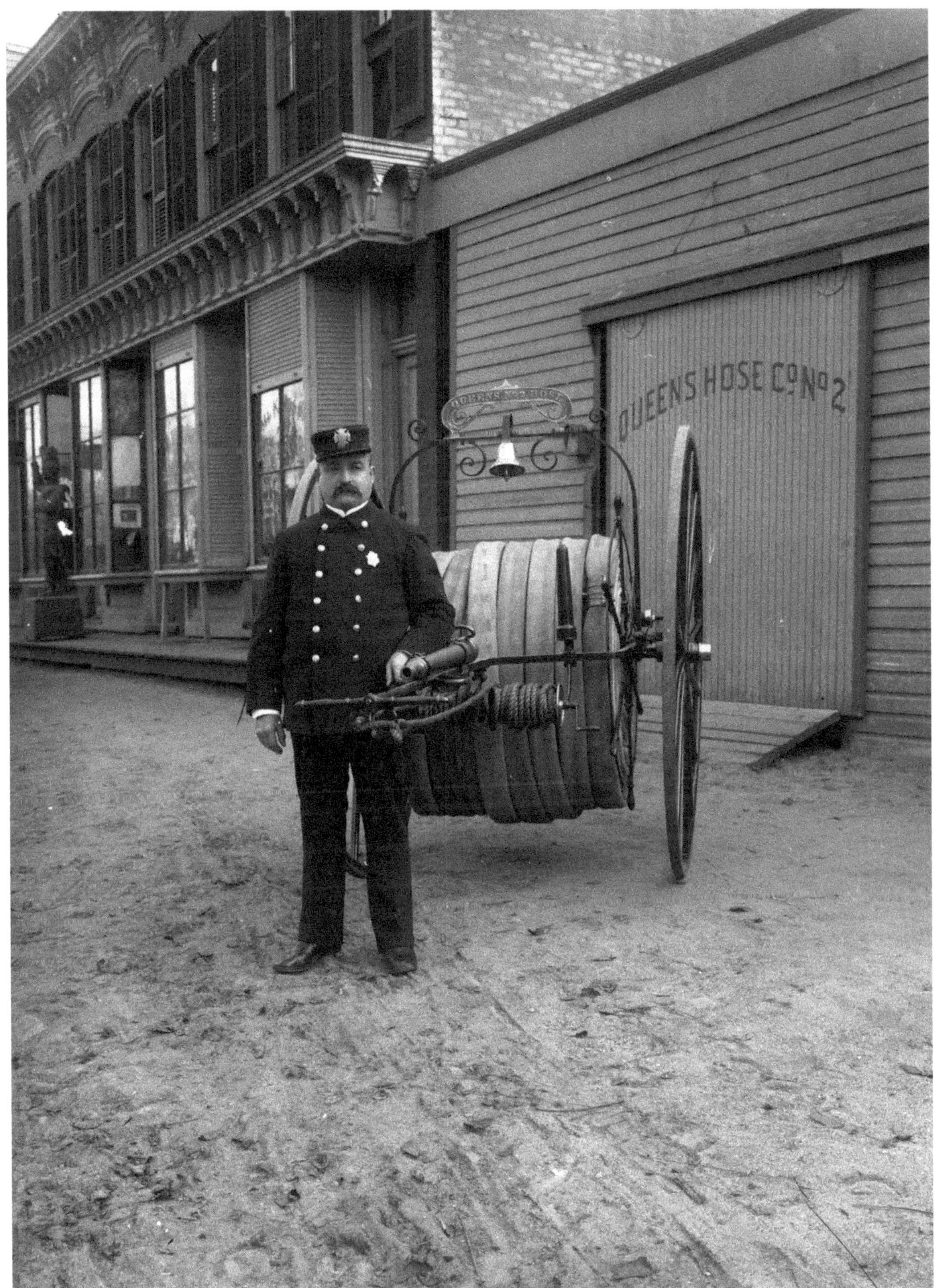

This fire fighter is identified as George Barb, of Queens Hose Company No. 2, located in Queens Village on the eastern side of the town of Jamaica. Mr. Barb is shown with a hand-drawn "hose cart"—cutting-edge fire-fighting technology at the time. Fire companies were proud of their organizations and frequently competed in parades and other public demonstrations.

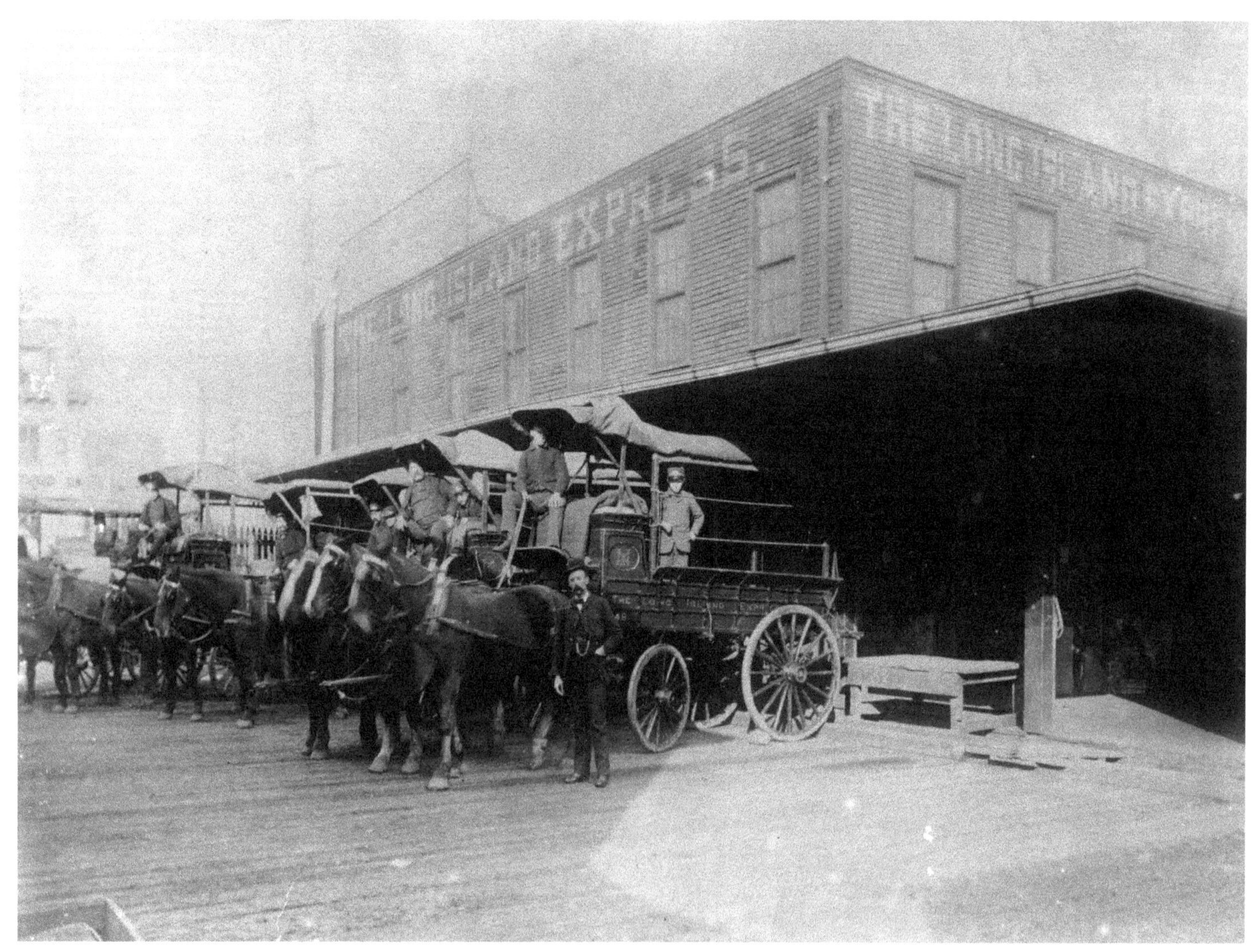

The Long Island Express was a baggage and trunk delivery service that was provided by the Long Island Railroad to its customers. Here a company of drivers pose atop their horse-drawn "trucks" outside the Express building in Long Island City.

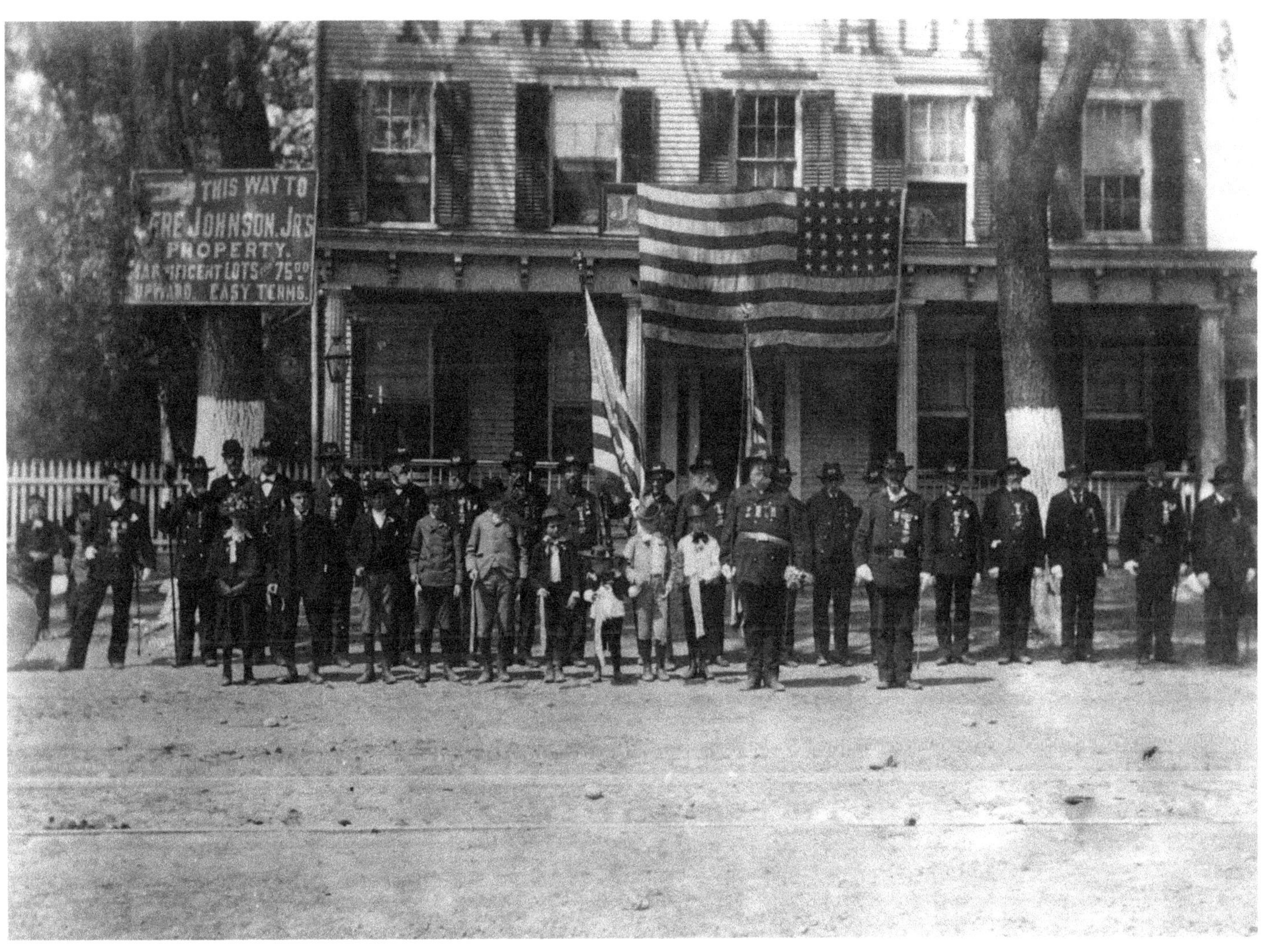

A group of Civil War veterans pose with local children on "Decoration Day" (now celebrated as Memorial Day) in front of the Newtown Hotel at the intersection of Broadway and Maurice Avenue on May 30, 1891, with the Stars and Stripes oddly displayed in reverse. The veterans are likely from the Robert Marks Post, Grand Army of the Republic.

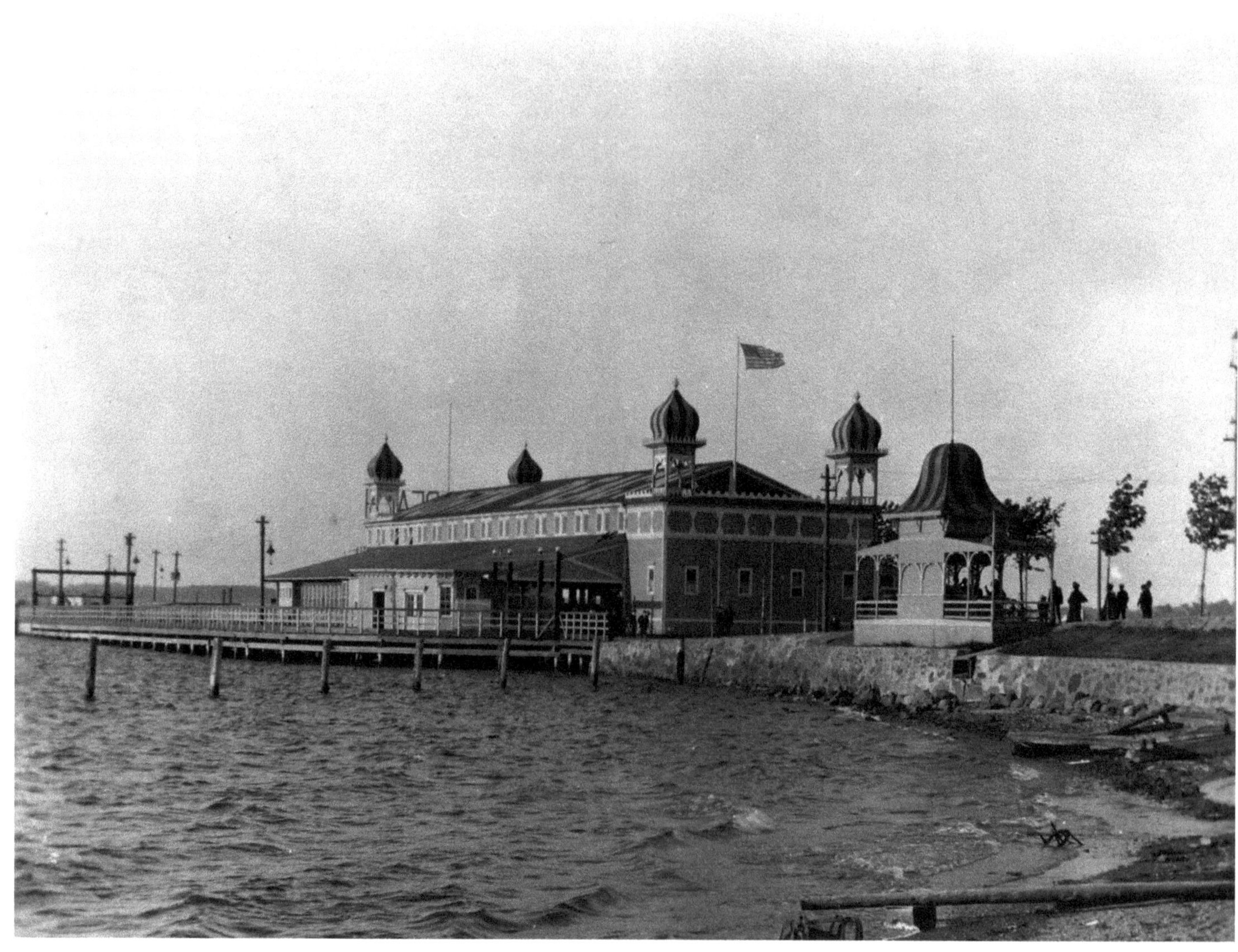

The 300-foot-long Grand Pier in North Beach (Elmhurst) accommodated steamships and ferries from upper Manhattan, the Bronx, and eastern Queens. The fanciful pavilions, which were part of the casino resort atmosphere and featured food and live music, could accommodate 2,000 people. LaGuardia Airport now encompasses much of the original North Beach area.

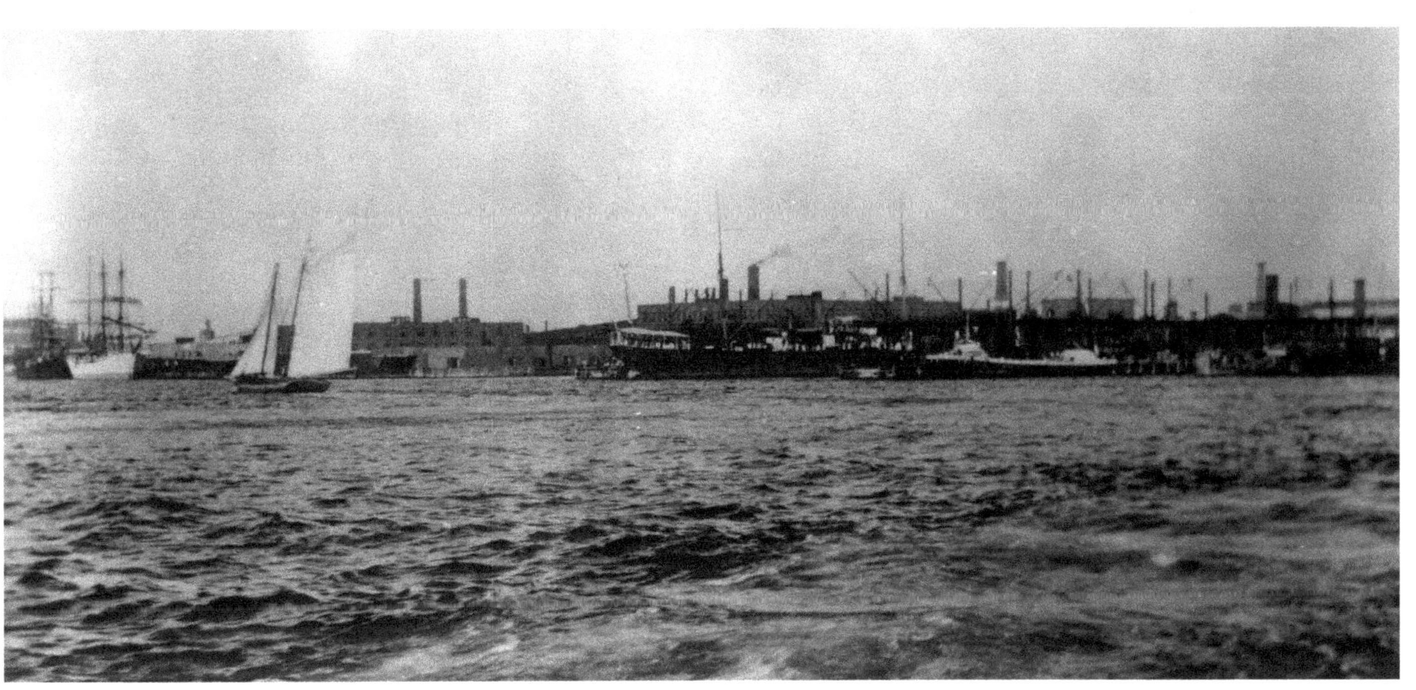

This view from 1895 illustrates the smokestacks and shipping ports that made Long Island City the industrial center of Queens. Today the area remains industrialized, although in recent years it has become a fashionable neighborhood of residential lofts, in former factory buildings, and high-rise condominiums with views of the Manhattan skyline.

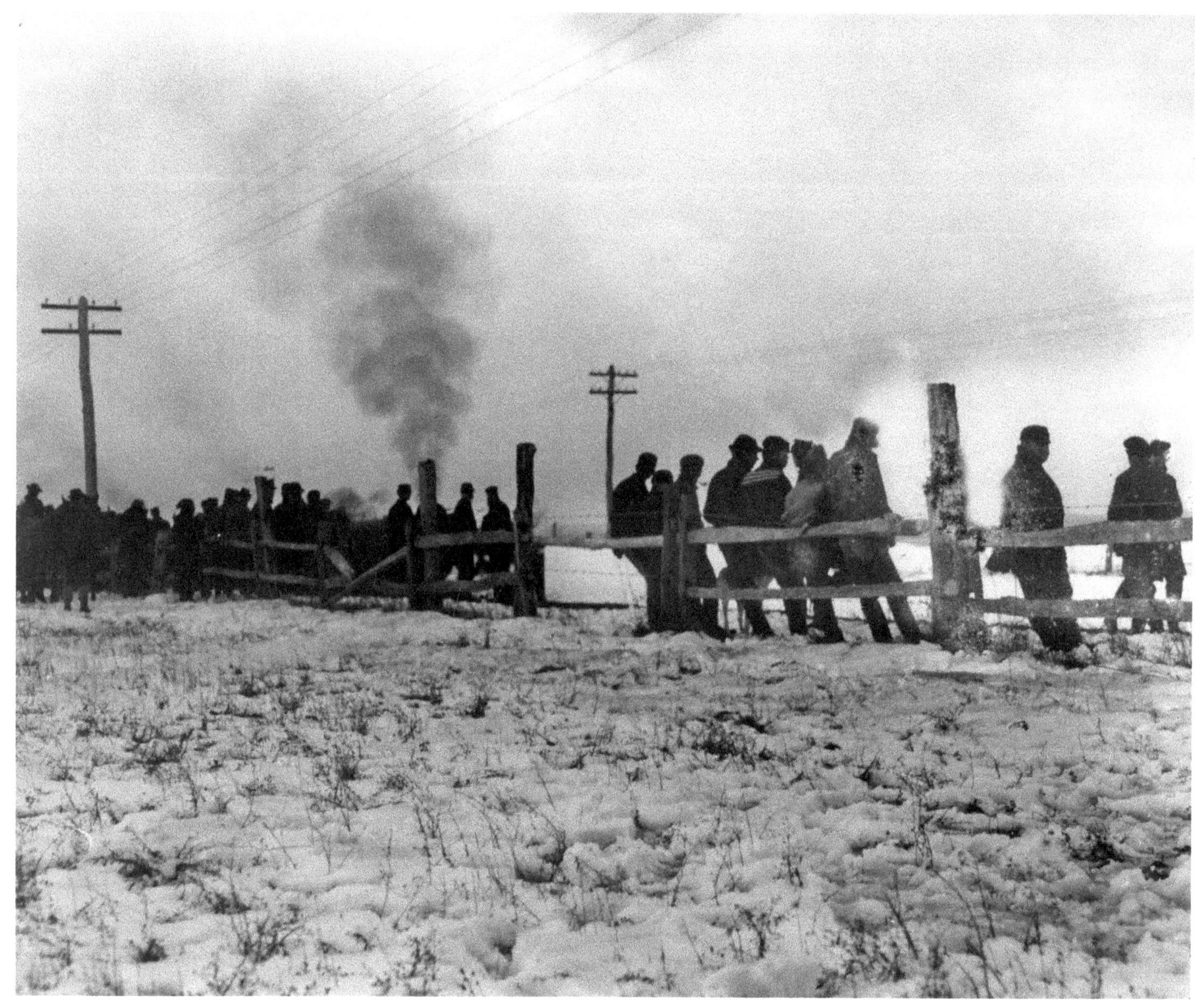

Groups of men lean against a fence in Queens Village in November 1898 looking at the scene of a massive Long Island Railroad accident involving the "triple-header" Russell "Wedge" snowplow. The trains were among the most dangerous to operate—as the rails were cleared, their flanger blades threw snow against engine windows, dimming visibility.

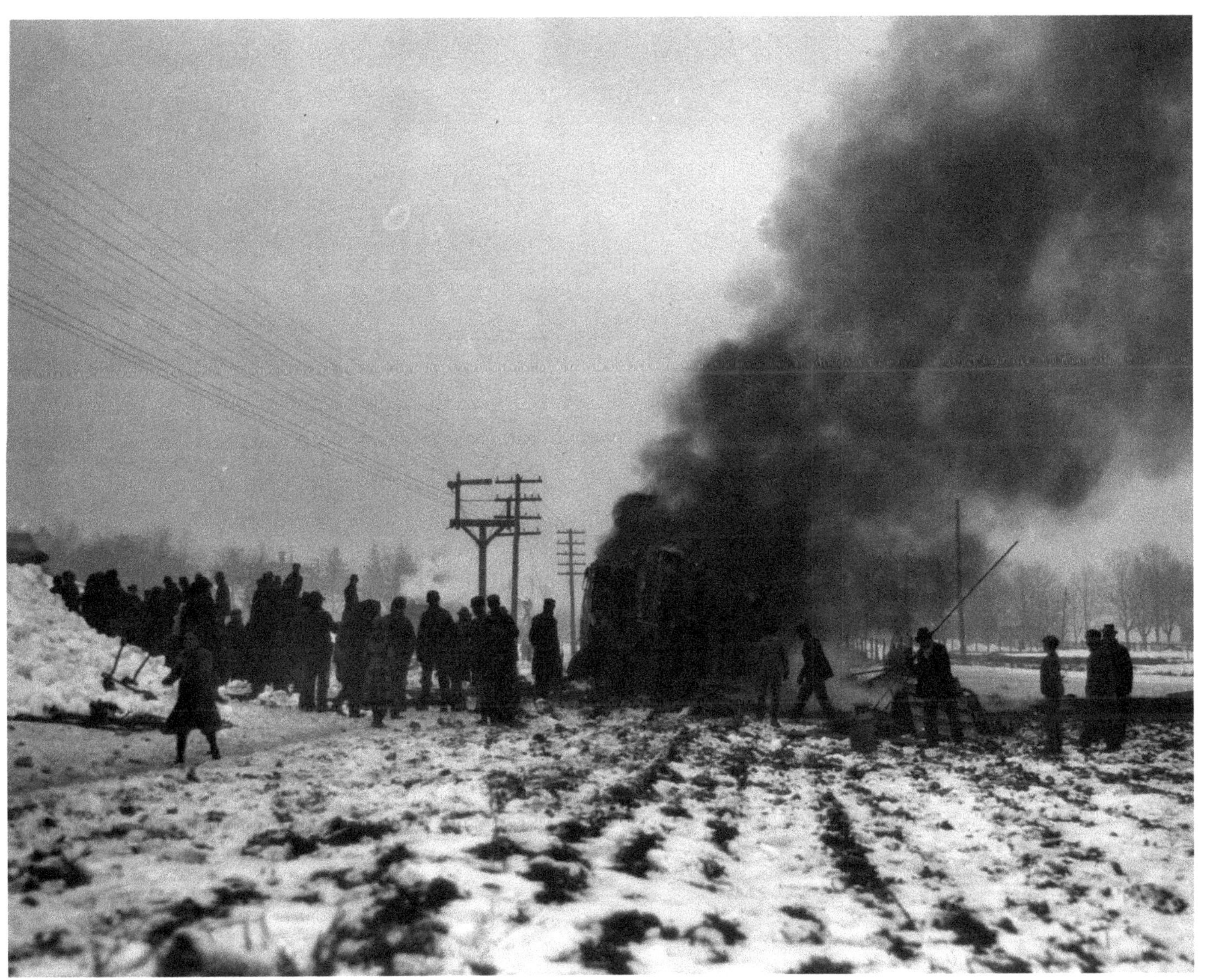

Amid the burning wreckage following the derailment in November 1898, large groups gather at the site, in Queens Village, on what is now the eastern border between Queens and Nassau counties.

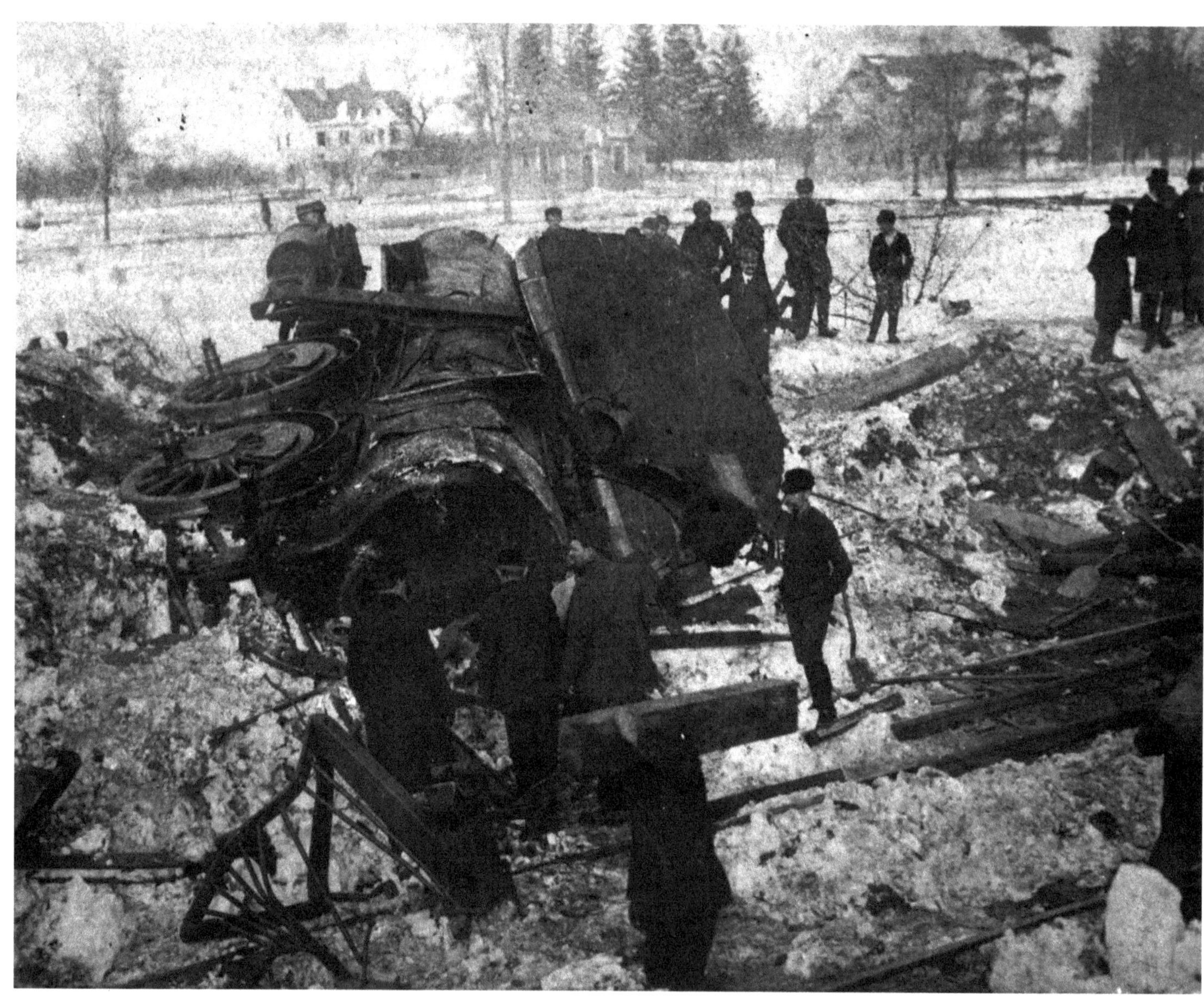

The derailed and burned Russell Wedge plow engine lies on its side in utter ruin.

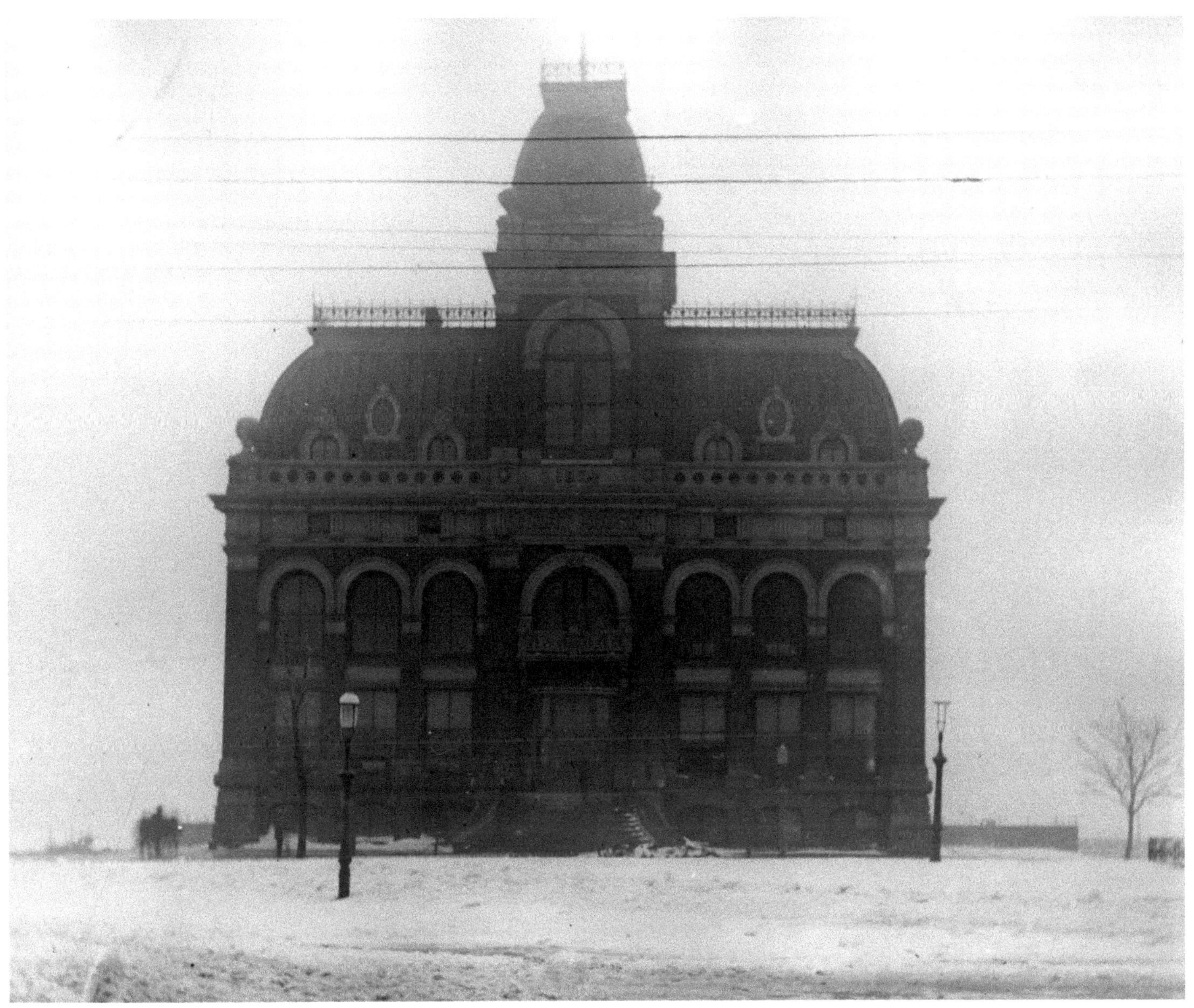

The Long Island City Courthouse was built between 1872 and 1876—overcoming scandals and budget overruns. The building was built in the French Empire style and stood more than two stories tall. Gutted by a fire in 1908, it was redesigned by Long Island City architect Peter M. Coco, who replaced the original design (seen here in 1899) with Neoclassical elements. The courthouse remains in use by the New York State Unified Court System today for hearings in Queens County.

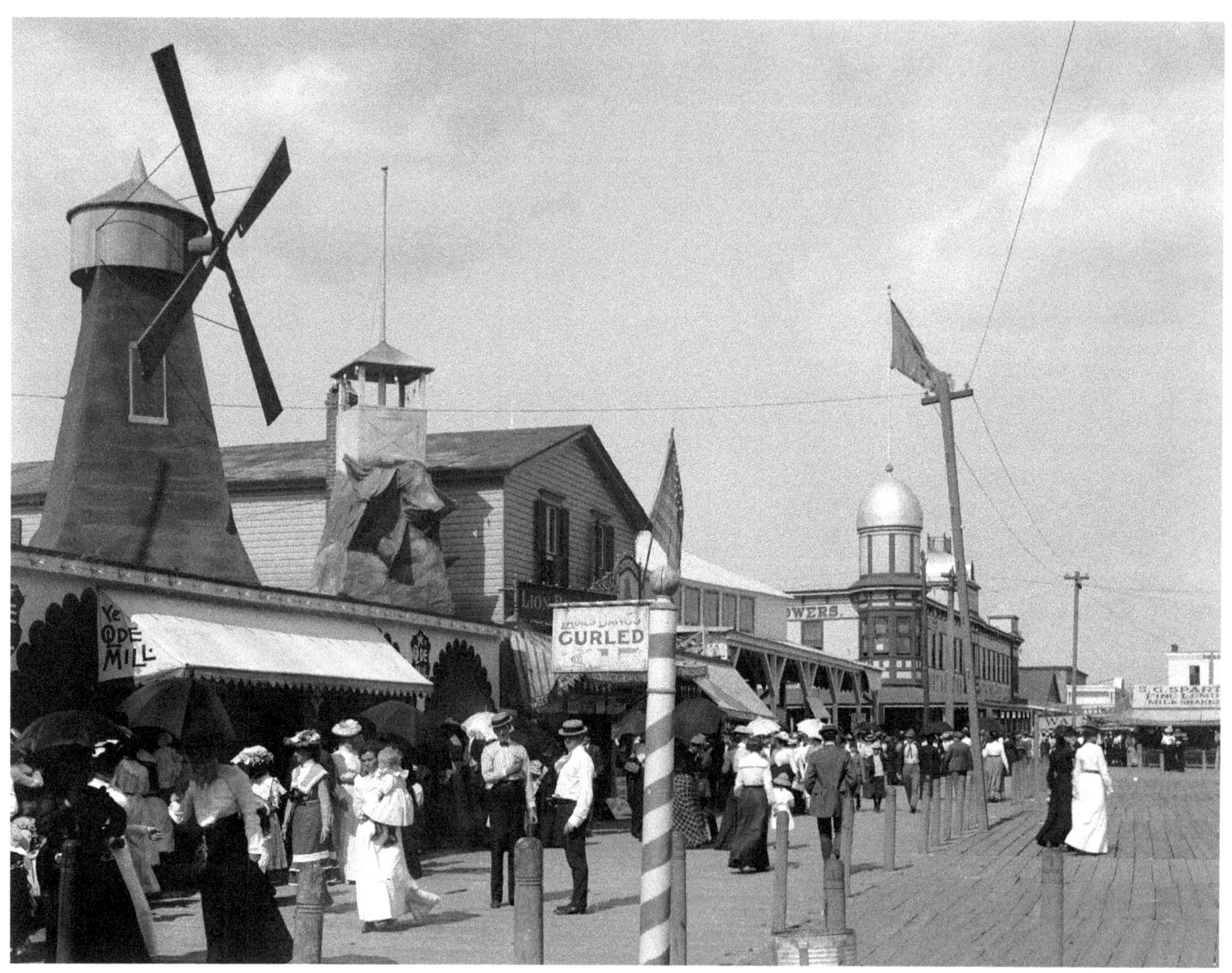

The Rockaway boardwalk continued to be popular in the early part of the twentieth century. Seen here in 1900 is an establishment called "Ye Olde Mill"—perhaps built to give visitors a sense of "old Queens," which had experienced significant changes in the past decade.

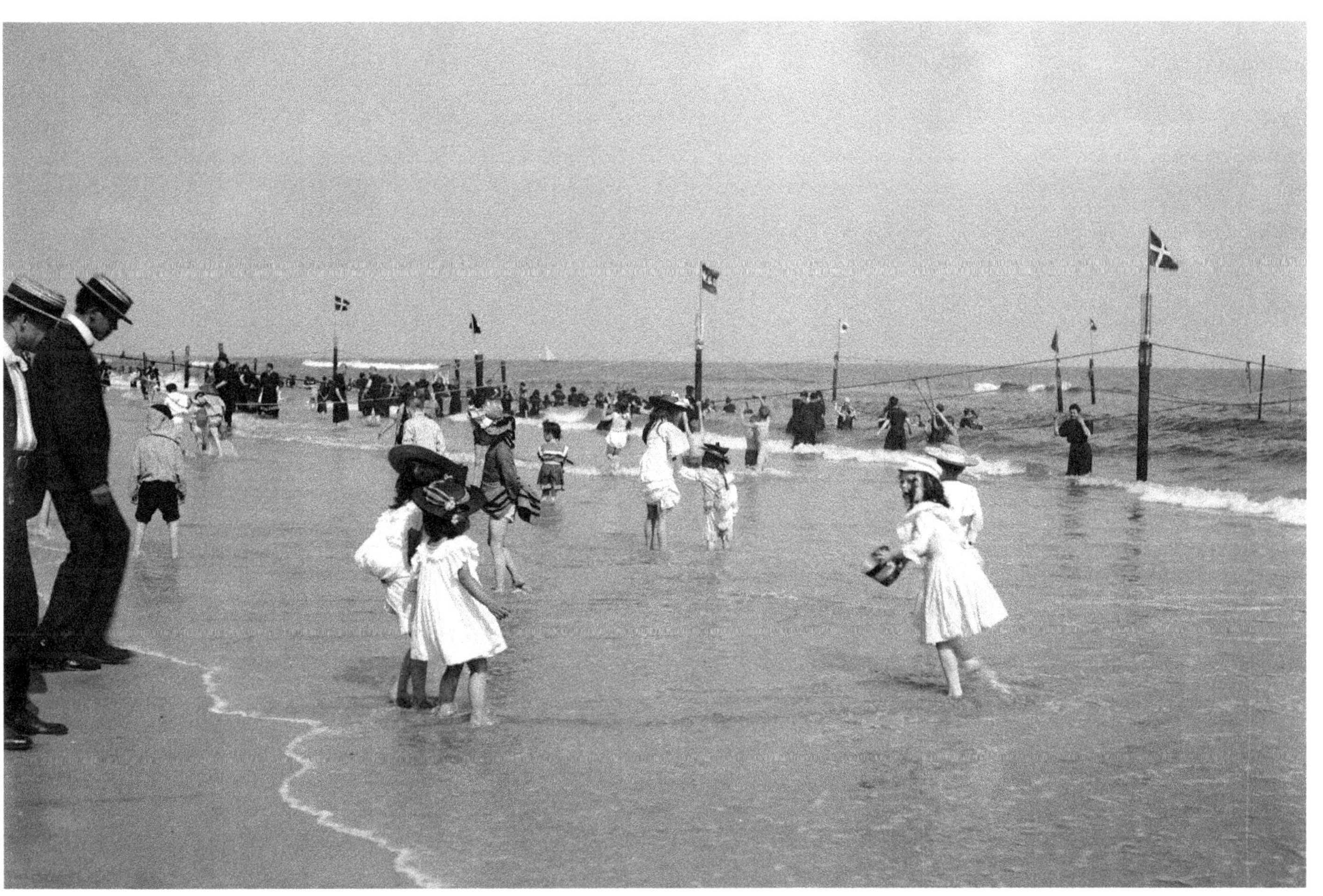

In the early twentieth century, Americans dressed up for the beach. Here children frolick in their Sunday best (minus stockings and shoes) while adults watch over them. The ropes visible in the image were strung out into the surf to assist the able-bodied with rescues, since beachgoers often did not know how to swim and the undertow could be dangerous.

The LIRR played an important role in the development of Queens in the twentieth century. Seen here in the winter of 1900 is a 4-4-0 engine, carrying both passengers and freight from Long Island City to points east.

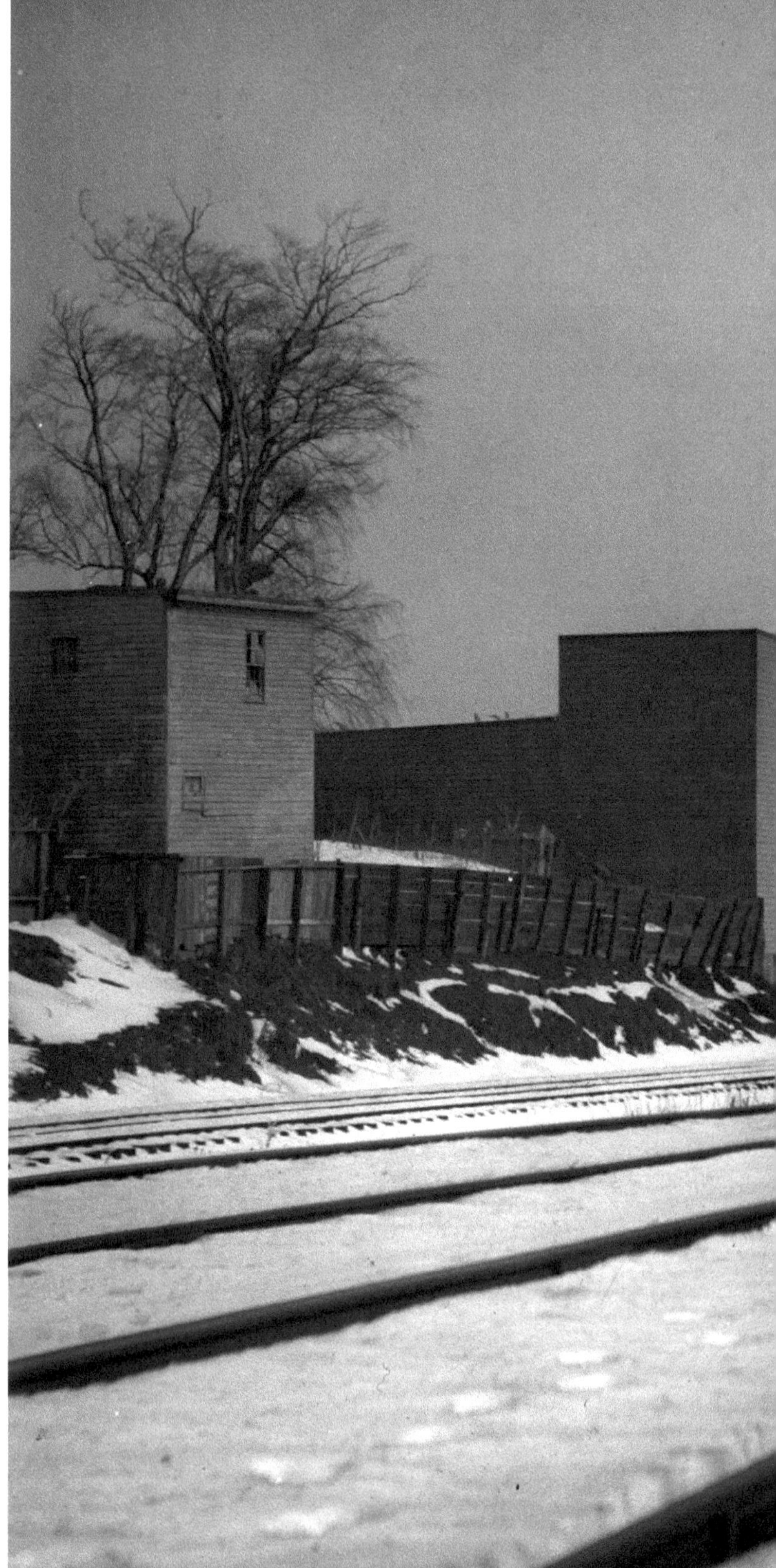

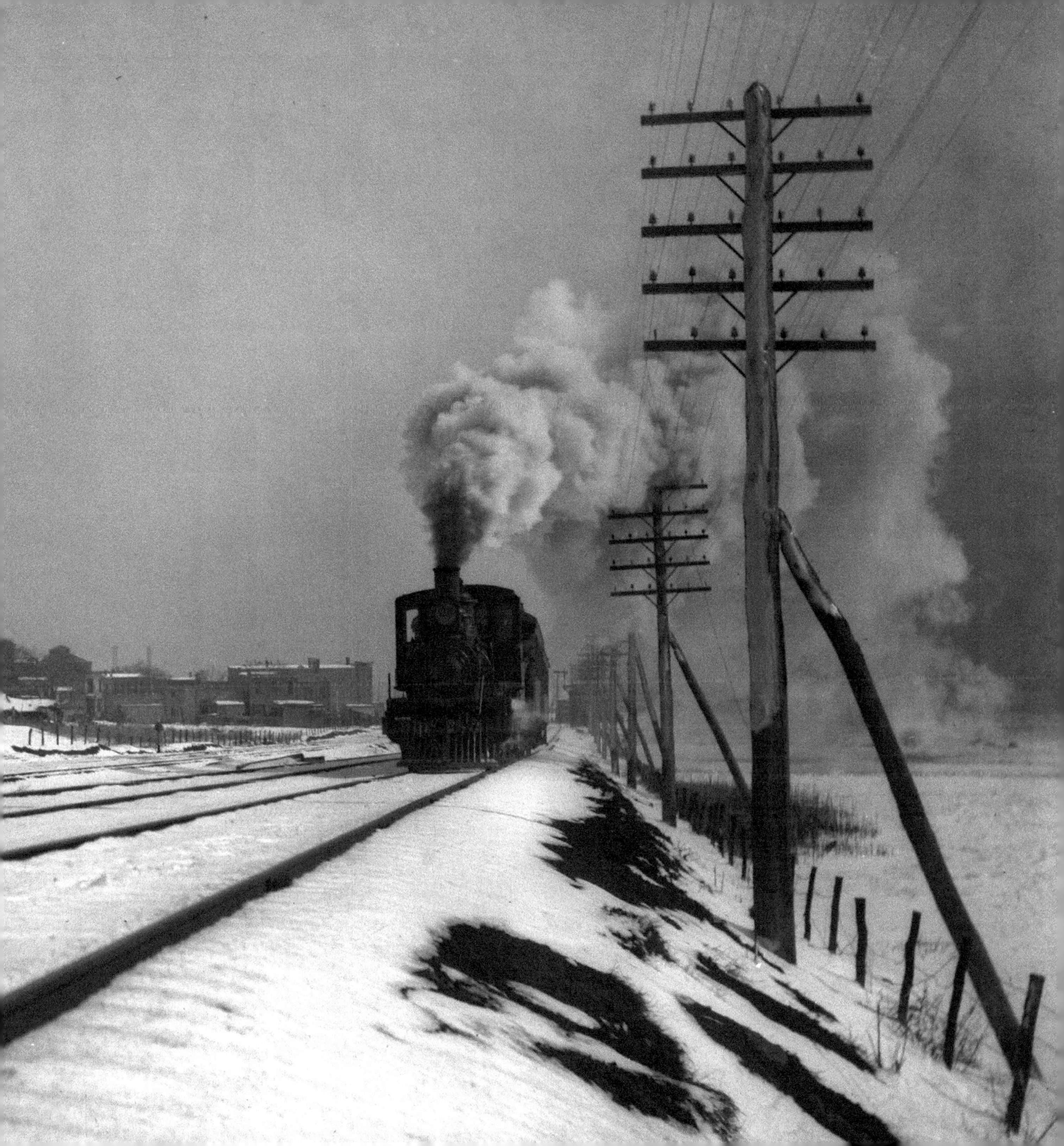

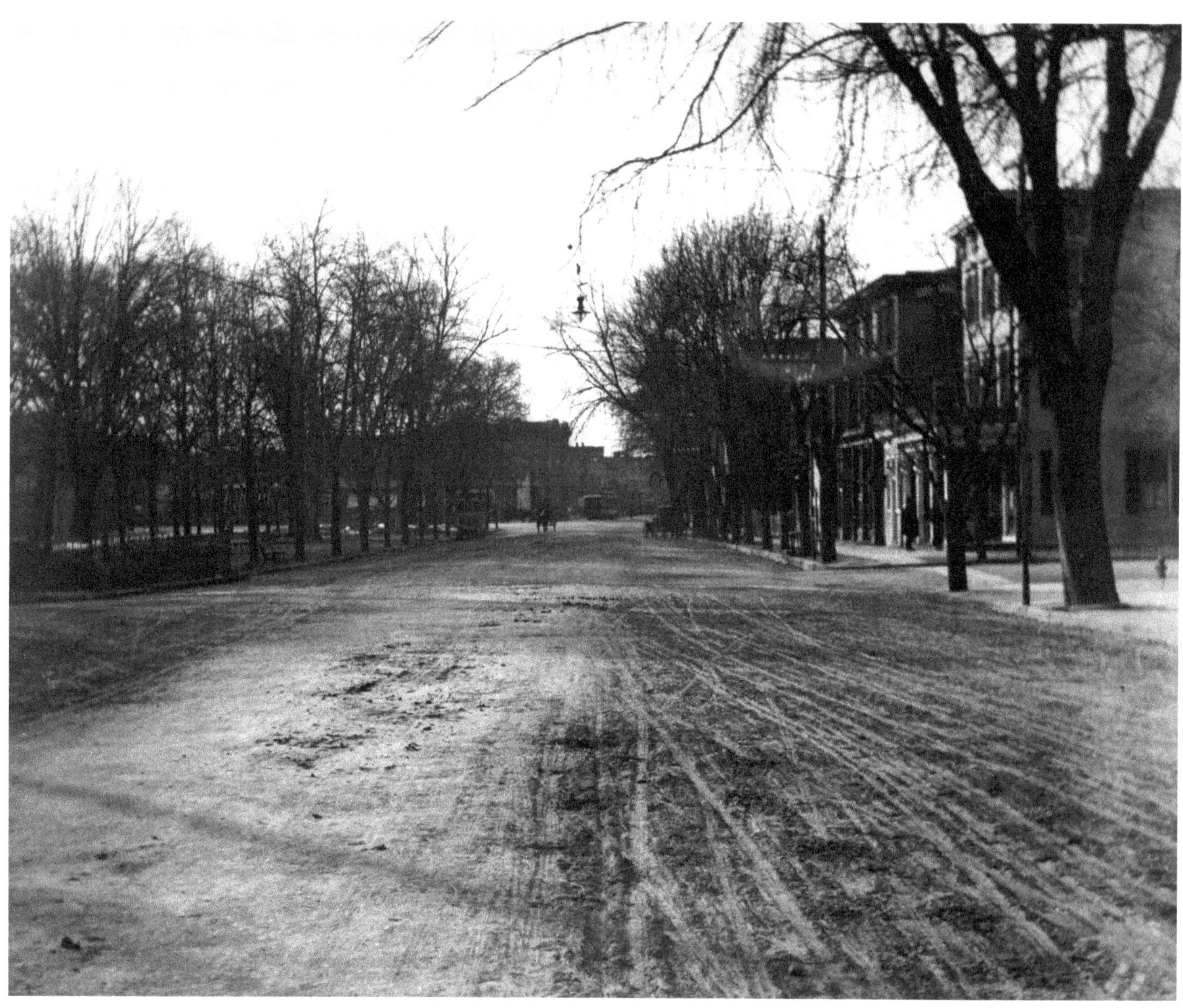

A view of Flushing's Broadway looking west. Since renamed Northern Boulevard, this was a main street, bisecting the borough and continuing into Nassau County. To the far left of the frame in an area known as Flushing Greens is a Civil War monument, erected in 1866 as a tribute to the men of Flushing who perished fighting for the Union. Daniel Carter Beard Square is located today in the wooded area visible at left.

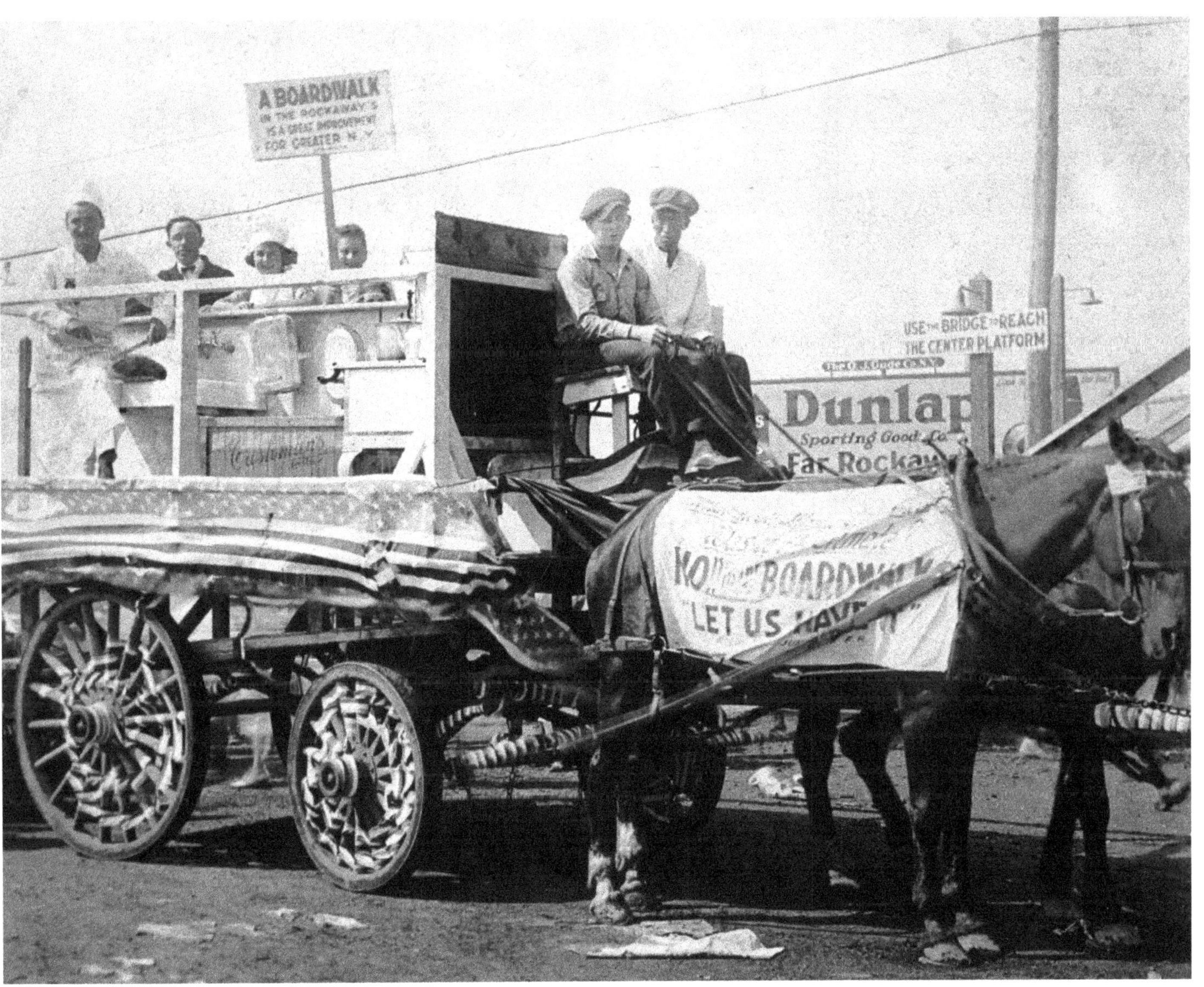

In a showing of some turn-of-the-century civic activism, a horse-drawn carriage drives through Far Rockaway in 1900. The signs push for the Rockaway boardwalk, which served the peninsula for 80 years with an amusement park and other attractions complementing the nation's largest urban beach.

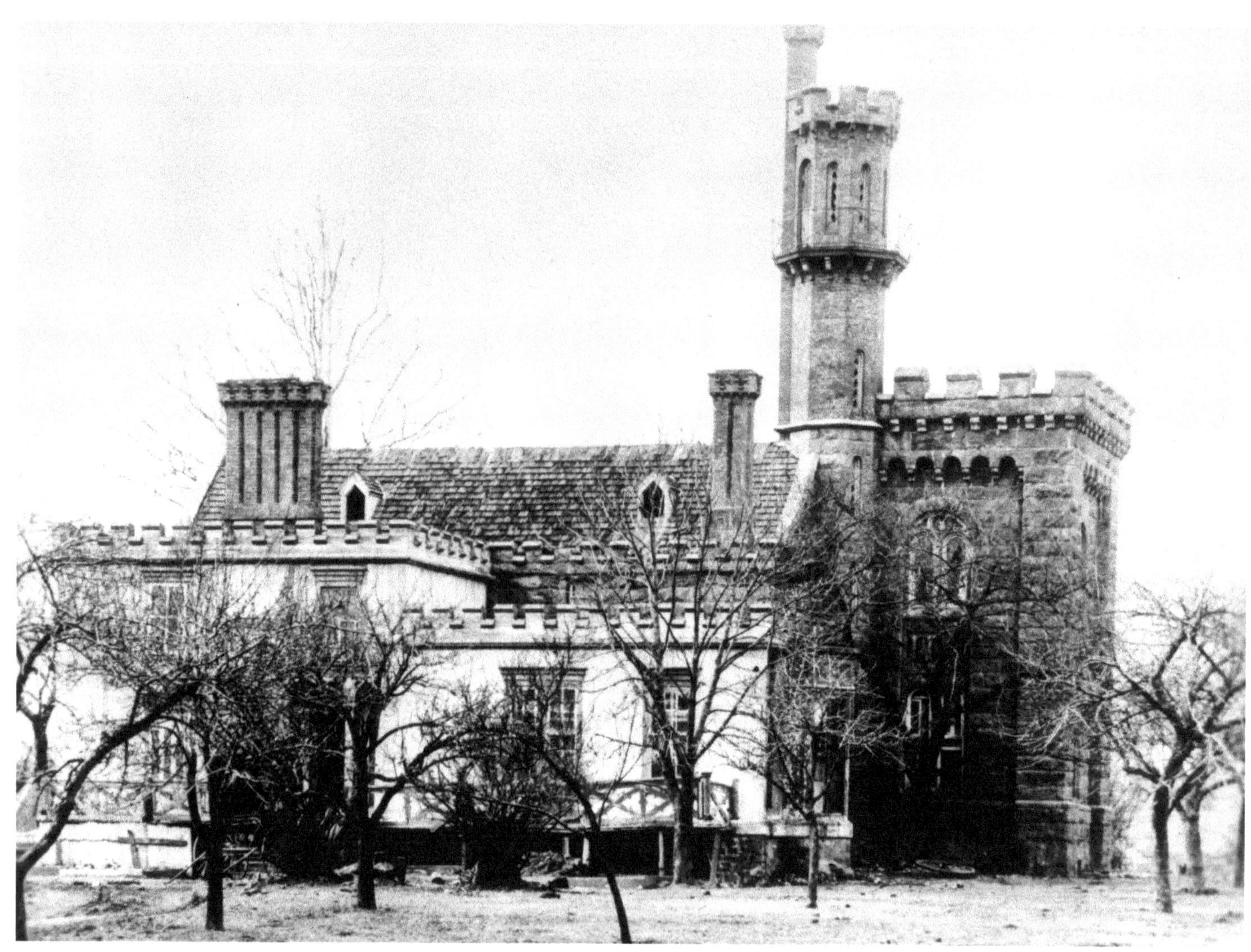

Bodine Castle was located at 43rd Street and Vernon Boulevard. The house is representative of country villas once built in the riverside resort of Ravenswood, Long Island City, by wealthy New Yorkers. The structure fell into disrepair in the twentieth century and was demolished in 1966, when ConEdison began building its massive power plant.

The Bridge to Unstoppable Progress (1900–1929)

Queens was once rural—at the edges of New York society. But as the railroads and subways expanded, as roads and bridges were built, the wheels of progress started to roll. With progress came jobs and development, bringing not only immigrants seeking the American dream, but also those from Manhattan and Brooklyn seeking more space and new opportunities.

The ferries had long connected Long Island City and its environs to Manhattan, but with the completion of the Queensboro Bridge in 1909, the borough now had a direct link to Manhattan. Improved transportation gave streetcars access to and from Queens. The automobile, which soon ceased to be a novelty as Henry Ford and his competitors drove them one after another off the assembly lines, joined the fray and soon the great stream of Long Island commuting began.

Queens had always been a center for recreation, and North Beach on "Bowery Bay" in Elmhurst became a hotspot, as did the newly built resorts along Rockaway Beach. These destinations were no longer just seasonal—with the improved modes of transportation, permanent residents were moving in. Housing booms turned the farms and marshes into neighborhoods like Bayside, Queens Village, Forest Hills, and Jackson Heights.

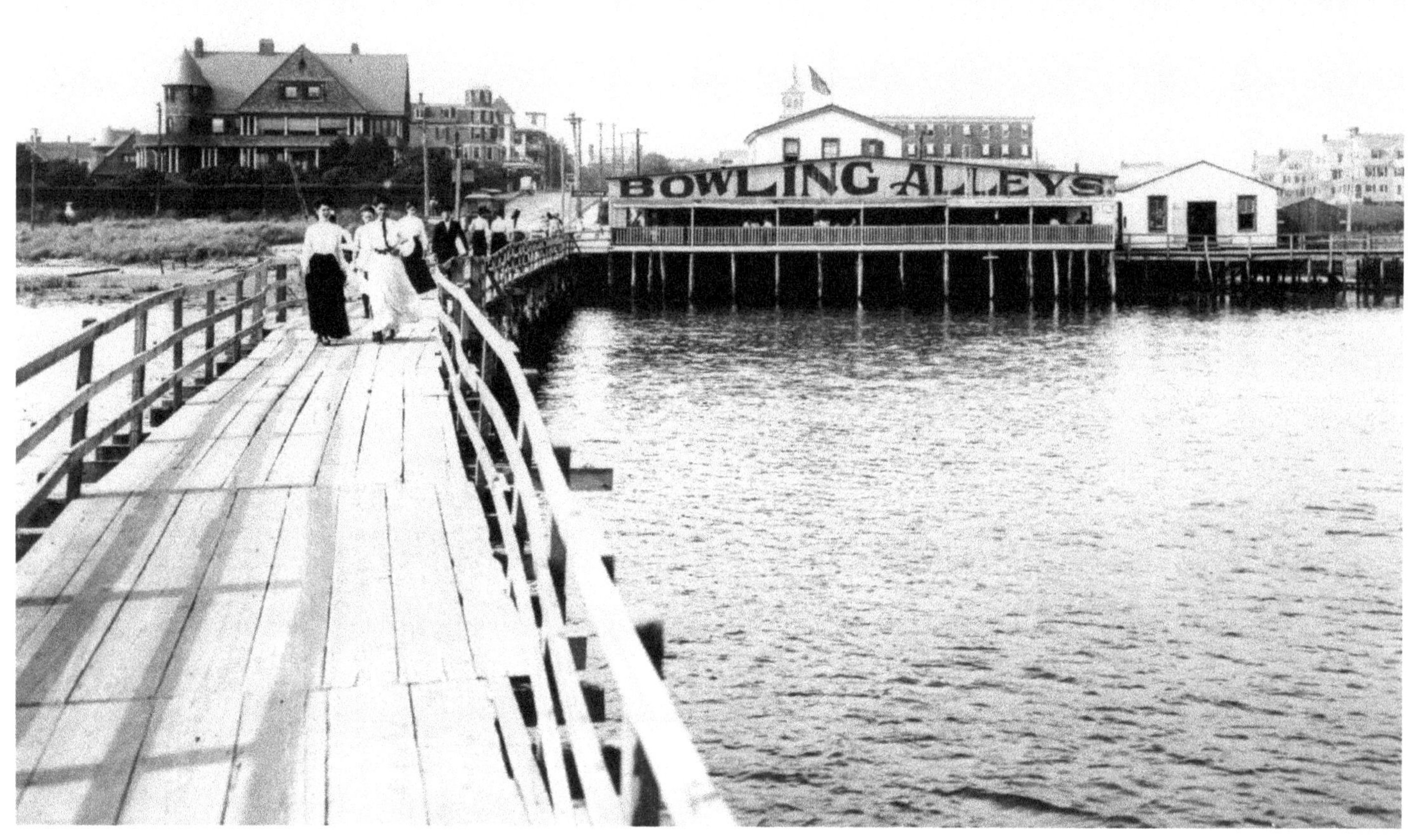

A pier extends into the waters at Far Rockaway around 1902. With the railroad running out to the Rockaways, "New York's Playground" was opened up to new leisure seekers, from the wealthy to the working man, as well as an influx of new locals who worked at the hotels, restaurants, and in the building trades. Visible in the background is the Central Park Bowling Alleys.

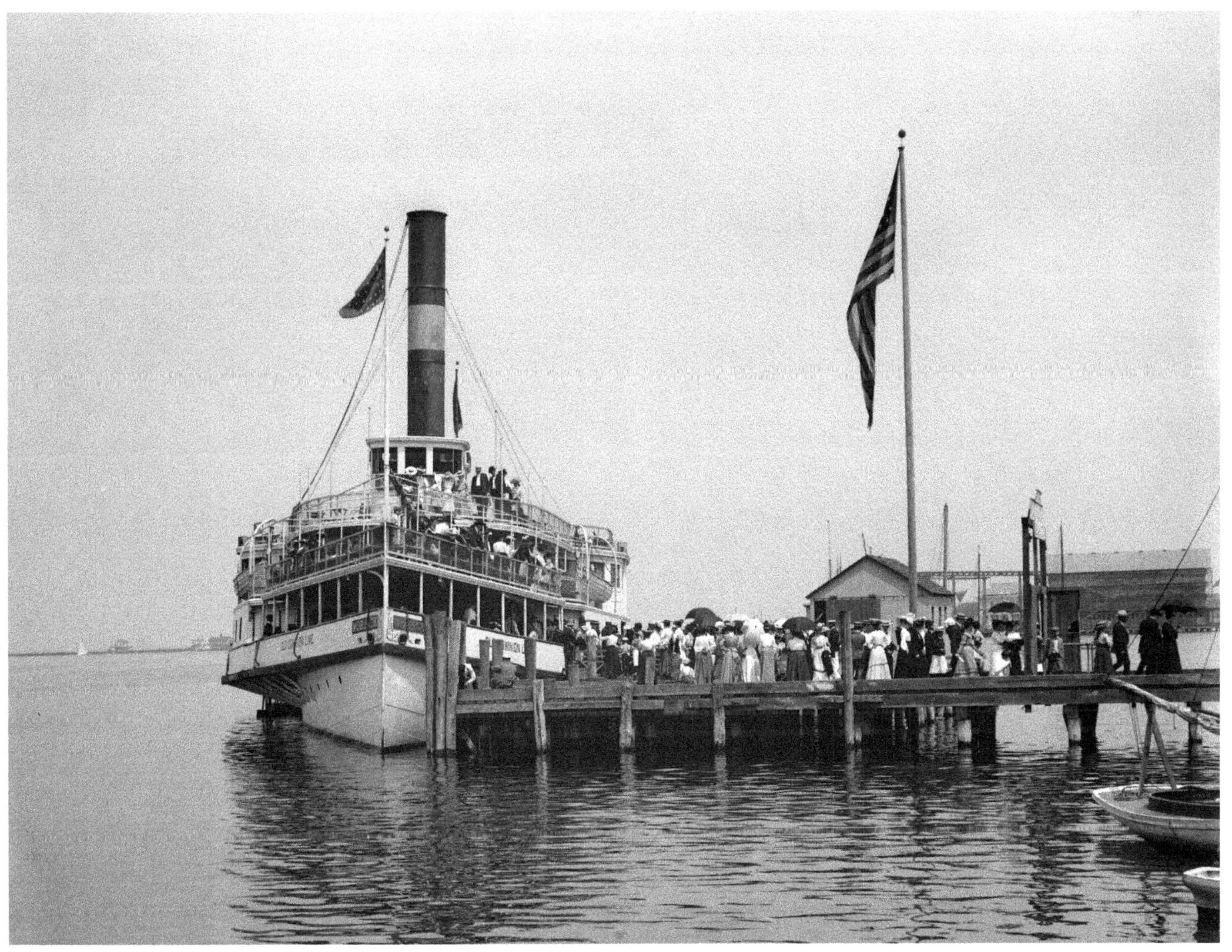

The steamship *Mobjack* takes on passengers at Rockaway Island early in the new century. Although Rockaway is actually a peninsula, there were no bridges for visitors and new residents to travel over until the late 1930s. Steamships thus served as an important conduit.

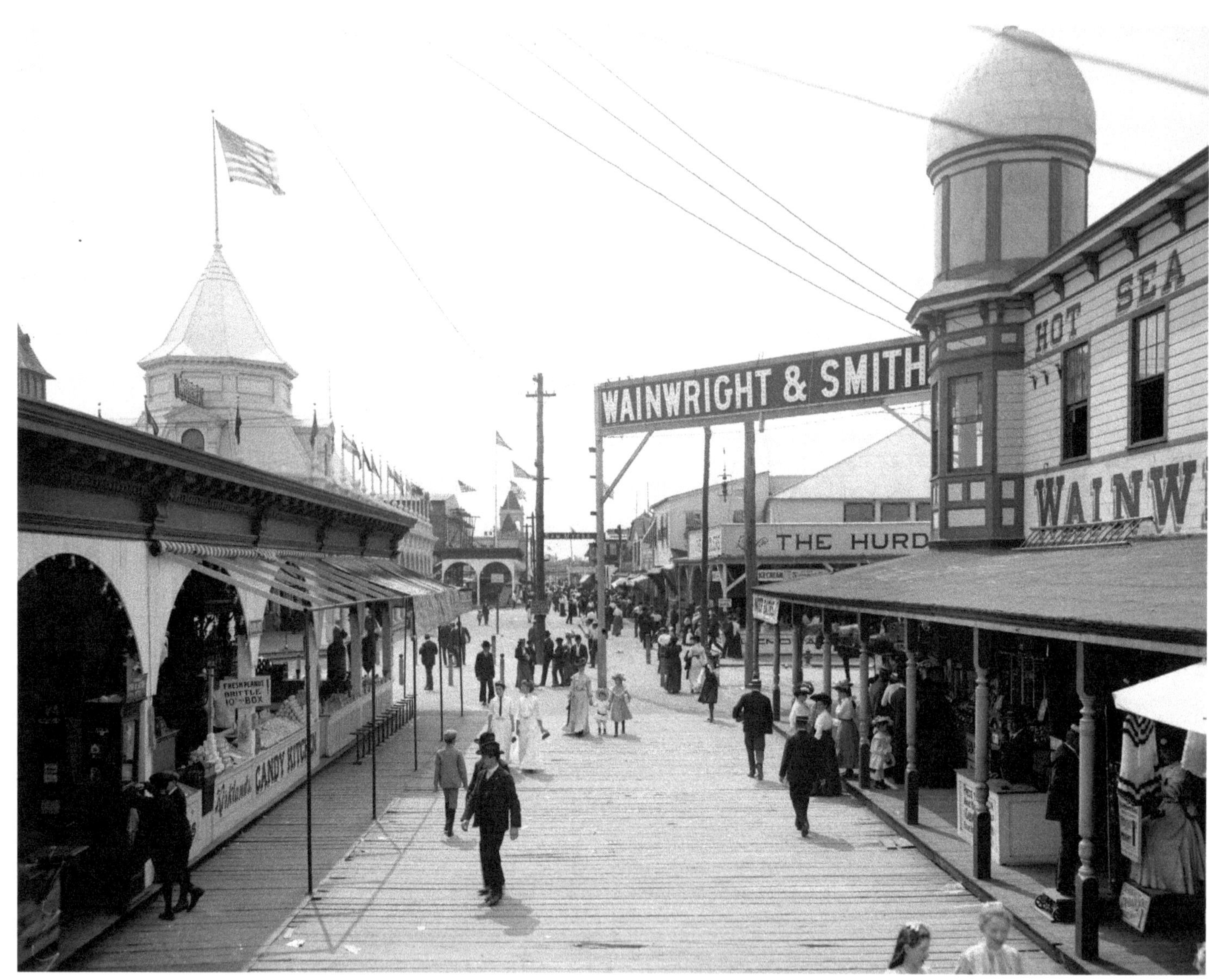

A view of the Bowery at Rockaway Beach in 1903. This was one of the amusement pavilions built by developer William Wainwright. The pavilions included dancing, dining, bars, and bathing areas, and formed some of the first streets in Rockaway, stretching from Rockaway Beach Boulevard across the boardwalk to the shore.

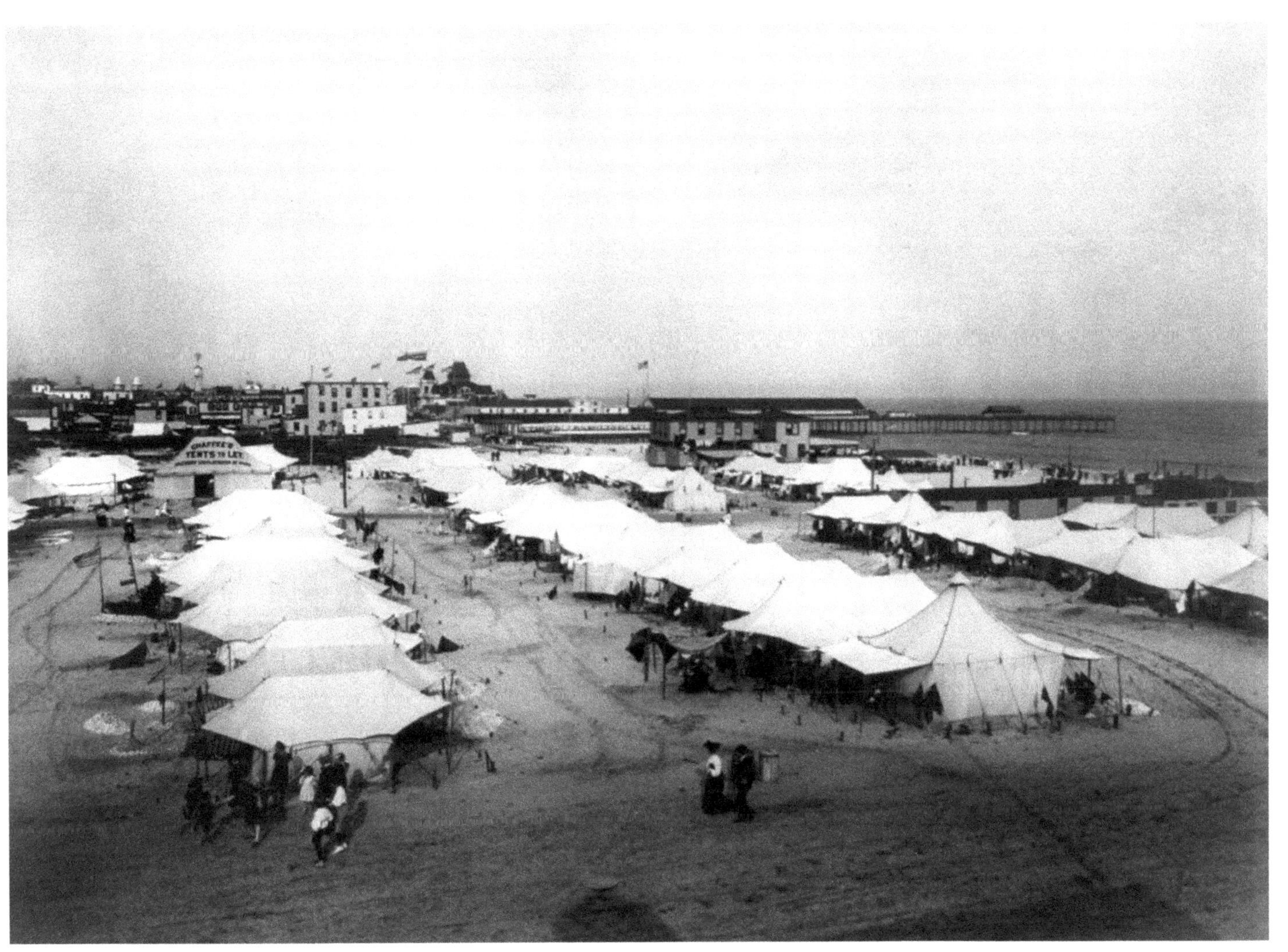

With the railroad providing greater access to the beach, the working man and middle class flocked to "tent cities" like these, which provided low-cost camping on the Atlantic shores for those who could not afford boardwalk hotels. Many families would rent a tent for the entire summer and return to the same camp each year.

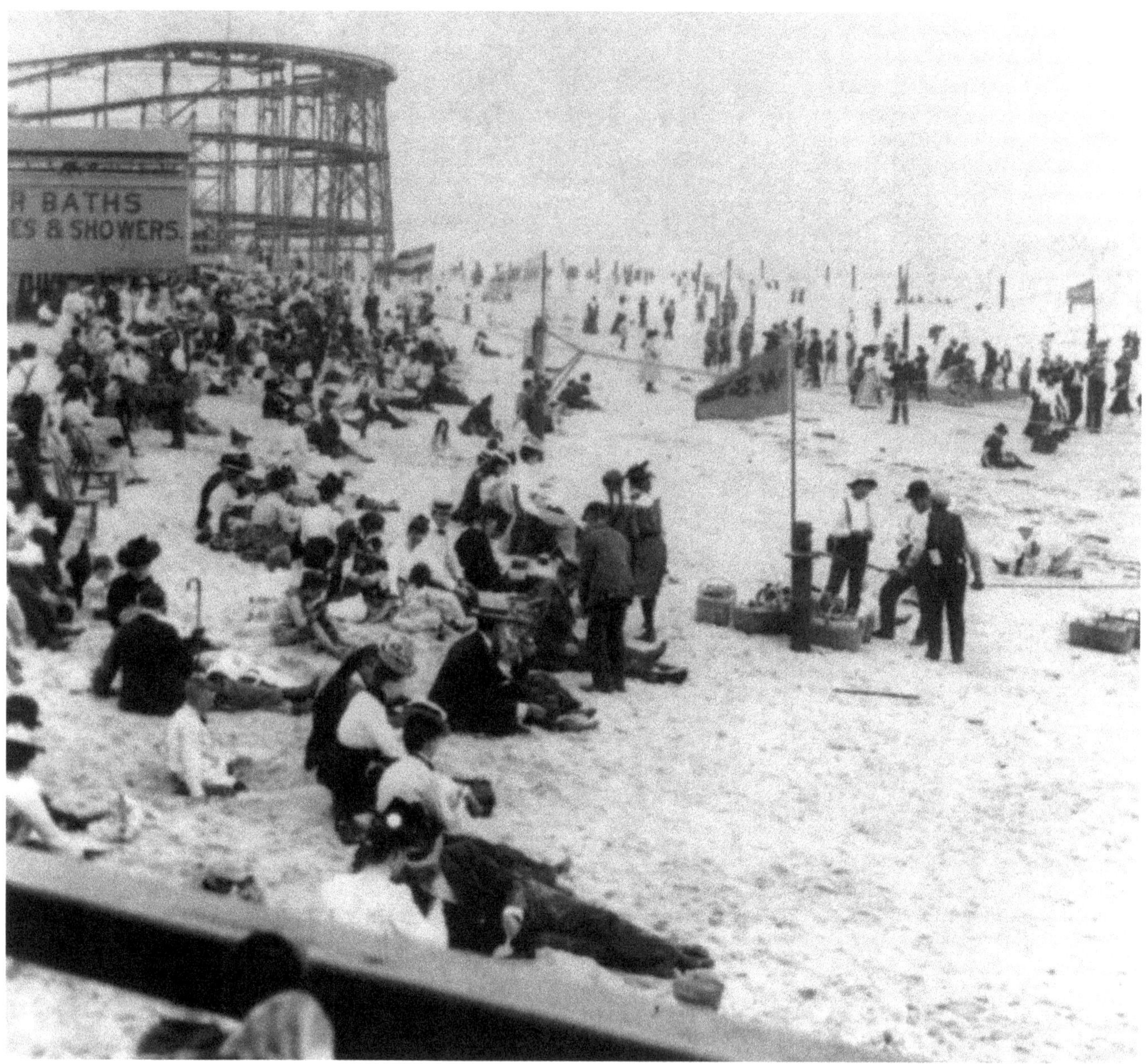

The famous Rockaway Playground was opened by LaMarcus Thompson in 1902, with one of his "gravity highways" or roller coasters, as seen here at upper-left. Thompson had also opened a coaster in Coney Island, which he ran until his death in 1926. The coaster was renamed the Atom Smasher in 1950, and the park operated in various incarnations until 1985.

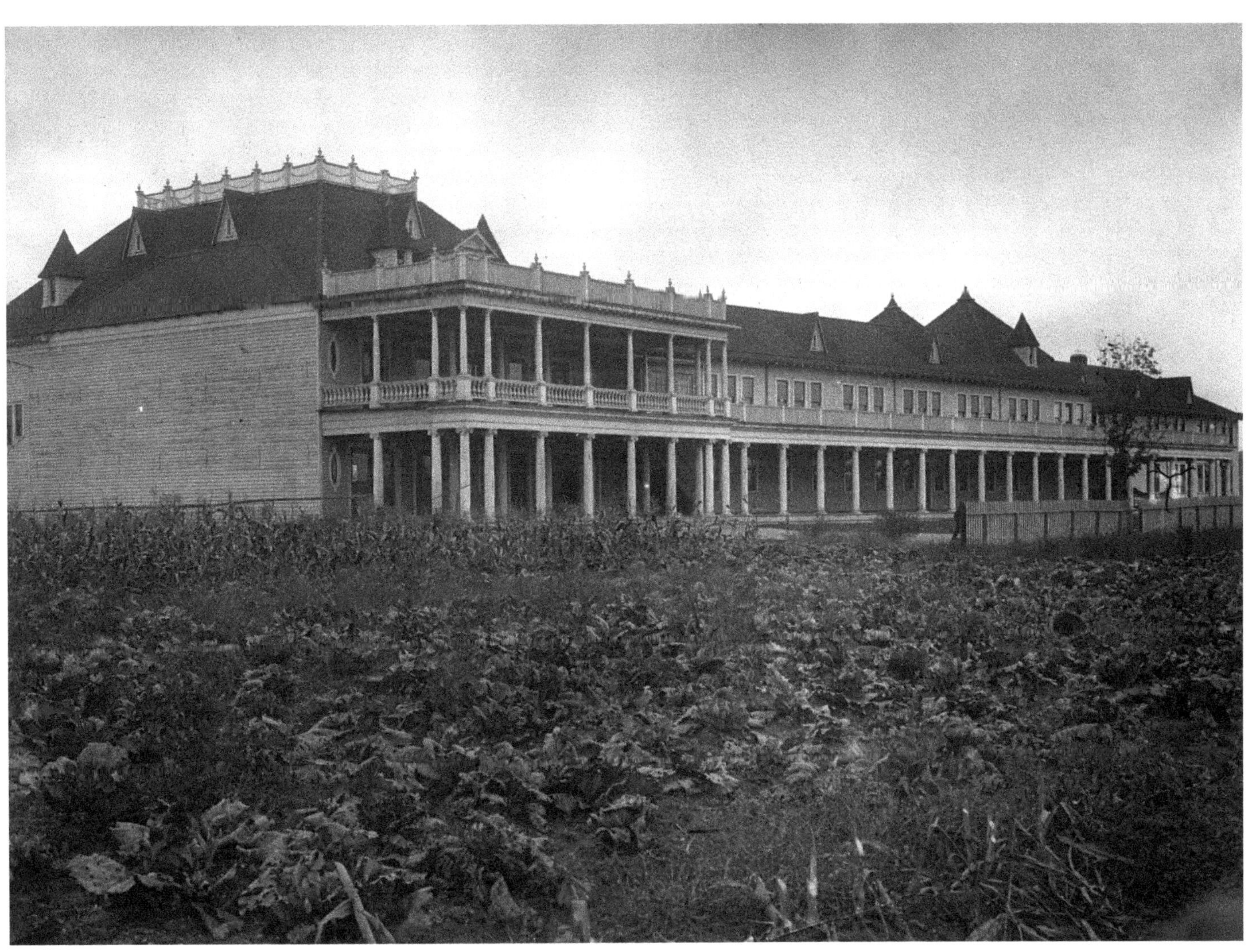

The Interstate Park Casino stood just to the south of the Long Island Railroad station that brought scores of people to the Rockaway Peninsula. Developers had plans to rival Atlantic City far to the south, but were unsuccessful. This photograph shows the casino in 1904 and a large vegetable garden in the foreground filled with cabbages and cornstalks.

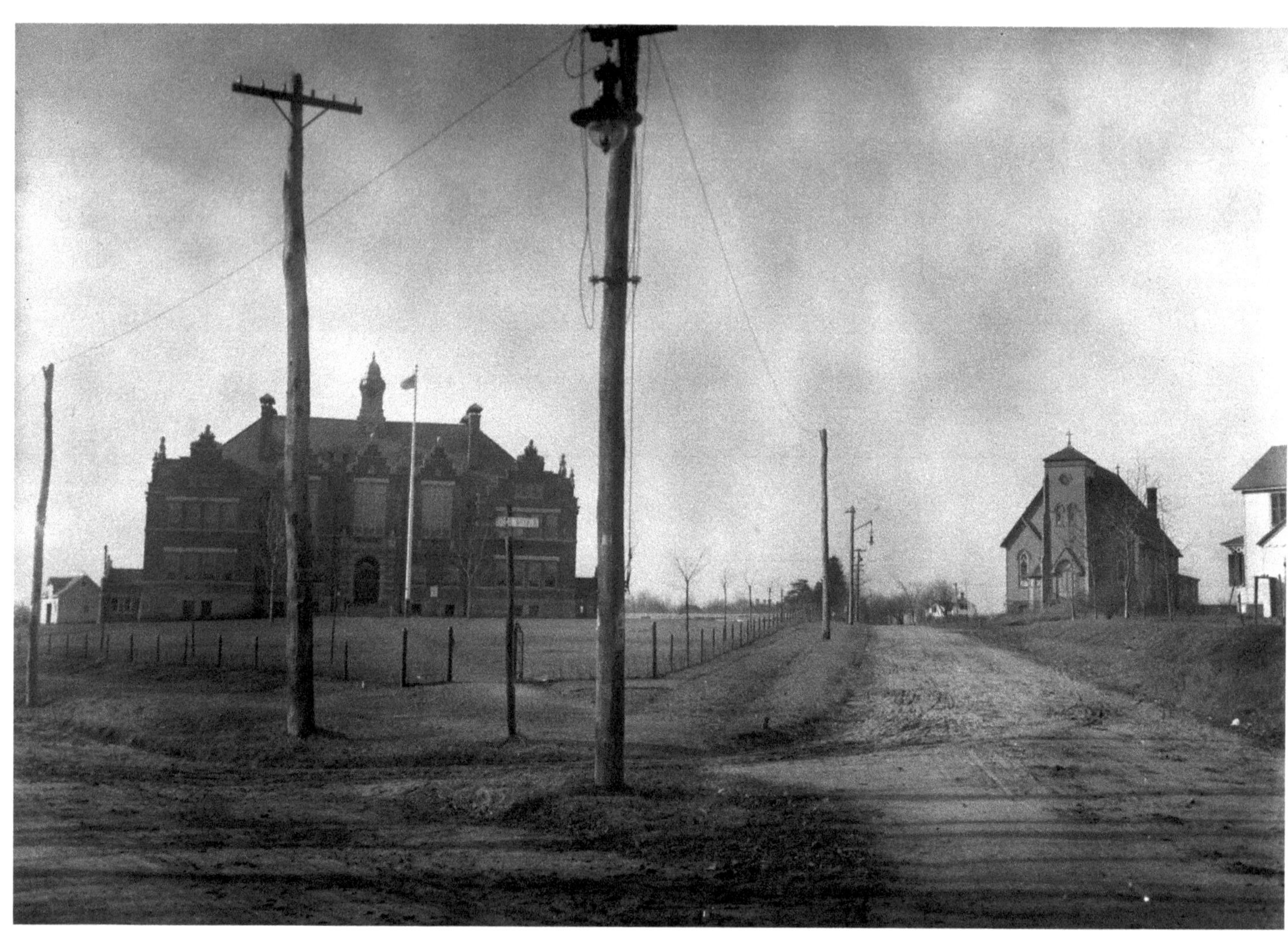

To the left is Public School 34, across from St. Joachim and Anne Catholic Church in Queens Village. Both structures were built on farmland at the end of the nineteenth century. This photograph taken in 1905 shows the great open spaces that still existed in Queens in the early years of the twentieth century, but the borough quickly lost its rural character as development continued over the next two decades, when Queens Village was part of a housing boom.

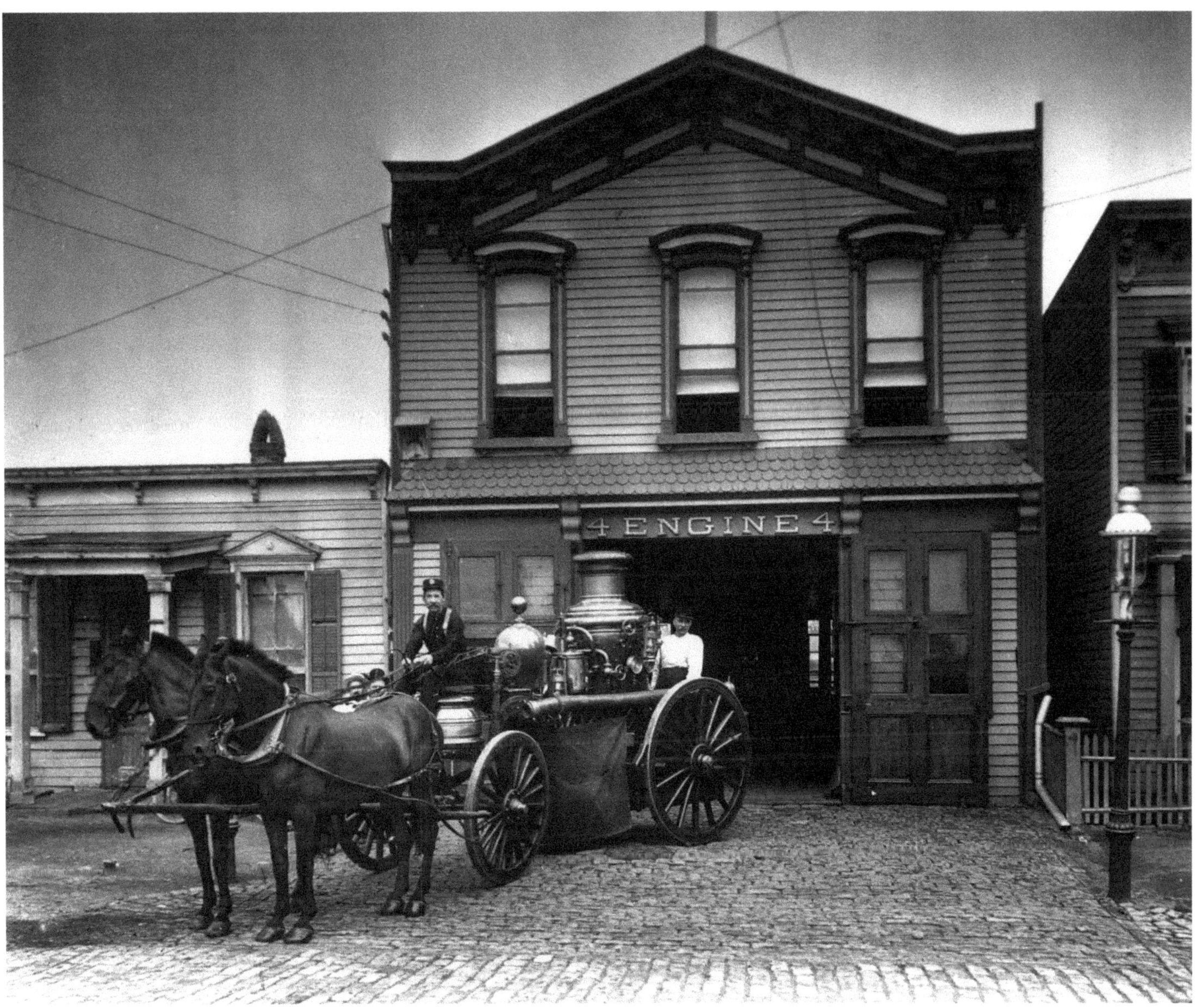

Fire fighters with Maspeth Steamer Engine No. 4. Despite bitter resistance, in 1898 once the boroughs were unified as part of New York City, fire department volunteers were replaced by professionals after insurance companies lobbied the governor. Seen here in 1908, this steam pumper is representative of the types of equipment available in the era to fight blazes across the city. As the internal combustion engine gained sway in the next decade, horses and steam would give way to motorized fire engines and equipment.

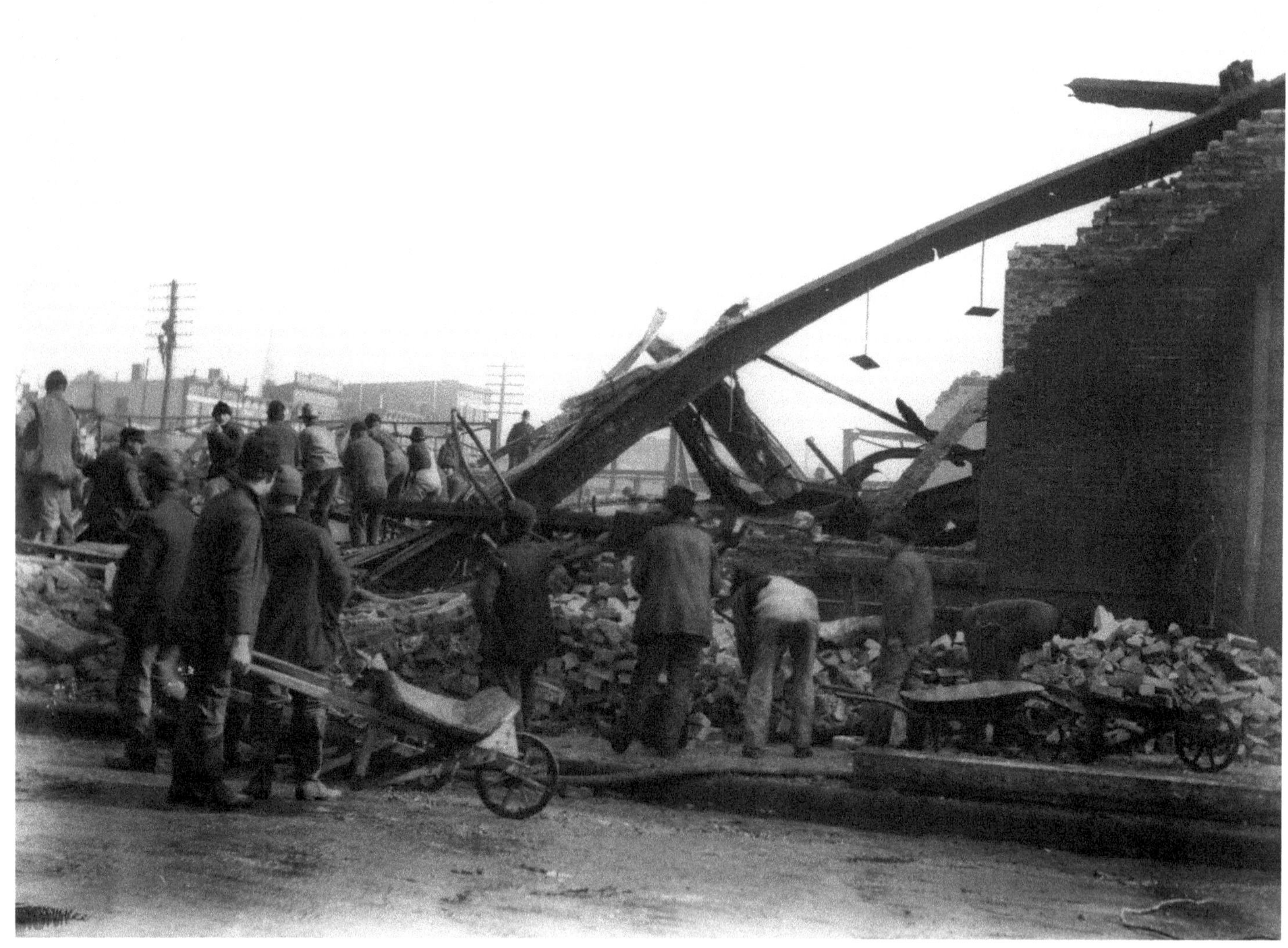

The aftermath of a massive fire at the Long Island City terminal for the Long Island Railroad in December 1902. According to news reports at the time, employees had to jump from the windows to escape, although there was only one injury reported. The fire was said to be so intense that the red-brick building collapsed on itself within 30 minutes, despite every engine from Brooklyn, Queens, and Manhattan being called in to assist. The station had earlier been rebuilt in 1891 at a cost of $200,000 after a fire destroyed the terminal, which stood at the end of the main line. The newer terminal was rebuilt in 1903.

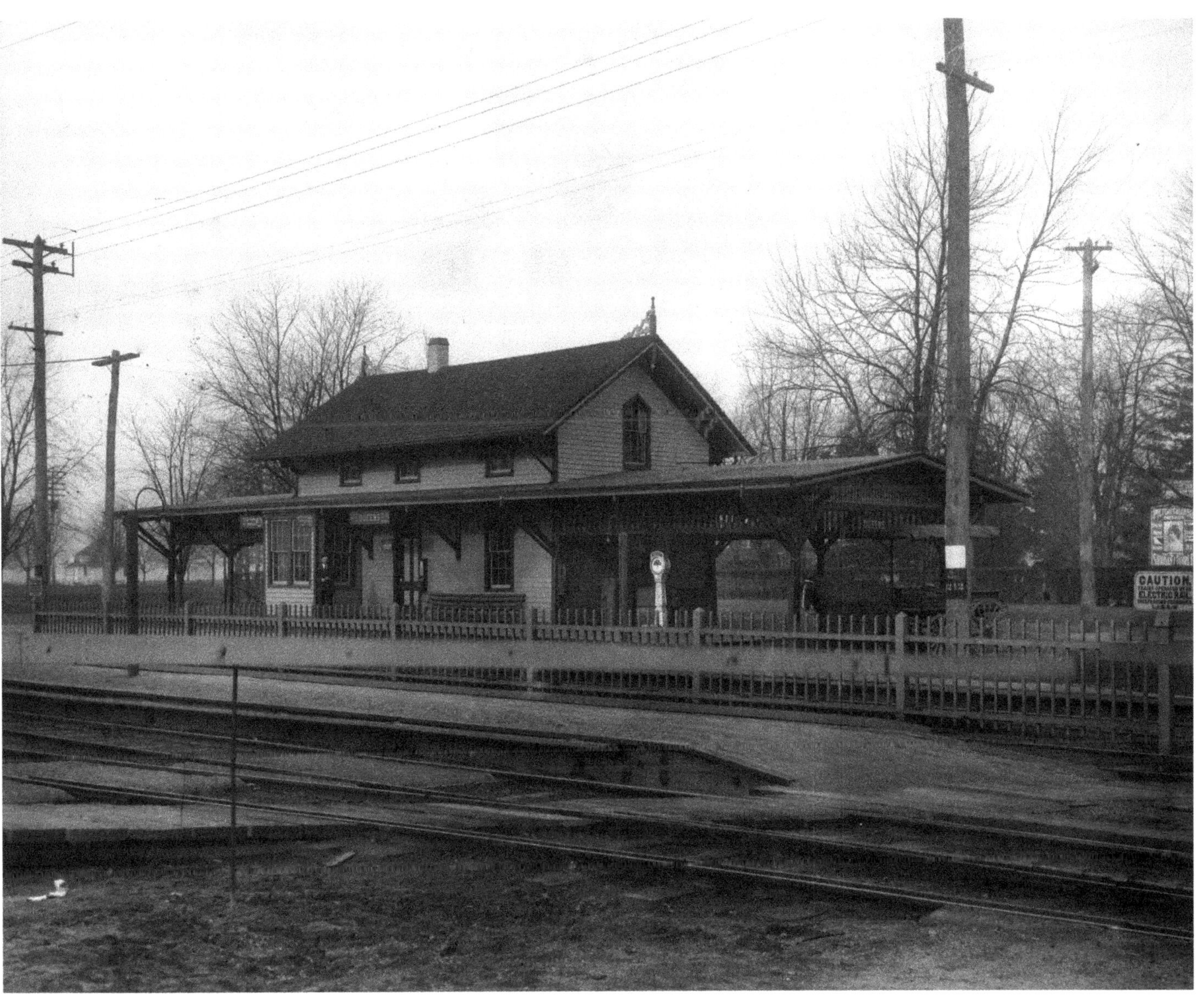

The Queens Village Long Island Railroad station, on the eastern edge of the borough, is seen here in 1909. By the 1920s, the area was in the midst of a housing boom that converted what was once farmland into a large neighborhood adjacent to Jamaica, the county seat.

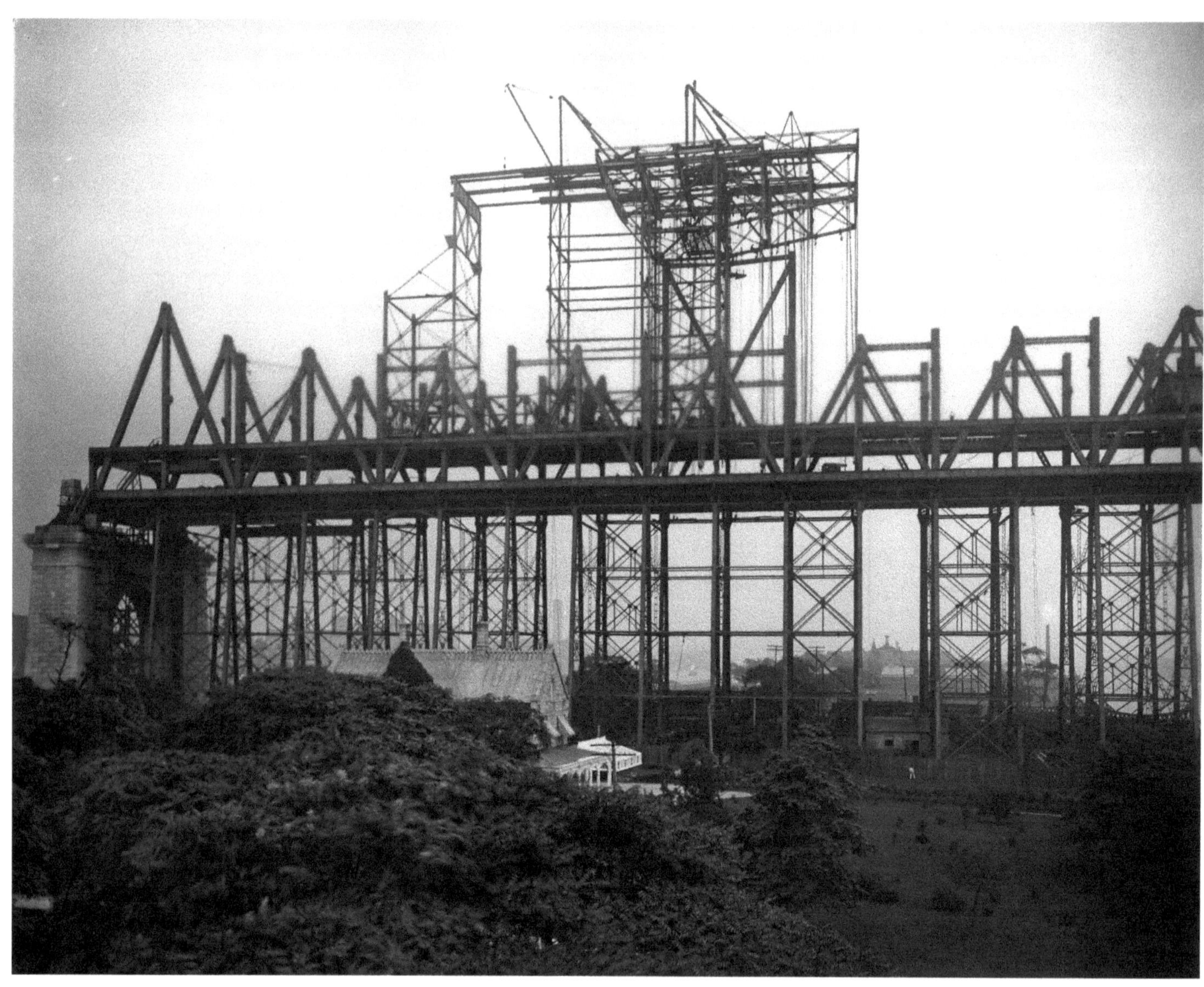

The construction of the Queensboro Bridge forever changed Queens, providing for the first time a direct link over the East River to Manhattan. Construction is shown here in 1906, as the bridge crosses Blackwell's Island (Roosevelt Island) in the center of the river. The view is to the north, toward the Bronx, with Queens on the right and Manhattan to the left. The bridge would be completed in 1909 at a cost of $18 million and 50 lives lost.

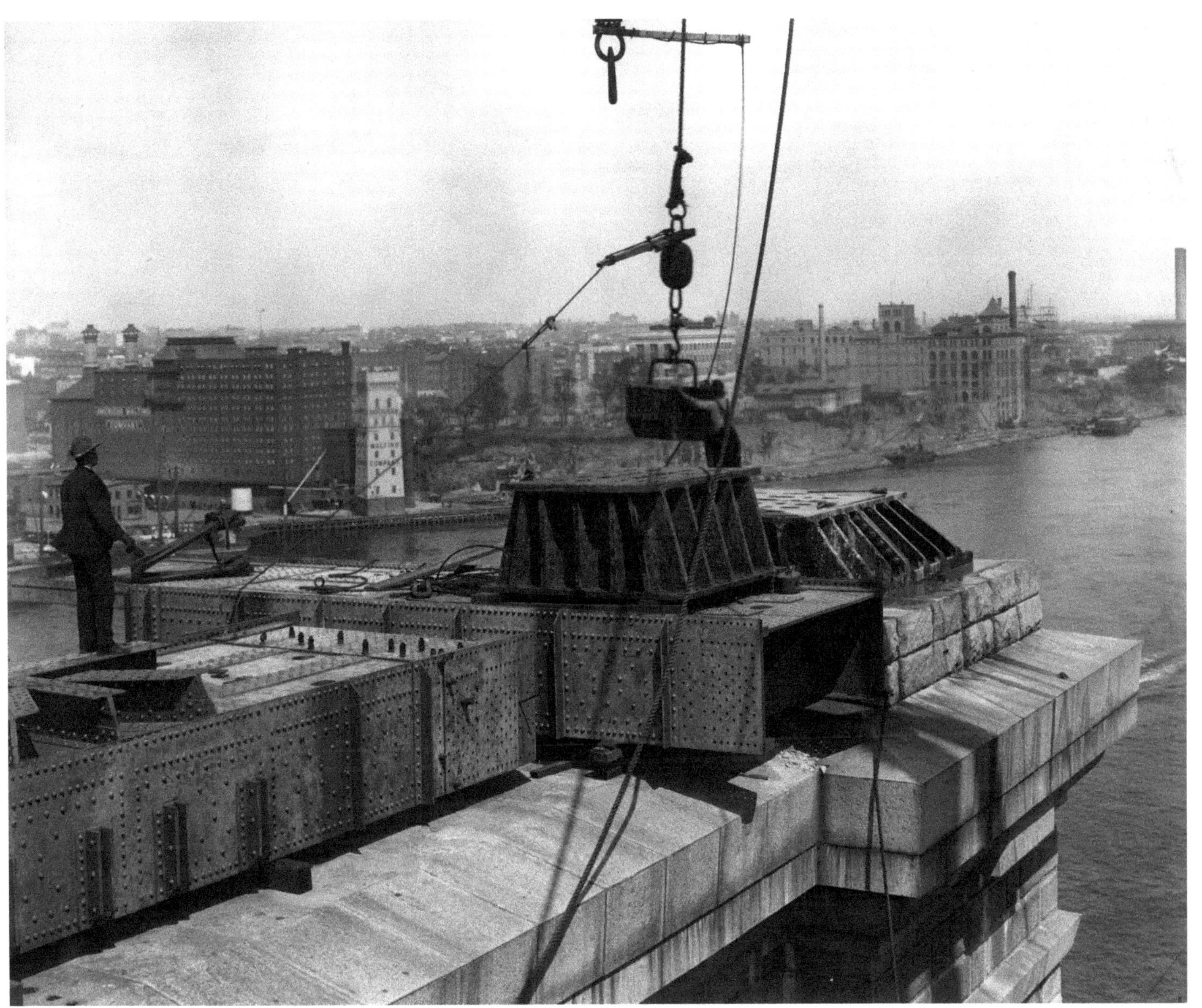

Although the Queensboro Bridge lacks something of the charm of the Brooklyn Bridge spanning the same river just a few miles to the south, its construction ended the isolation of Queens from Manhattan. The bridge remains the only overland crossing directly between the two boroughs. As evidence of the backseat Queens takes to "the City," New Yorkers today commonly refer to the bridge as the "59th Street Bridge" for the Manhattan street the bridge connects to, despite the bridge's official name.

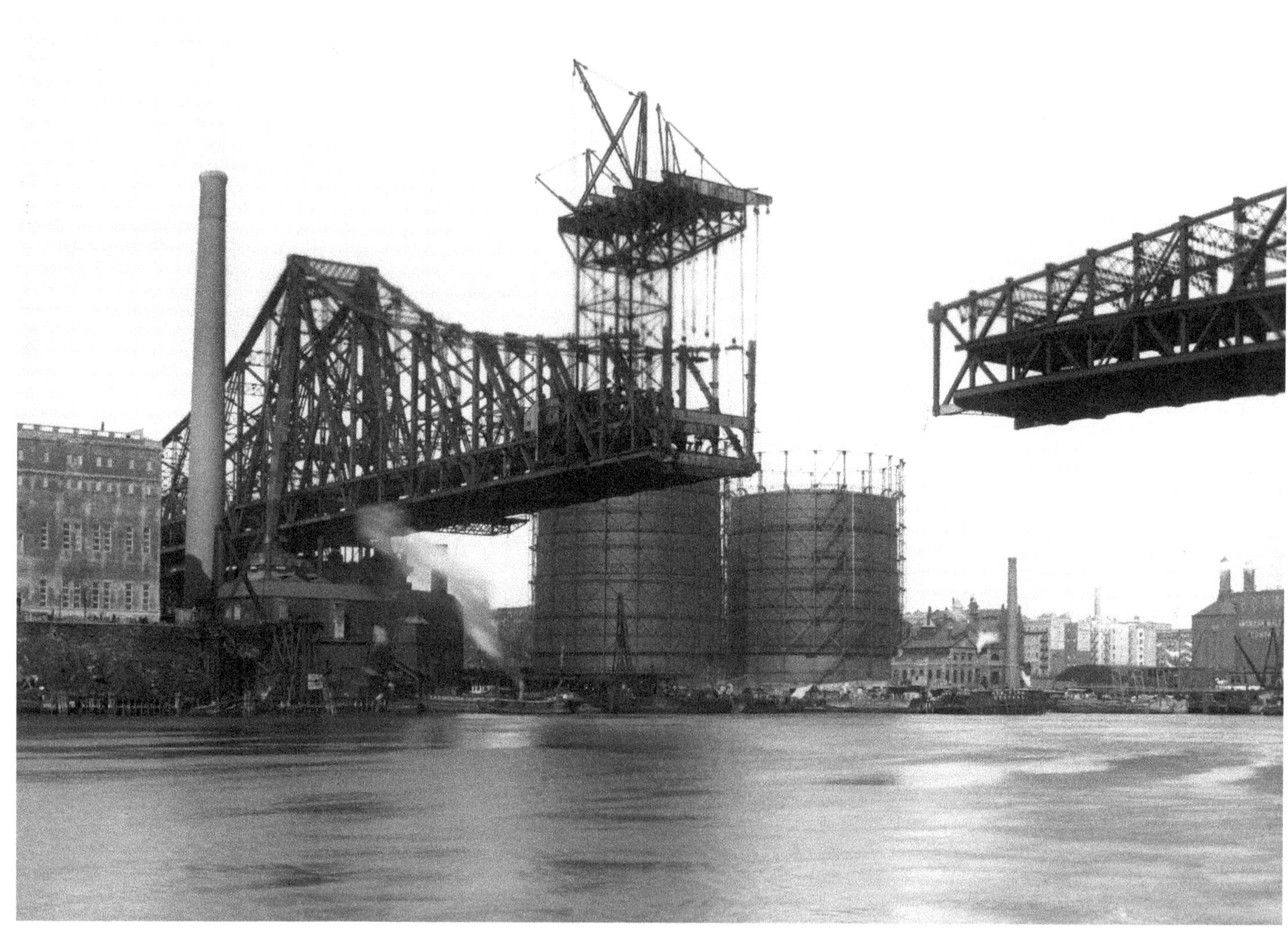

About a year prior to the opening of the Queensboro Bridge in March 1909, the span of the bridge is nearing completion. The bridge is a double-cantilever, two-level bridge, with one span on either side of Roosevelt Island, to which it also connects. This photograph was taken from the island.

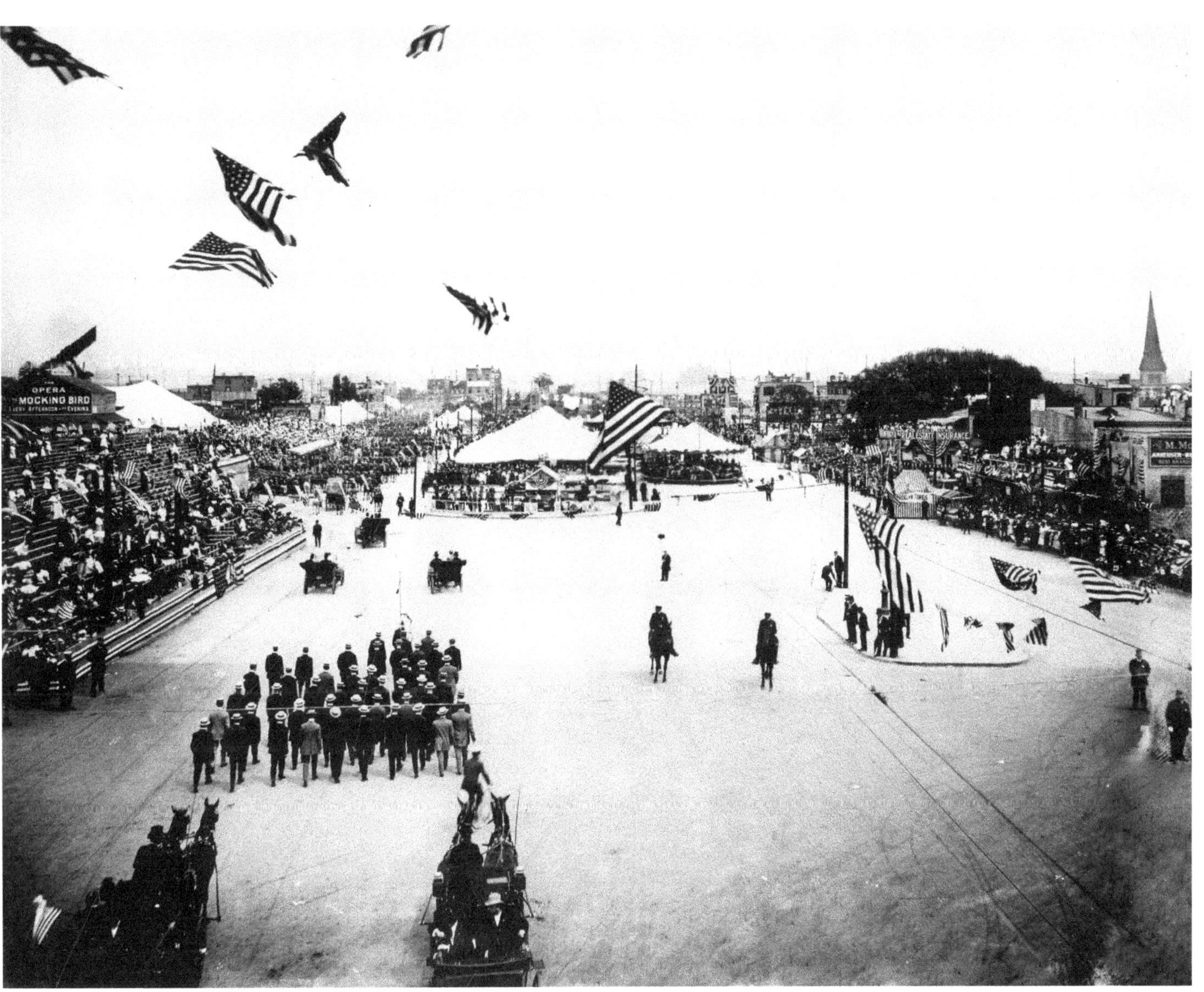

Opening Day ceremonies for the monumental bridge in June 1909 were held with great fanfare, as Queens was finally united with Manhattan, perhaps the most important event in the history of the borough. The base of the Queens side of the bridge was transformed into Queensboro Plaza, seen here looking east from the bridge. The plaza was used as parade grounds for the ceremonies.

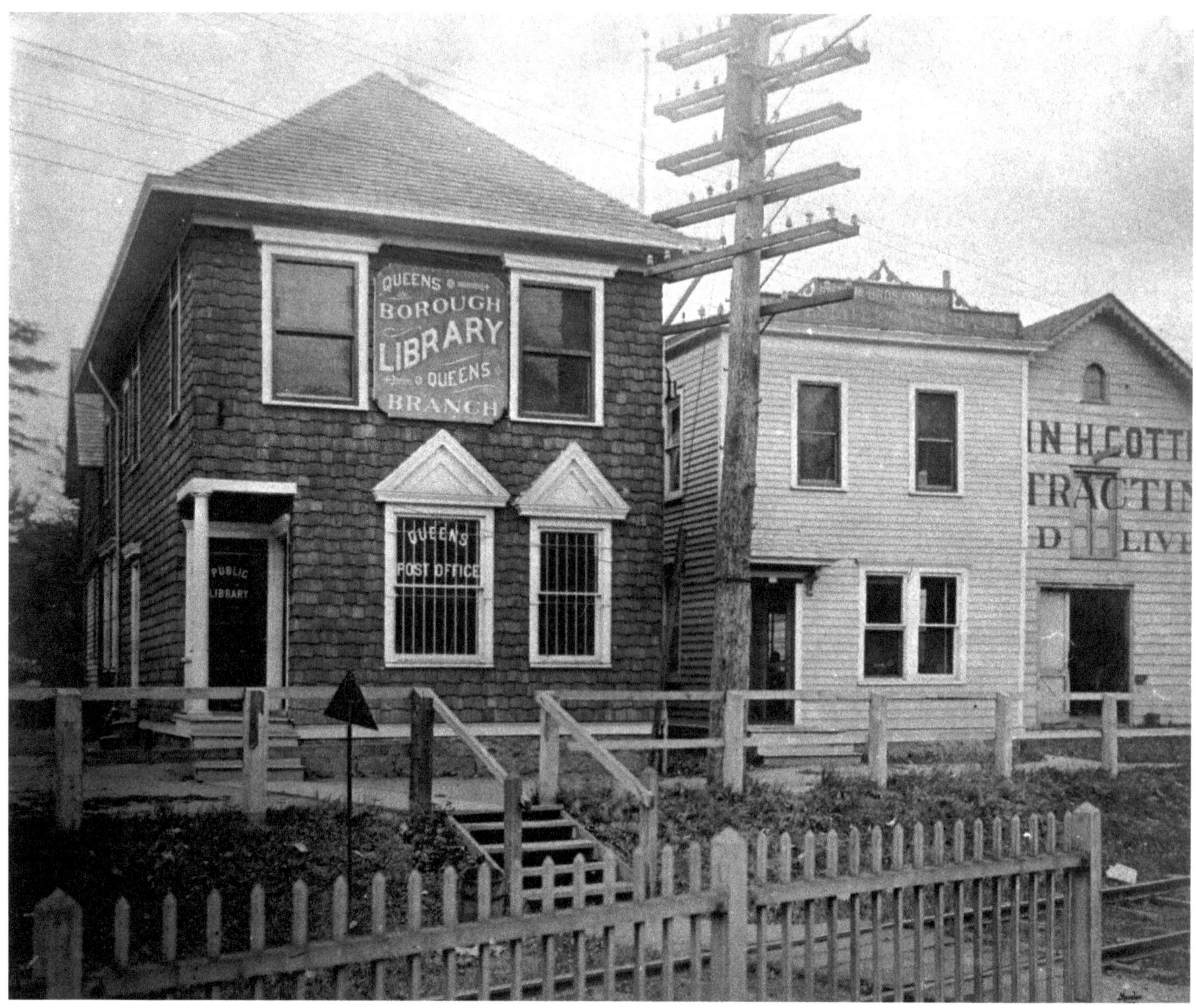

The Queens Village branch of the Queens Public Library shared its building with the Queens Post Office shown here in 1910. Because the population of the borough was still spread out across the large area of the borough, the libraries were often operated from storefronts and stocked by a traveling library system—which was so popular that it eventually led to permanent branches being established across Queens.

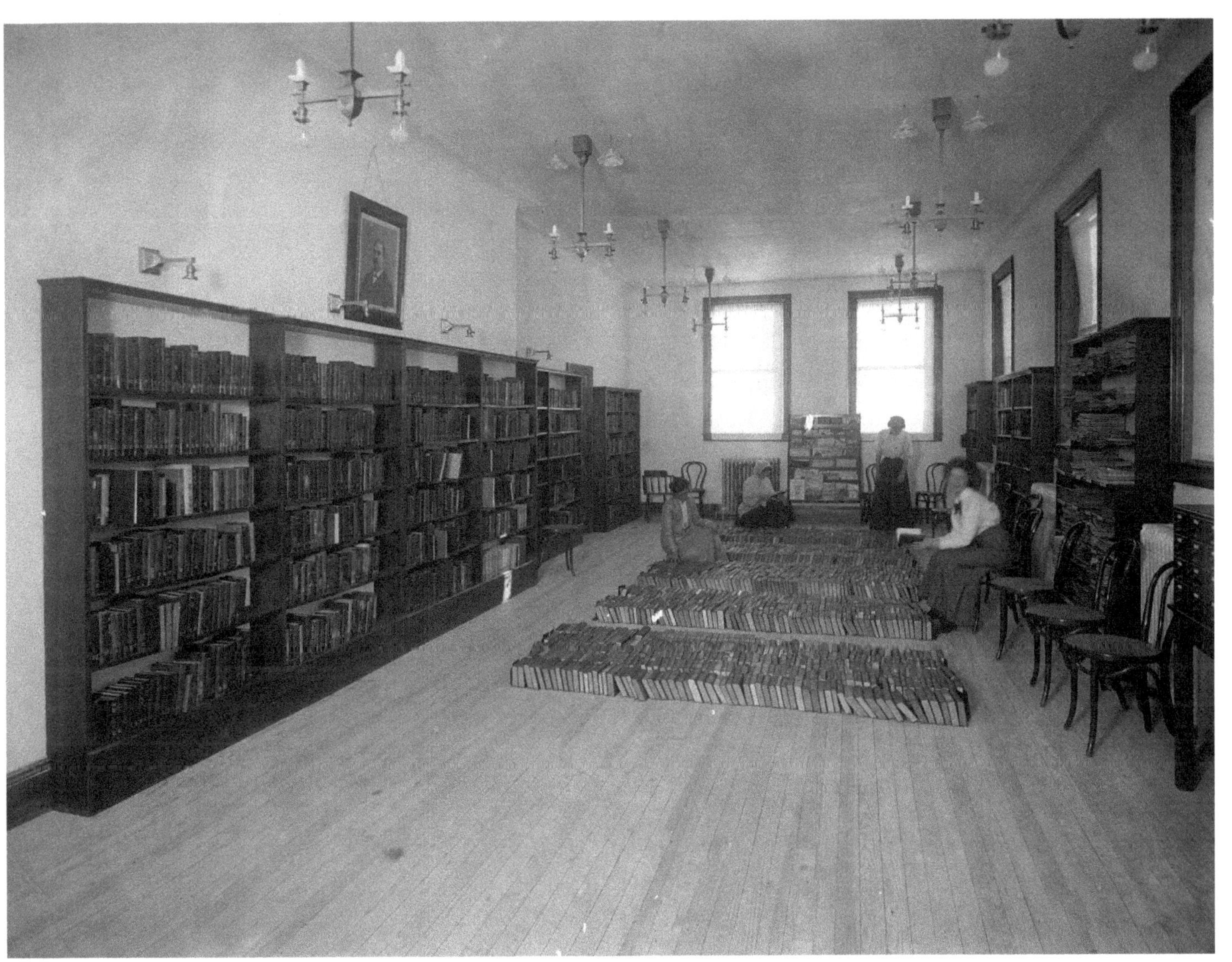

Librarians are seen preparing books for the stacks in 1910. The Queens Borough Public Library is one of the largest in the United States and is separate from the New York Public Library and Brooklyn Public Library. The library was consolidated in 1901 by New York City, which combined the various libraries from the towns and villages that existed in Queens County prior to its incorporation as a borough of New York City.

Fire fighters at Hose Company No. 2 are seen here reading books just dropped off by the traveling library service, while in between alarm runs. The fireman at right is holding a book titled *Motor-Car Principles*—perhaps dreaming of trading the horses for a newfangled motorized fire engine.

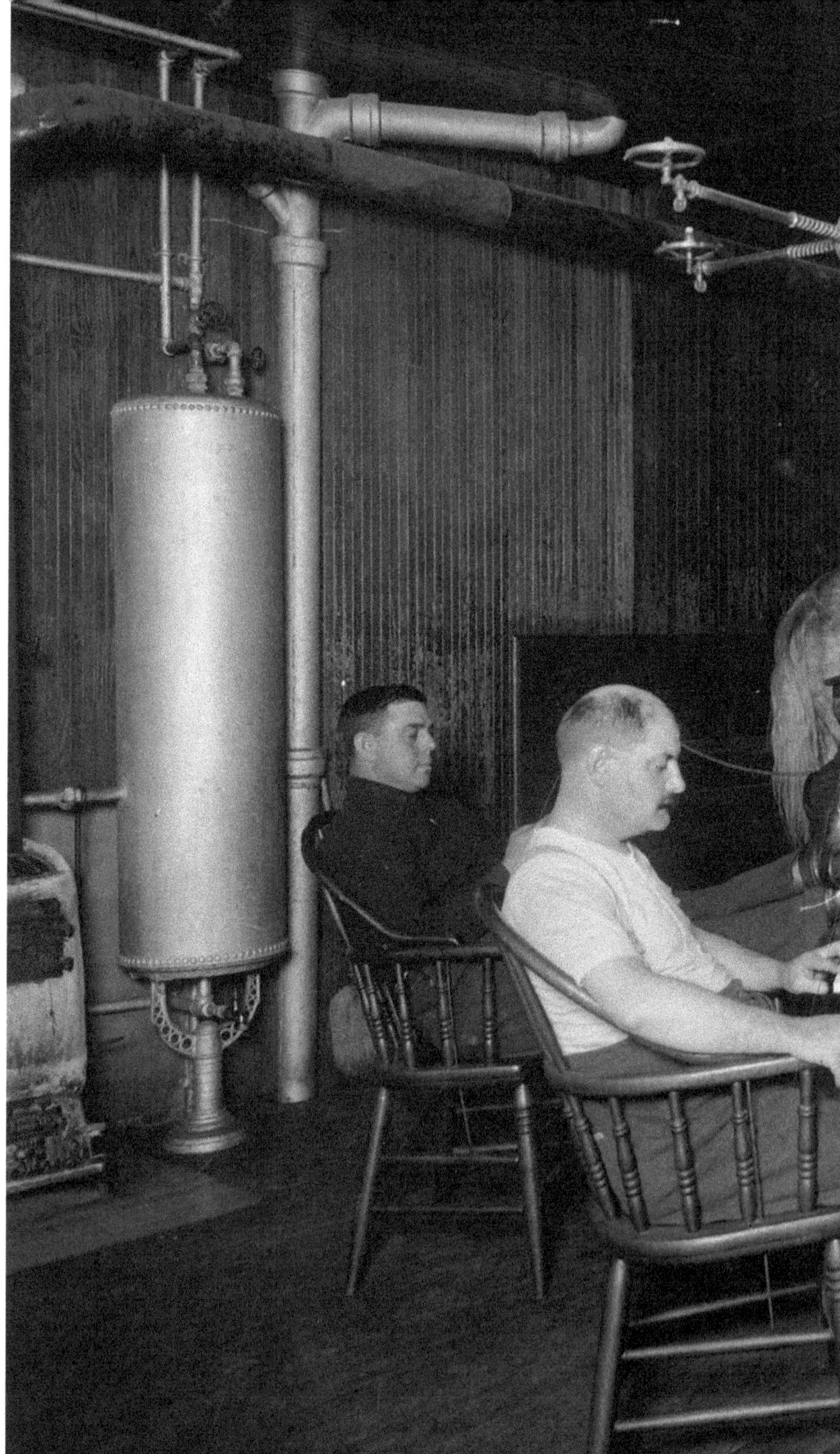

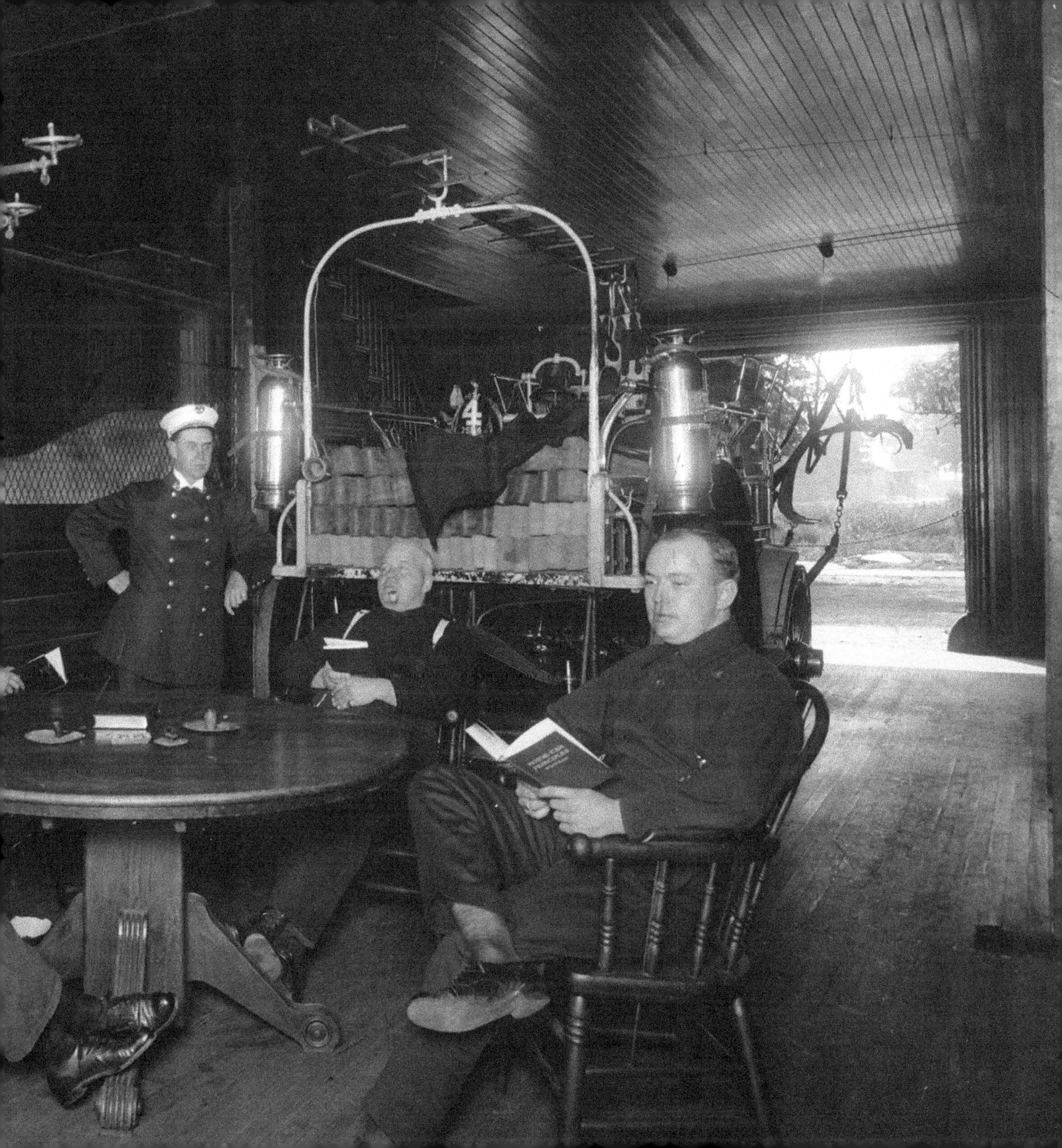

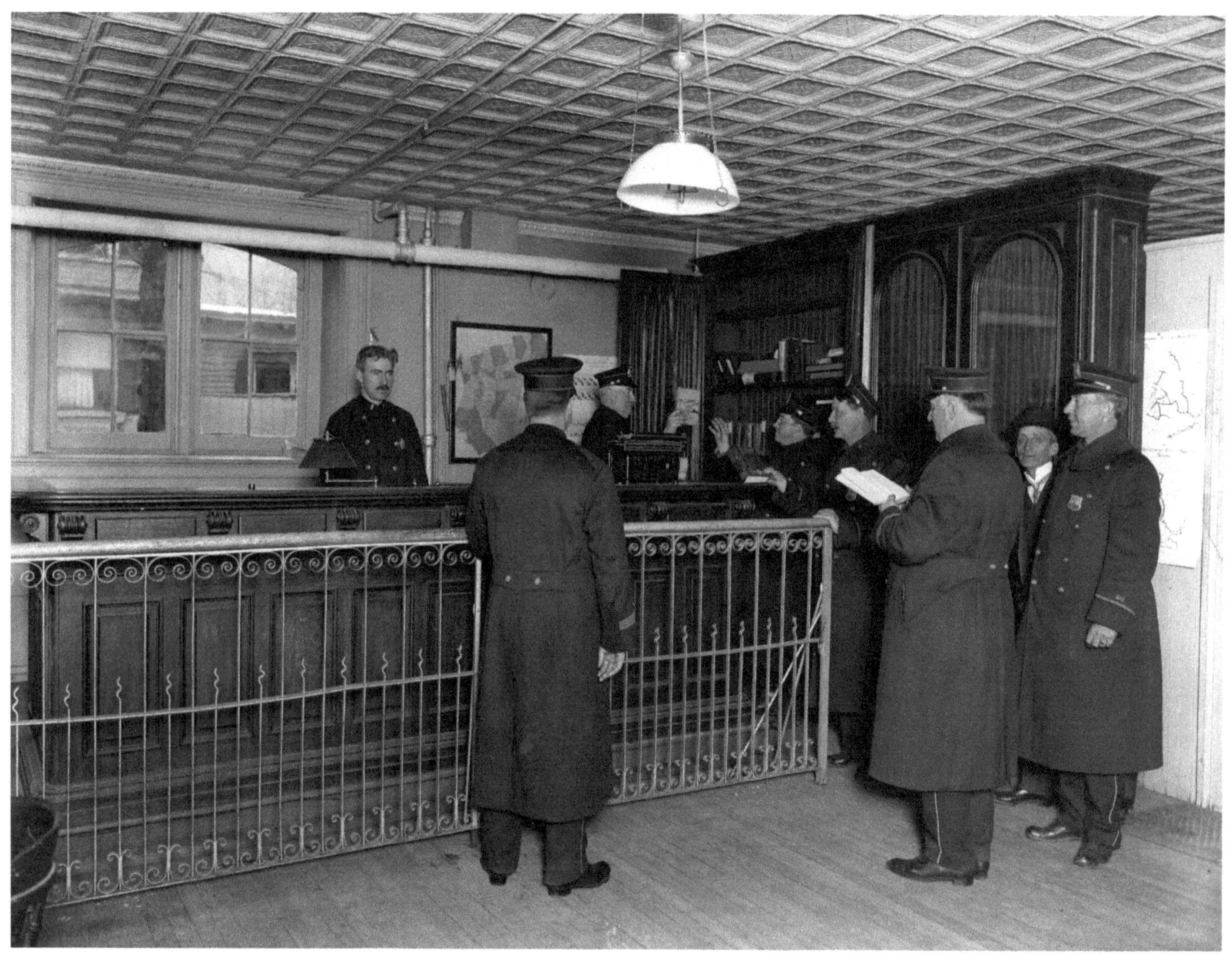

The police department also received visits from the traveling library. This precinct appears to have its own lending library behind the main desk.

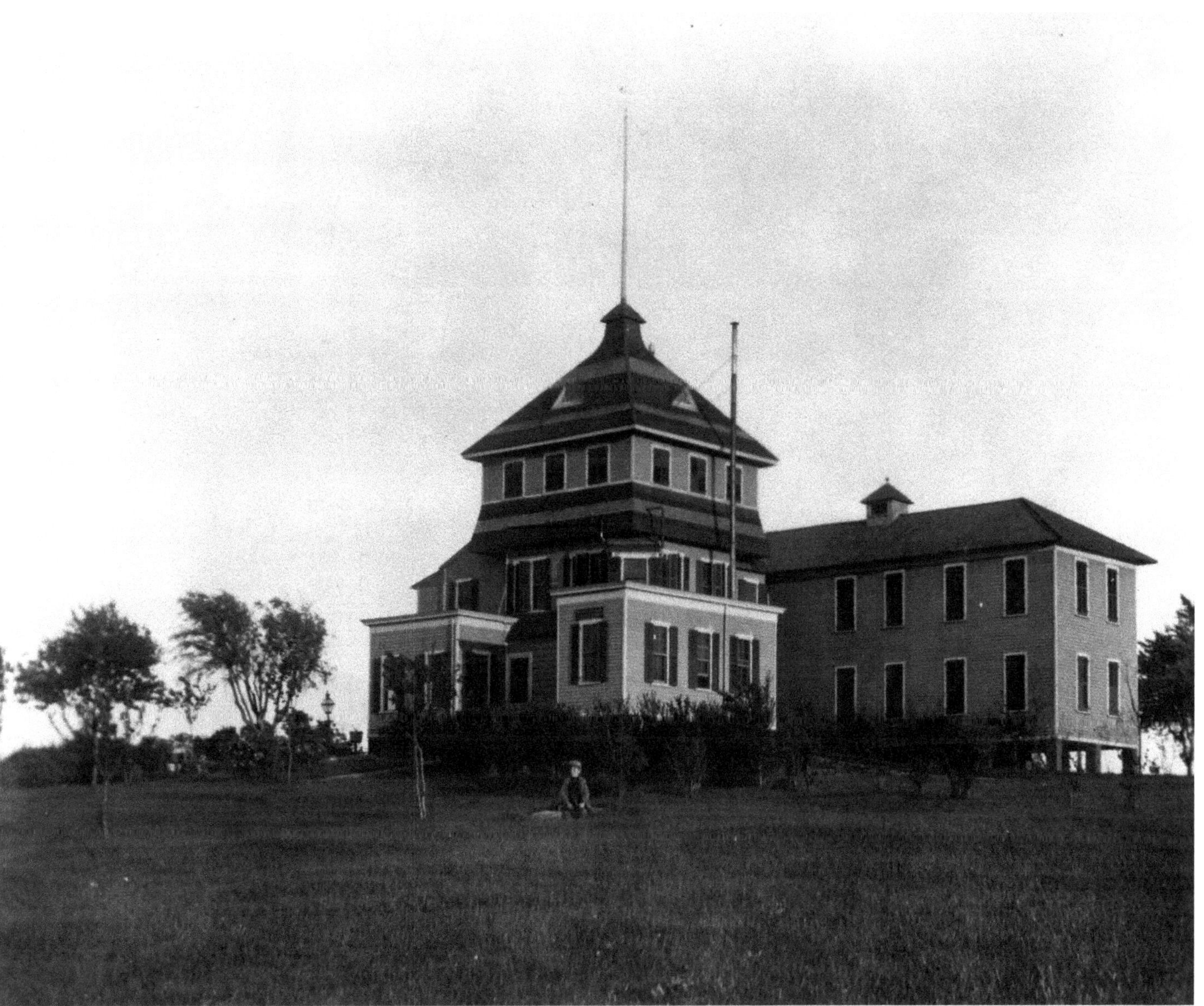

The 74th Sub-Precinct building at North Beach rivaled the Grand Pier for its stateliness. Seen here, the station operated mainly in the summer months and sat on a landscaped property befitting the resort area it served and protected. North Beach was also called "Bowery Bay" as part of a marketing plan devised by its main investors, piano maker William Steinway and brewer George Ehrets.

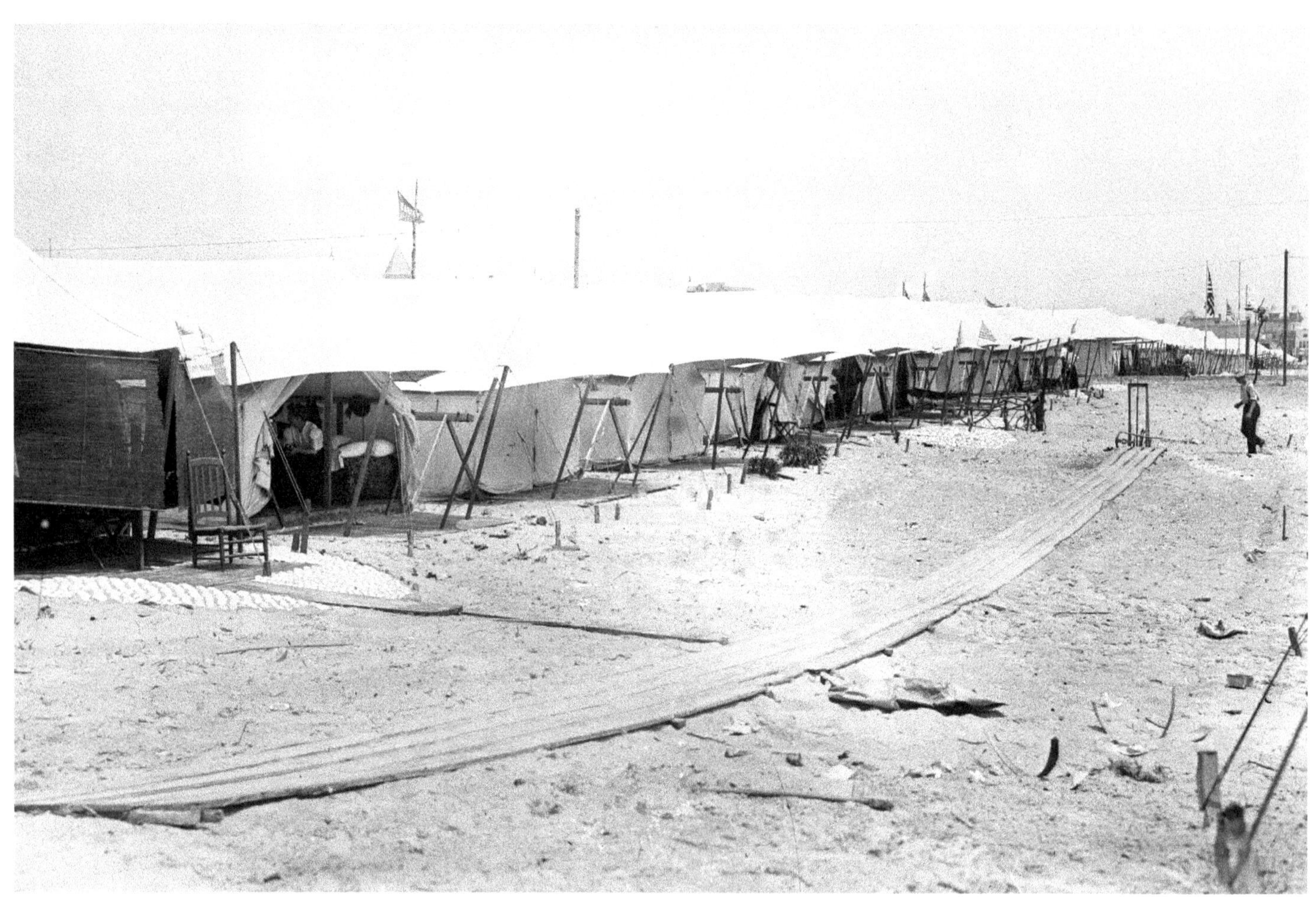

A close-up look at one of the many tent cities that filled the beaches of Rockaway along the Atlantic in the summer, providing respite for New York's everyday folks. The makeshift boardwalk laid across the sand made walking around the camp much easier.

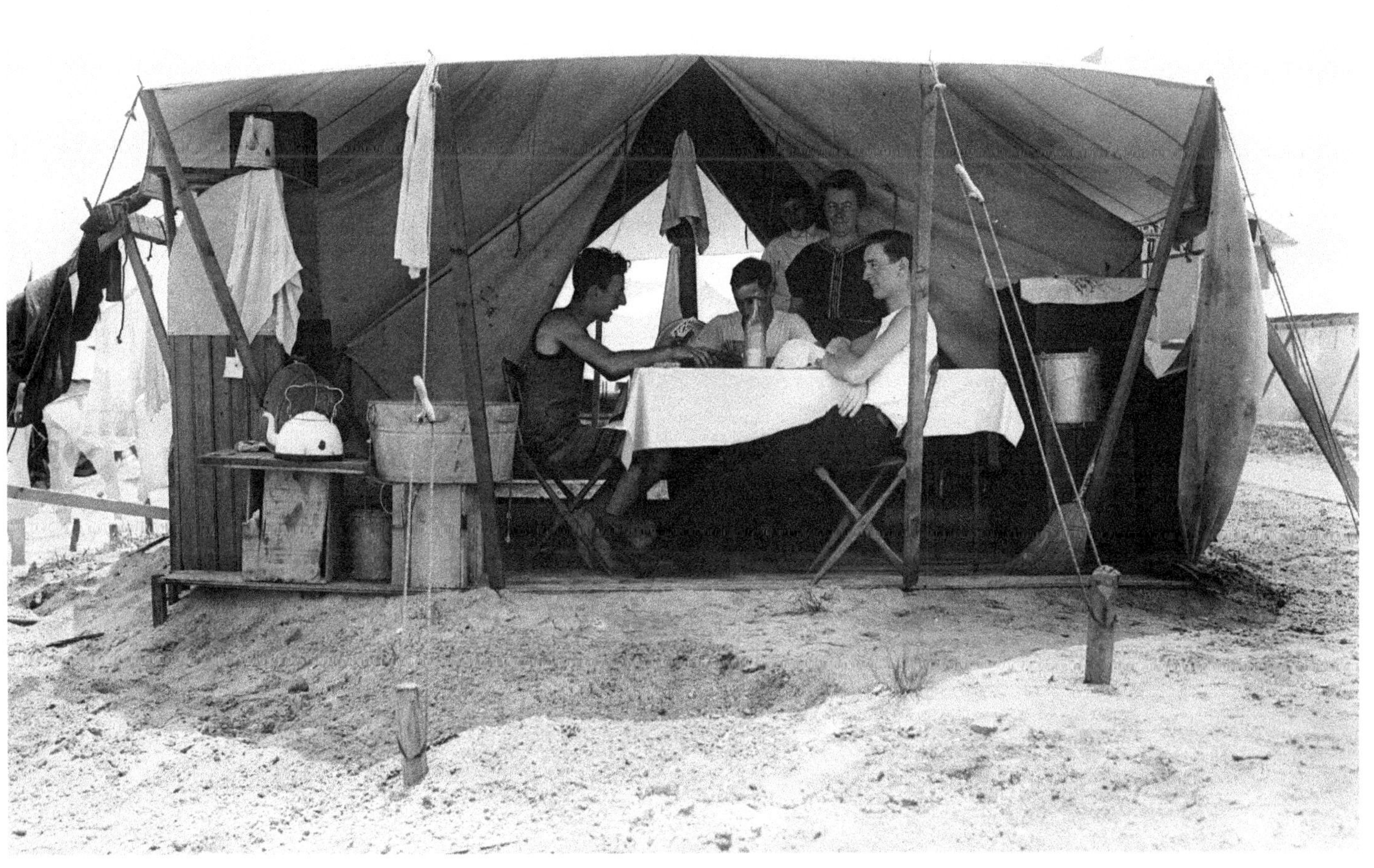

A more intimate look at the inside of one of the tents in the camps at Rockaway Beach. Here in 1910 a family enjoys a card game on the sand—complete with all the refinements of home, including a white tablecloth and a teakettle.

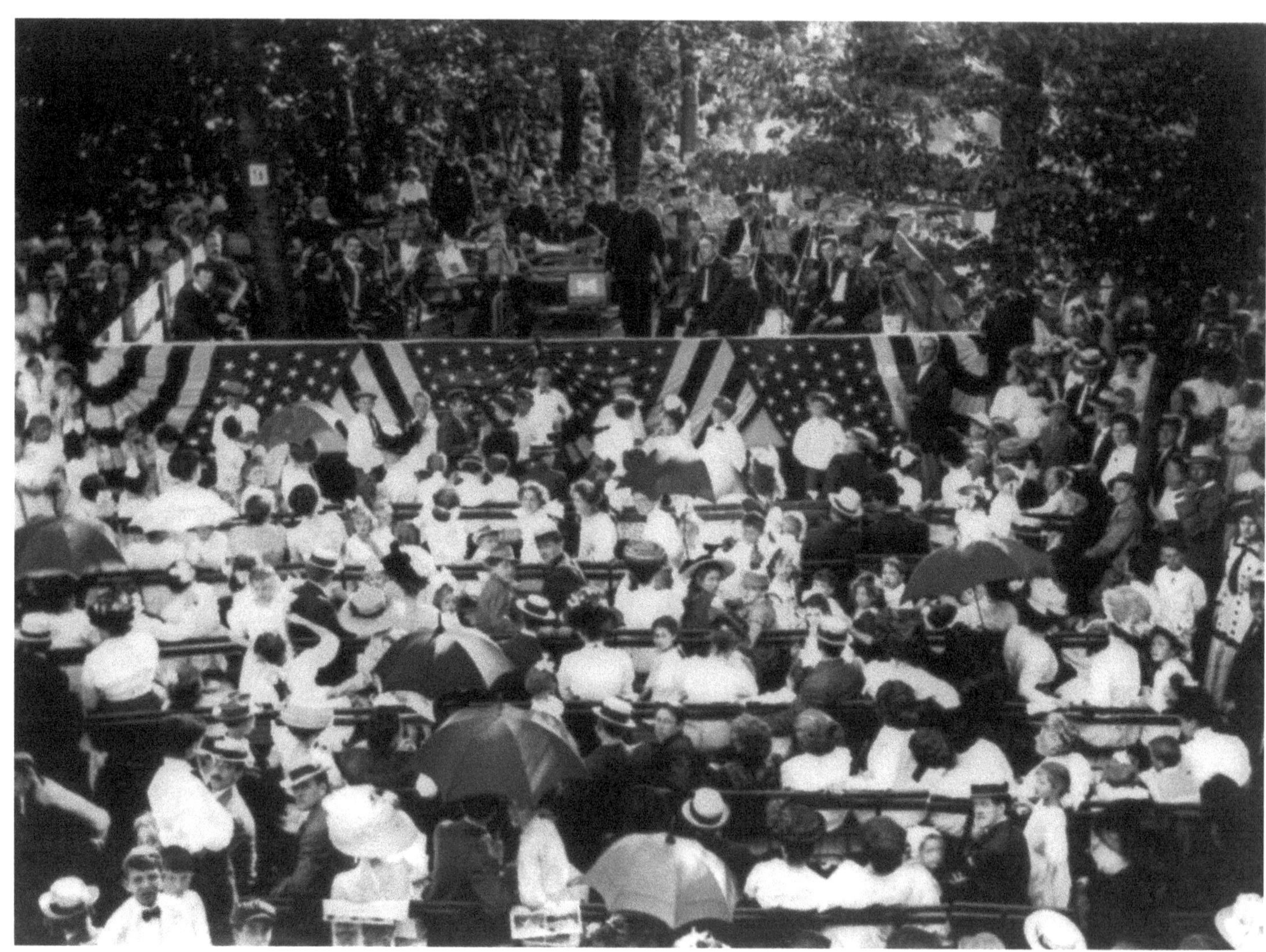

On Sunday afternoons at Forest Park in the 1910s, bandleader George Seuffert, Sr., led free concerts for the public. Musicians and audience at this performance have taken an intermission to look back at the cameraman. With hilltop views of Long Island Sound, Forest Park was established in 1898 with a central drive designed by legendary landscape architect Frederick Law Olmsted.

In sharp contrast to the rustic Rockaway Beach camps, two New York & Queens Company trolley cars ply Borden Avenue (here facing East at Front Street) in Long Island City, on the opposite side of the borough. The sky is crisscrossed with electrical and telephone lines, demonstrating the technological progress the borough experienced after the turn of the century. To the left of the frame are a number of beer gardens that once did business in the area.

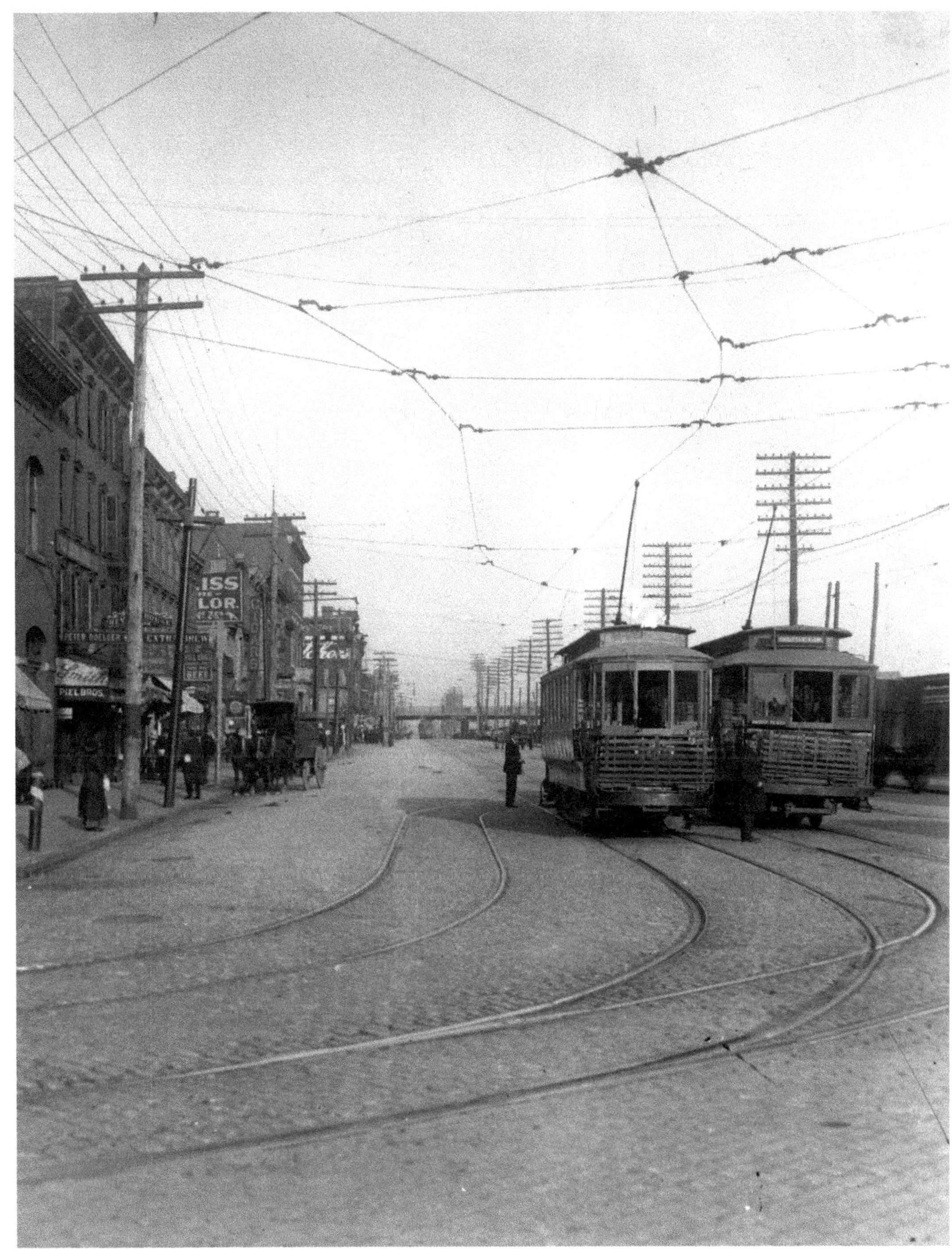

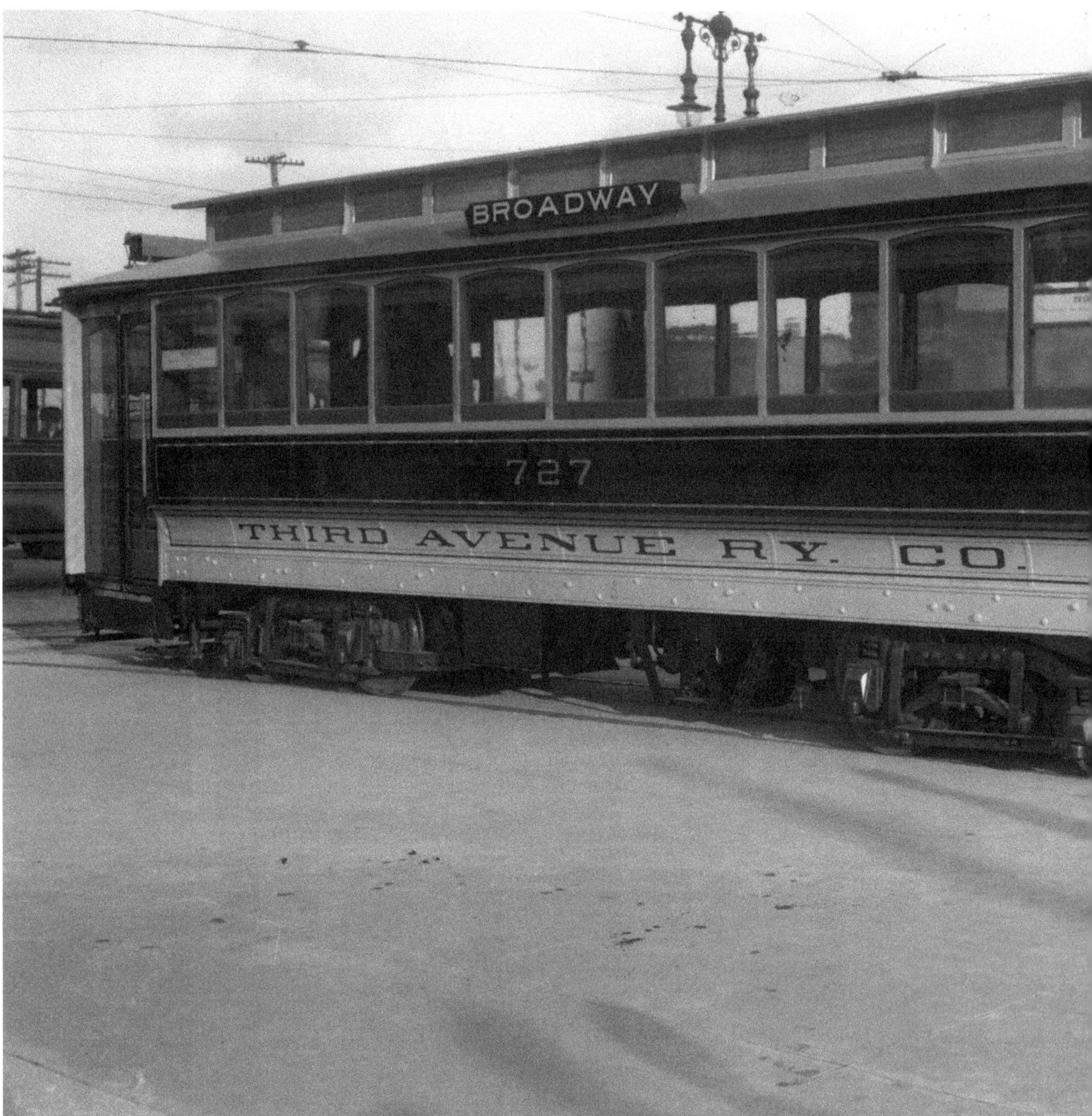
BROADWAY
727
THIRD AVENUE RY. CO.

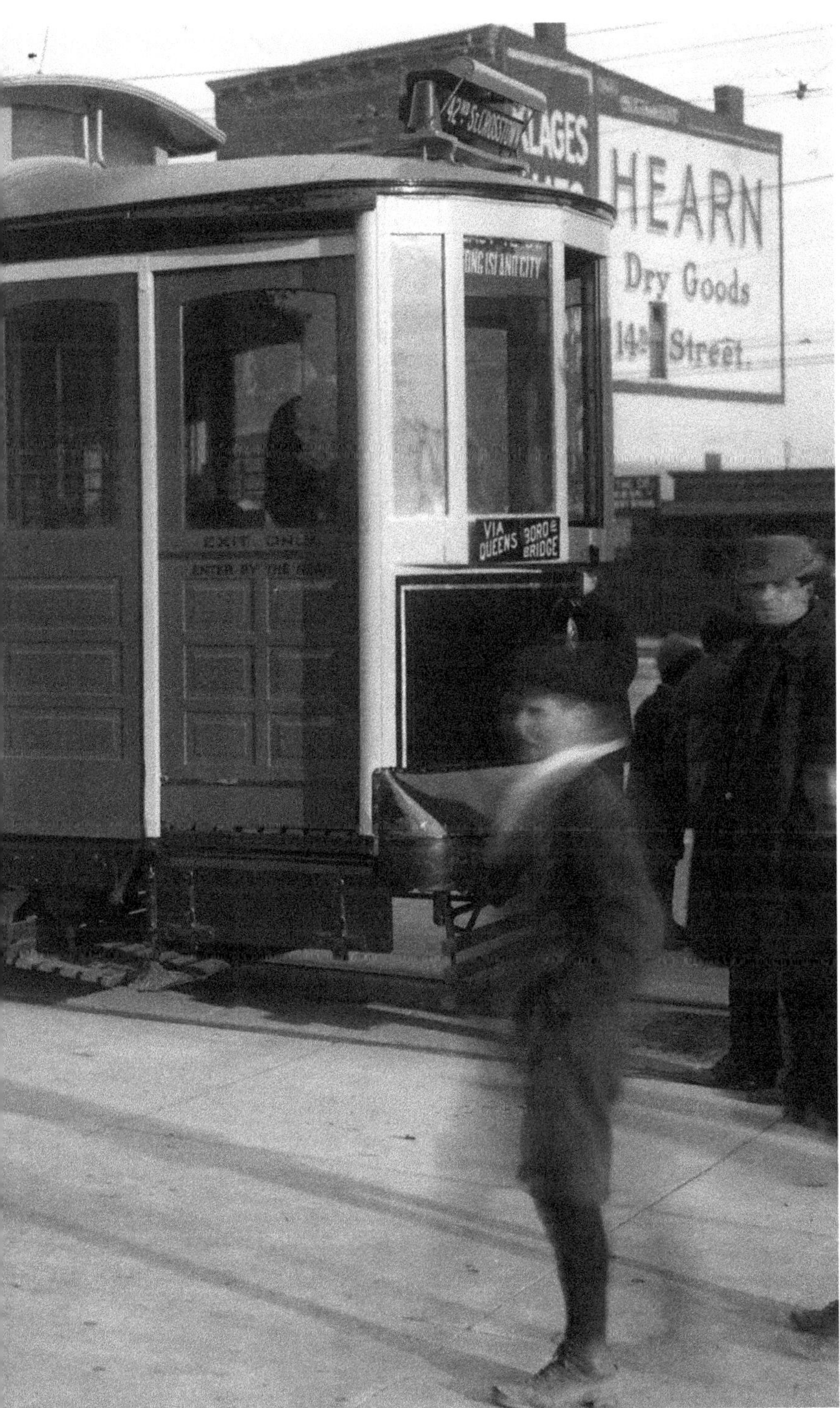

The Third Avenue Railway Company's 42nd Street crosstown streetcar at Queens Plaza. The car identifies its route as "Broadway" on the side and "via Queensboro Bridge" at front, indicating that this train ran over the Queensboro Bridge. Early on, the top level of the bridge carried trains and had a mid-bridge station for transfers.

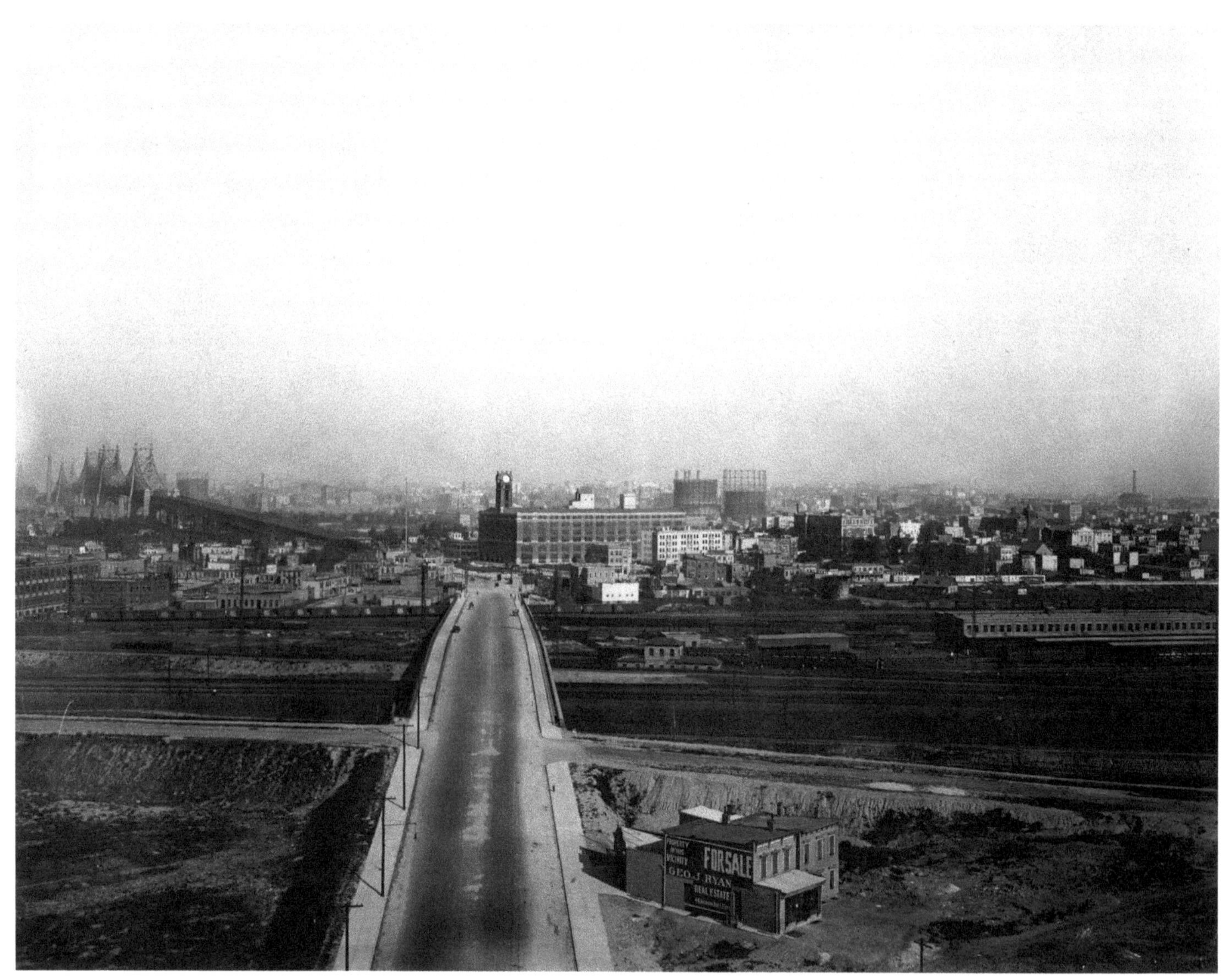

A western view of the Sunnyside Yards, just in front of the Queensboro Bridge, which is visible in the left background of the frame. The yards still exist and are in use by the Long Island Railroad and Amtrak. In some respects, the area today retains an industrial charm, although high-rises punctuate parts of the skyline, including the massive glass Citibank Building that stands across from the Long Island City Courthouse.

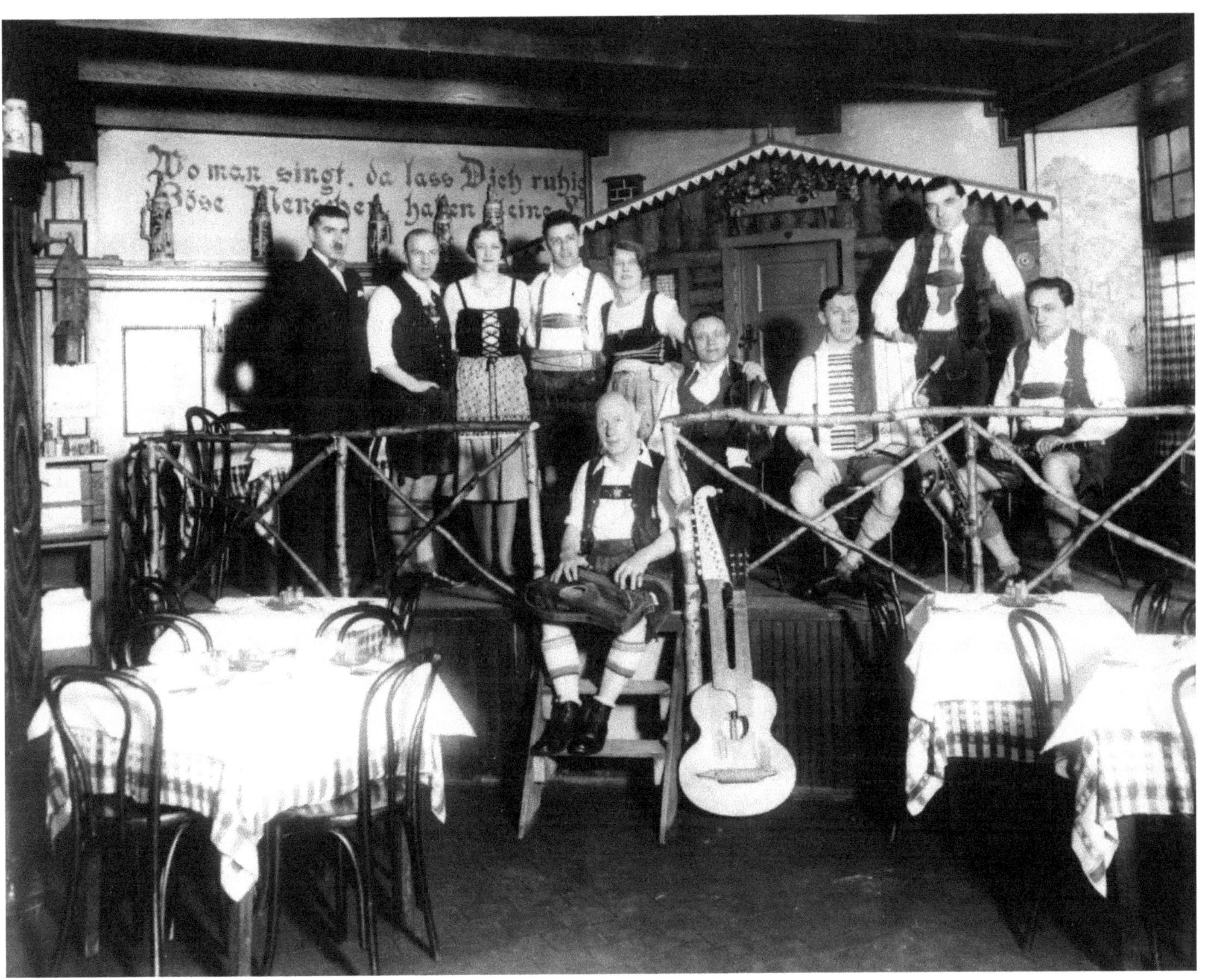

The staff joined entertainers for a photograph on the stage at Gostl's Original Munchner Platzl, a traditional German Hofbrauhaus that celebrated the Bavarian heritage of Long Island City in 1910.

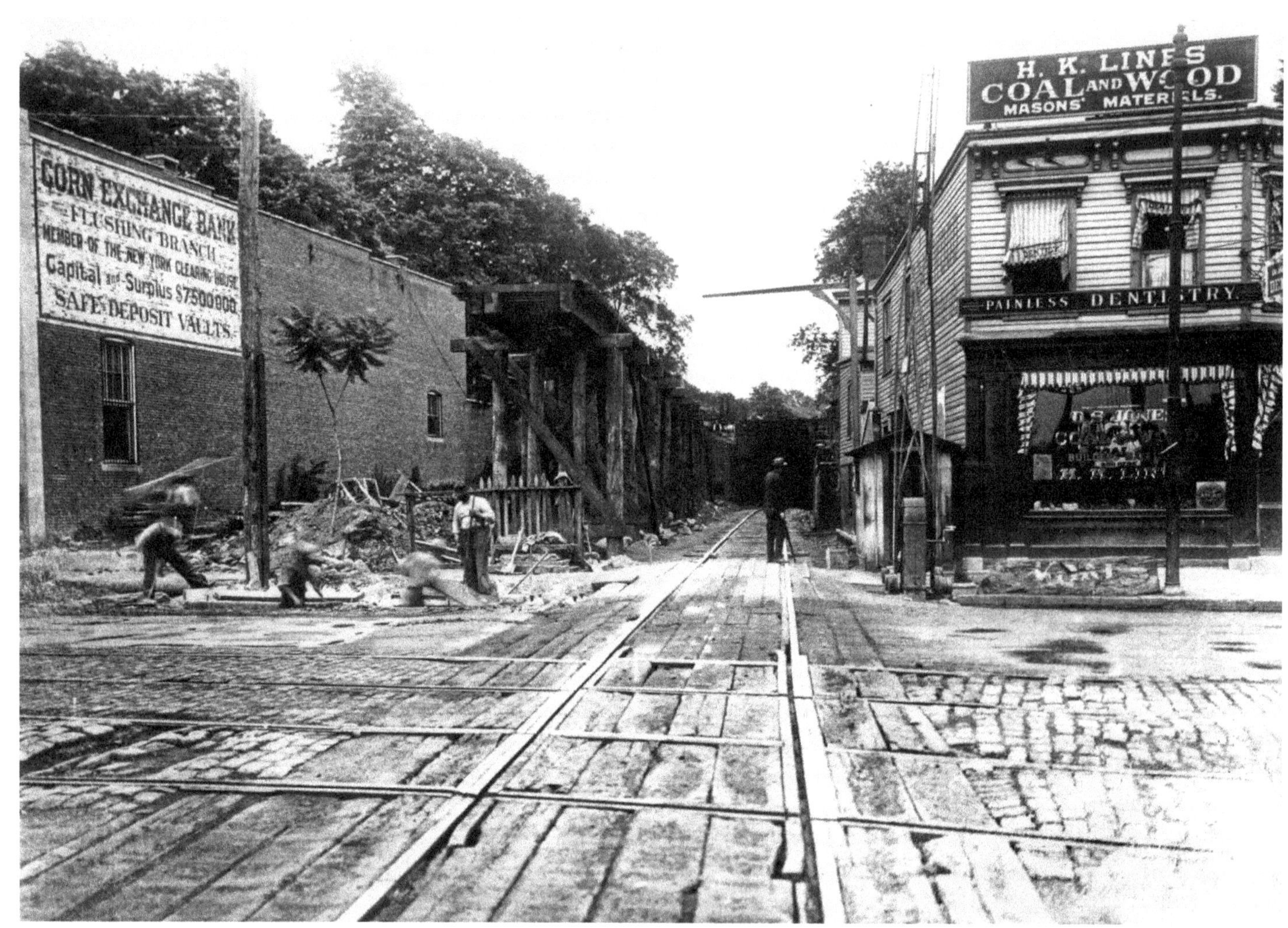

Made famous by F. Scott Fitzgerald's *The Great Gatsby*, the Long Island Railroad's "Gold Coast" line still runs along the North Shore of Long Island, through the Queens neighborhoods of Woodside, Flushing, Bayside, Douglaston, and Little Neck. Seen here in 1912 is the crossing at Main Street, in Flushing.

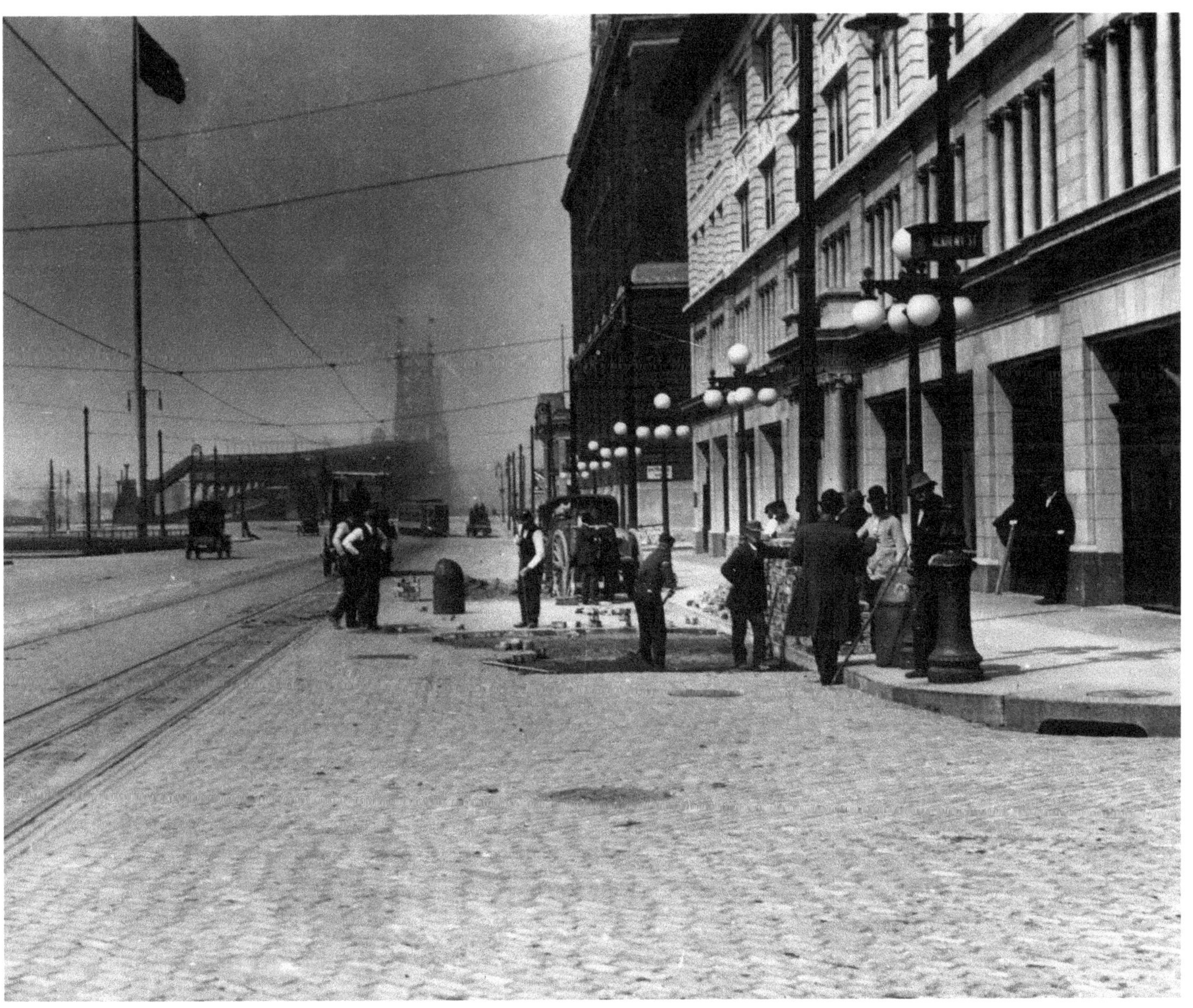

A view looking west from the north side of the Queensboro Bridge Plaza, near 29th Street in Long Island City, around 1912. The area continued to be developed and was characterized by the wide, paved streets and charming architecture and street fixtures seen here to the right in the frame.

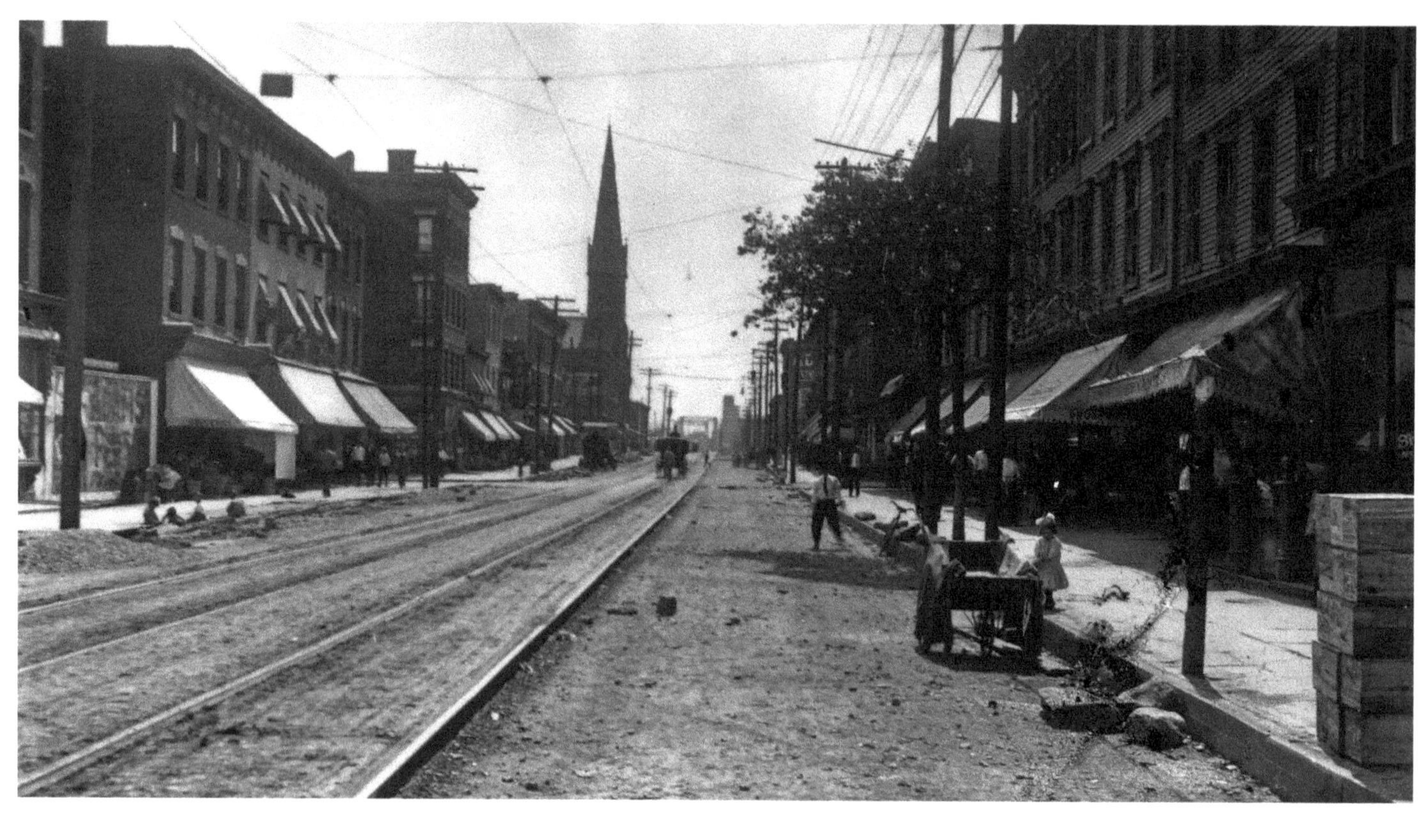

Just a few blocks from where the bridge brought paved streets, in 1915 this stretch of Vernon Boulevard (Avenue) near 47th Avenue remained unpaved, despite the tracks running down the thoroughfare.

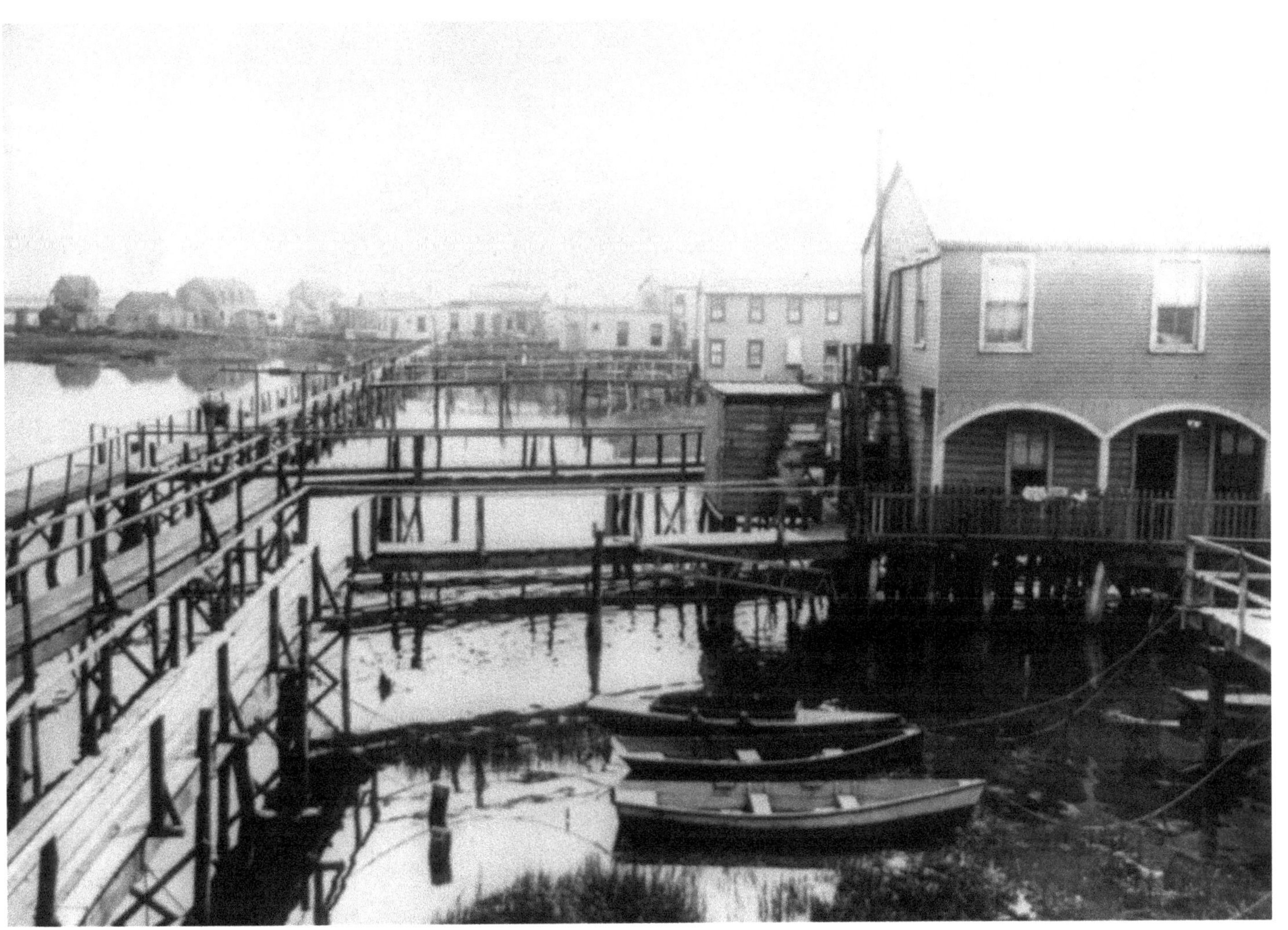

The inlets and marshes on the edge of Jamaica Bay were part of a housing boom in the second decade of the twentieth century. This scene from around 1915 shows houses built on stilts into the bay, with gangways connecting the homes and the mainland, rather than sidewalks. Small boats are moored near some of the houses. Communities like this one still exist in south Queens, west of John F. Kennedy Airport.

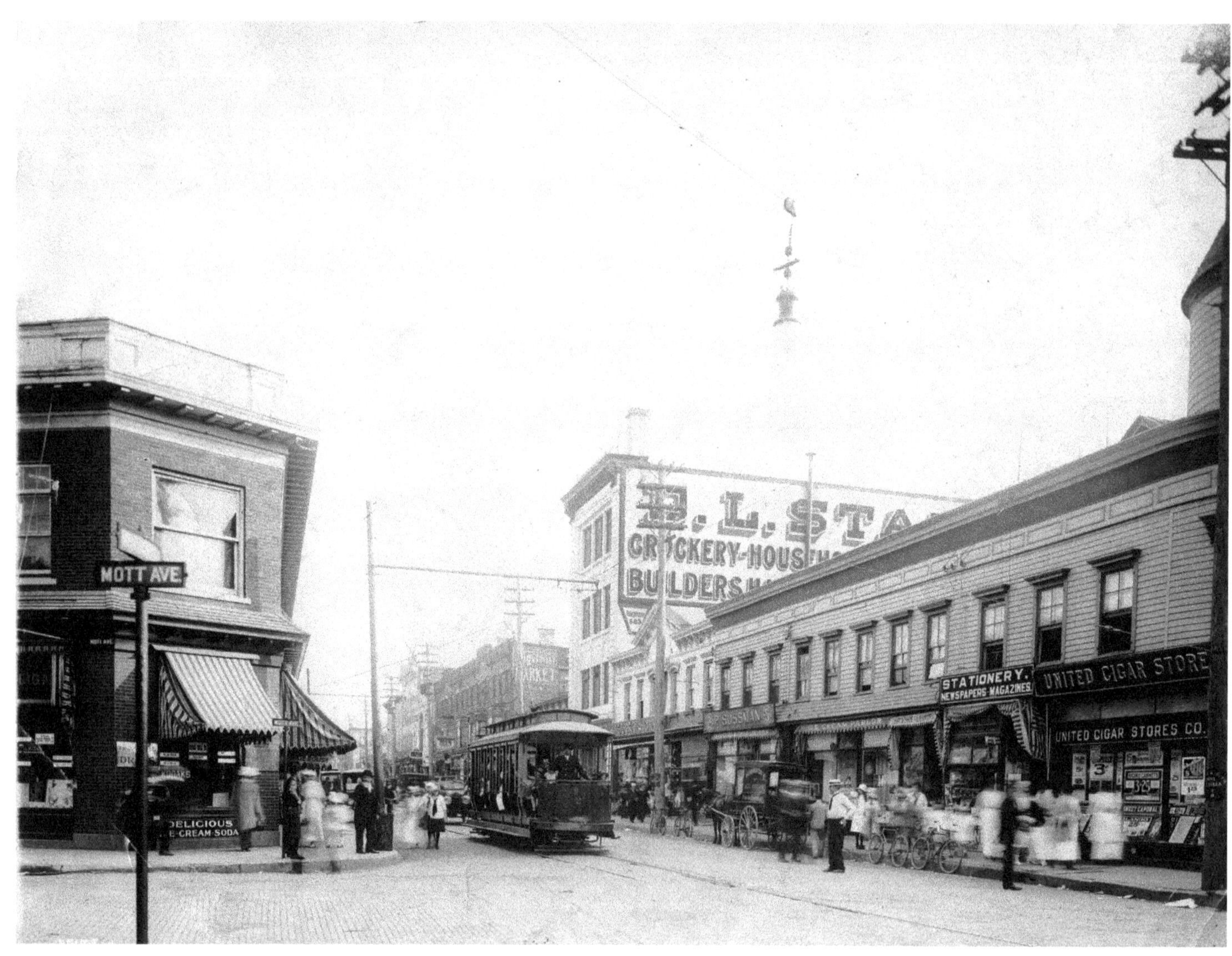

Although known for its seaside pavilions and amusements in the summertime, Far Rockaway was (and is) a community of locals who are accustomed to living on an isolated strip of land on the Atlantic Coast, yet still within the borders of New York City. Here in 1916 is a busy day along Mott Avenue at the intersection of Central Avenue.

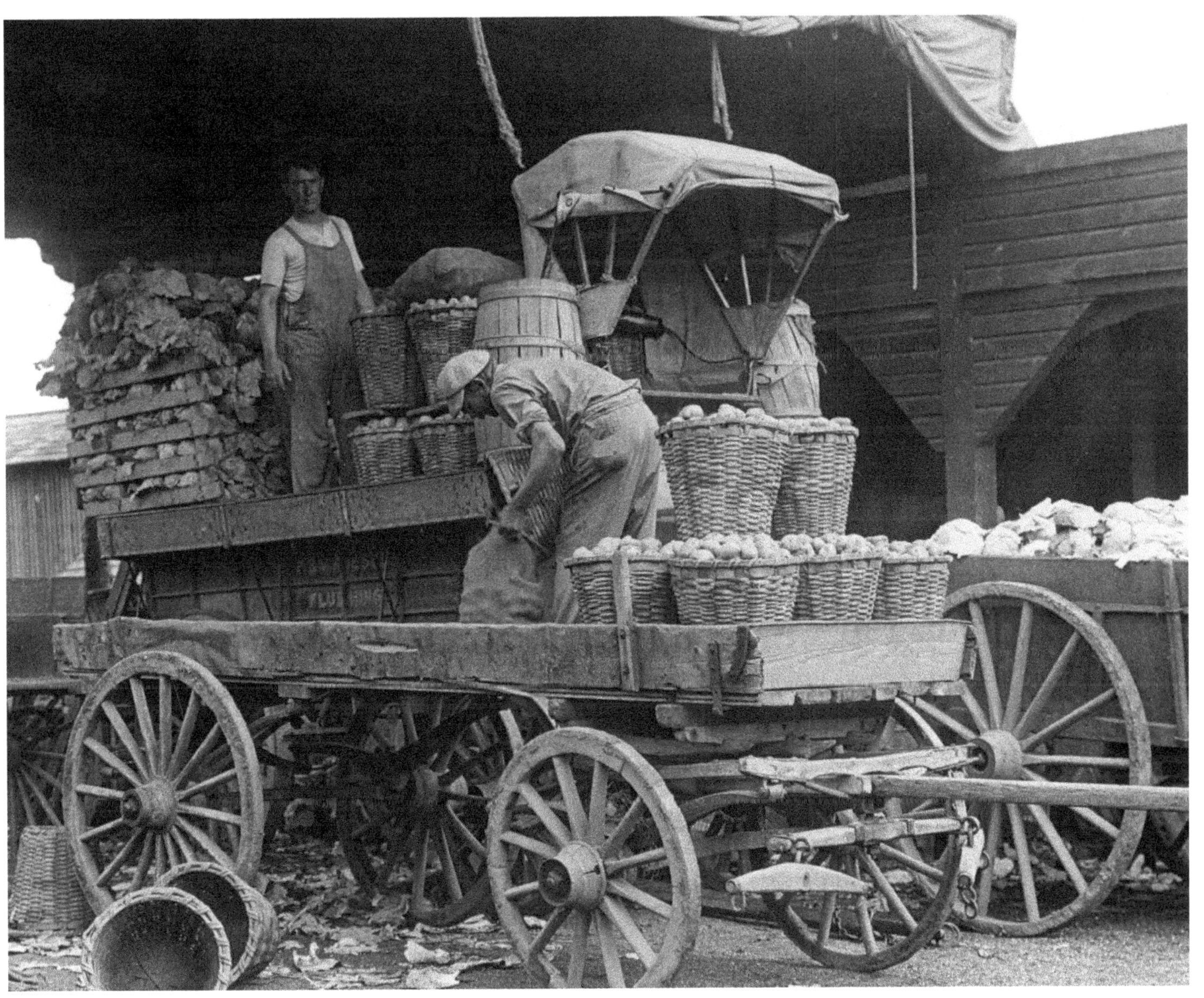

Two farmers load a wagon with cabbages and potatoes at this truck farm near Jamaica, Queens, in the 1910s. The borough was still known for agricultural production in the years leading up to the encroachment of suburbia.

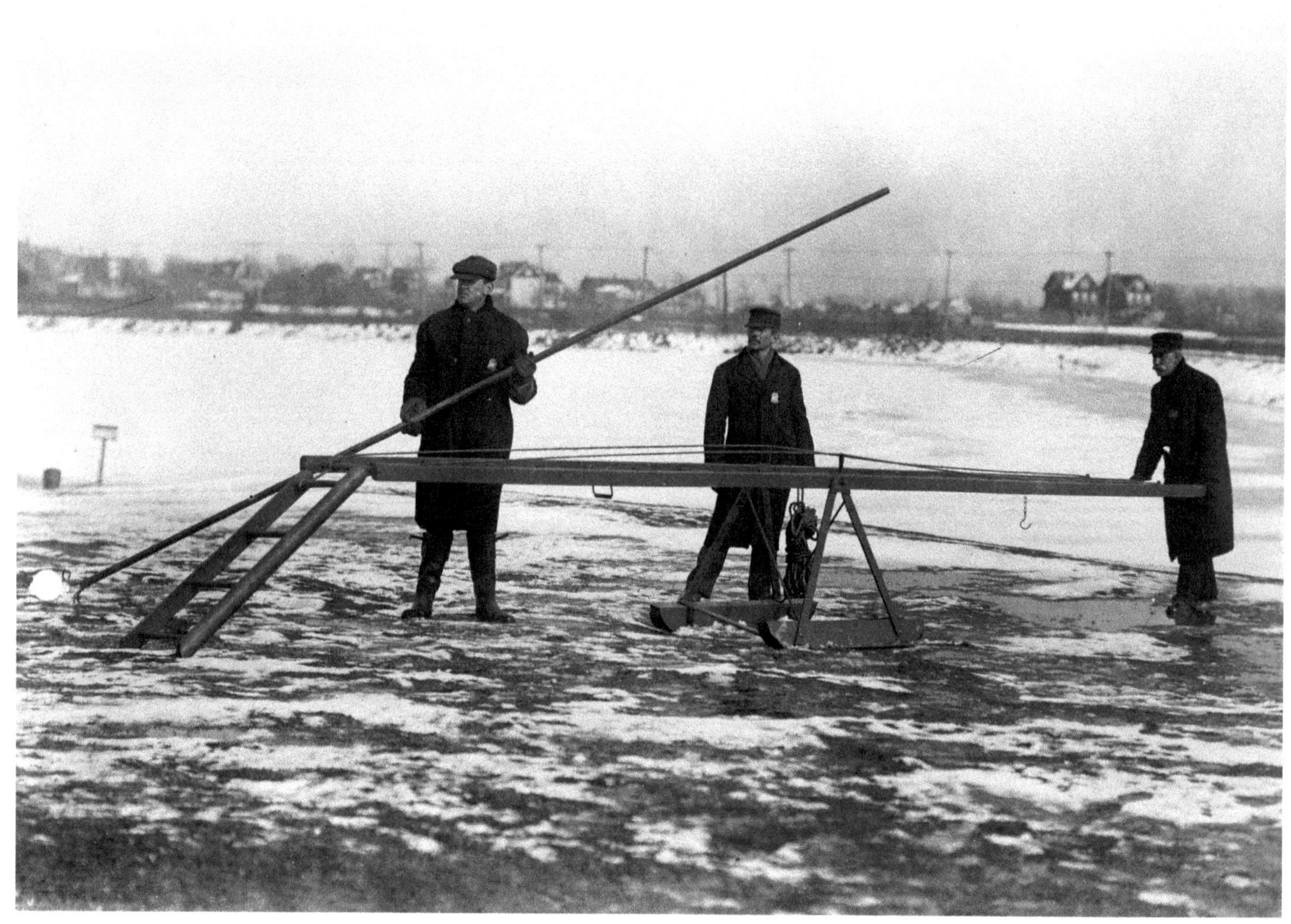

On a frozen pond in Queens stands George Hanlon, the foreman of the Department of Parks for Queens. Hanlon and crew were on hand with an apparatus designed to rescue hapless skaters fallen through the ice.

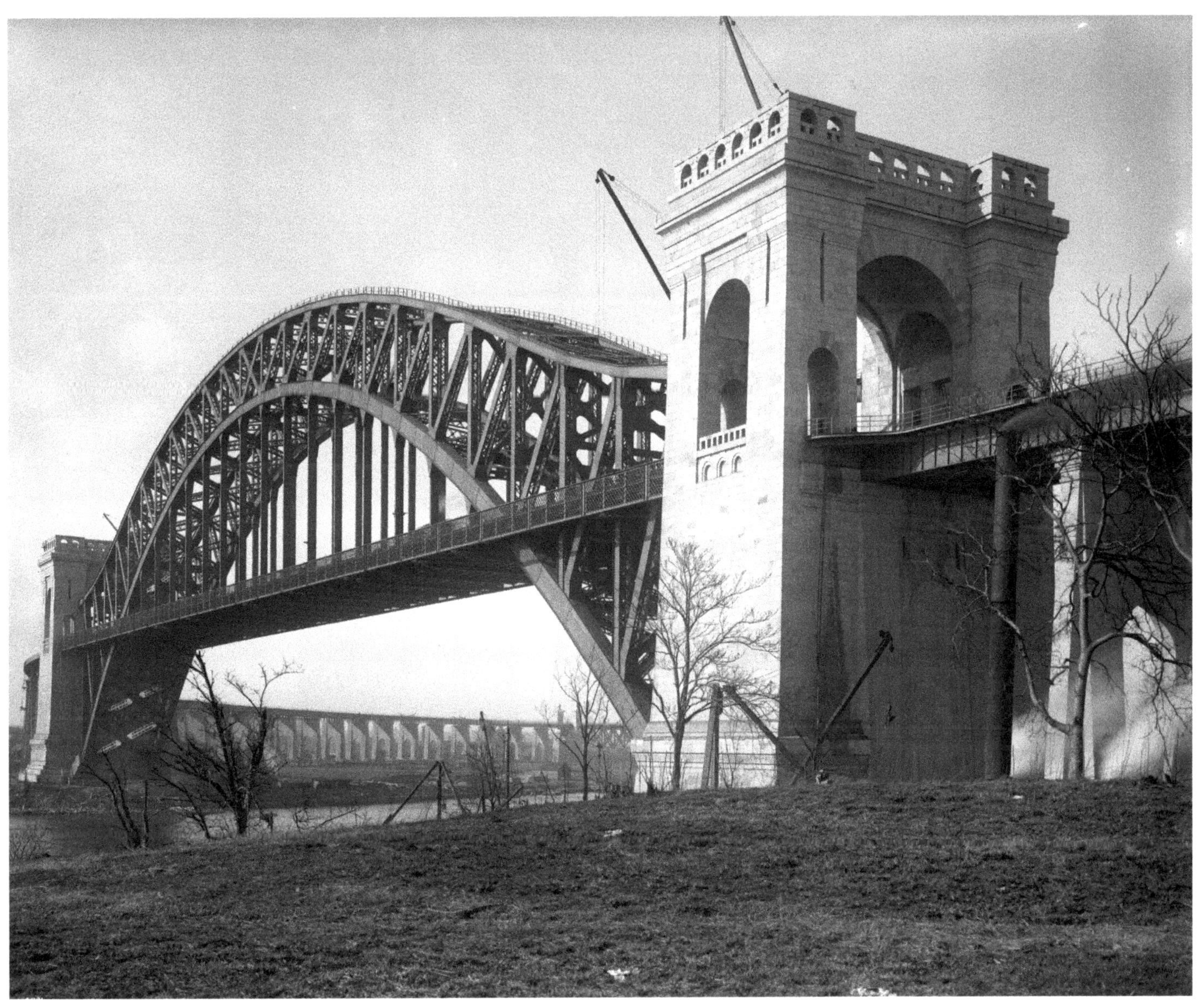

The Hell Gate Bridge opened in 1916 in Astoria as a railroad bridge spanning an area of the East River known as Hell Gate. The bridge was designed by Gustav Lindenthal, who had completed work on the Queensboro Bridge some years earlier. With little formal education and lacking a degree in civil engineering, Lindenthal had taught himself to build bridges, immigrating to America to find the opportunity denied him in Europe.

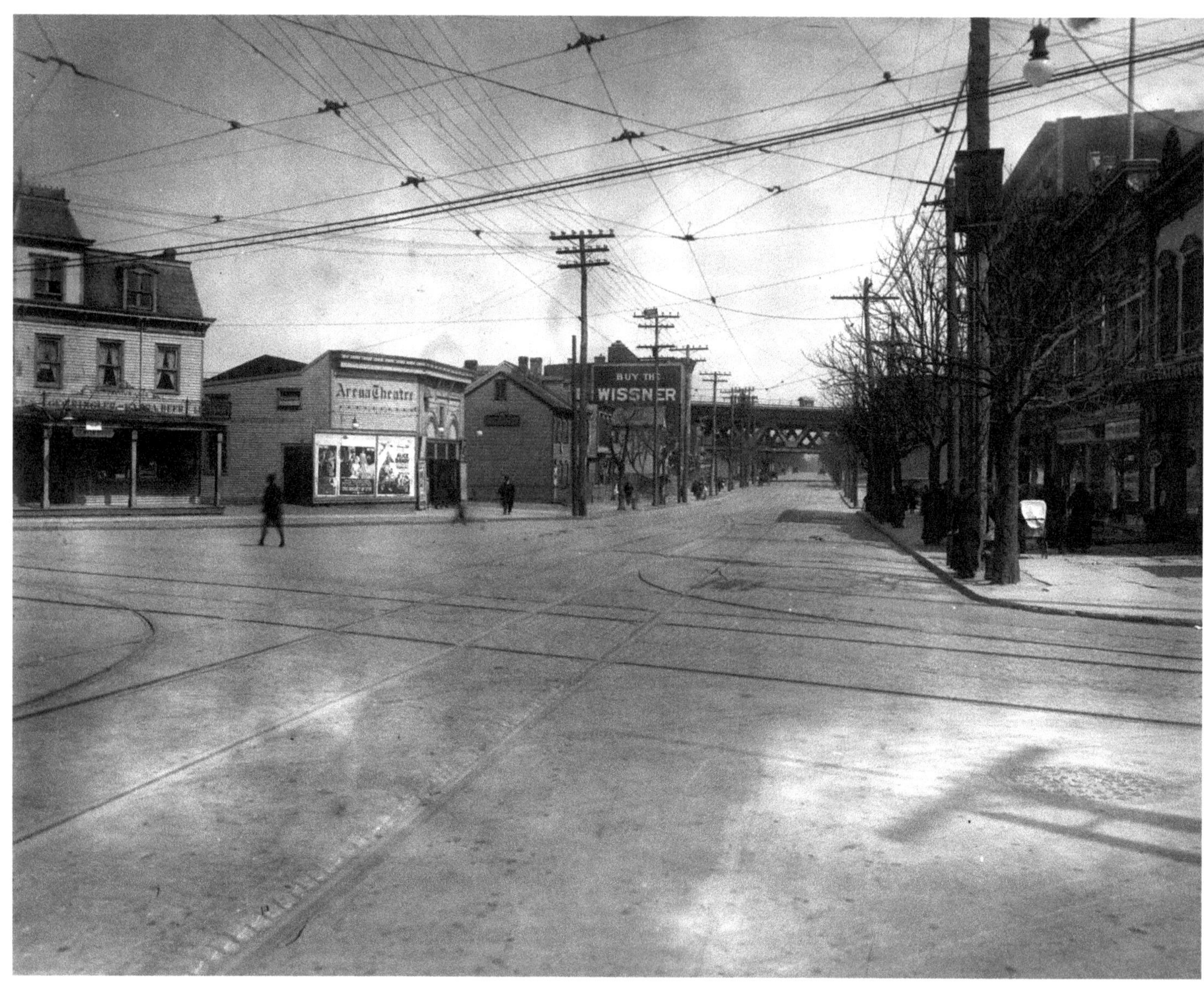

This is Steinway Street in Astoria, facing north from what is now Astoria Boulevard (formerly Flushing Avenue). To the left is the Arena Theatre, one of the first cinemas to open in Queens during the silent film era. The large sign to the north advertising the "Wissner" is likely for the Wissner Piano Company—strategically placed on the street named for the founder of the rival Steinway & Sons brand.

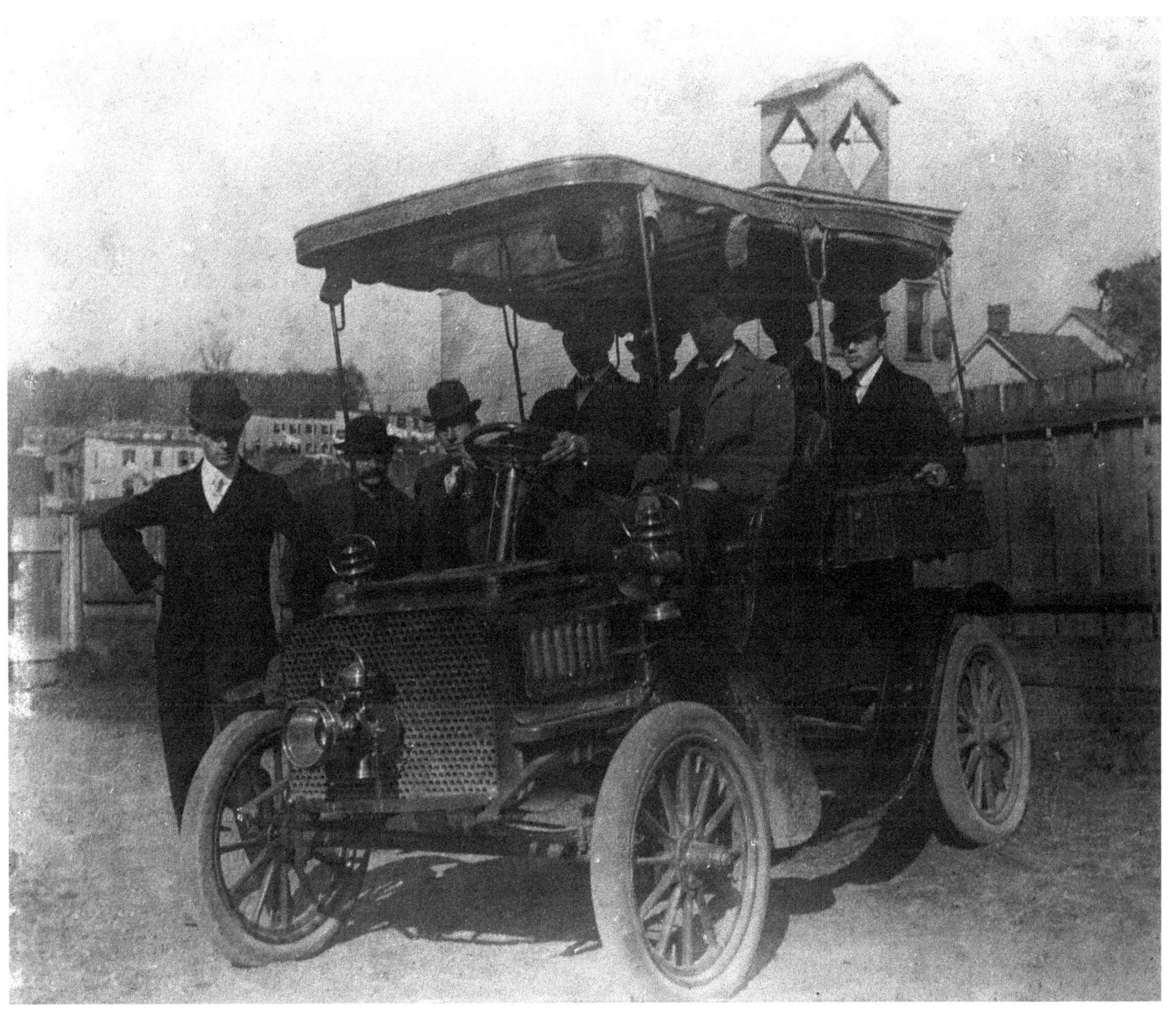

The automobile increasingly supplanted public transportation, the horse-and-buggy, and other conveyances, giving commuters and travelers greater mobility across the vast borough.

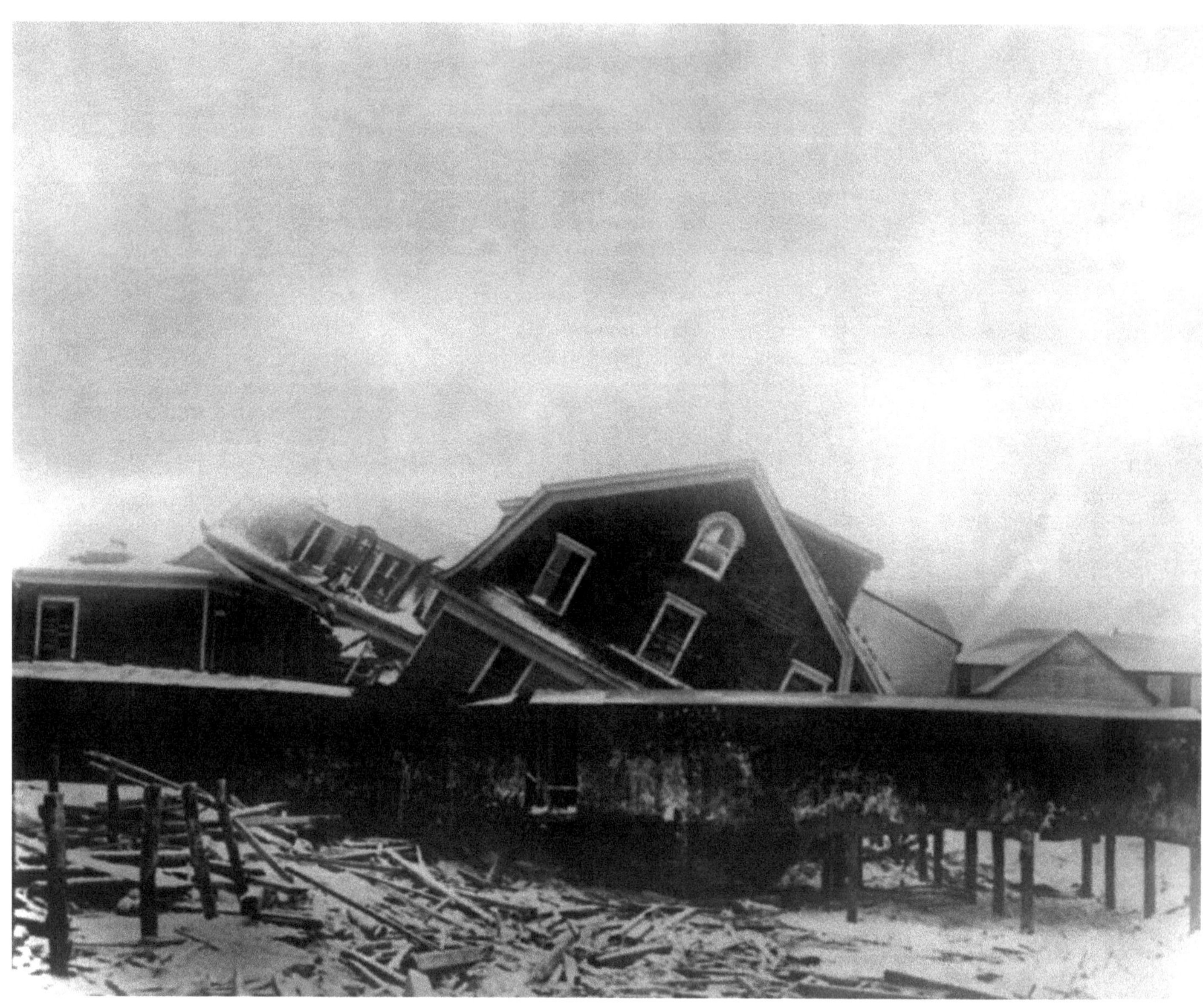

In February 1920, a punishing storm ravaged the Rockaway peninsula, with high tides destroying buildings along the coast and parts of the boardwalk and leaving only ruins.

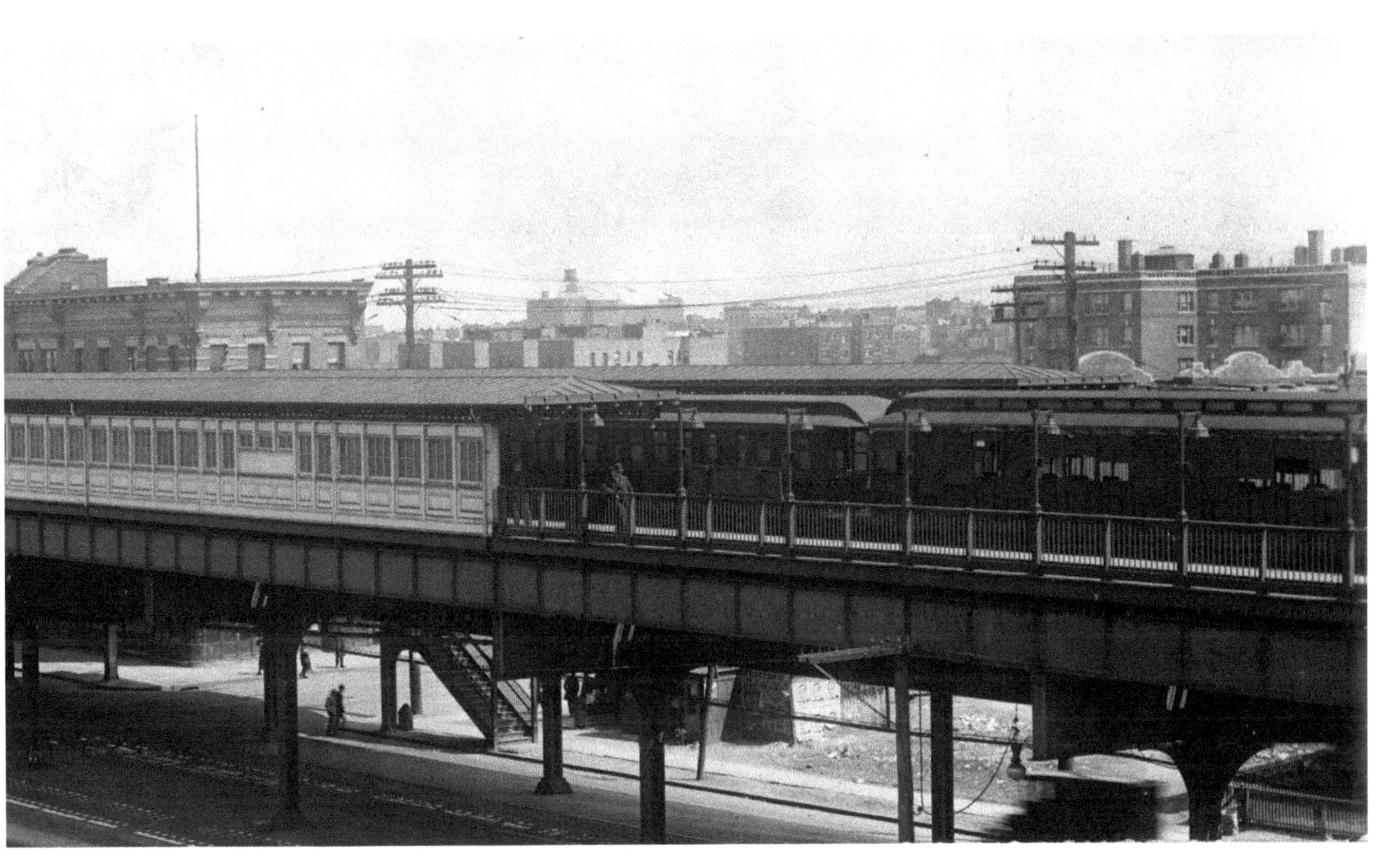

The west side platform of the Broadway Avenue subway station in 1922. These elevated tracks made rapid transit service possible and are still in use today.

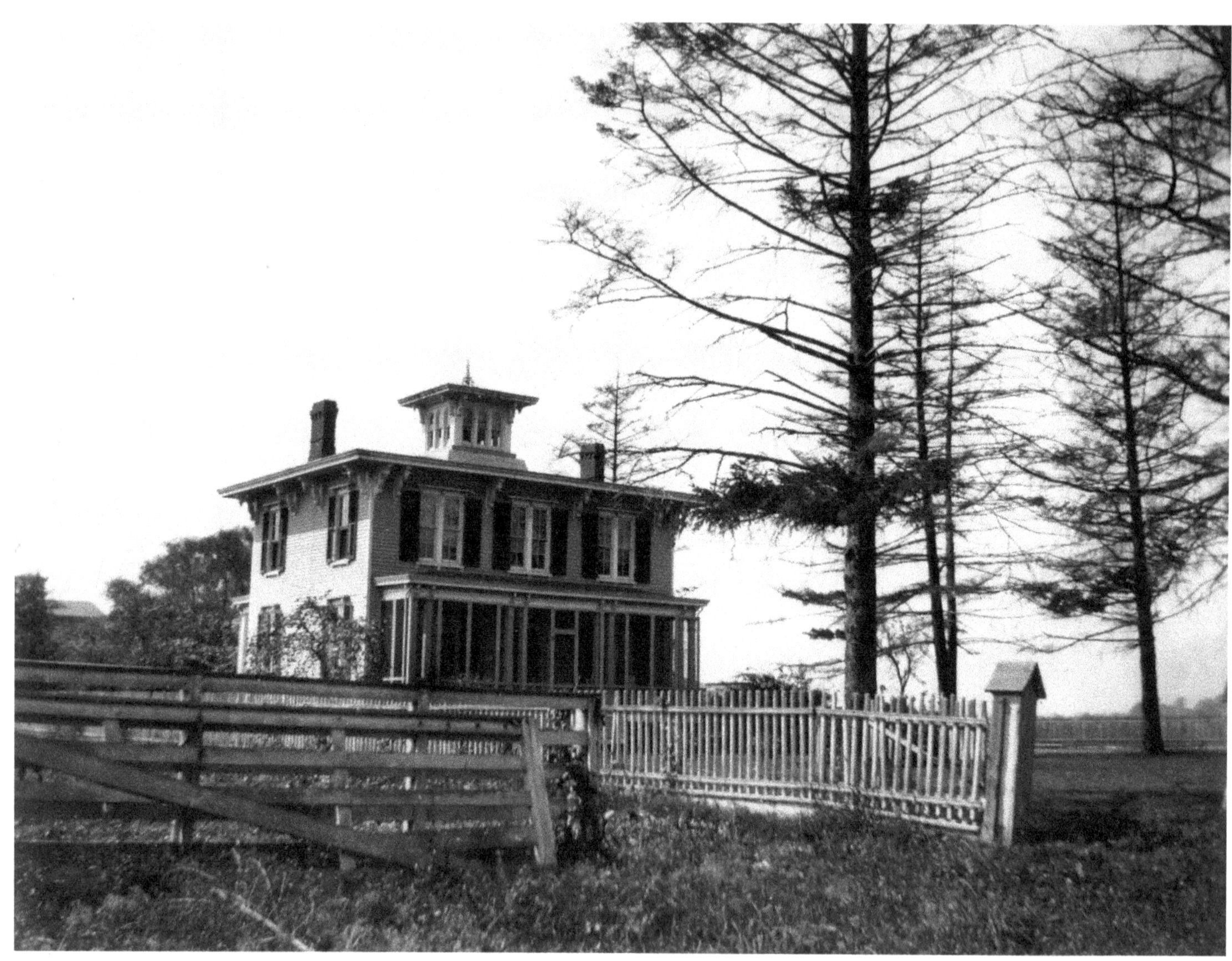

George E. Van Siclen's house on what is now Springfield Boulevard and Hollis Avenue. The Van Siclens were one of the oldest families on Long Island and operated a farm in what was later established as Queens Village. The farmland succumbed to development in the 1920s, when a housing boom sparked the building of large residences for commuters, who established some of the earliest suburban areas of the county.

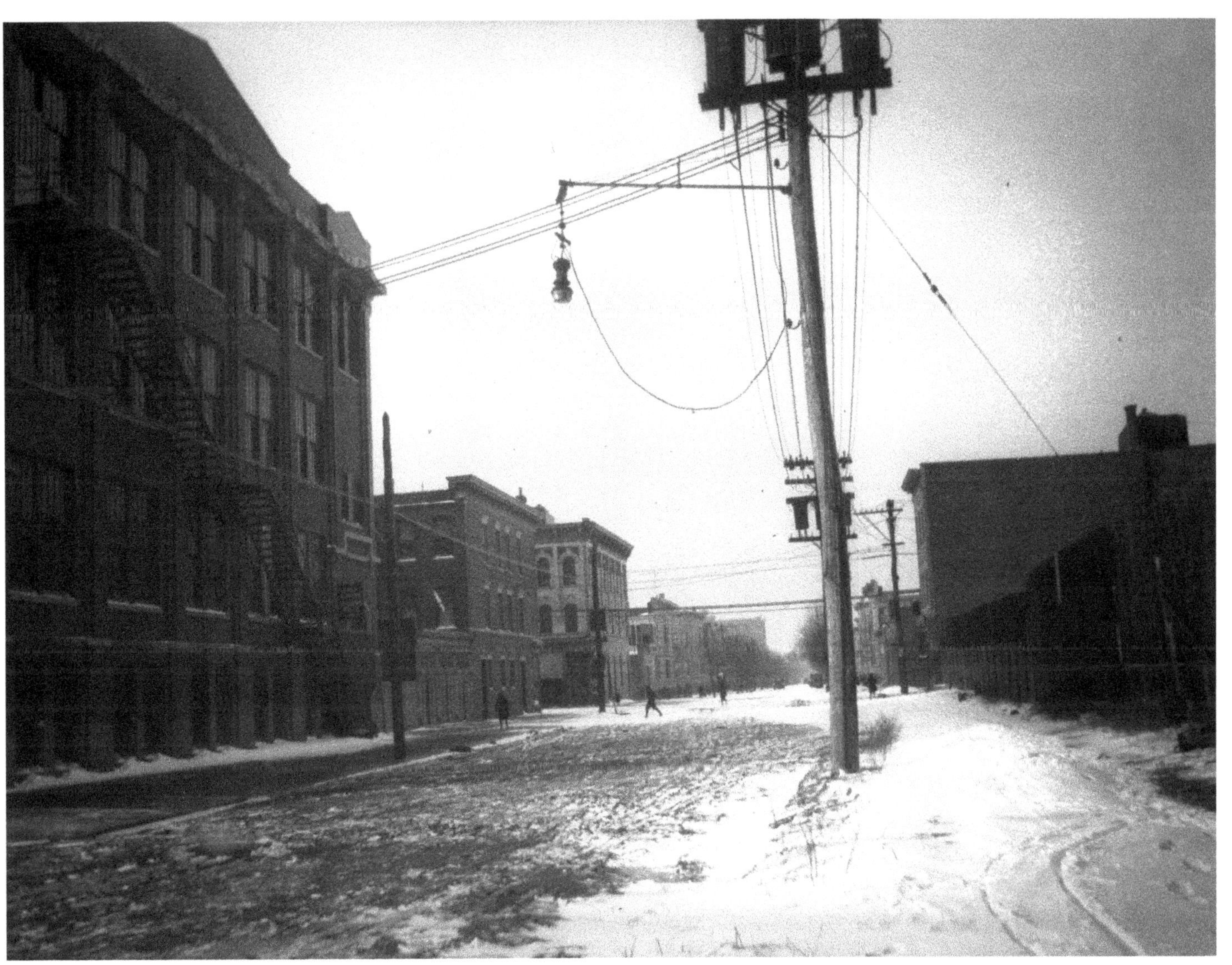

A factory on the Brooklyn-Queens border, between Bushwick and Ridgewood. Seen here on a snowy day in 1922, the factory on the left displays a "Help Wanted" sign.

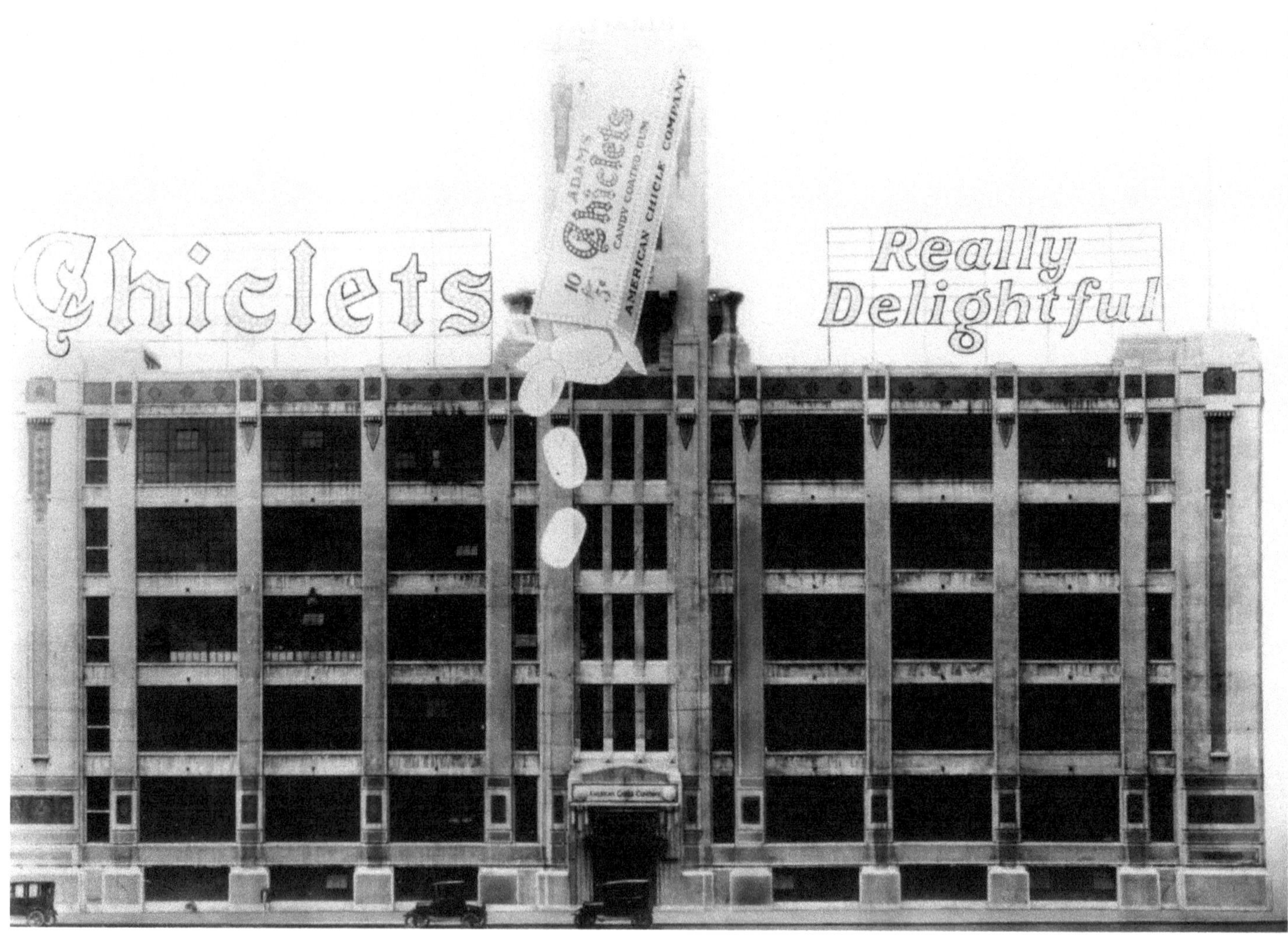

The American Chicle Company at Degnon Terminal in Long Island City (at Thomson Street) displays a new billboard for Chiclets gum in 1923. The building spanned 60 city lots, had an internal courtyard to accommodate railroad sidings, and cost $2 million to build. The company was actually a "chewing gum trust," manufacturing its products for various brands in the United States and imported gum from the Yucatan region of Mexico.

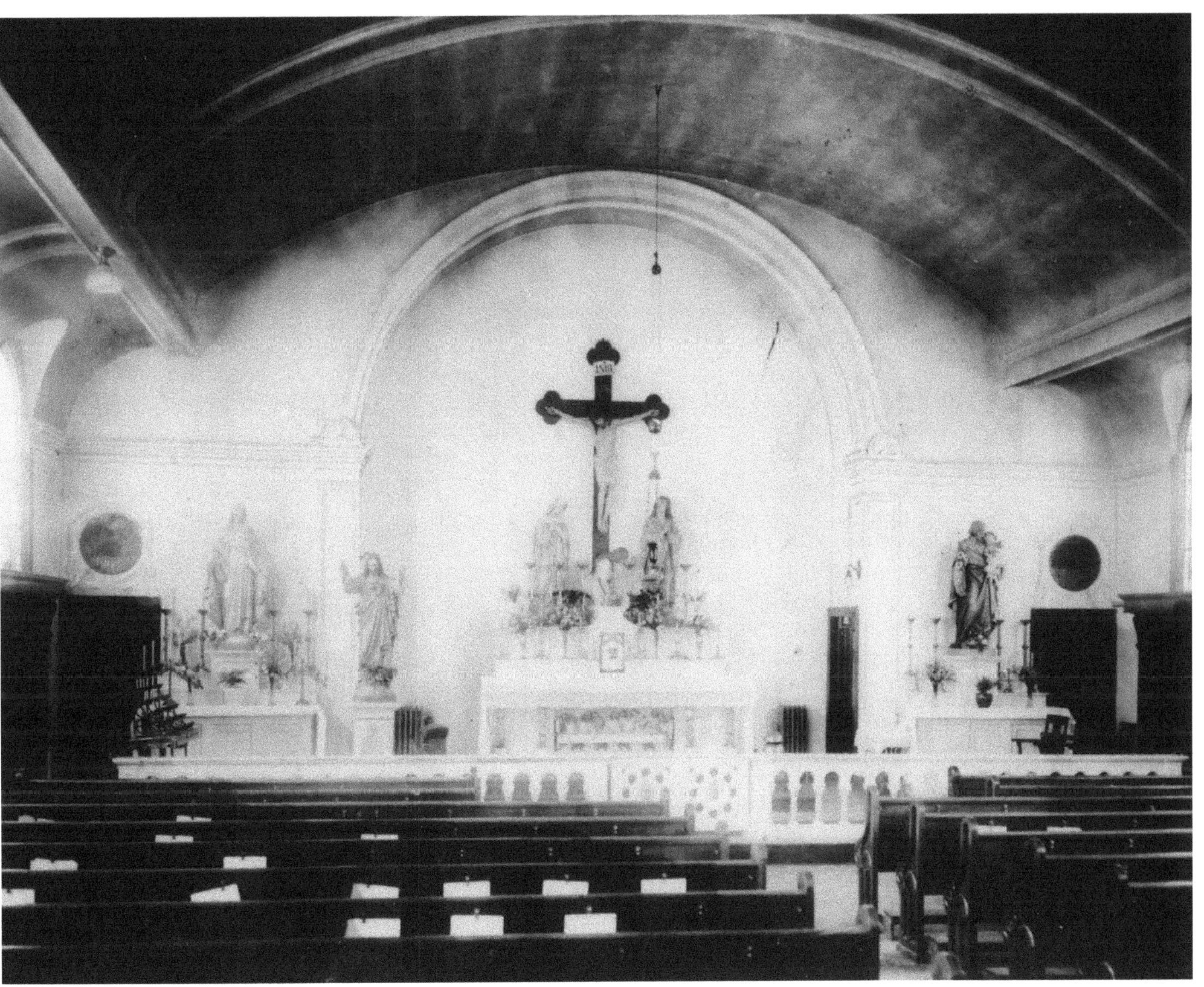

The interior of Our Lady of Grace Roman Catholic Church, built in 1924, located in the neighborhood of Howard Beach—a small peninsula formed by Jamaica Bay to the south, Shellbank Basin on the west, and Hawtree Creek on the east. The northern part of the area was originally a goat farm used to provide skins to glove manufacturer William Howard. He developed the area, which eventually included a pier, casino, railroad station, and beaches—which drew investors and eventually formed enough of a neighborhood to merit building the church.

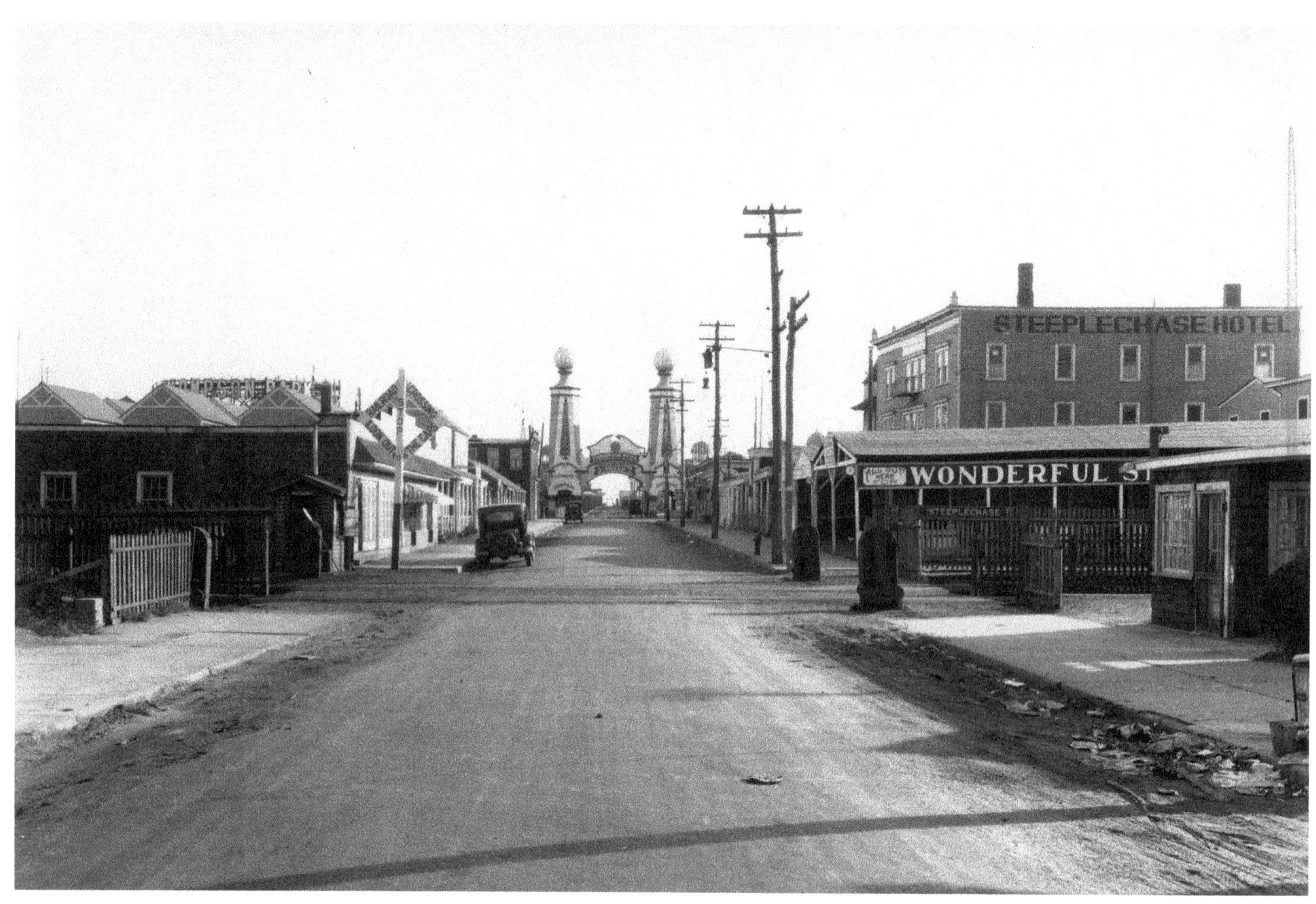

Looking south down Ward Avenue (Beach 98th Street) across the Long Island Railroad crossing, near the Steeplechase LIRR station—named for the Steeplechase Park and the Steeplechase Hotel visible in the distance. The stop was also used by the Ocean Electric Railway's trolleys. It was later used by the IND Rockaway Line. Today the Beach 98th Street elevated subway station stands in roughly the same location.

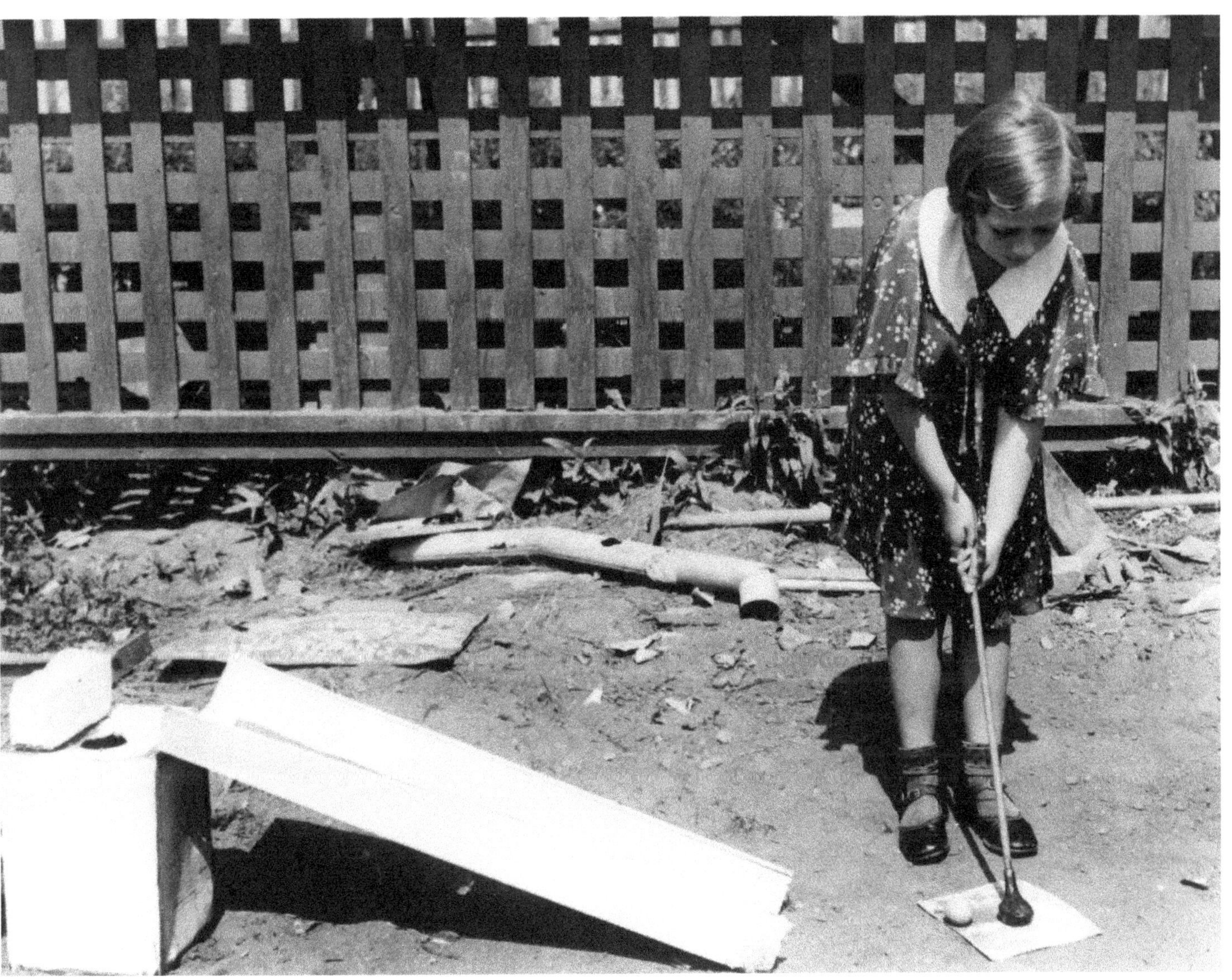

Little Dorothy Messina practices her putt on a homemade miniature golf course in Ozone Park. The neighborhood was originally developed in the late nineteenth century and expanded as the LIRR opened a station east of Howard Beach. In 1914, an elevated railroad line made the area even more accessible for commuters seeking a suburban life. With the expansion of Woodhaven Boulevard all the way to the Rockaways, the area was opened to vehicular traffic and development boomed.

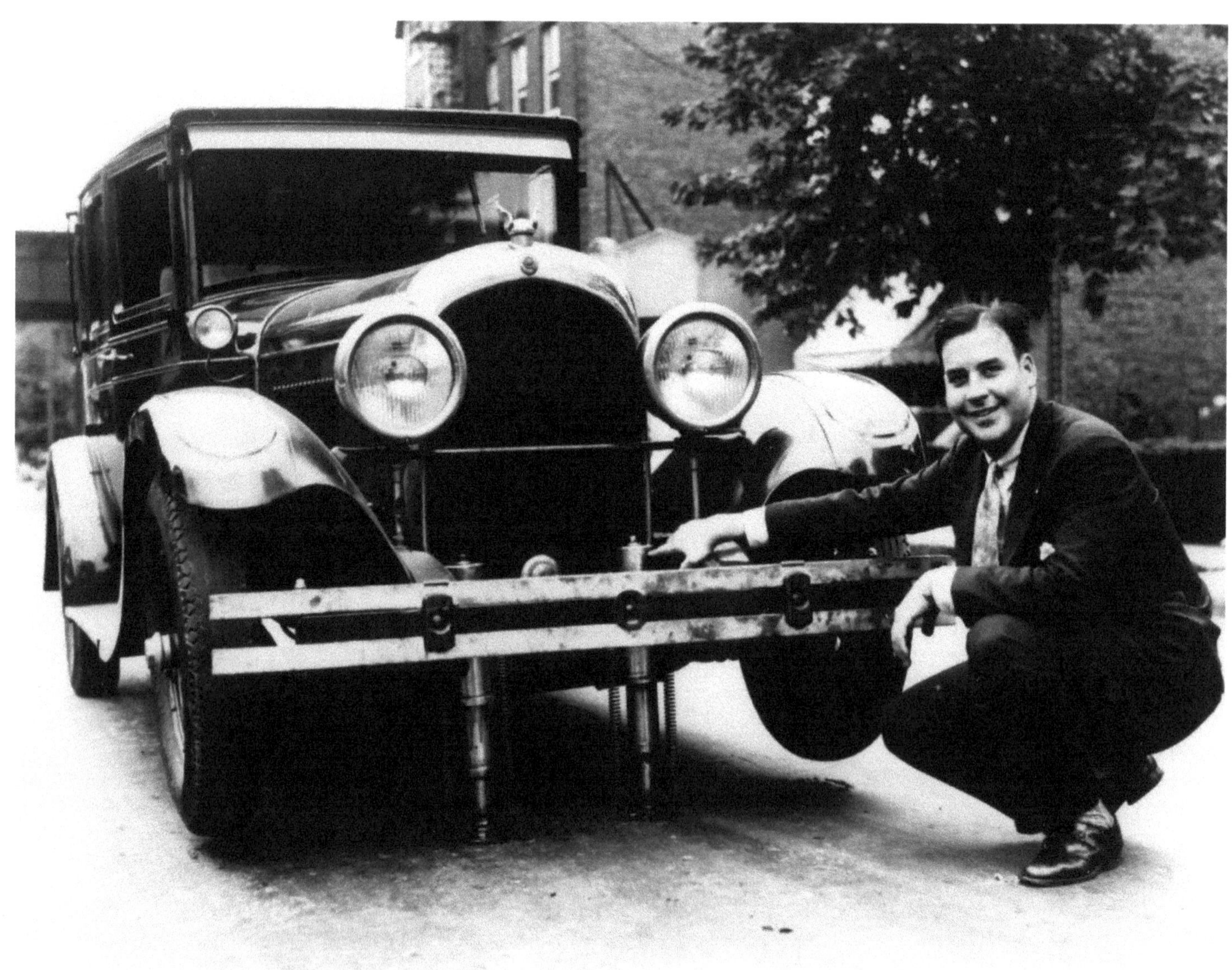

With the rise of the automobile in the 1920s came the rise of mechanical problems with the automobile. Here Enrique D. Paez, Jr., of Jackson Heights, displays his automobile's front end, suspended by two jacks—just the thing for auto mechanics needing access to the trouble beneath.

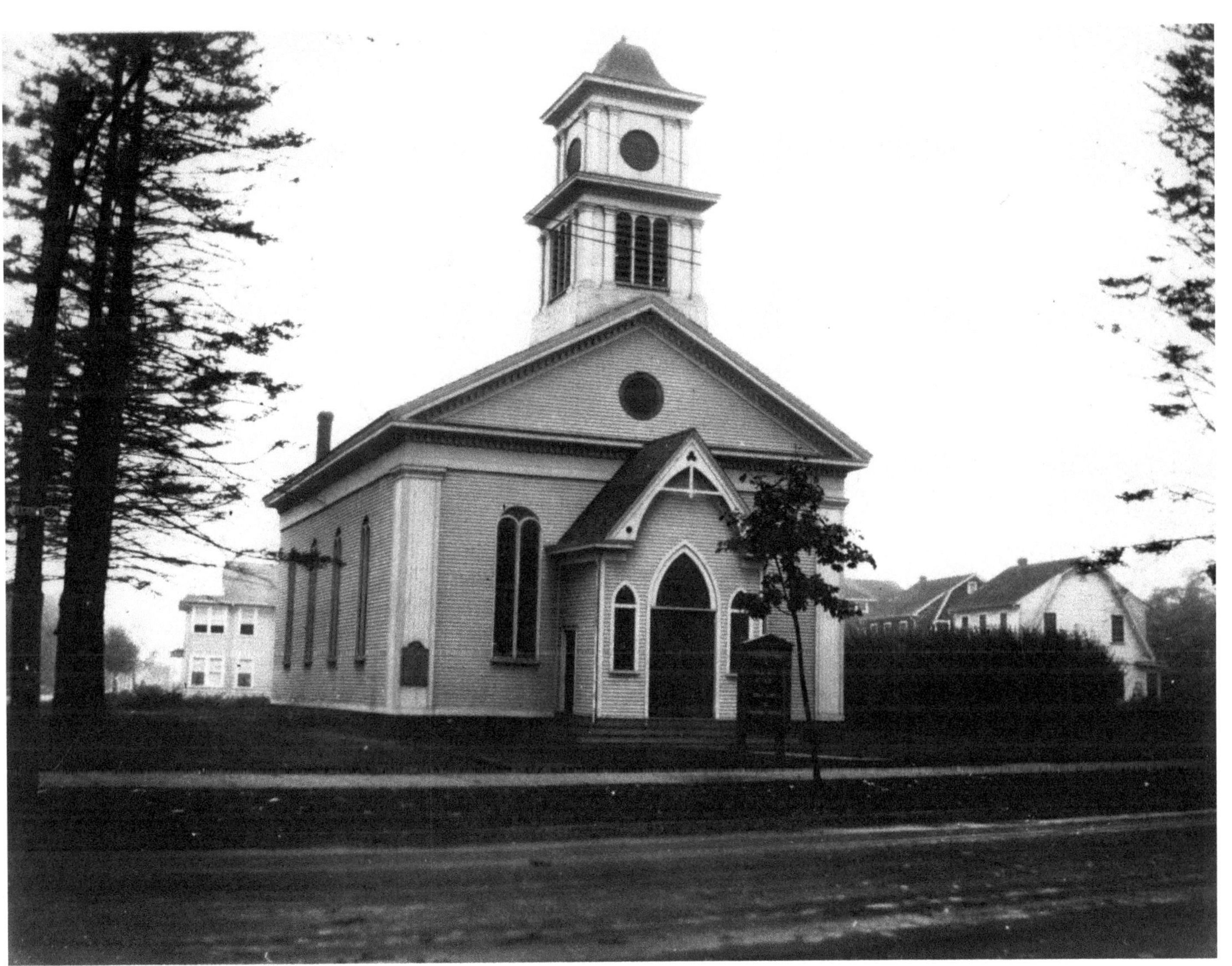

The Dutch Reformed Church in Queens Village, in 1922, located on Jamaica Avenue near Springfield Boulevard. It was founded in 1858 as the Reformed Protestant Dutch Church of Queens, and parishioners included the large Van Siclen farming family.

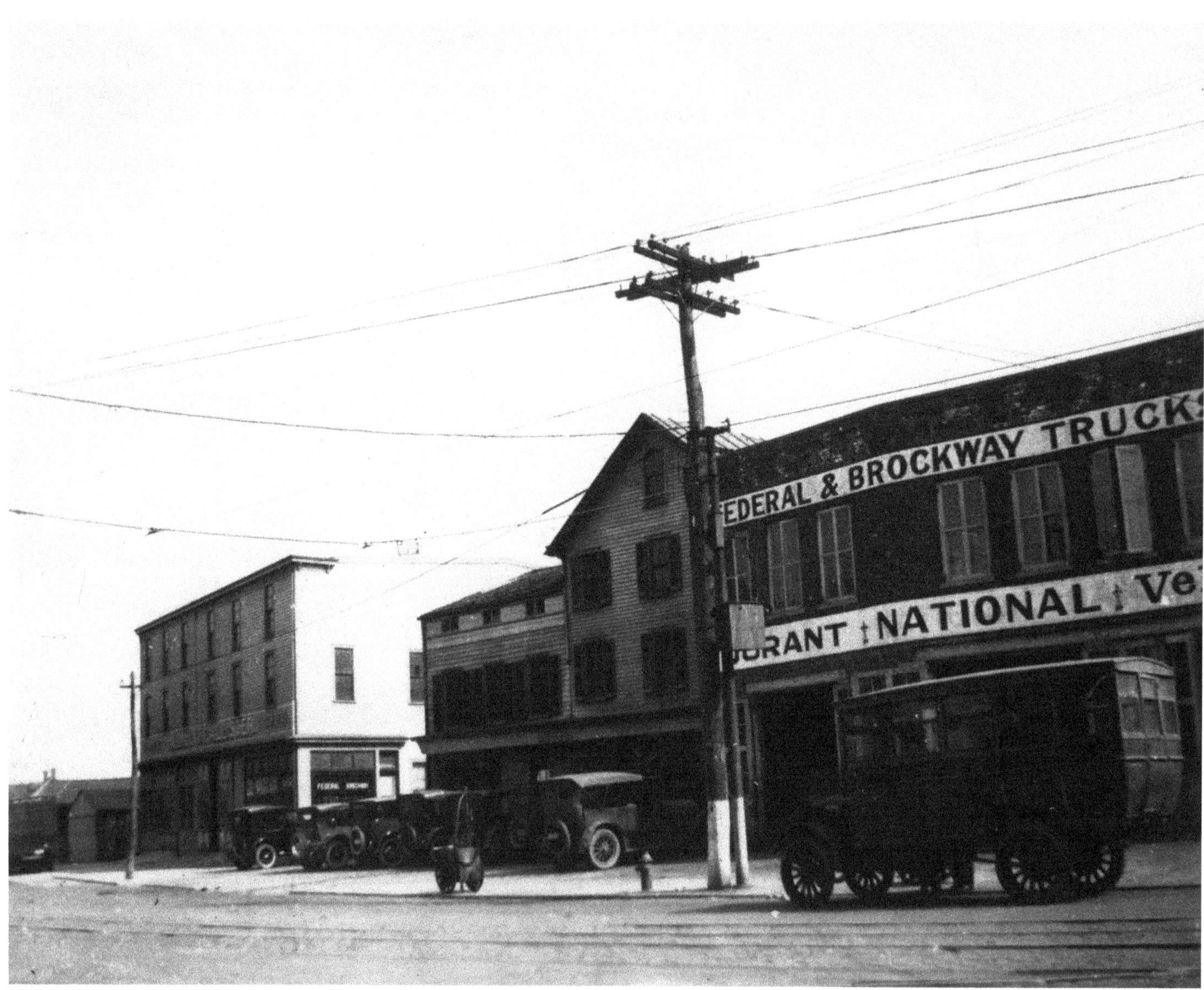

A wagon shop at the northeast corner of Jamaica Avenue at Hempstead Turnpike in Queens Village had opened in 1853 to serve area farms. As the housing boom continued in the 1920s and the area became more residential, proprietor Thomas Callister expanded into selling new and used cars and trucks, with an early version of his showroom visible at center.

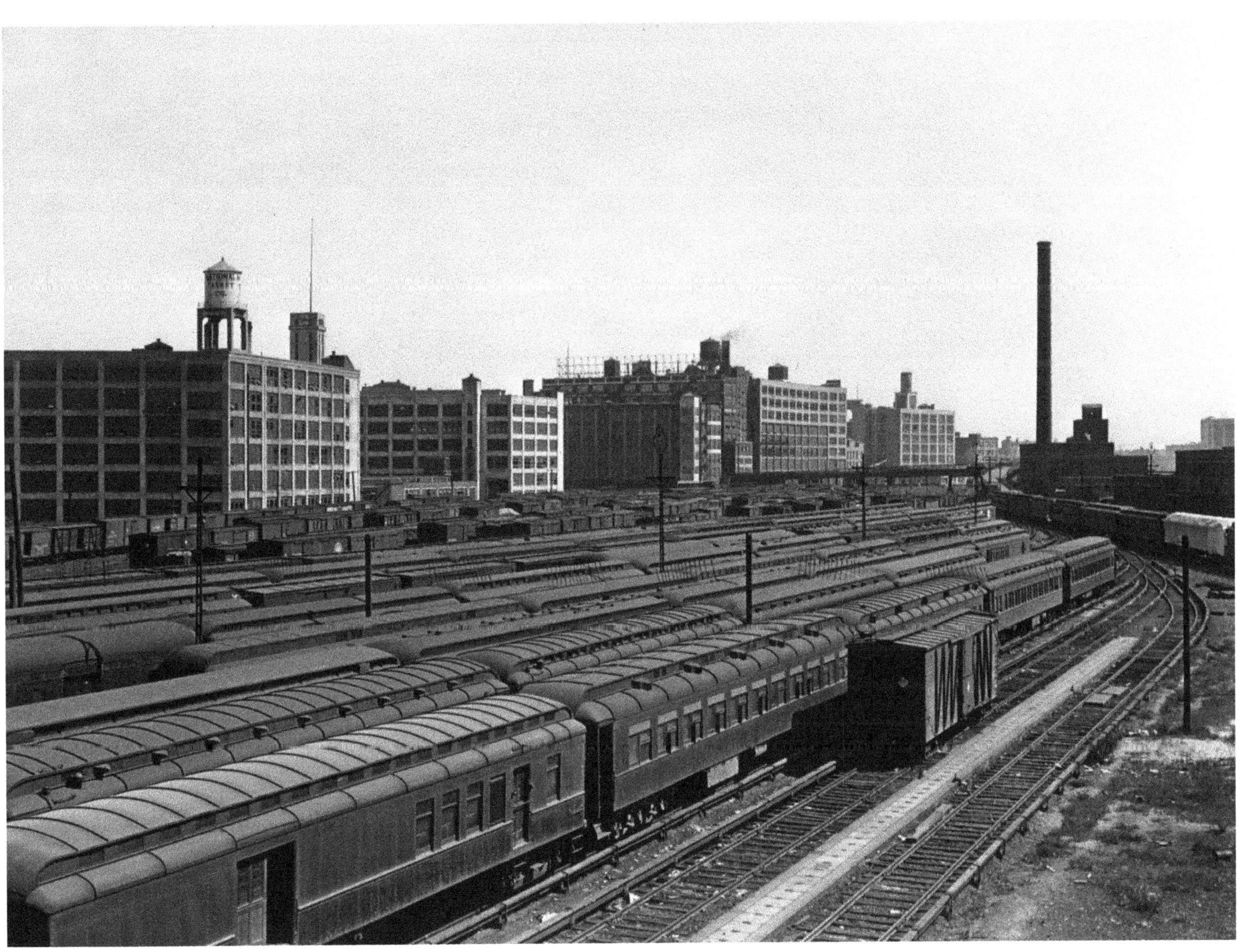

Vibrant commercially in 1922, Long Island City enjoyed an advantageous location across the East River from Manhattan. The rail yards in this view are heavy with passenger and freight cars.

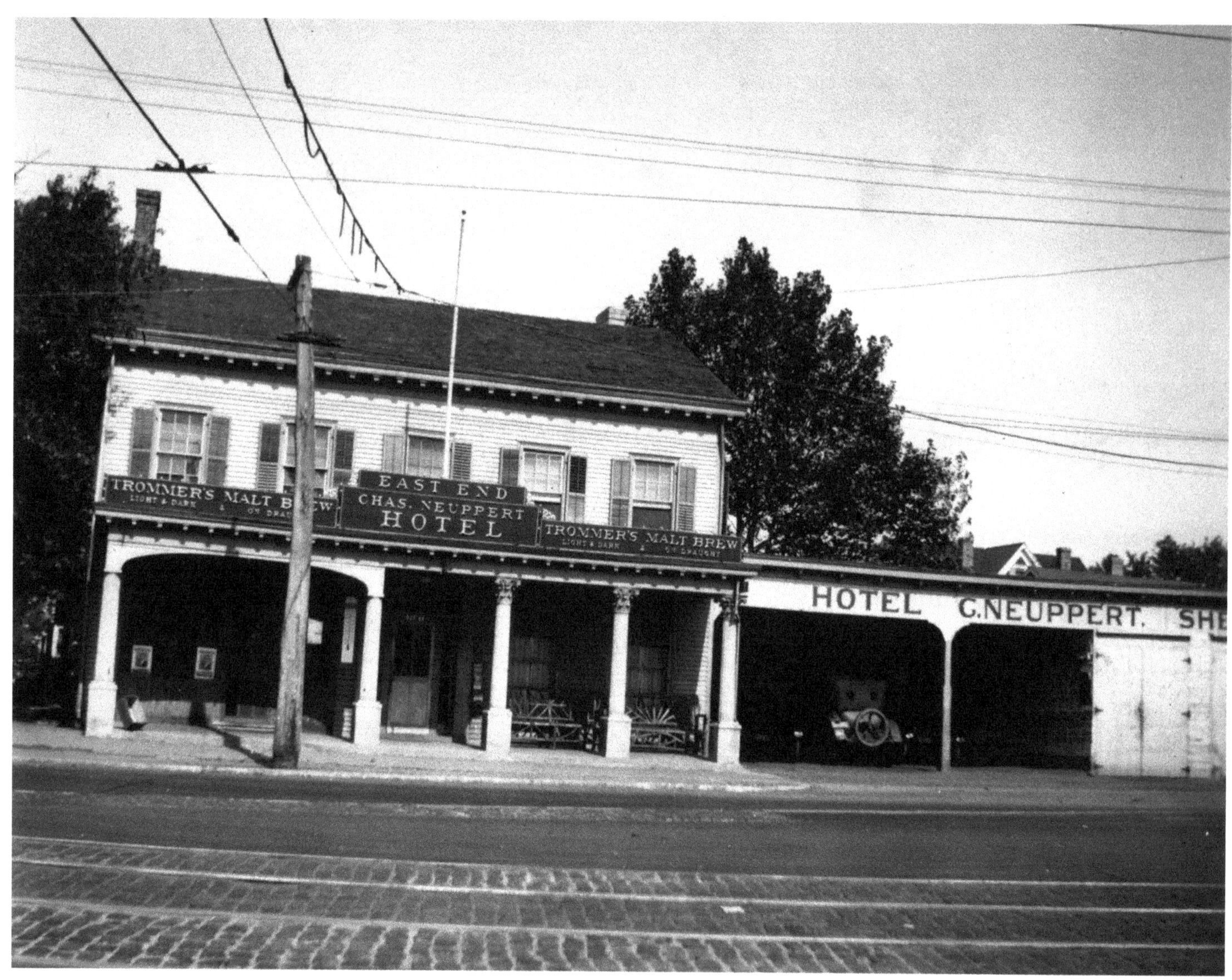

The "East End" generally refers to the eastern tip of Long Island—yet here, a hotel on Jamaica Avenue is named the East End Charles Neuppert—evidence of the Manhattan attitude that Queens was worlds away. The signs advertise Trommer's Malt Brew, a beer brewed in nearby Bushwick, Brooklyn.

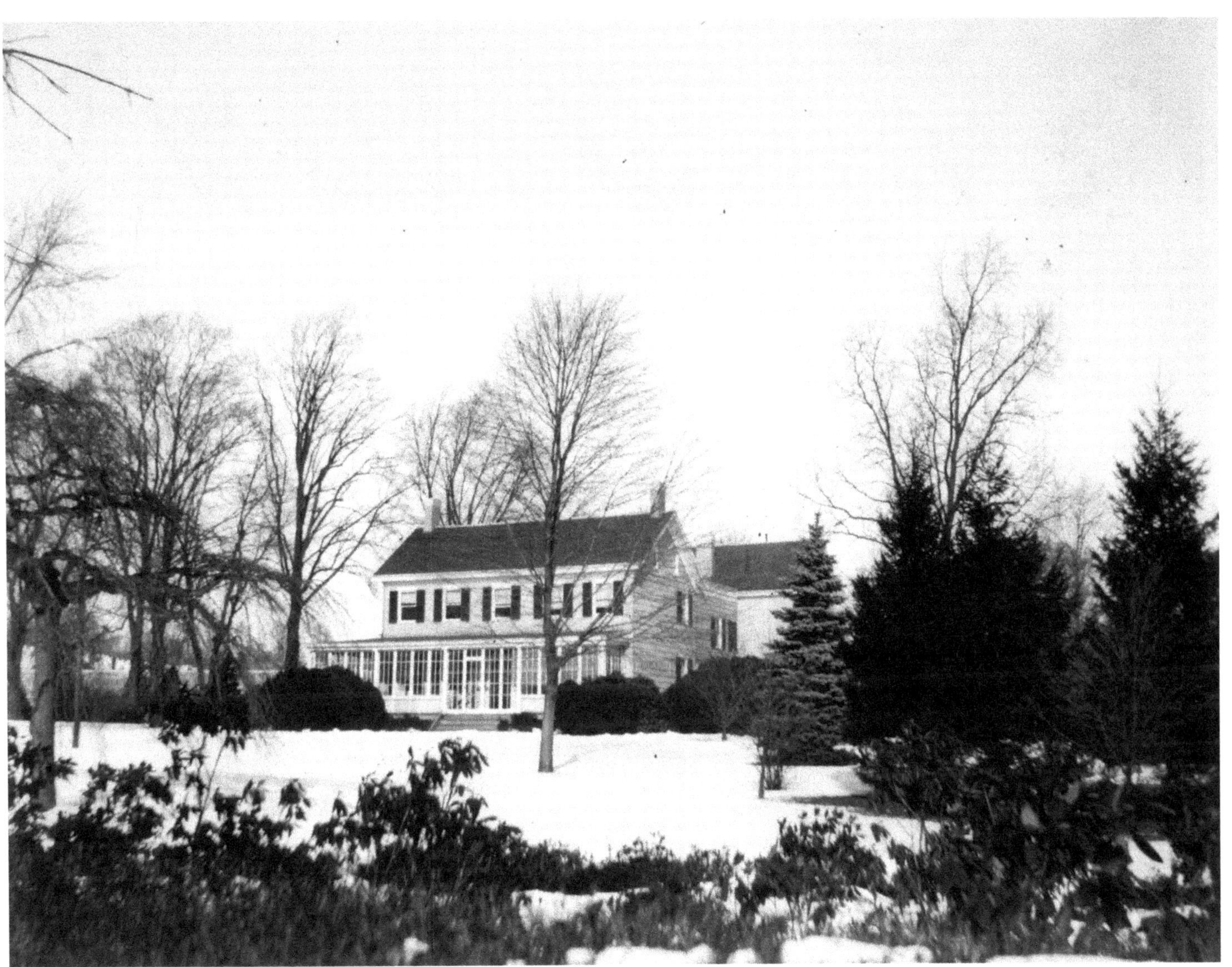

The H. C. Poppenhusen House in Queens Village was turned into a hotel in 1896. The mansion stood at what is now the corner of Braddock Avenue and Winchester Boulevard, in front of the Creedmoor Rifle Range. Conrad Poppenhusen was a German immigrant who founded College Point in northern Queens and built the causeway that connected it to Flushing—now known as College Point Boulevard. The Poppenhusen Institute, built in 1868, hosted the nation's first free kindergarten and the building remains in use.

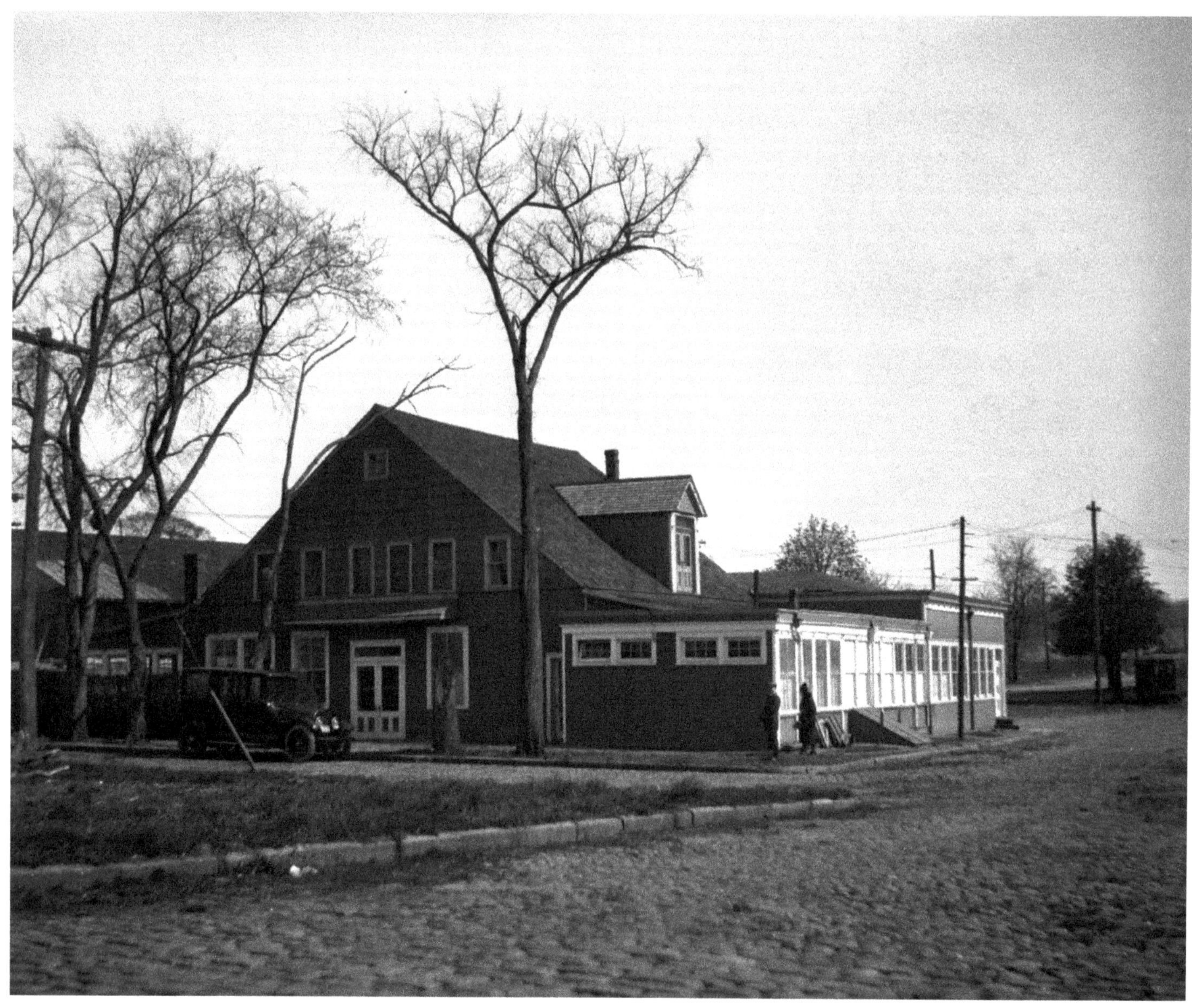

In East Elmhurst, near the Old North Beach area, a large frame-house with many additions stands in what could be a country lane around 1925—if not for the cobblestone streets and the trolley car seen in the distance, clearly identifying this as at least a quasi-urban neighborhood.

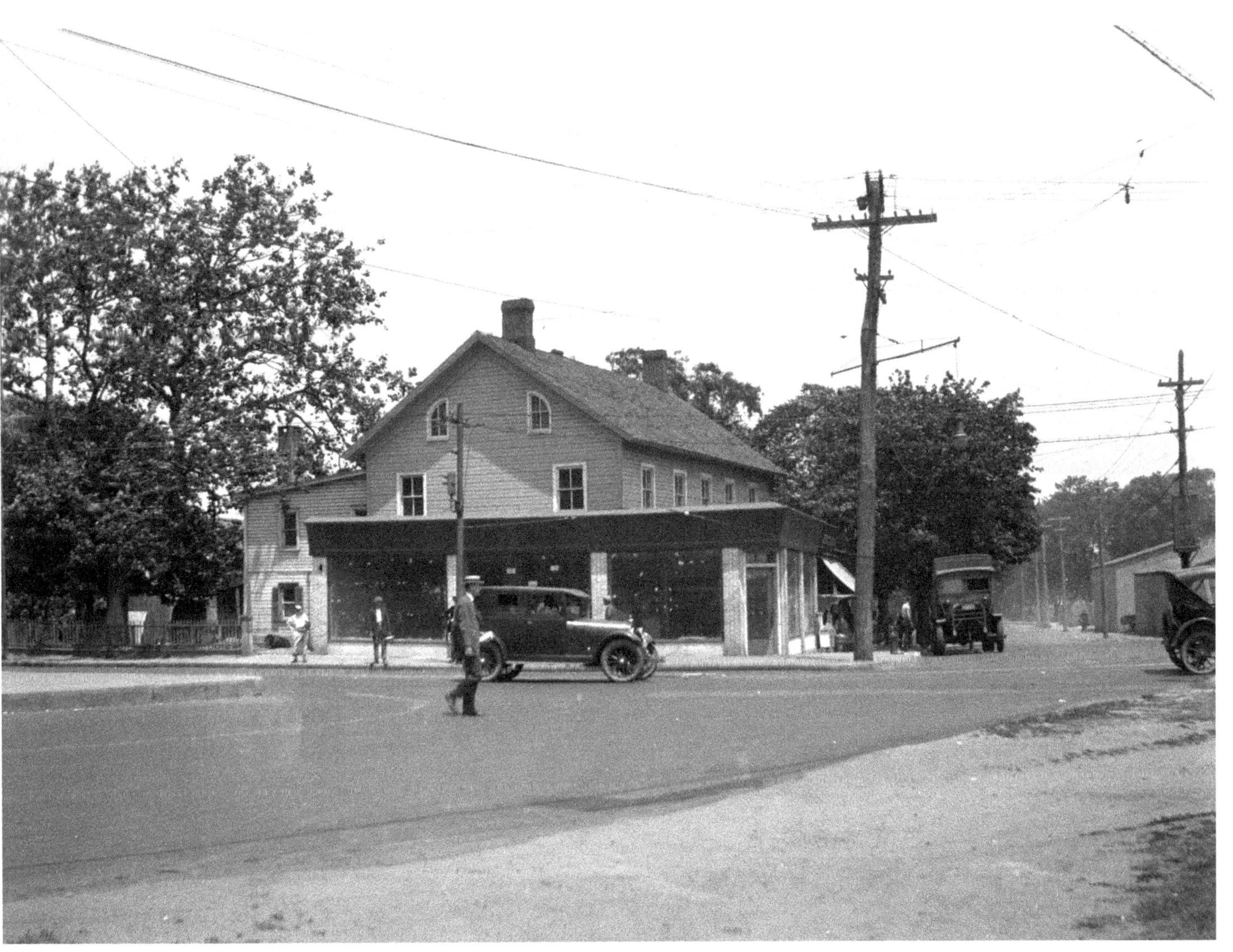

Another of the high-peaked, large frame-houses that were built across the borough in the housing boom of the 1920s. This house has not only been extended, but also has a retail establishment and adjacent grocery, well placed on a busy corner with ample foot and automobile traffic.

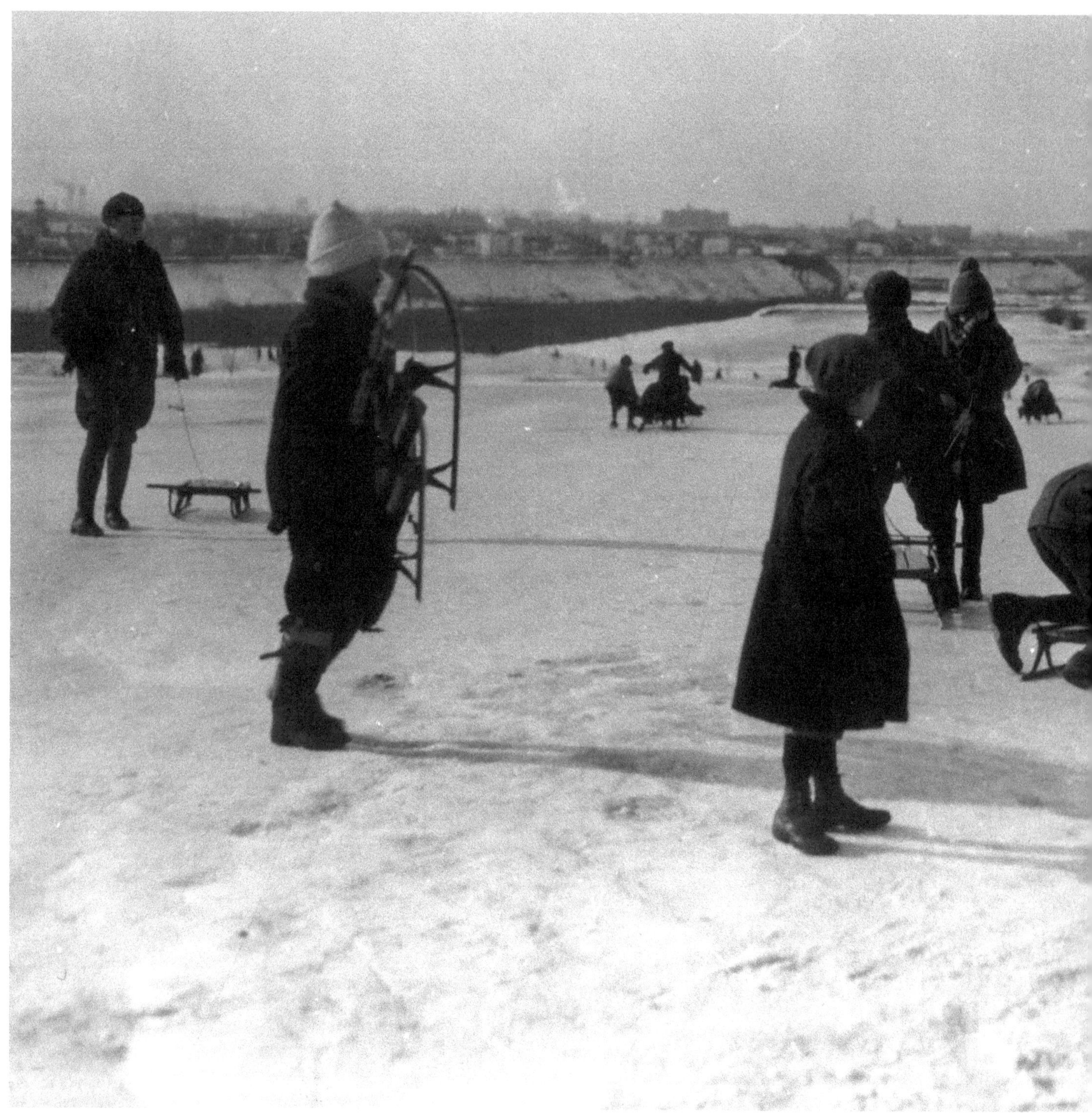

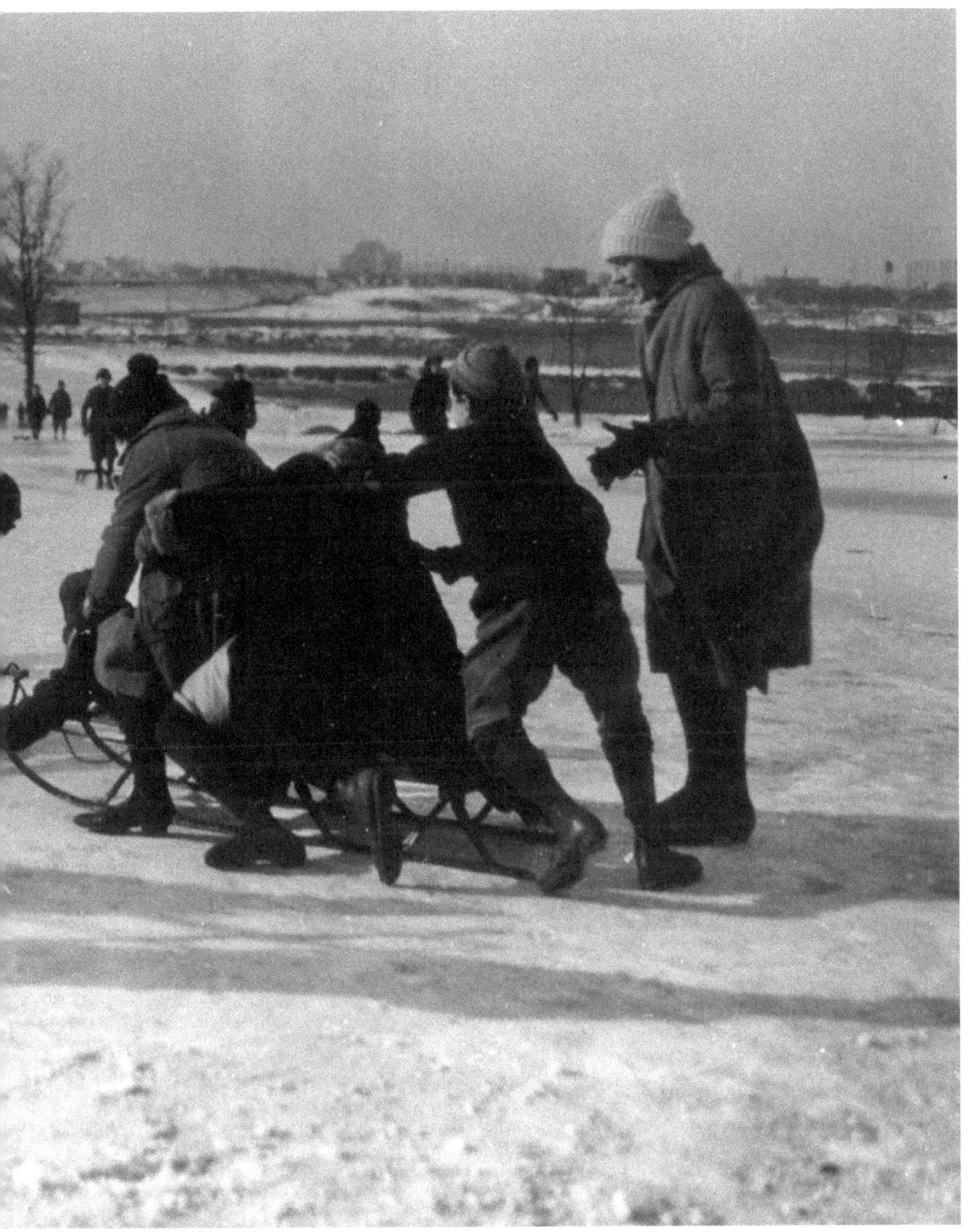

Children take advantage of a snowy day in the open spaces of Jackson Heights in the winter of 1925. Today, the area is densely packed with a mix of residential and commercial buildings as diverse as the population that lives and works in the area.

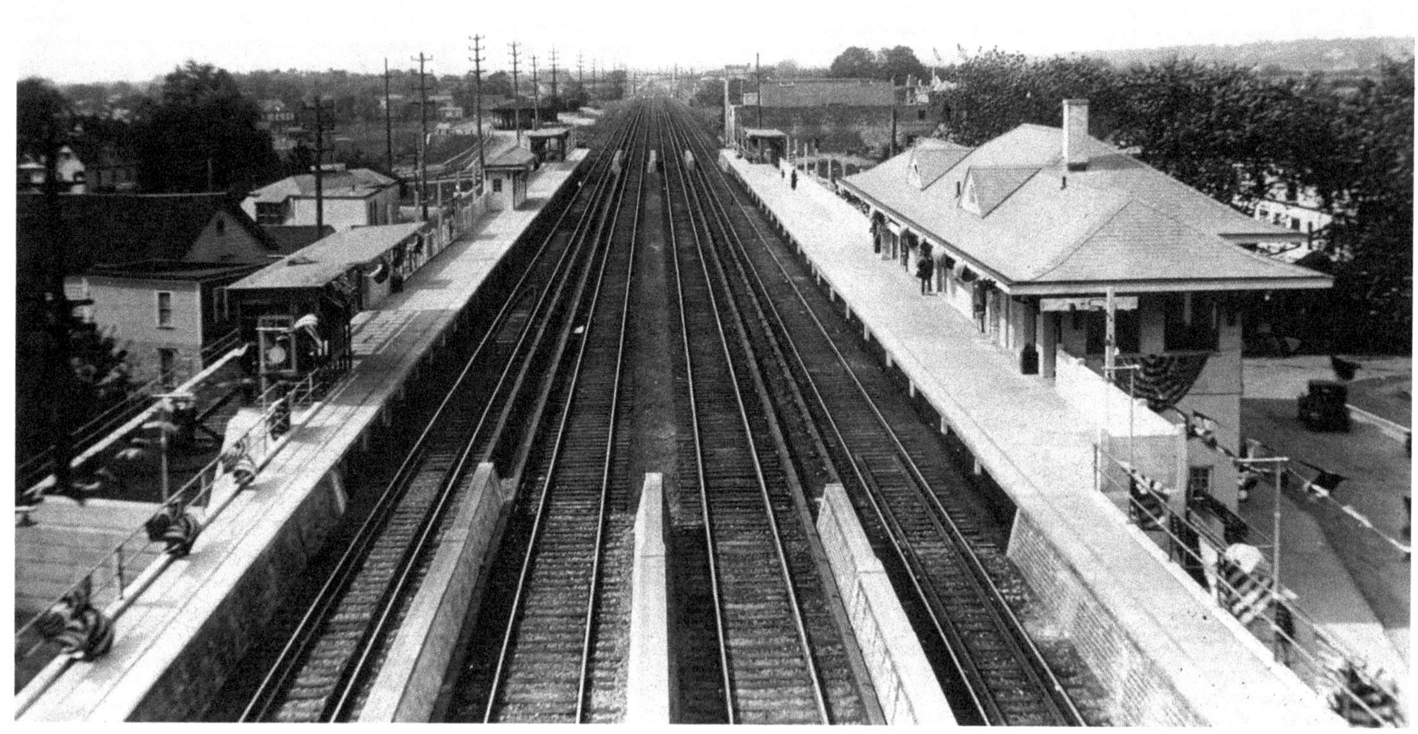

Row houses and large homes went up by the hundreds in eastern Queens, leading to a renovation of the Queens Village Long Island Railroad station in 1923. The LIRR made such growth possible, allowing commuters to settle in the countryside located about a dozen miles from Manhattan.

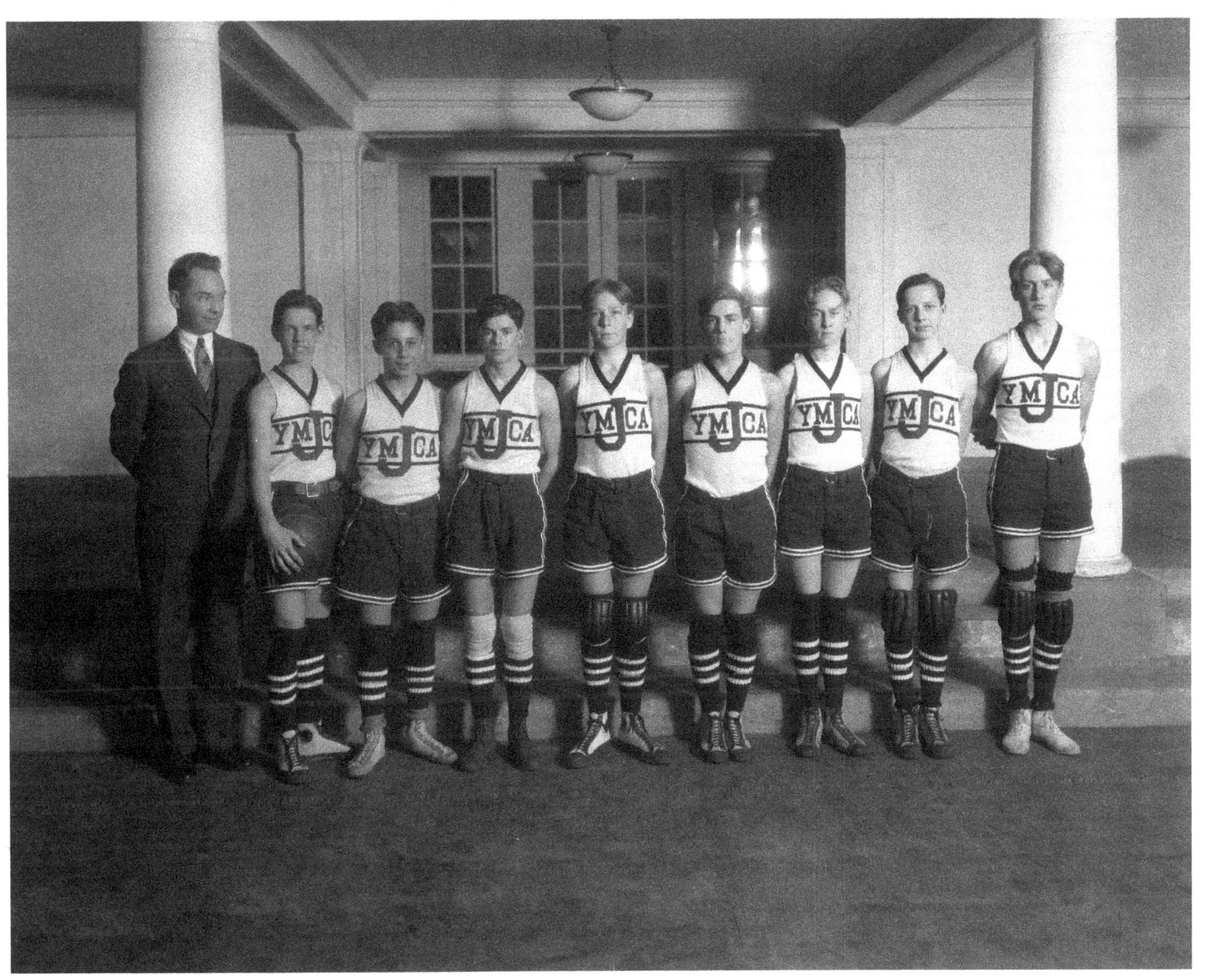

Basketball continued to grow in popularity across New York City, with assistance from organizations like the Y.M.C.A., which sponsored local teams and provided gymnasium space. Here a group of teenage boys from Queens are listed as the 1925-26 Y.M.C.A. Champions of Greater New York.

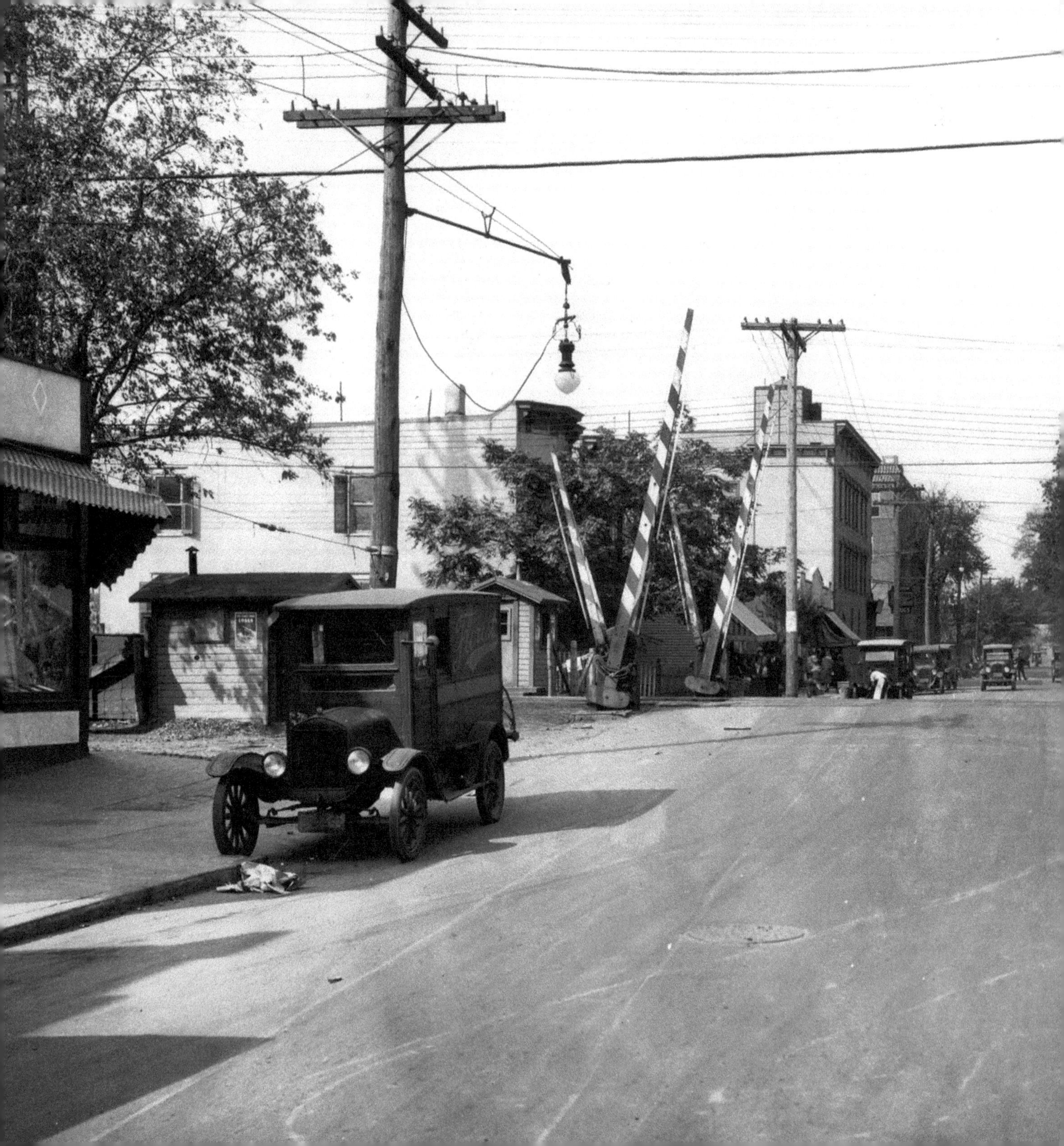

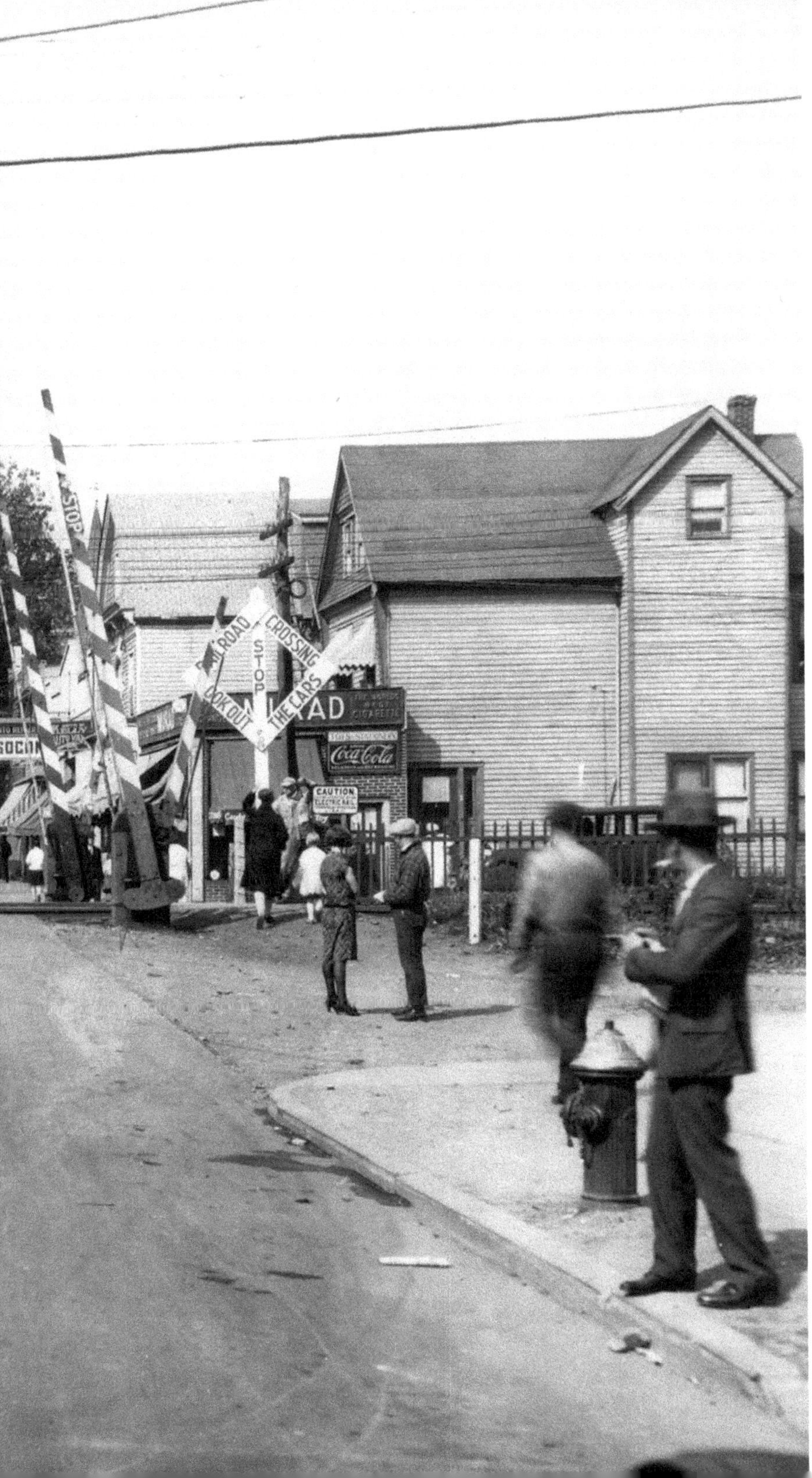

The neighborhood of Corona, between Flushing and Elmhurst, was served by the Long Island Railroad with the Alburtis Street Station crossing near 45th Avenue and what is now 104th Street. The no. 7 elevated subway train has replaced the railroad, which now bypasses the area between Flushing and Woodside.

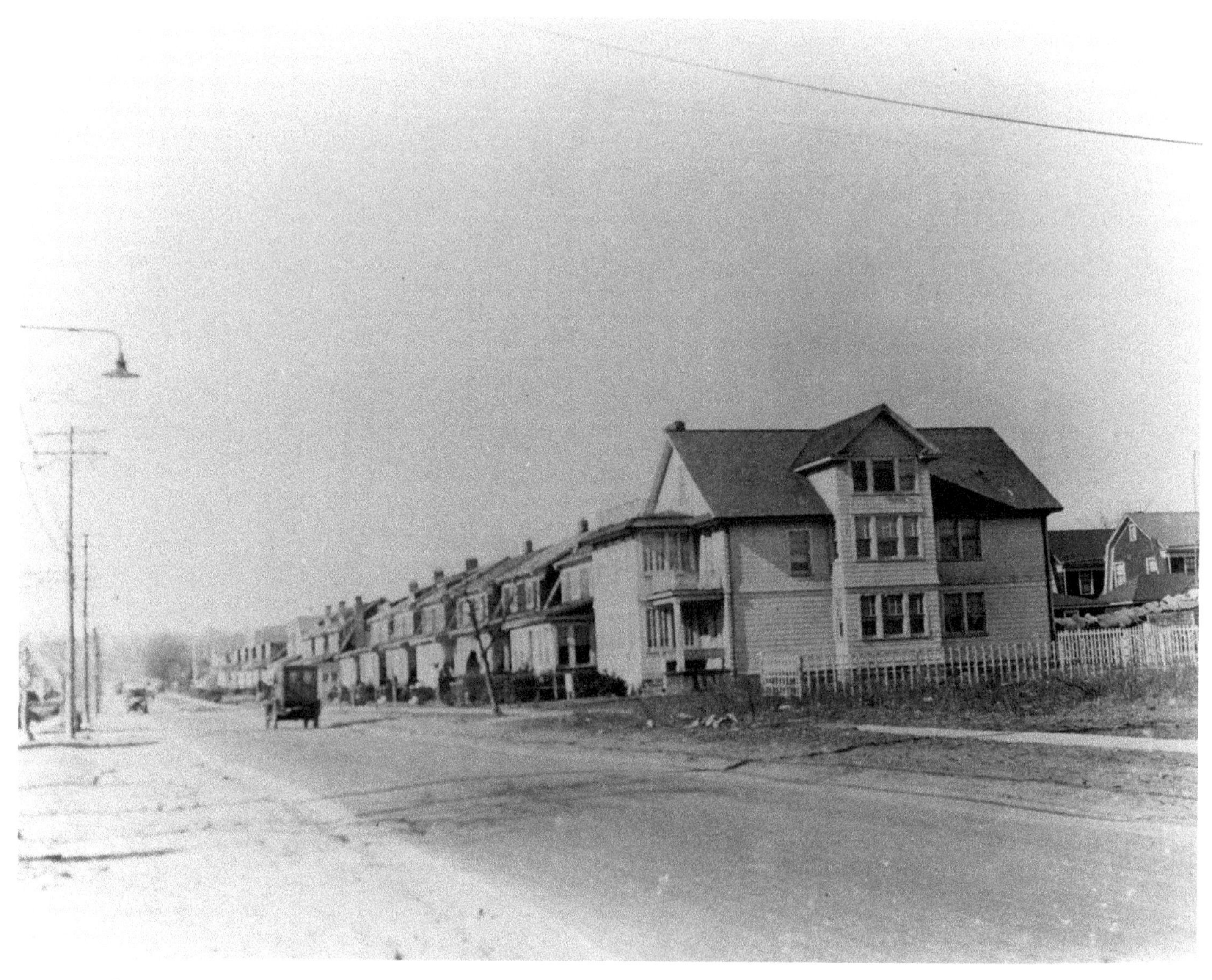

These seemingly endless, nearly identical row houses are evidence of the housing boom that led to the explosive growth of Queens Village in the 1920s. This shot is a look at Springfield Boulevard near 93rd Avenue in 1927.

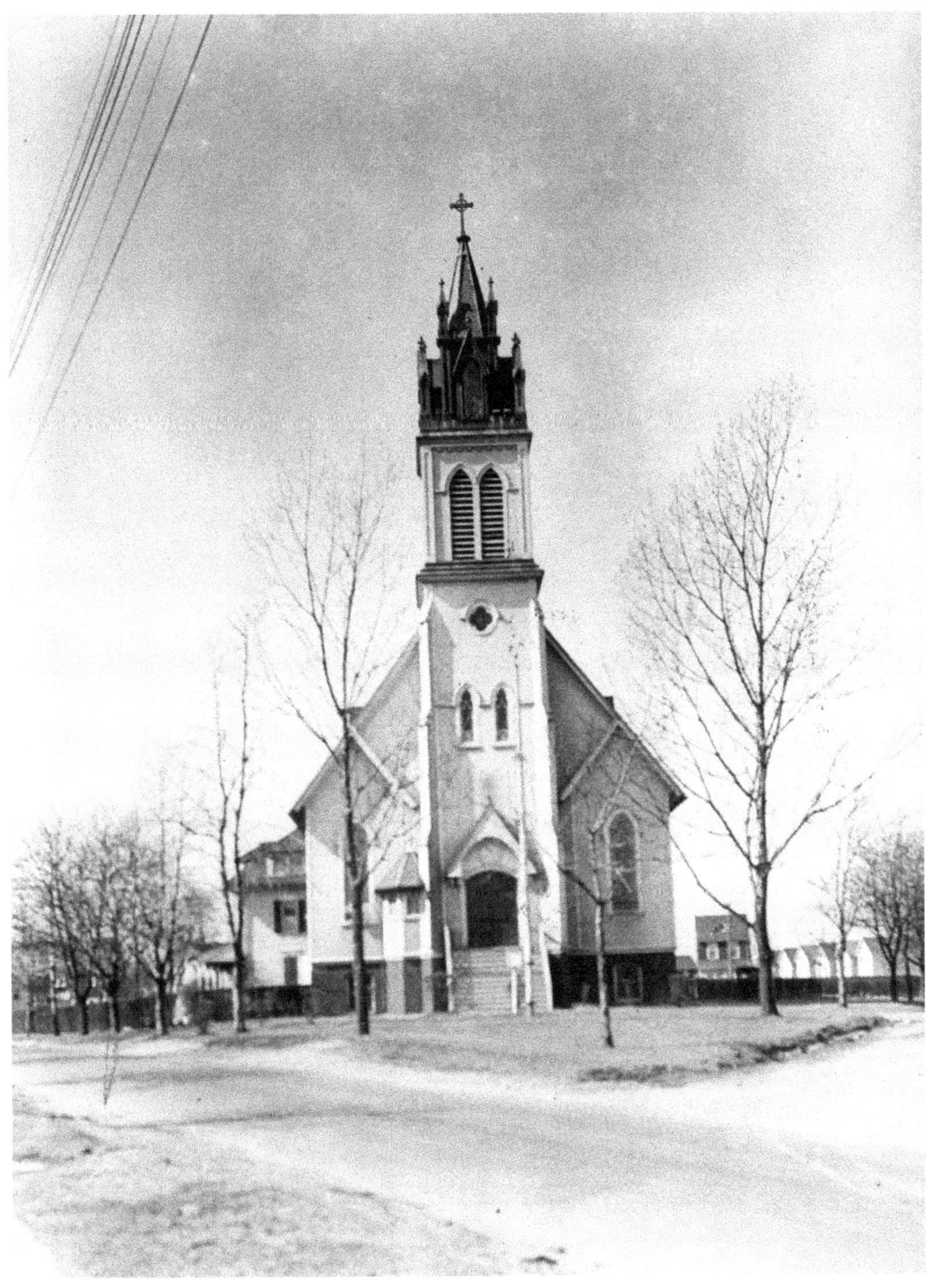

St. Joachim and Anne Catholic Church in Queens Village in 1927. In 1905, the church stood alone in a rural setting. Located on Hollis Avenue, it was now surrounded by roads on both sides with houses lining the streets in the distance, marking a final chapter in the great farming history of the borough.

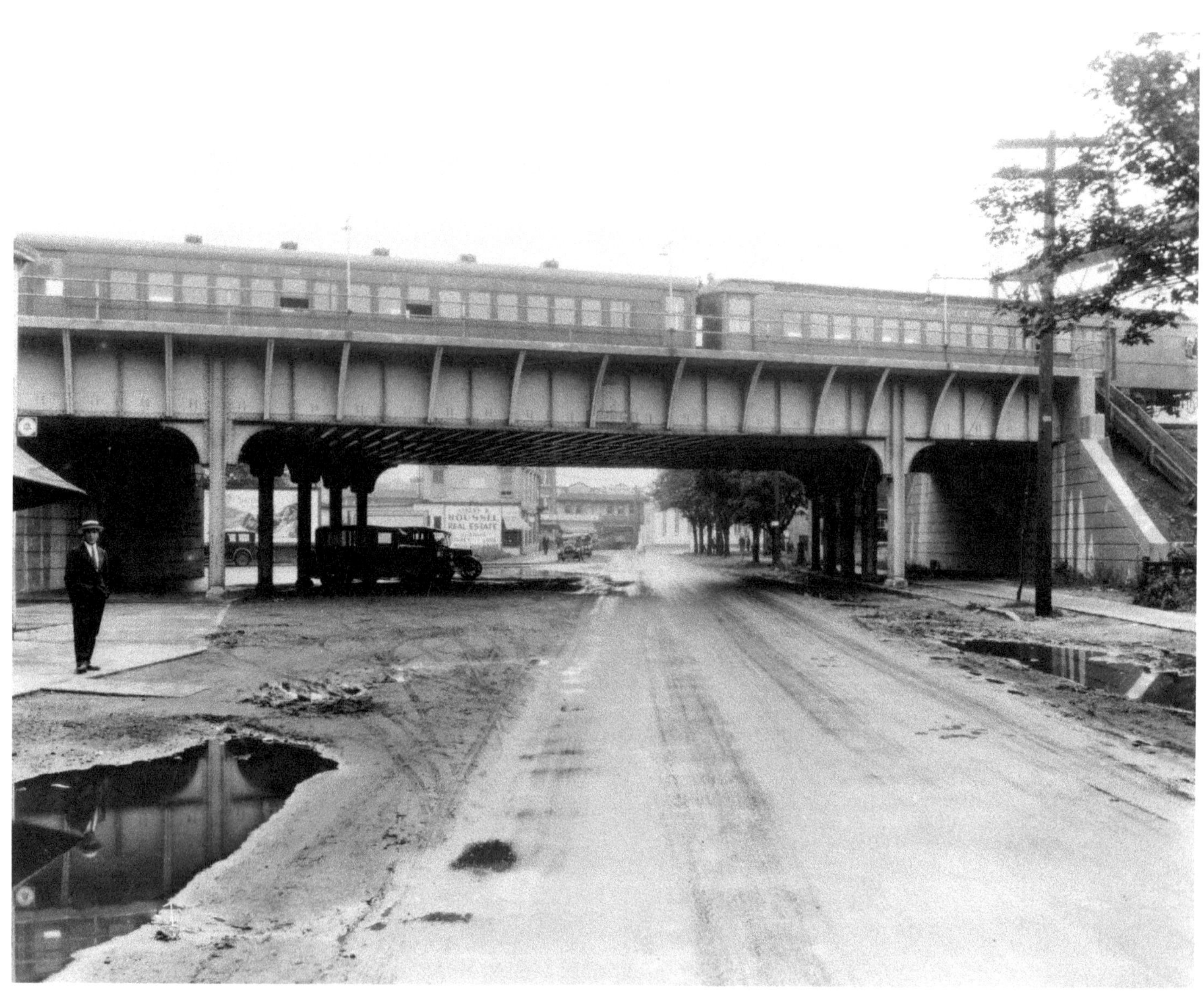

Although the new Queens Village Long Island Railroad station made commuting to Manhattan easier for commuters, it also brought the ugly trappings of urban modernity to the once pastoral area. This conflict is manifest in the unpaved road running beneath this train trestle at Springfield Boulevard, just south of Jamaica Avenue, and the tightly packed shops and homes in the background.

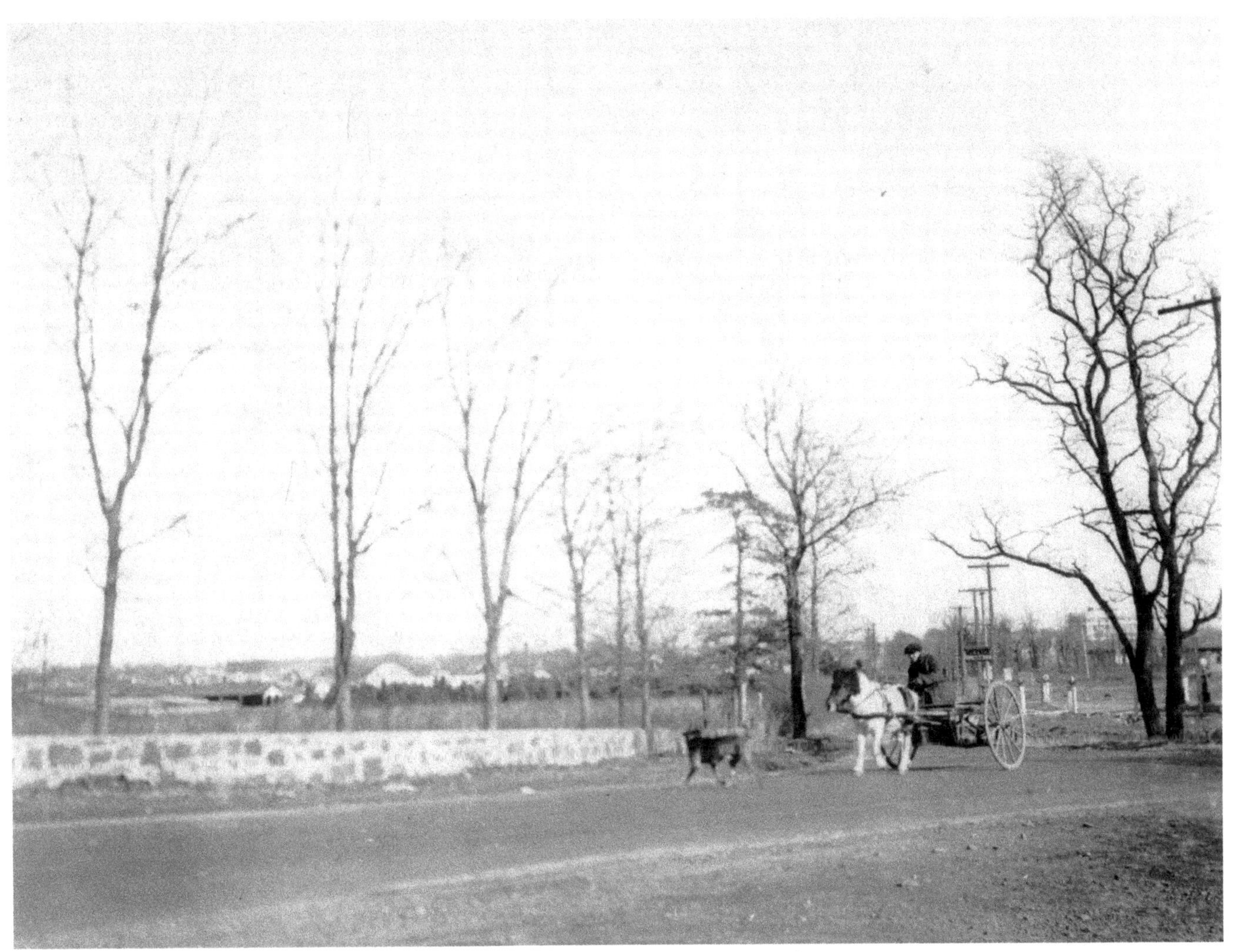

Despite the development, some lands remained open. In the distance at far-left, homes and other development can be discerned, but on this stretch of Braddock Avenue near Springfield Boulevard in Queens Village in 1927, this pony-drawn cart with a dog surveying the road, does not look out of place. The intersection marked the boundary between the Third and Fourth wards of the county, early political divisions.

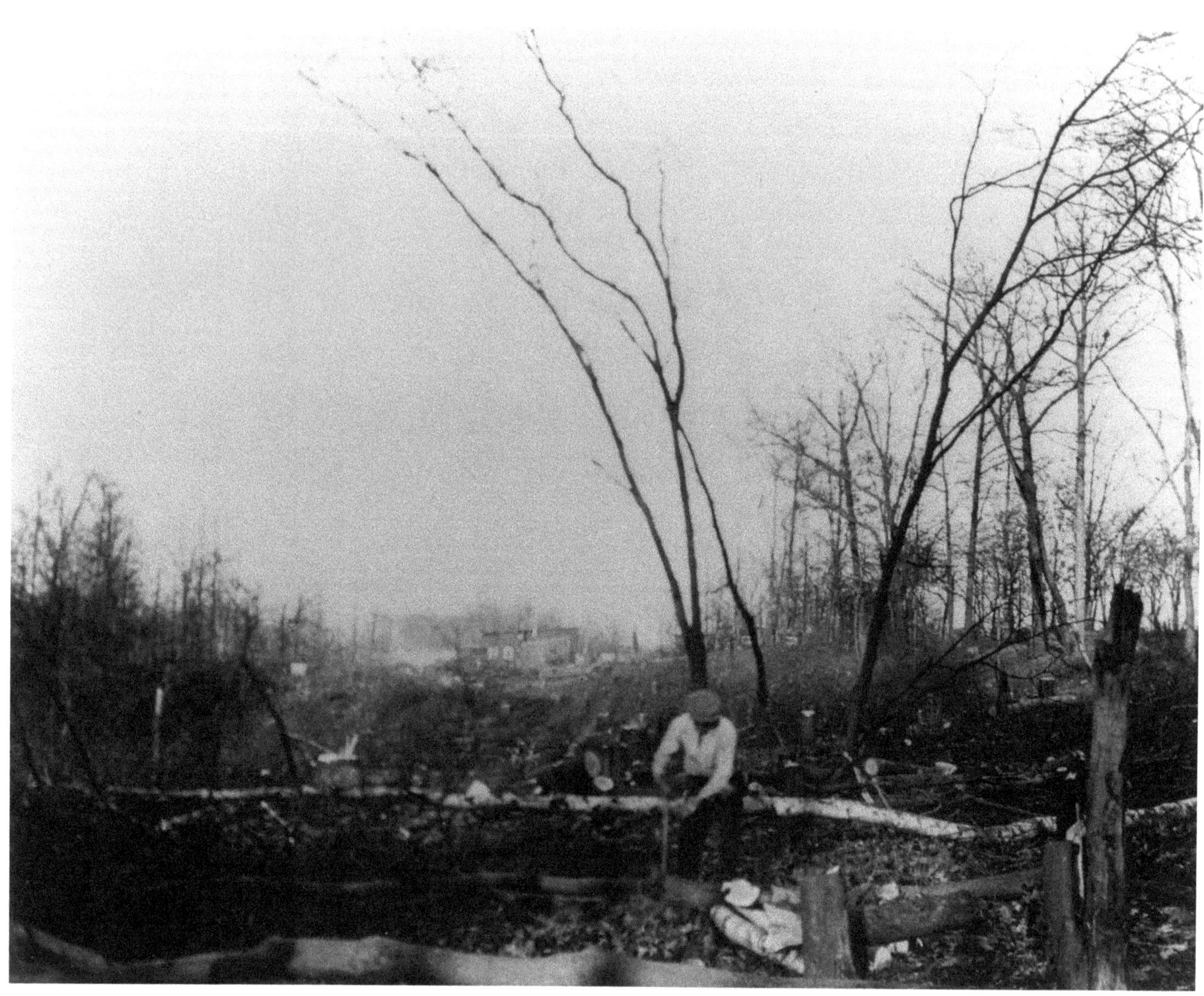

In order to bring greater development to eastern Queens, roads had to be cut through the wilderness, which required crews to clear trees from the forests. This may be an early extension of Hillside Avenue from Jamaica to Hollis and Queens Village.

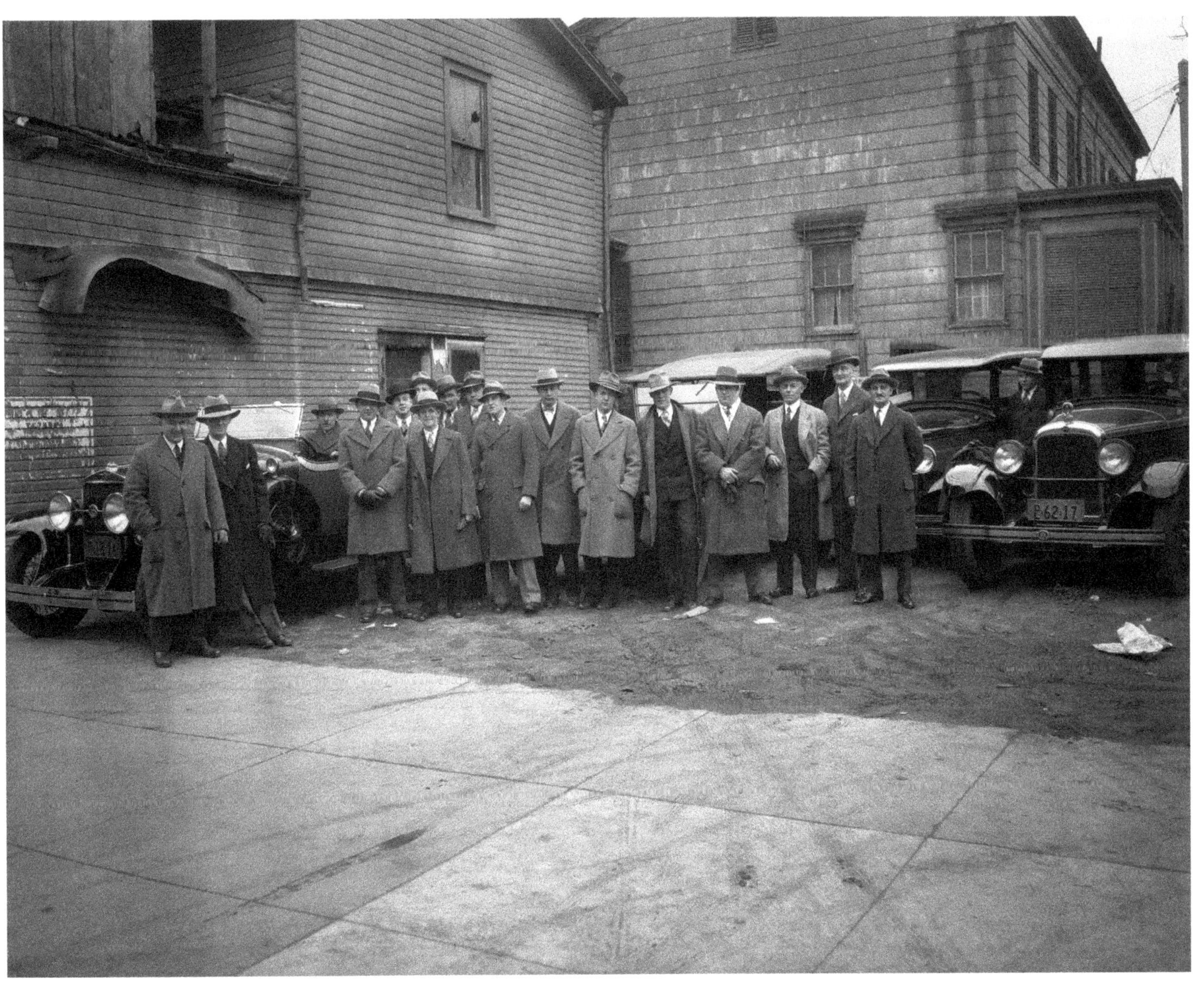

A photograph by the Long Island Press showing Mayor James John "Jimmy" Walker's automobile trip to the Borough of Queens in 1927. Known as "Beau James," the jazz age mayor is seen here touring the city during a time of great prosperity, prior to the 1929 stock market crash.

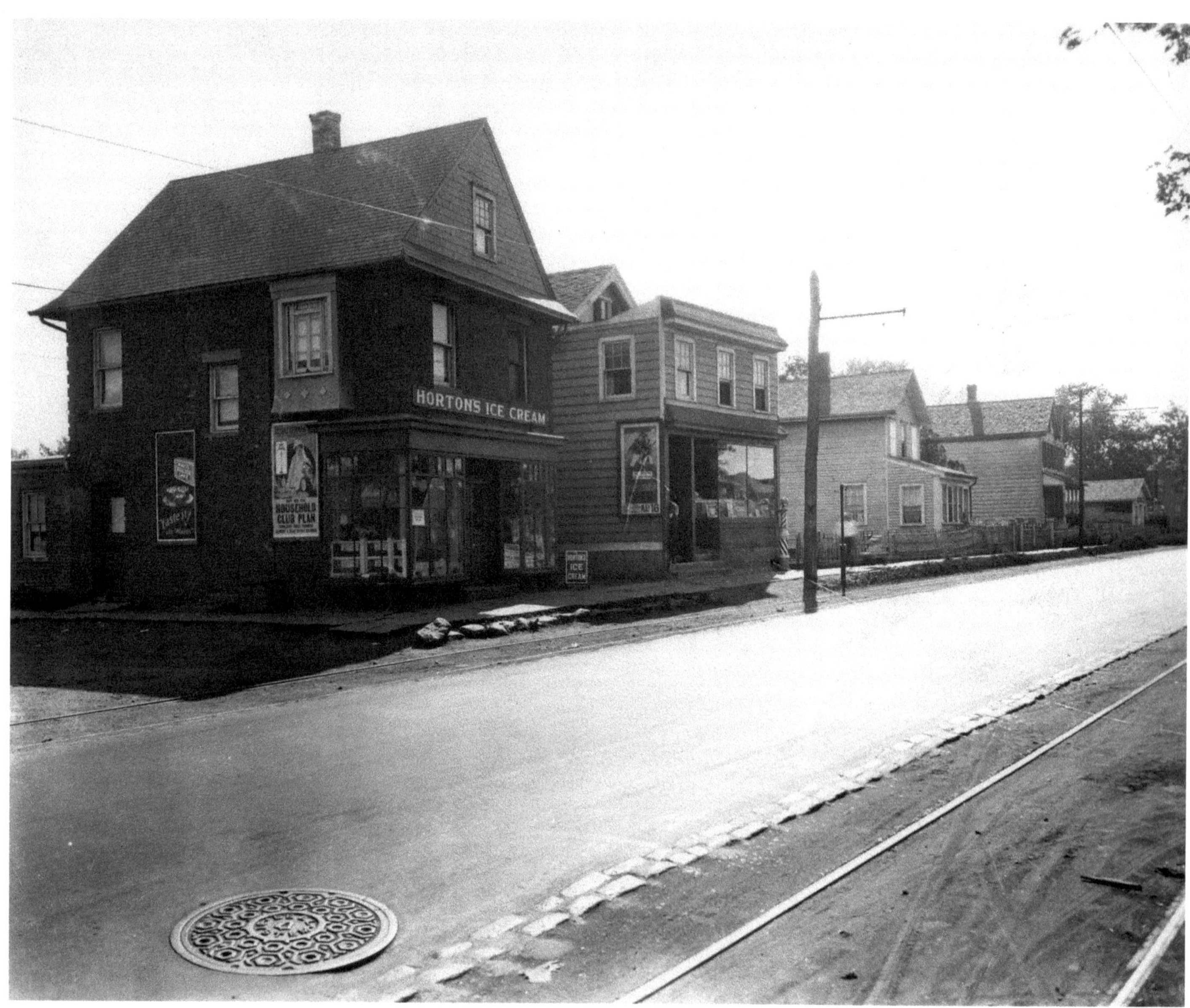

A paved Hempstead Turnpike near 217 Lane, in Queens Village, just a few blocks from the junction with Jamaica Avenue. This street shows a traditional New York City manhole cover in the foreground, evidence of the sewage system that was part of many public works that improved the burgeoning borough in the twentieth century.

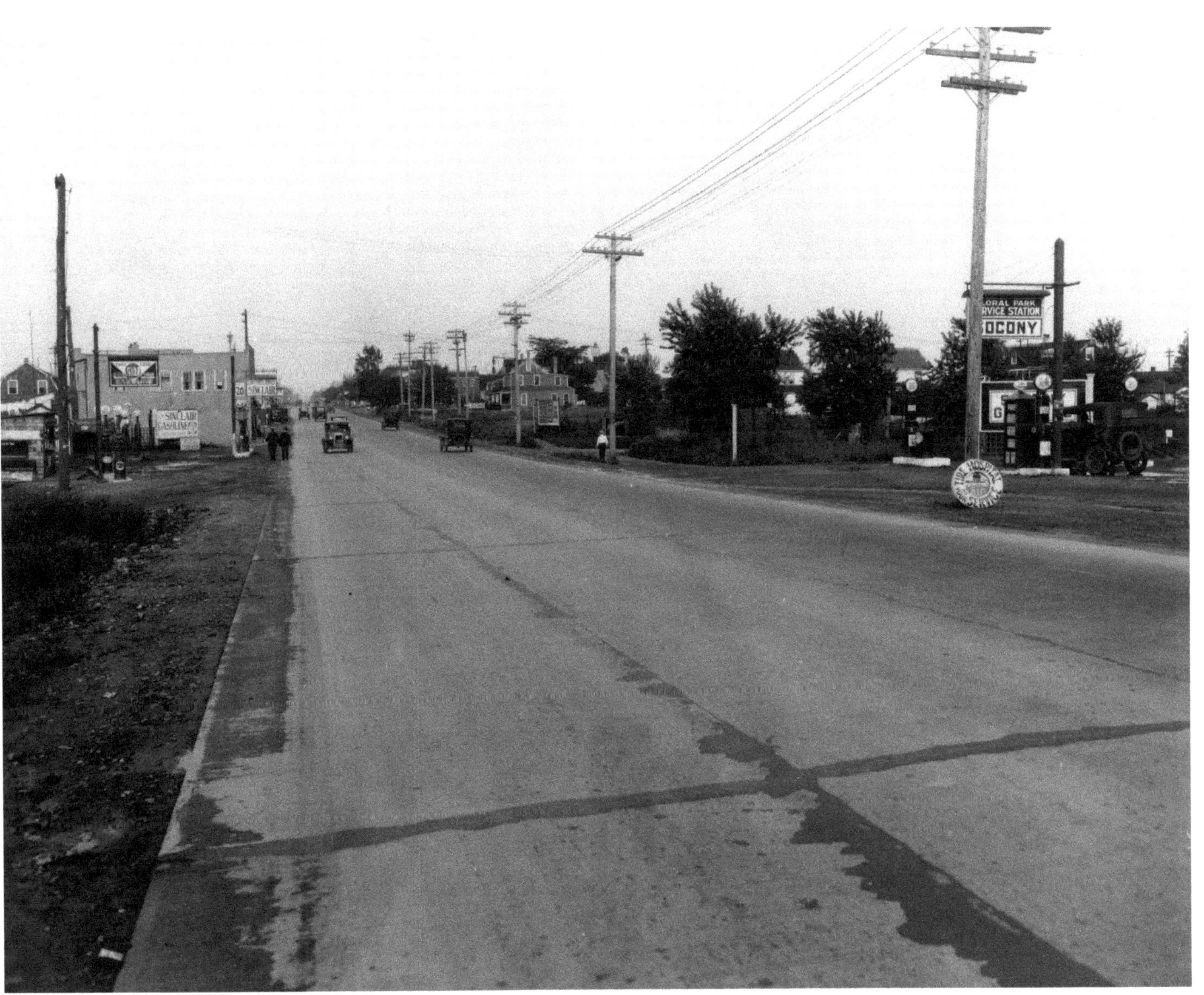

Floral Park on the eastern edge of the borough is actually bisected, with part of the neighborhood in Queens and the rest in the town of Floral Park in Nassau County. This 1928 photograph was likely made near the border between the counties, where Jamaica Avenue turns into Jericho Turnpike. At right is a service station advertising Standard Oil Company of New York (SOCONY) gasoline—a commodity quickly becoming essential to the "suburban" lives of eastern Queens residents. The white tire against the utility pole at right advertises whimsically, "Tire Hospital at Your Service: Flats Fixed."

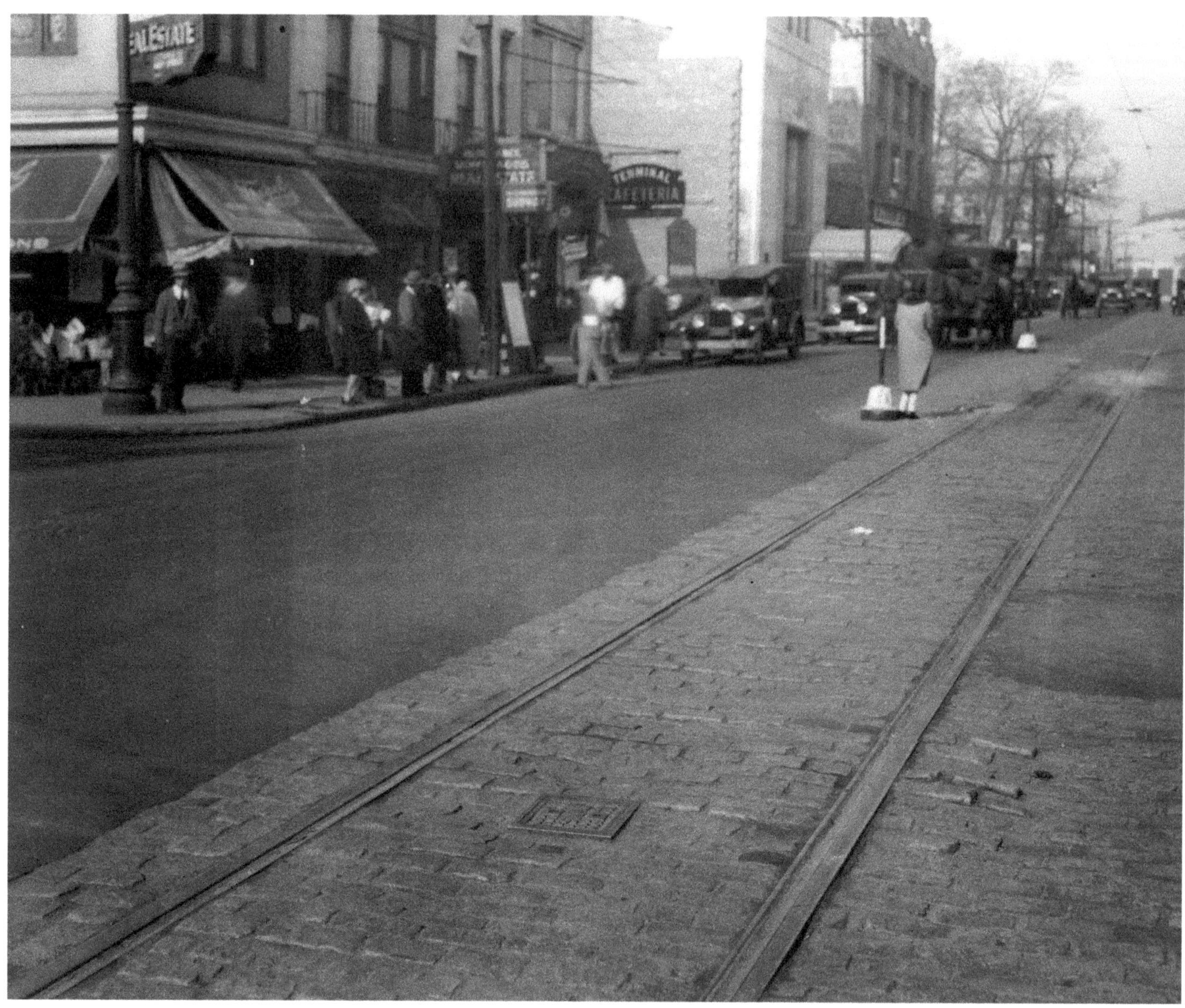

Flushing Main Street in 1928, with dual streetcar tracks running down the center. This is a view facing north, from the Roosevelt Avenue intersection, with a look at the Terminal Cafeteria near 39th Avenue. This intersection today is one of the busiest in the borough, with the no. 7 terminal, the Long Island Railroad station, and dozens of bus lines converging amid banks, chain retail stores, and dozens of small merchants.

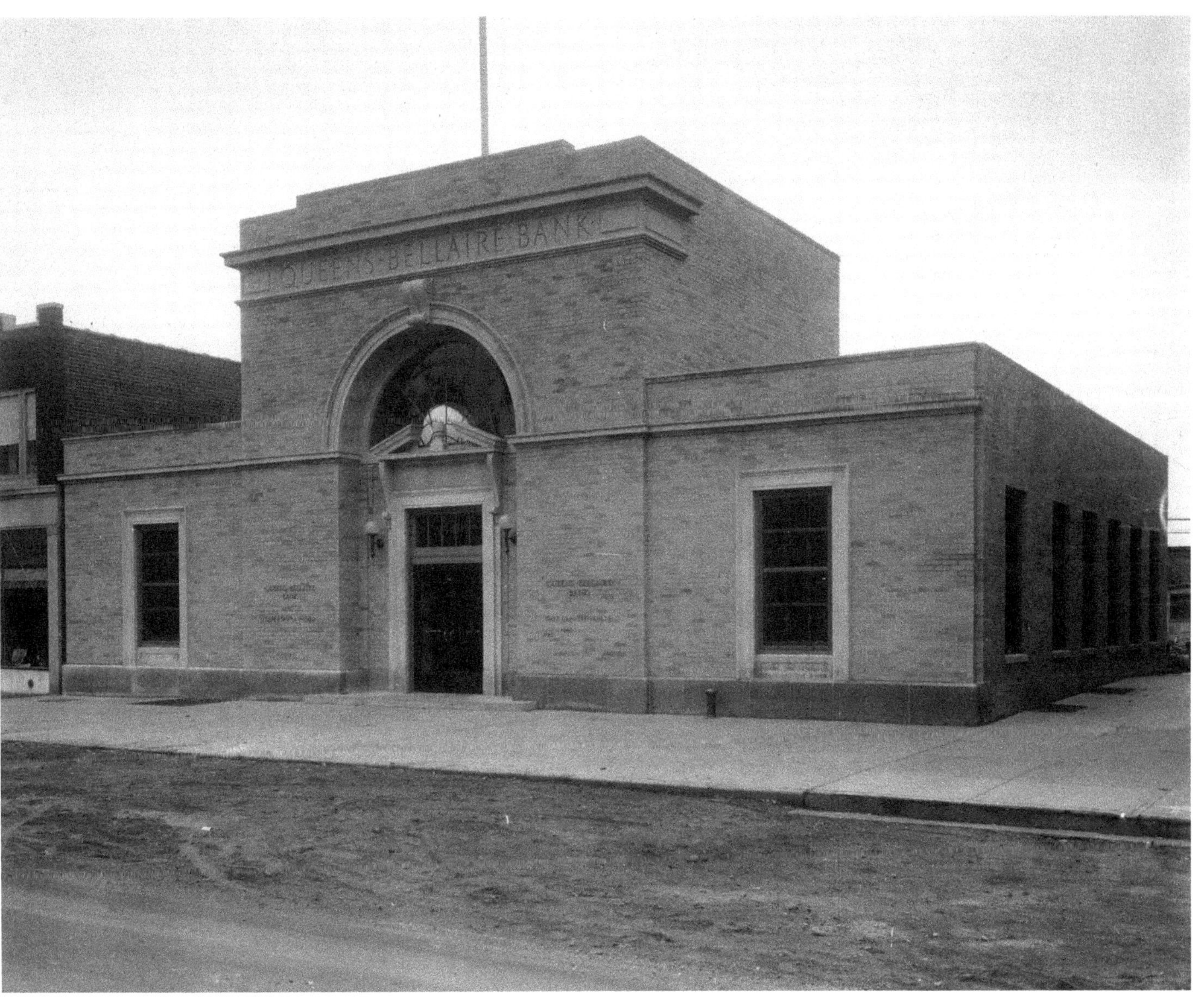

The Queens-Bellaire Bank, established in 1921, is seen here on Jamaica Avenue near 215th Street. Bellaire is a subsection of Queens Village, which today encompasses three zip codes.

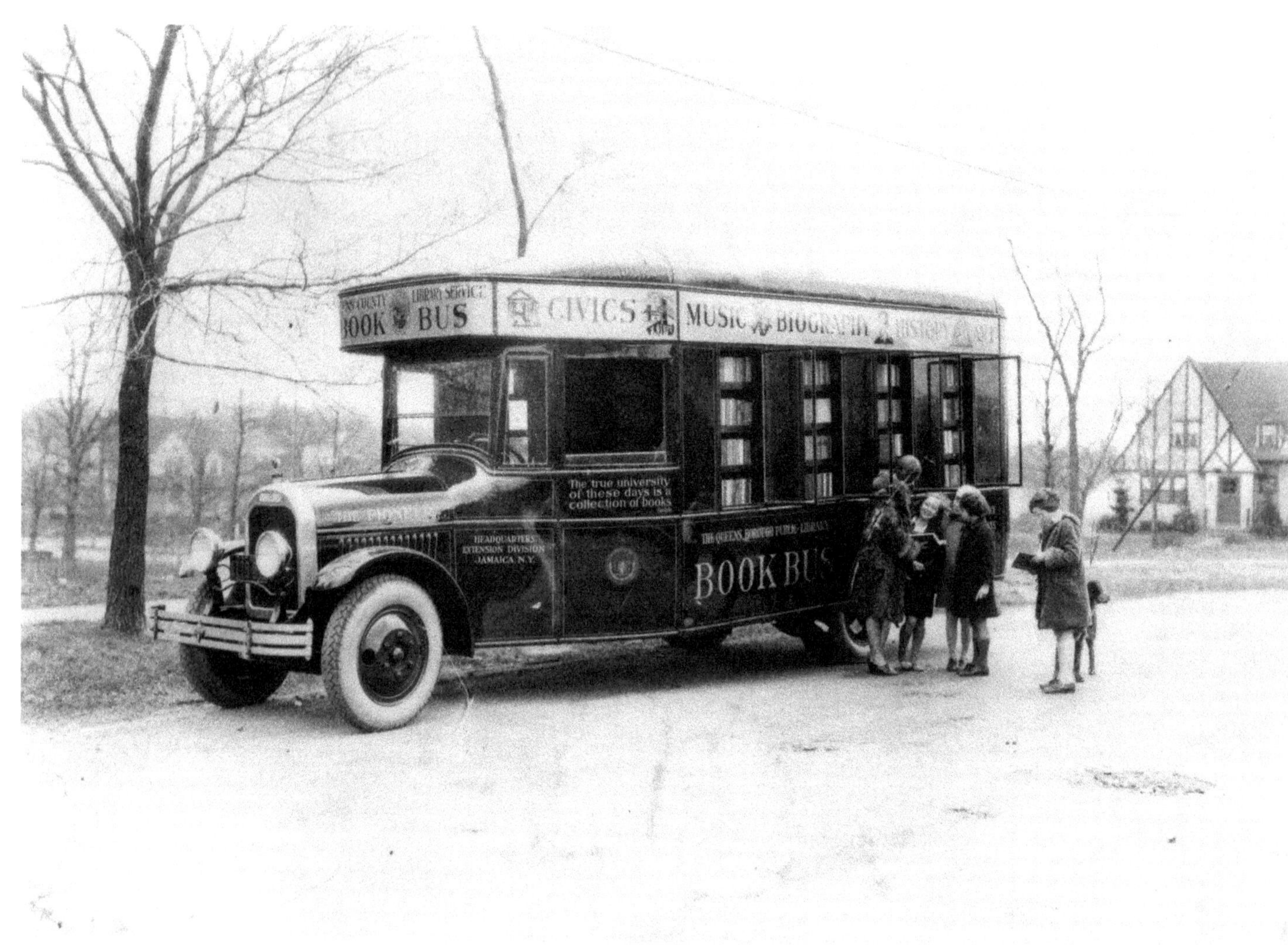

The book bus "Pioneer" makes a stop for young readers in a Queens neighborhood. The vehicle was Queens' first traveling library and featured bookshelves that literally opened to the public for browsing.

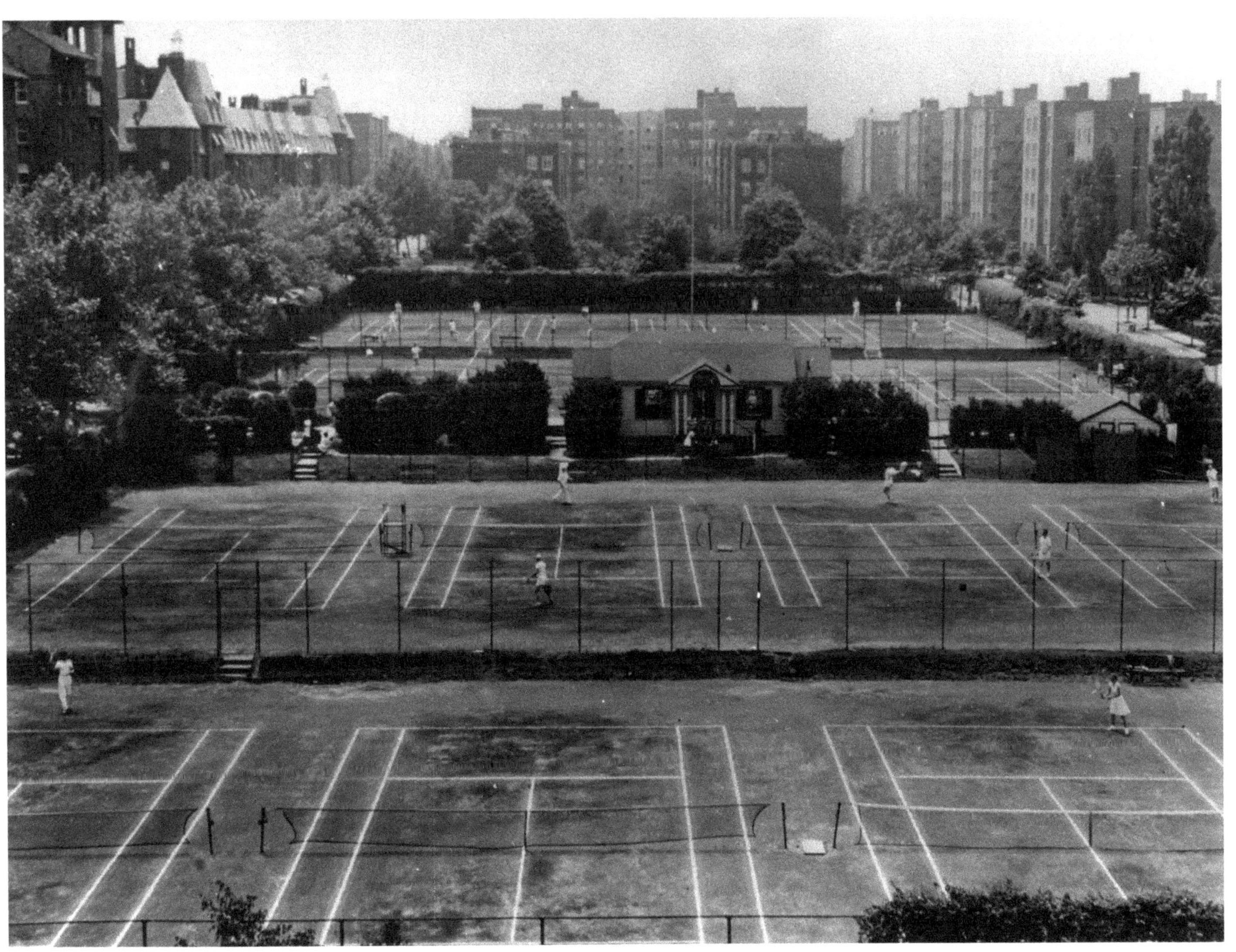

This 1928 shot shows the landscaped grass tennis Tournament Courts in Jackson Heights, with players wearing the traditional all-white outfits for club play—including long skirts for women. The surrounding buildings were not built until 1914, when the Queensboro Corporation transformed the former swampland into cooperatives and apartments, with large inner courtyards. The neighborhood is named for John C. Jackson whose Jackson Avenue (Northern Boulevard) forms its southern border.

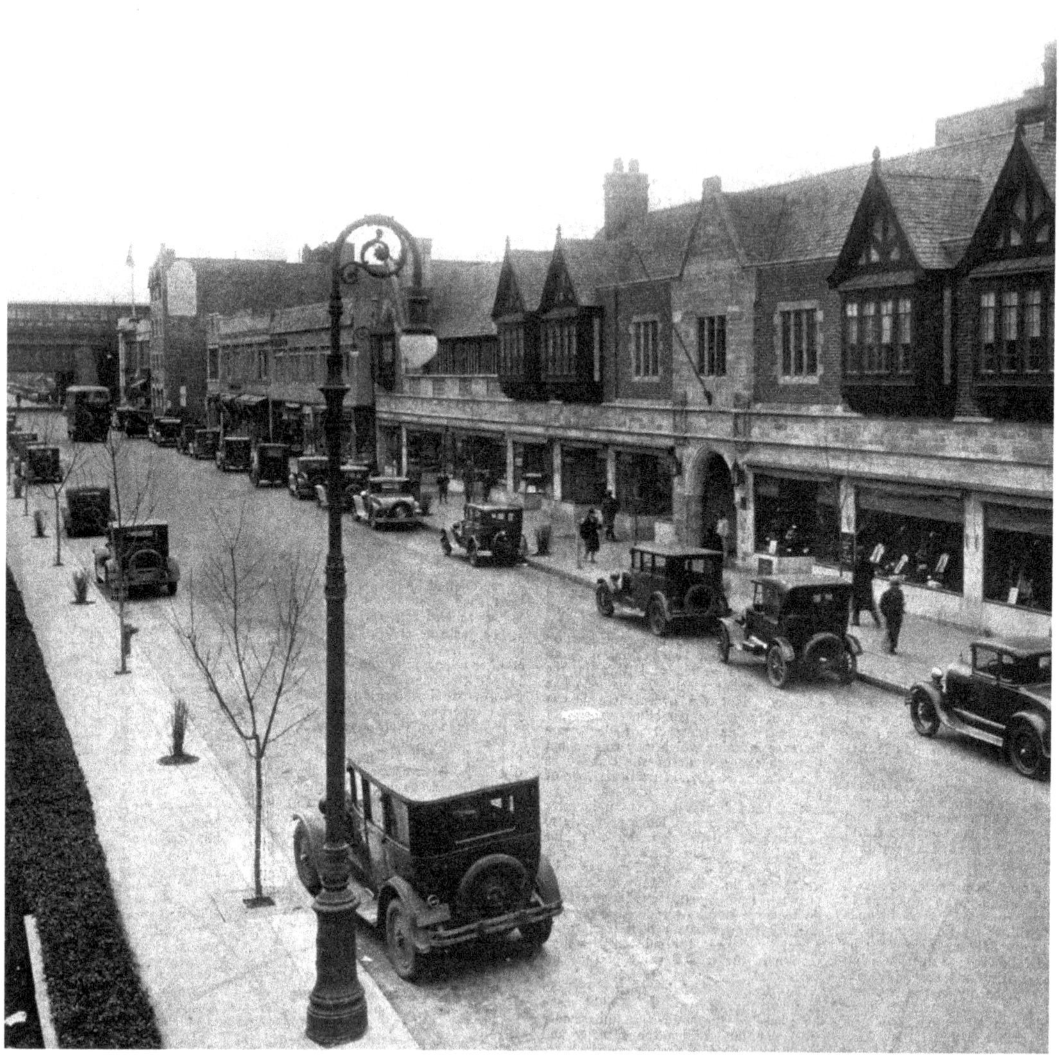

The main shopping strip in Jackson Heights has always been 82nd Street. Seen here at Roosevelt Avenue are the English Gables, designed by Robert Tappan specifically for the Queensboro Corporation, which had its headquarters in a large Tudor at the intersection of 82nd and 37th Avenue. Queensboro developed most of the area and was notoriously meticulous about controlling the neighborhood's character. Many of the facades still line 82nd Street today.

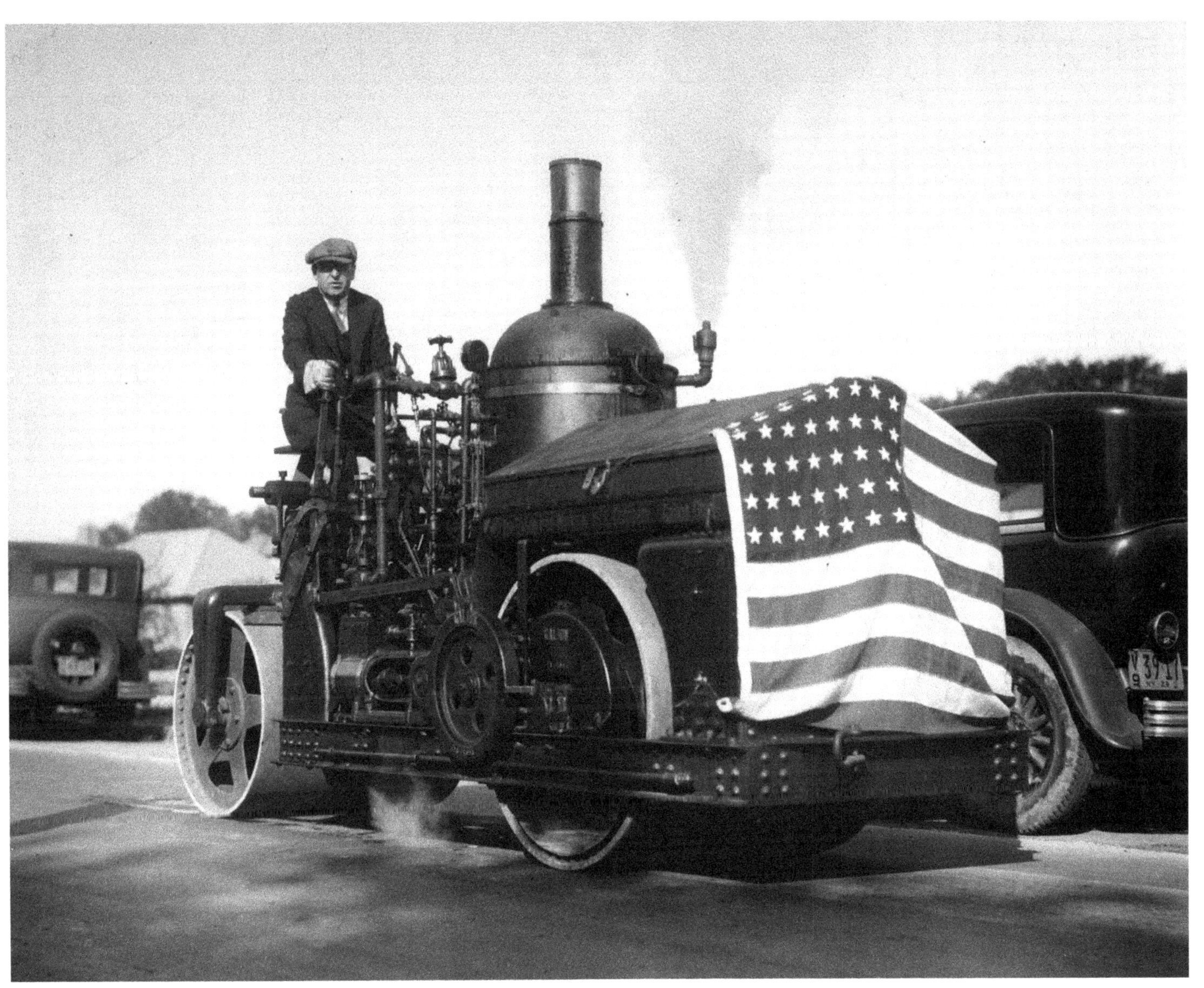

In 1929, the opening of this paved road was grand enough to warrant a celebration, as shown in the photograph. This patriotically decorated machine is a true steamroller (powered by a steam engine, at center)—and operated with Queens class by a Queens public works commissioner J. J. Halloran, who wears a three-piece suit and a tie.

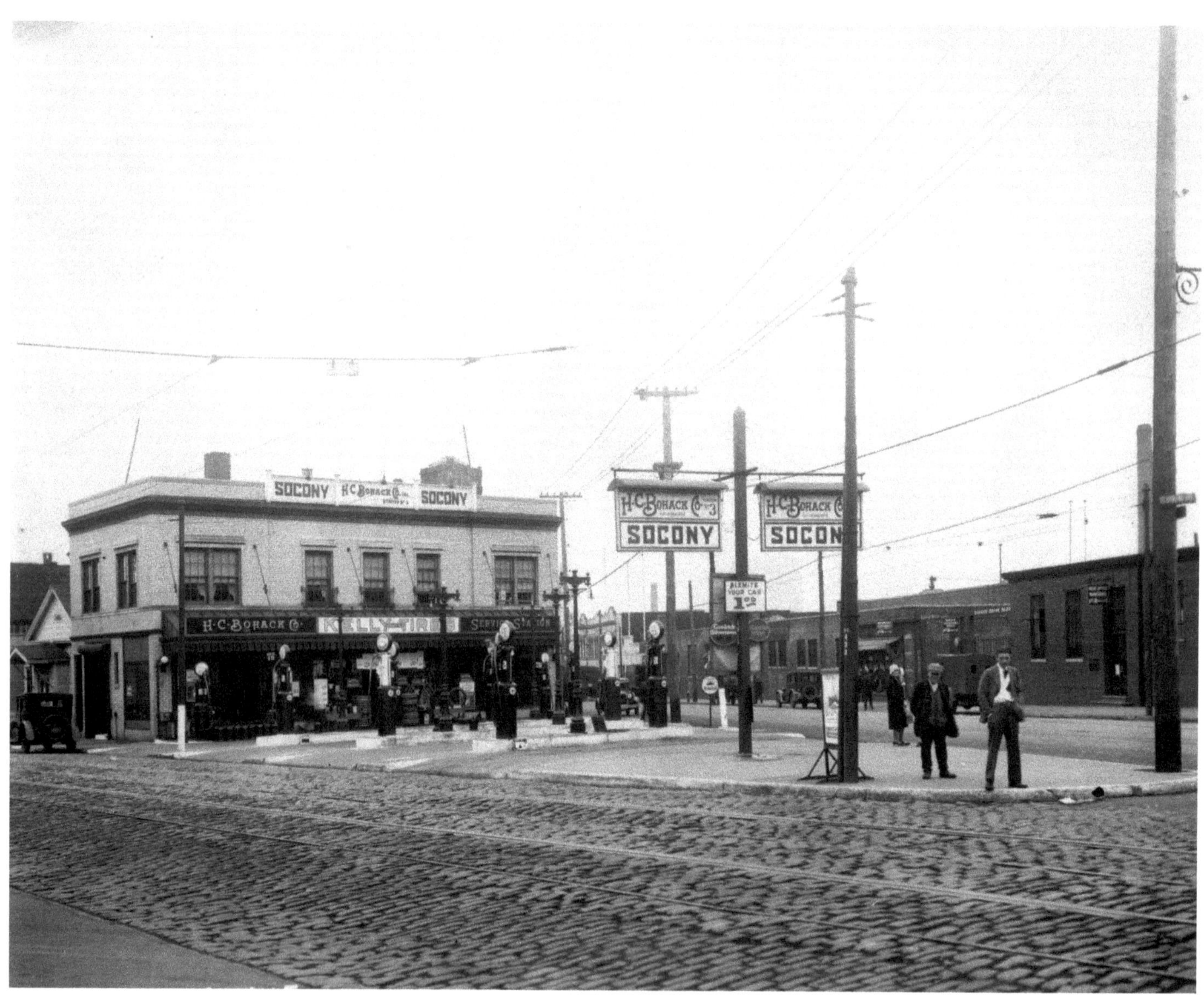

An H. C. Bohack Company grocery shared space with a SOCONY service station, in a bit of corporate synergy on Flushing Avenue in Ridgewood in 1929. Both companies operated many outposts across Long Island, with Henry Bohack expanding to 740 stores by the time of his death in 1931. In the foreground are the tracks for the no. 57 streetcar, which ran down Flushing Avenue to Brooklyn.

Era of the Great Depression

(1930–1939)

The housing boom of the 1920s slowed with the onset of the Great Depression, but from tenements to row houses to Tudor and Colonial mansions, the development of Queens would not be held in check. Whole neighborhoods sprang up where once there was nothing.

The Gala Amusement Park in North Beach, owned by the great Steinway dynasty that had owned part of Astoria for decades, was razed to make way for a new airport on the site—erasing summer memories for hundreds of thousands, but allowing millions to eventually visit—many of whom arrived from all over the world for the 1939-40 World's Fair, one of the most important events in Queens History.

Although the depression slowed growth, the federal Works Progress Administration found plenty to do with tax dollars in Queens, from the Art Deco design of the Maritime Sea Air Terminal at what would become LaGuardia International Airport, to building bridges, tunnels, and highways that provided even greater access into and out of the borough. The subways were consolidated and the Long Island Railroad continued to improve its service to points east.

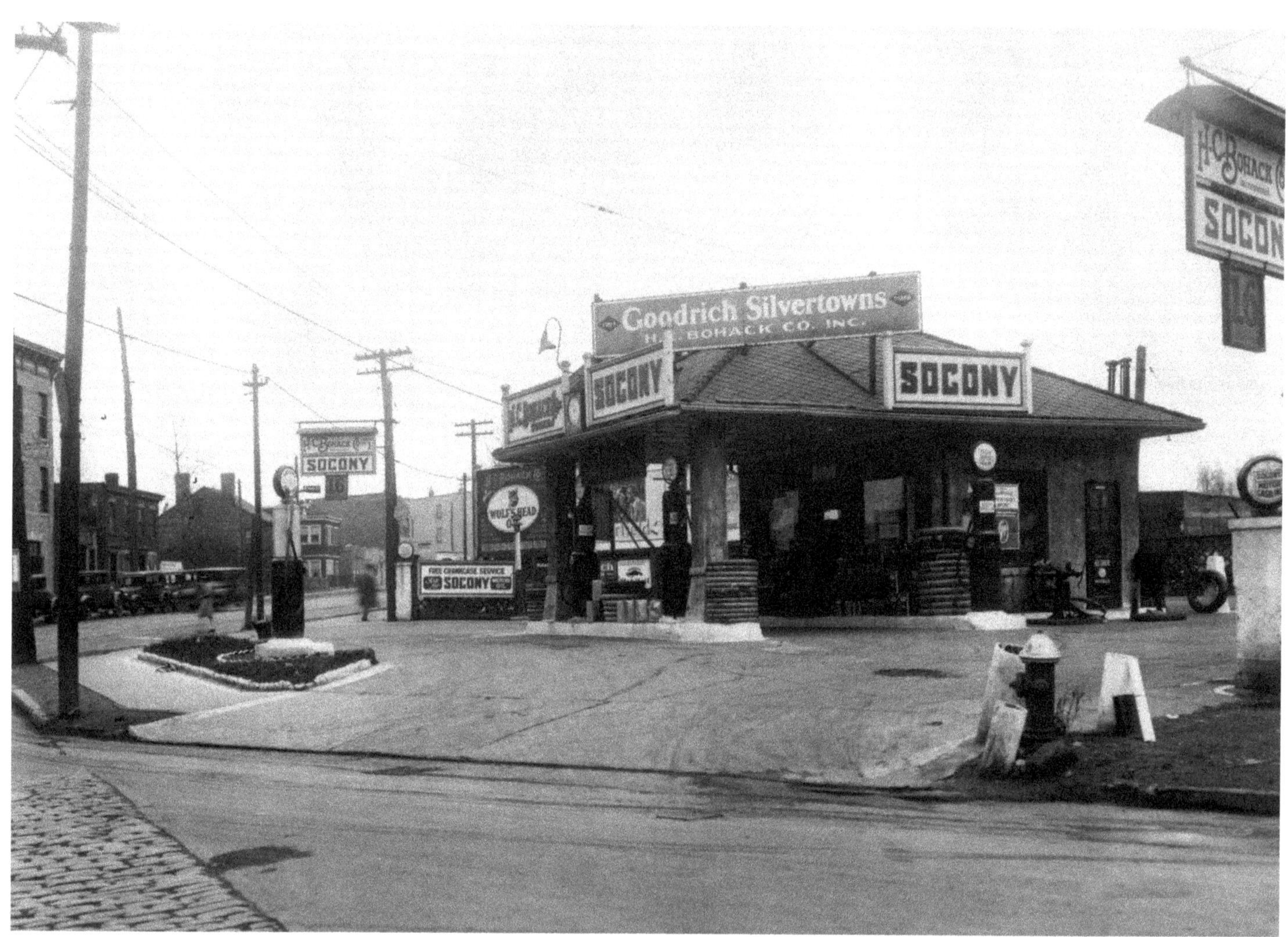

Bohack's flagship restaurant and massive headquarters originally encompassed 32 acres in Maspeth and Ridgewood. After Mr. Bohack's death, the area seen in this photograph bounded by Flushing Avenue at Metropolitan Avenue, facing east from Troutman Avenue in Maspeth, was renamed "Bohack Square." The headquarters had its own railroad access, a large bakery, and a fire department. Bohack's existed until 1977 when its properties were sold off following bankruptcy.

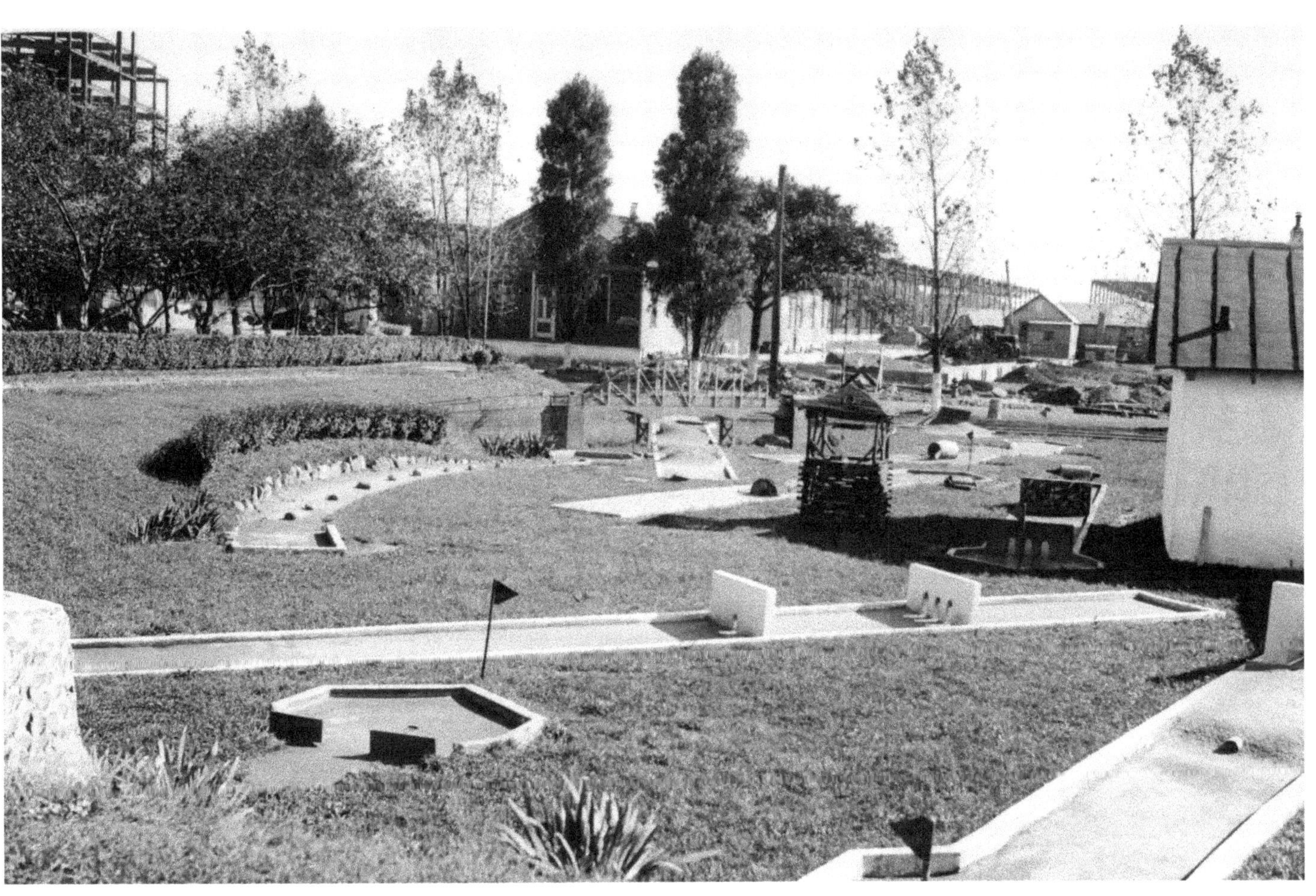

A miniature golf course was added to Riker's Island. This photograph from 1931 shows the course with the prison's chapel in the background, at upper-center. A baseball diamond was adjacent the course, located on what was known as "Old Prisoner's Row." A new jail opened on the island in 1932 to replace a jail on nearby Blackwell's Island (now Roosevelt Island). A permanent penitentiary opened on the island in 1935 and remained in use until 2000.

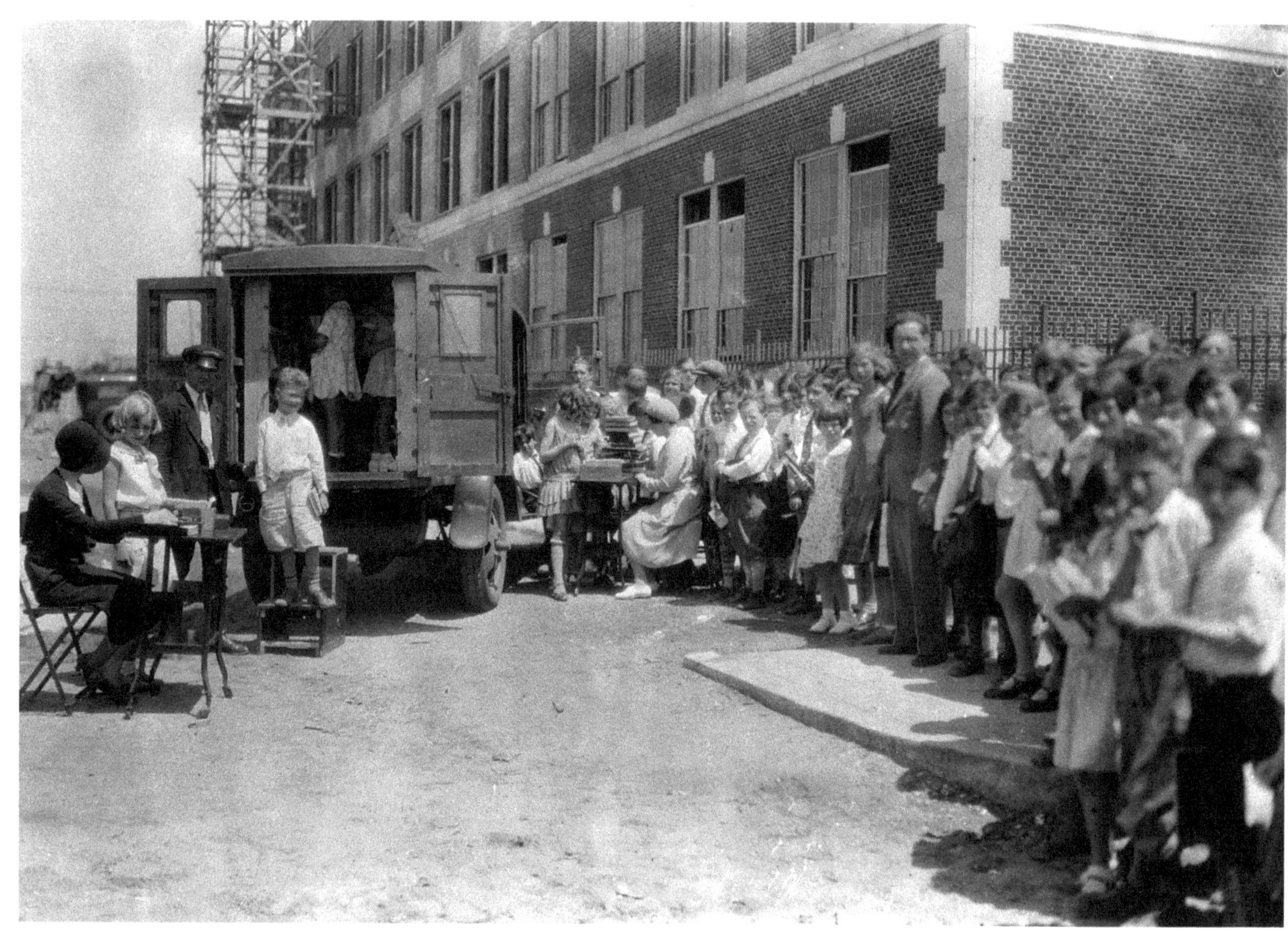

A mob scene outside a school as the Queens Borough Public Library's full-service bookmobile, complete with a uniformed driver, checkout desks, and two librarians makes a stop in 1930. The bookmobile operated until 1976, and was recently revived, serving neighborhoods when libraries are closed for renovations.

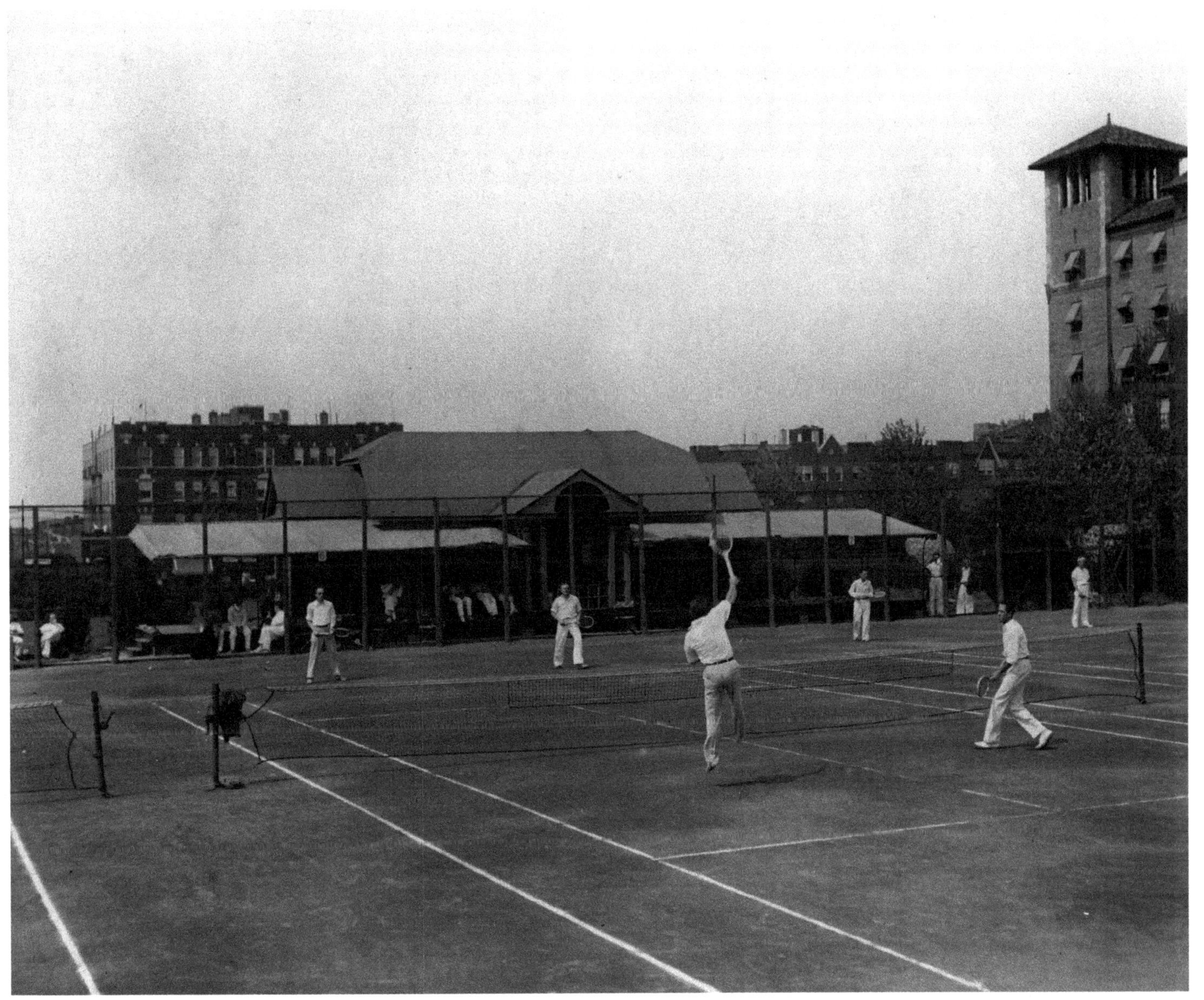

A view from the ground at the Jackson Heights Tennis Club's courts, an oasis among the multi-story tenements of the neighborhood. Located near 80th Avenue and Northern Boulevard, the club was situated in the center of the Queensboro Corporation's empire, which built the nation's first garden apartments in Jackson Heights in the 1910s.

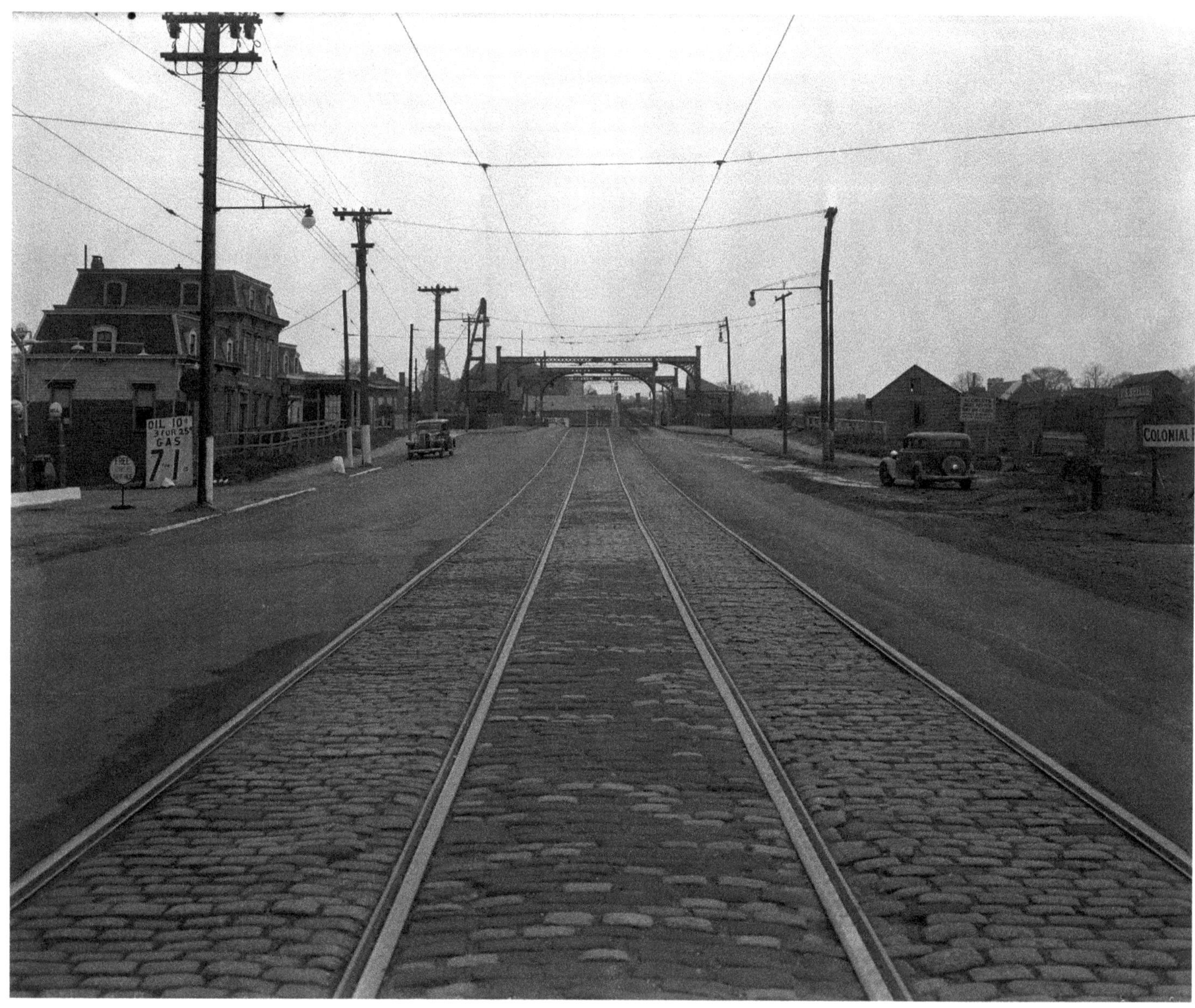

A view of Northern Boulevard in Corona in 1930, facing east toward the Flushing River Bridge. The tracks are for New York & Queens Company Railway streetcars. The river is actually a creek, flowing from Willow Lake in Flushing Meadows to Flushing Bay, which empties into the East River. The creek divides the borough into eastern and western sections.

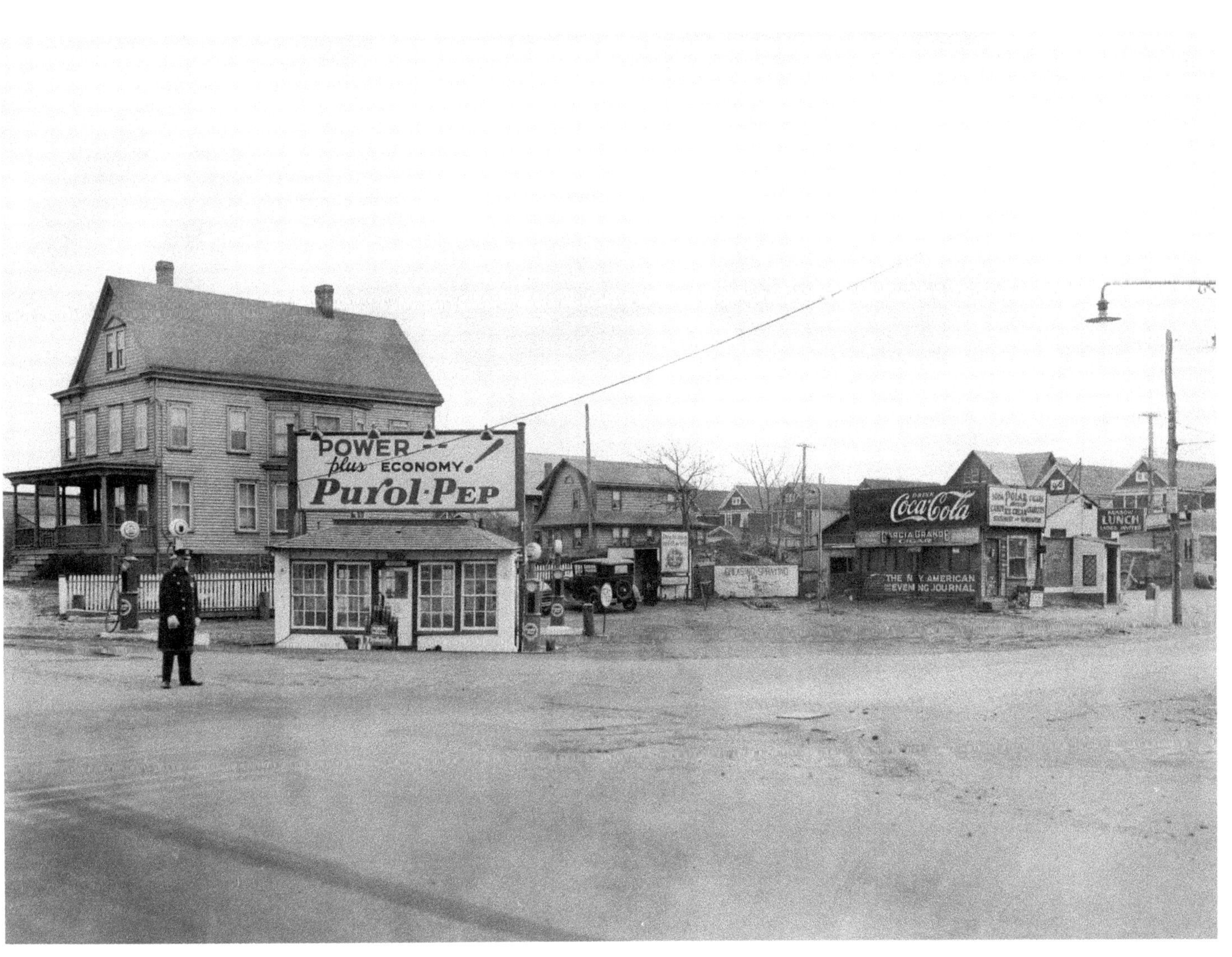

The Pure Oil Company produced Purol gasoline products, sold at service stations like this one located on Woodhaven Boulevard at Queens Boulevard. Purol Pep was gold in color and pumped from blue pumps, while Purol Ethyl was pumped from white pumps. A uniformed policeman, complete with full coat and white gloves, eyes the photographer in the middle of the intersection.

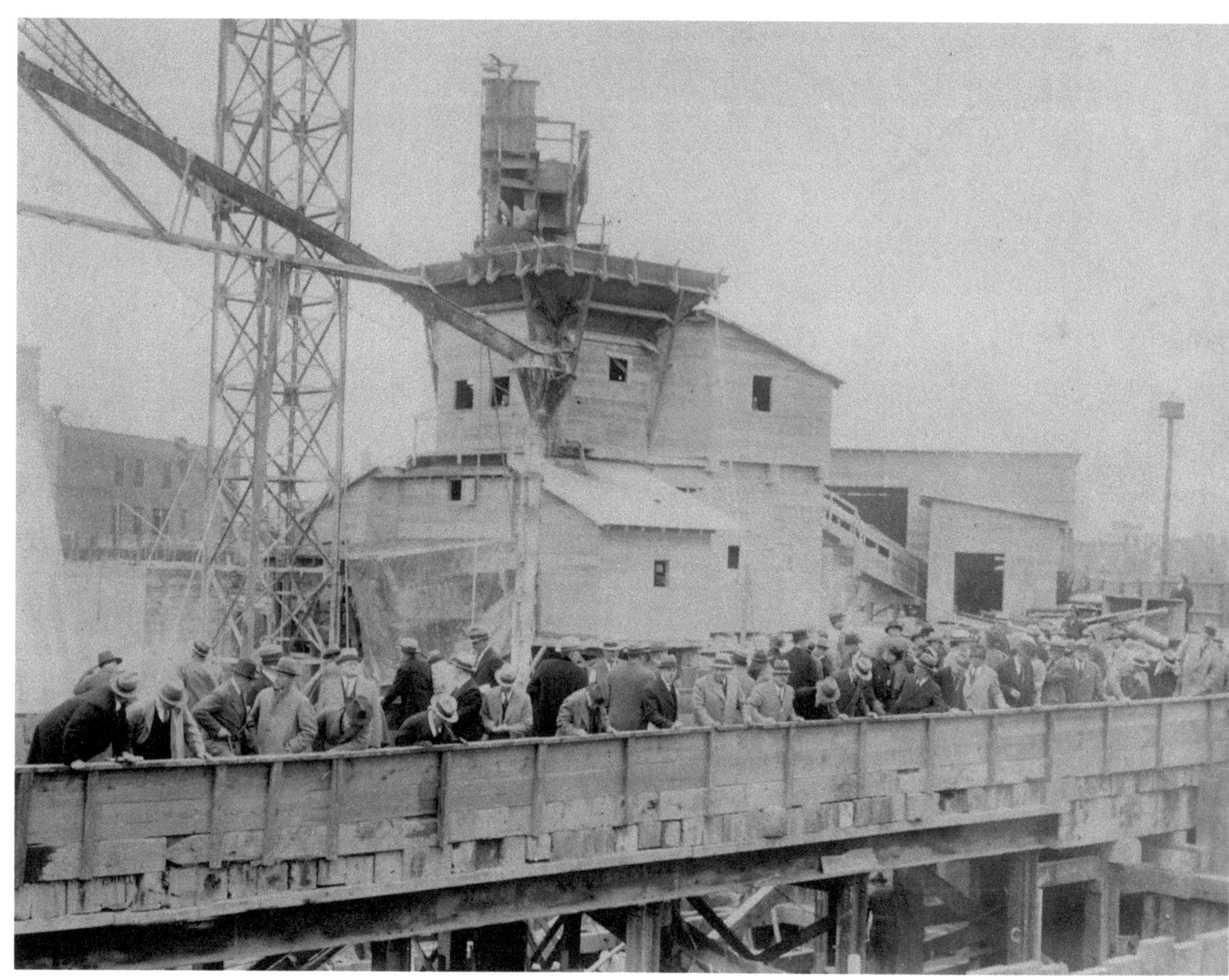

Two decades after the Queensboro Bridge was constructed, the Triborough Bridge was built at a cost of $60 million—one of the costliest public works projects of the Great Depression. The triple-span bridge connects Astoria to Ward's Island–Randall's Island, then forks to a bridge to the South Bronx and a bridge to East Harlem. With construction under way here in 1931, dignitaries are visiting the Queens side of the bridge. In 2008, the bridge was renamed for former New York senator Robert F. Kennedy.

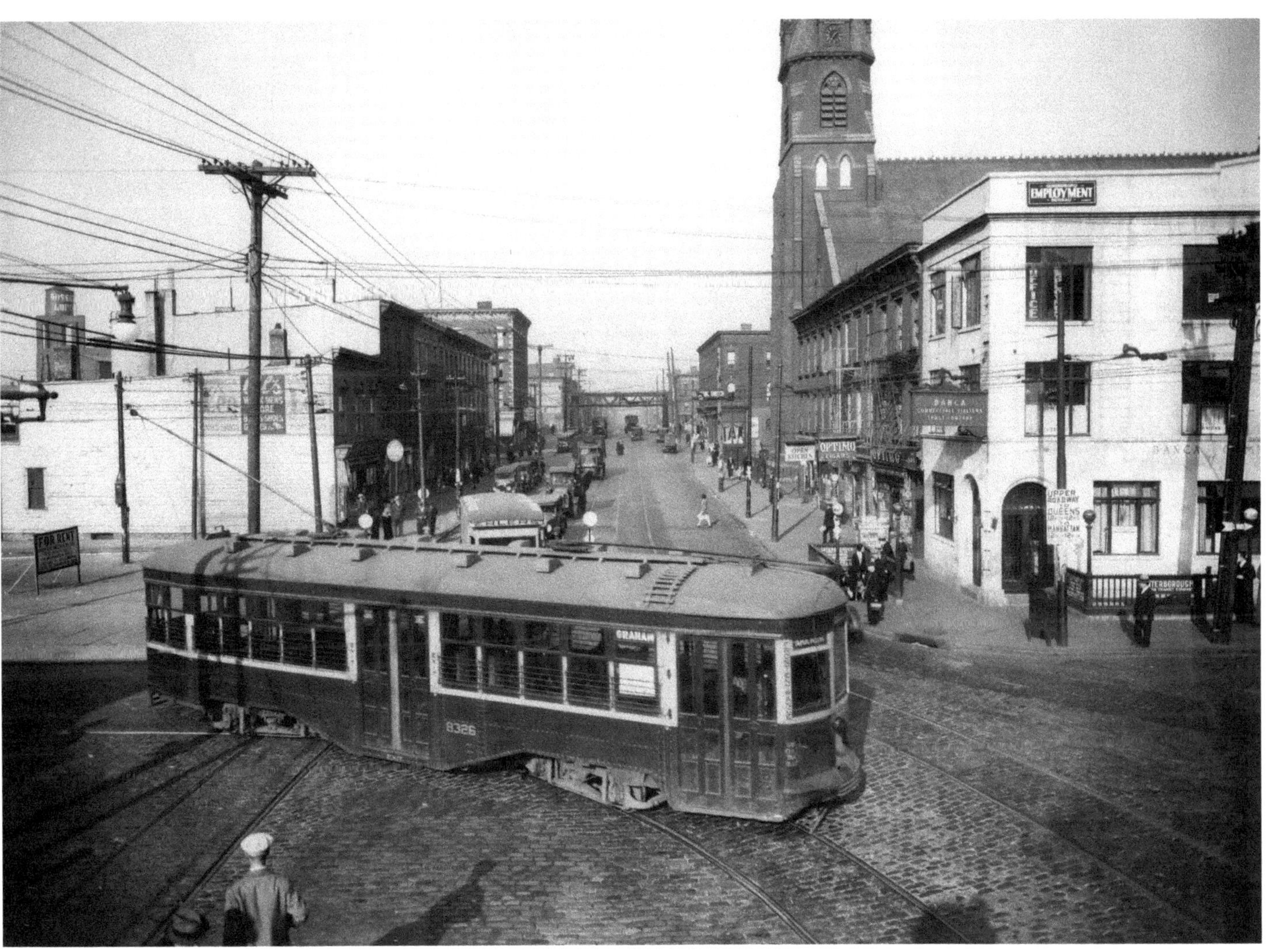

A busy day at Vernon Boulevard and 50th Avenue in Long Island City, near the entrance to the Queensboro Bridge. In addition to the bridge, transit options included the Park Row trolley, which swings past the Banca Commerciale Italiana Trust Company, the large white building to the right of the frame, flanked by the Interborough Rapid Transit subway entrances on the corner. In the middle distance is the spire of St. Mary's Roman Catholic Church, which had one of the largest congregations in the borough.

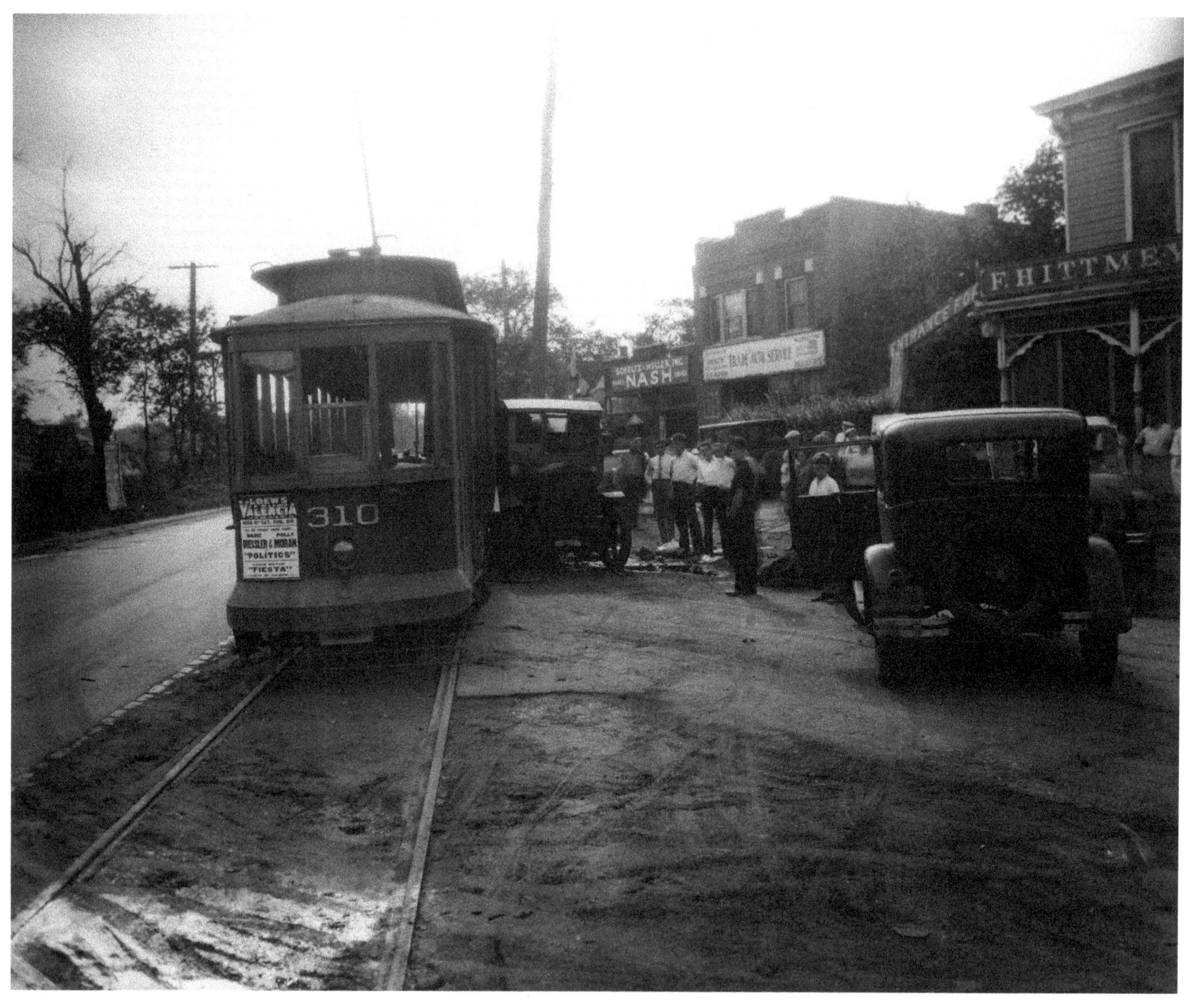

As populations swelled, so did the problems of modern urban life. A crowd gathers in 1931 to survey the damage caused by this driver, who appears to have sideswiped this Jamaica Central Railway Company no. 310 streetcar on Hempstead Turnpike.

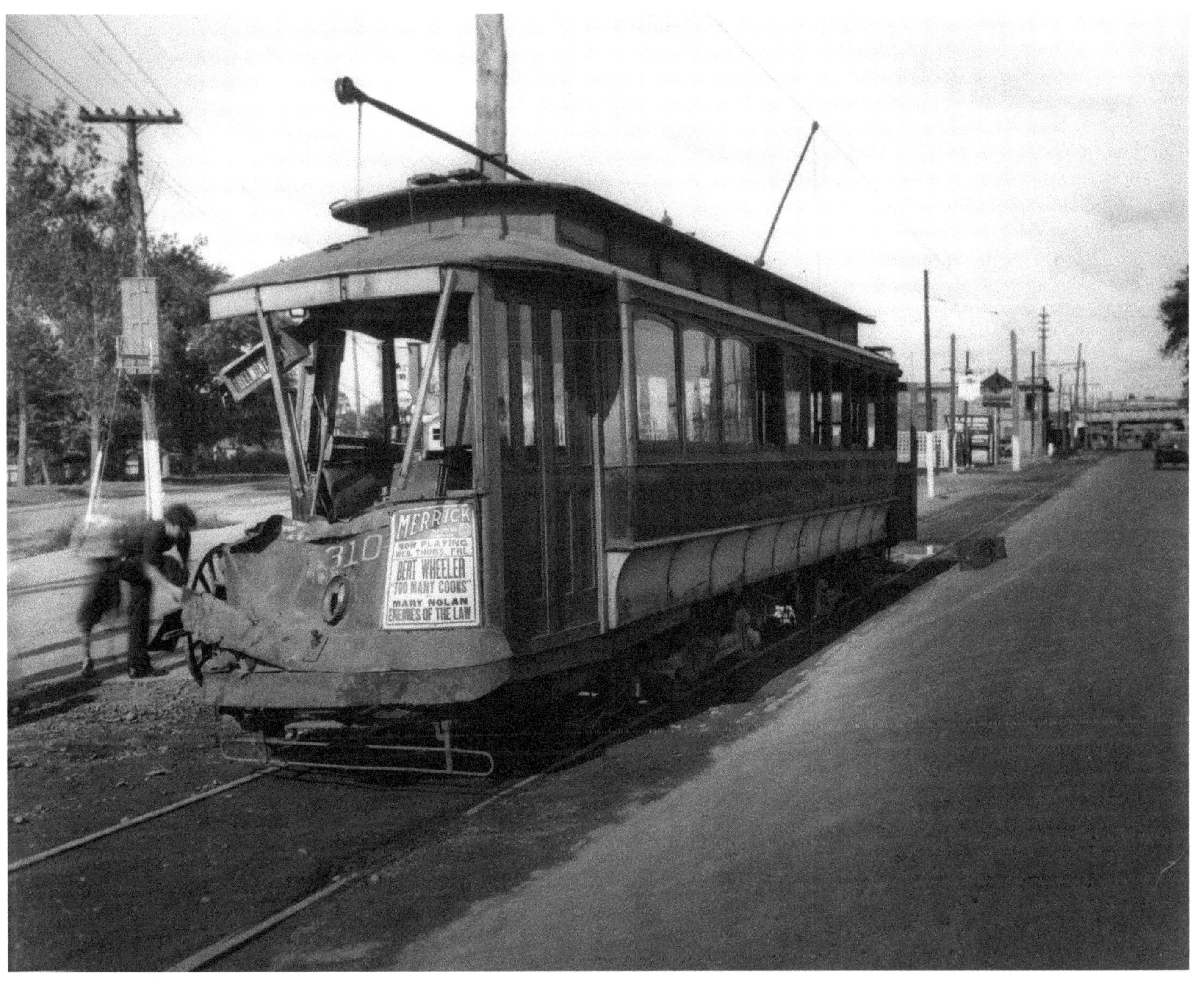

A view from the front of the serious damage to the no. 310 streetcar after the accident. This line ran from Jamaica out to the world-famous racetrack at Belmont Park, just over the county line.

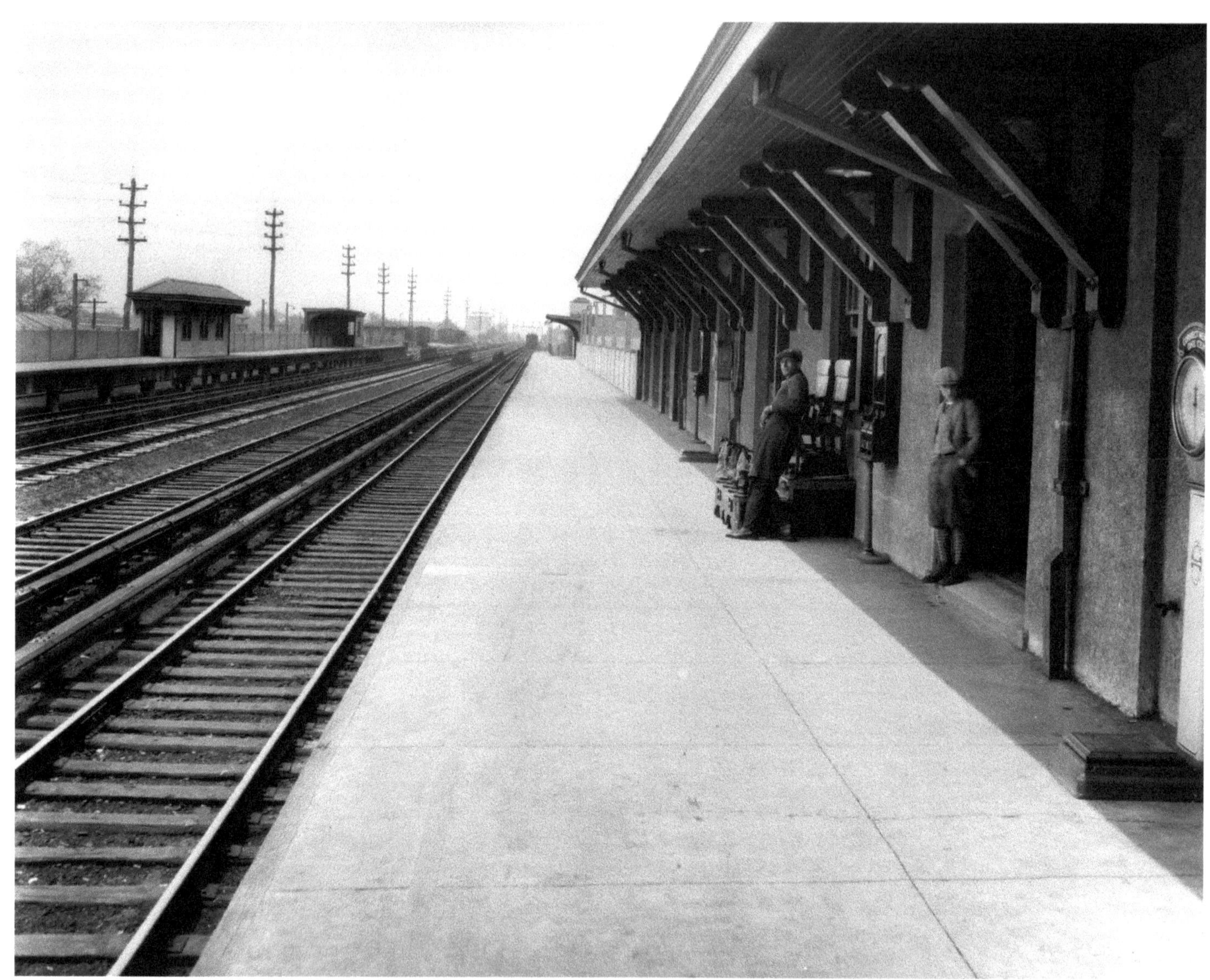

As commuters have done for more than a century, this view looks west, toward Manhattan, from this Long Island Railroad station in Queens Village. In the right foreground is a scale and toward the center is a shoe-shine stand—unsurprisingly deserted in this bleak 1931 photograph, as the boom in housing and development slowed with the economic meltdown.

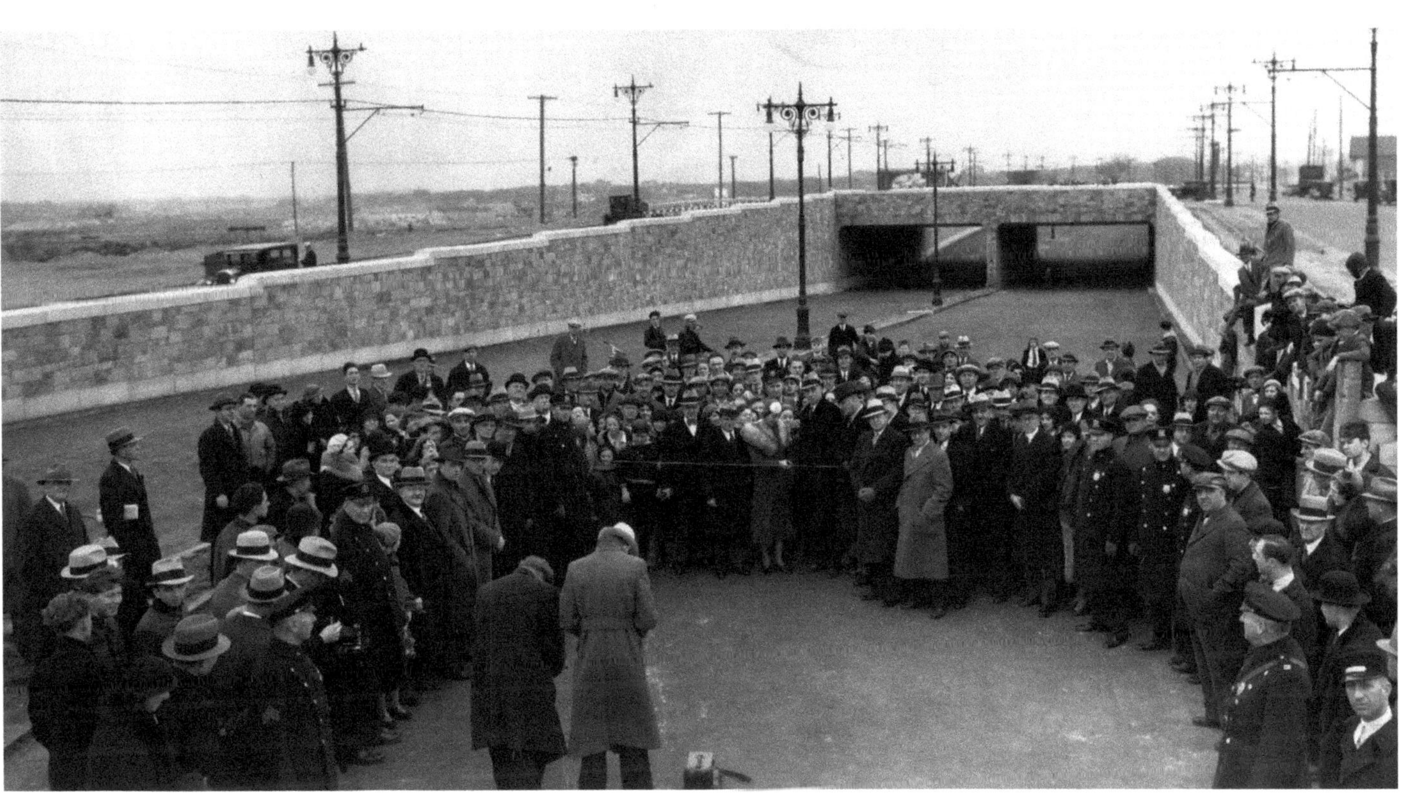

A historic event in 1932, when crowds gathered along with local politicians to mark the opening of the underpass at Queens Boulevard, in Rego Park at Woodhaven Boulevard, near Horace Harding Boulevard—a four-lane road that ran all the way to Shelter Rock Road in Nassau County (reportedly to allow its benefactor easier access to his country club). Within a decade, Horace Harding Boulevard was converted to an "express highway" and eventually transformed into the Long Island Expressway, which now runs from the Midtown Tunnel to the eastern end of Long Island.

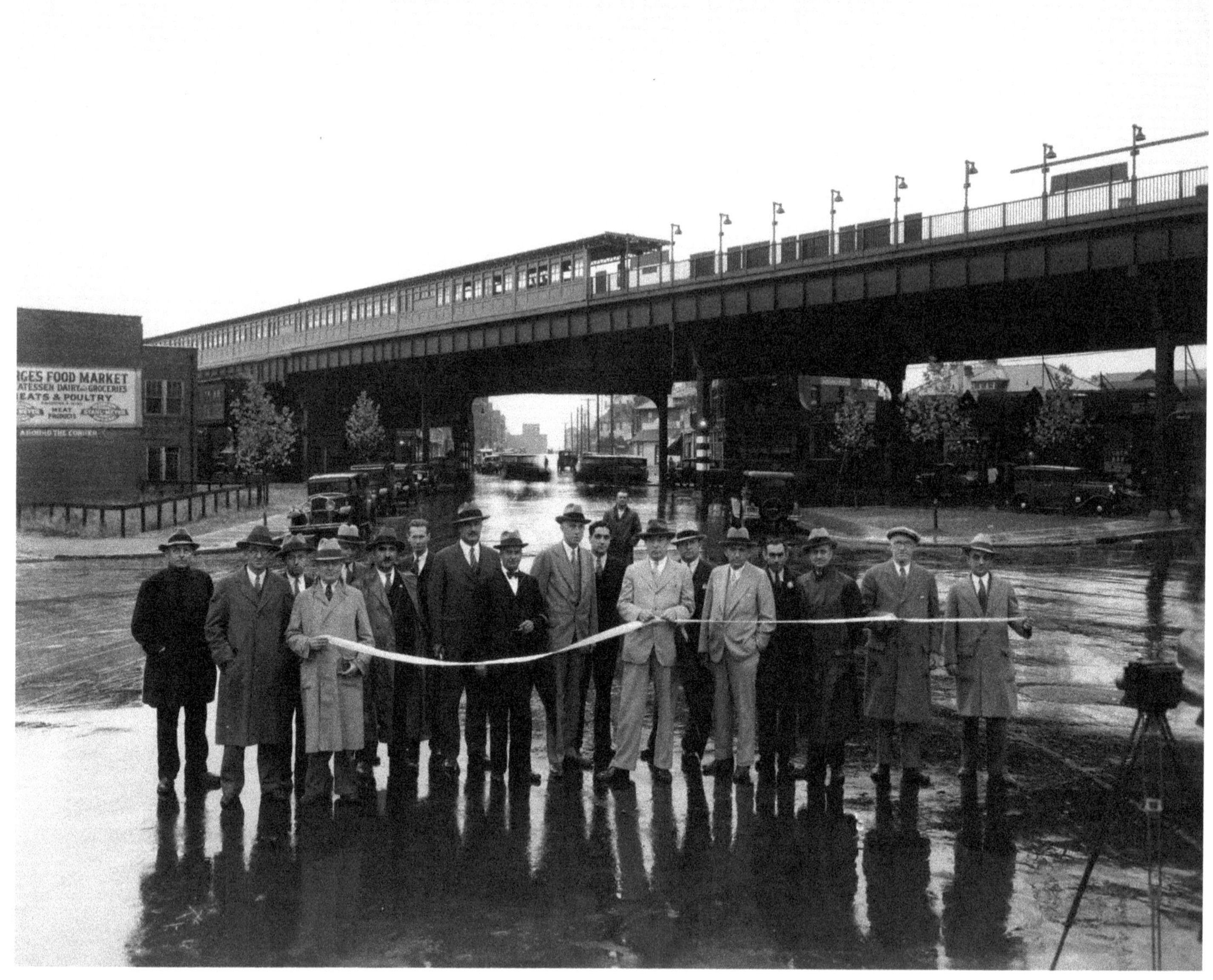

With newspaper readership very high in the 1930s, it seems that local leaders never missed a photo opportunity for ribbon-cutting ceremonies. Here is the opening of the large Independent Subway System's Queens Boulevard line, which connected to the IND's 50th Street station on the 8th Avenue line. This elevated trestle is located at 74th Street and Broadway and is one of the main transit hubs in Queens, on the border between Jackson Heights, Woodside, and Elmhurst.

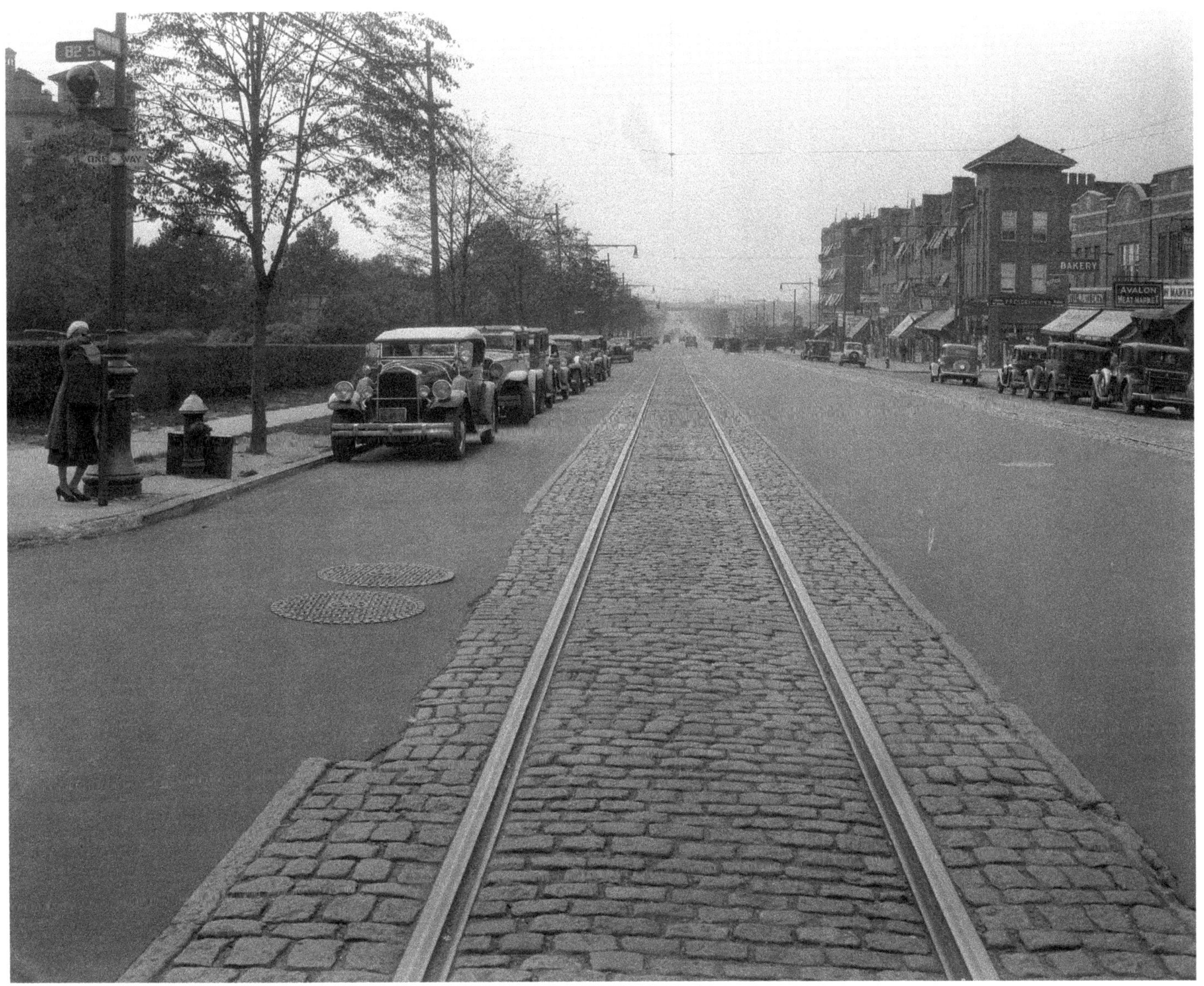

The intersection of Jackson Avenue (Northern Boulevard) and 82nd Street in Jackson Heights, with a landscaped garden behind the stone wall on the left, and a busy shopping district on the right, with parking clearly at a premium, even in 1933. The tracks are for the New York & Queens Railway Company streetcar, which served the area.

Following Spread: Springfield Boulevard and Hempstead Turnpike in Queens Village became a busy commercial district to serve the hordes of new residents in the area. In the left background is Breitfeller Auto Sales, across from Queen's cigar shop and the offices of Wacker dentistry. The tower of Grace Lutheran Church is visible in the middle right.

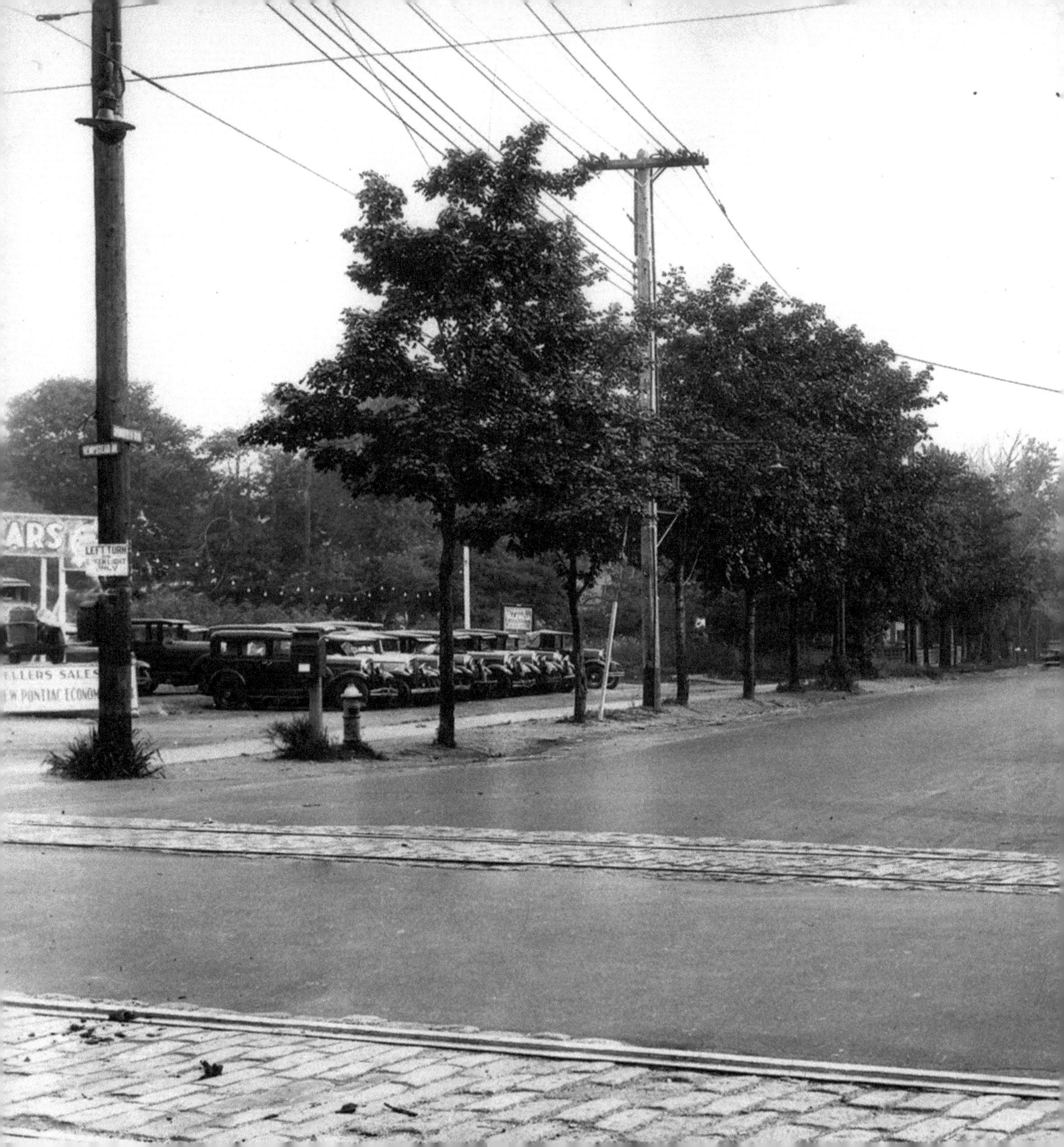
LEFT TURN
SALES

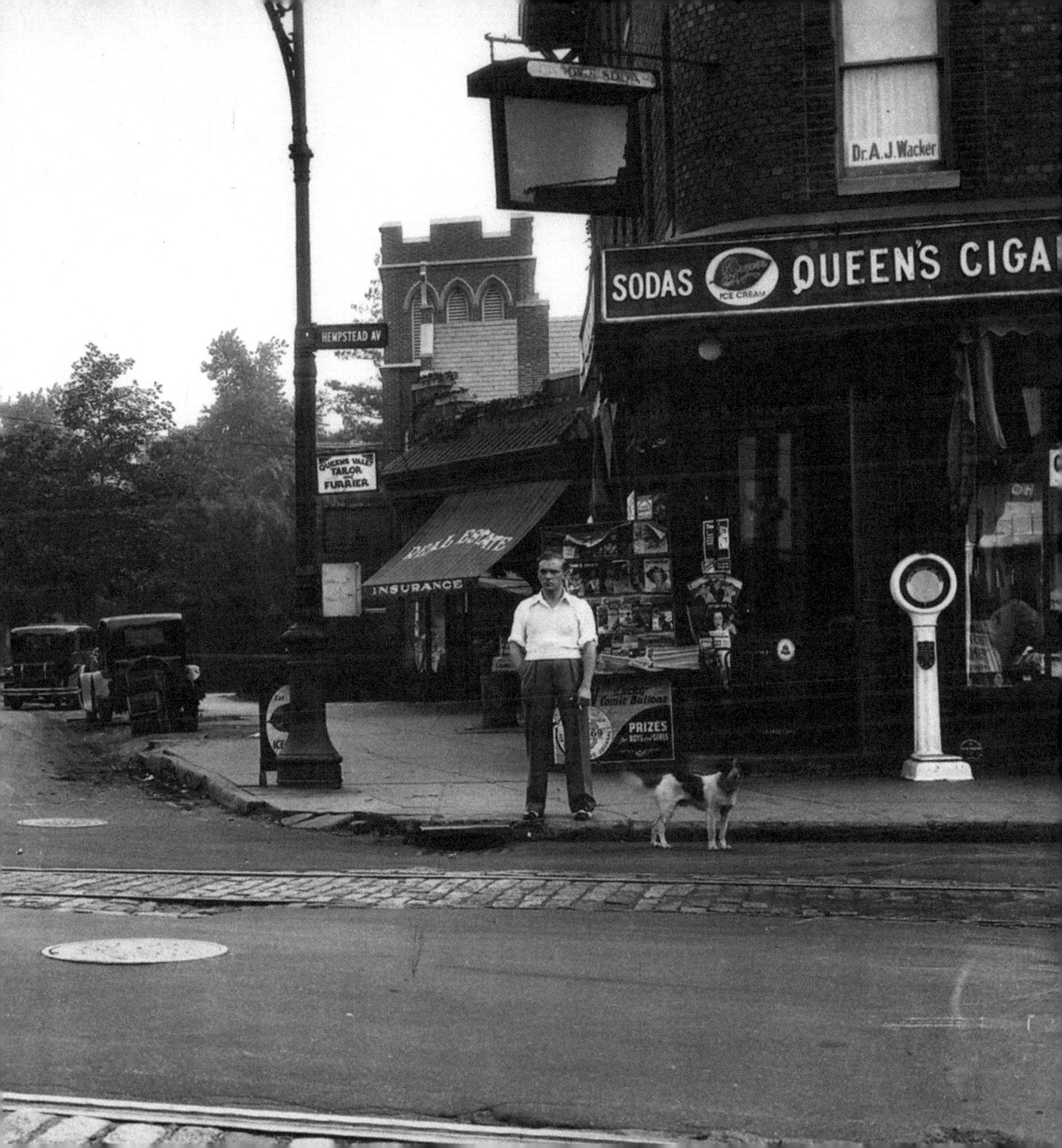
Dr. A. J. Wacker
SODAS
ICE CREAM
QUEEN'S CIGA
HEMPSTEAD AV
QUEENS VALLEY TAILOR FURRIER
REAL ESTATE
INSURANCE
PRIZES

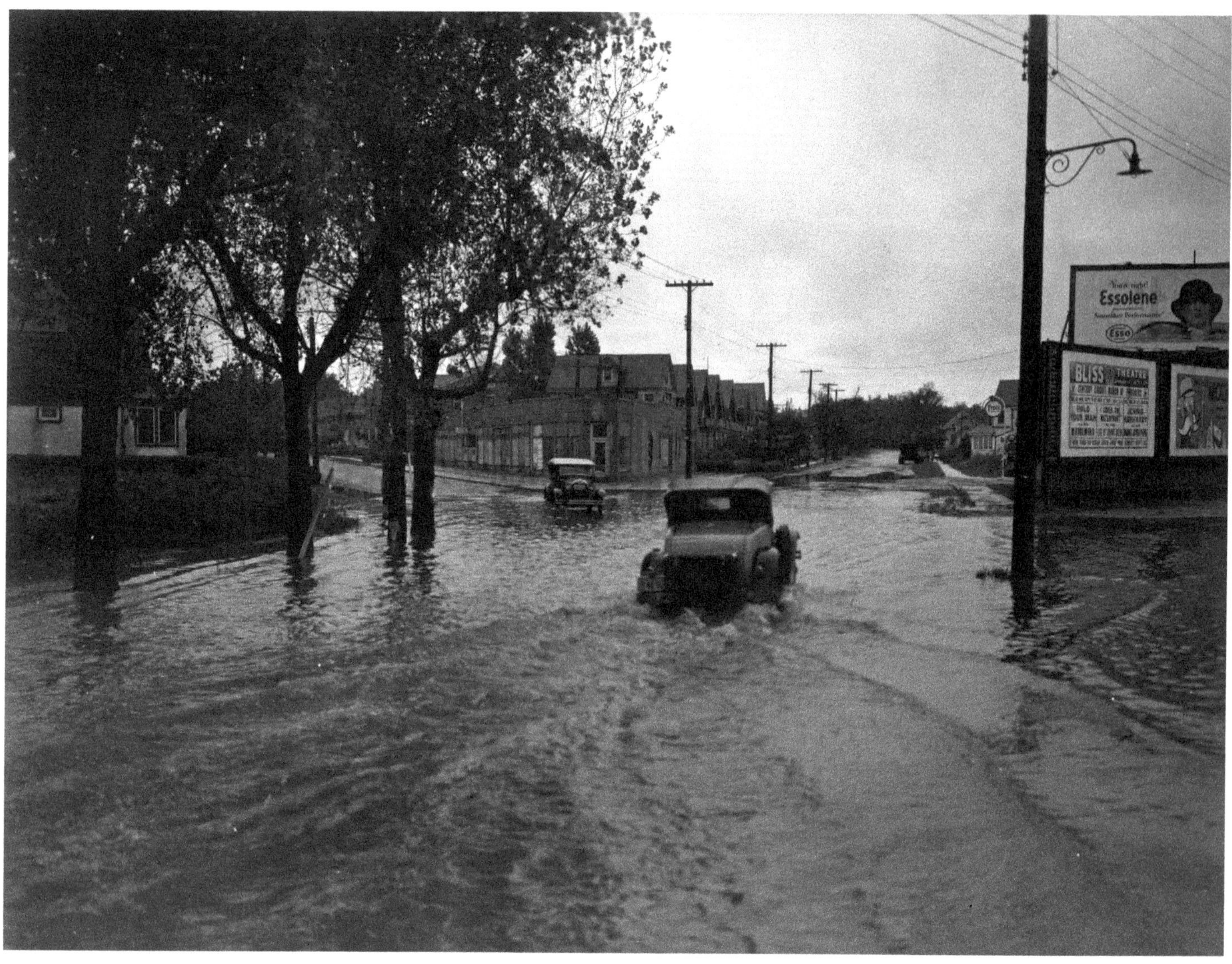

This car wades through waters left by one of many hurricane-force storms in 1933, attempting to cross St. James Avenue on 51st Street near Queens Boulevard in Elmhurst. The hurricane season of 1933 had the most Atlantic Ocean hurricanes on record until 2005, and the city was battered and flooded, despite advances in sewage systems and public works across the city.

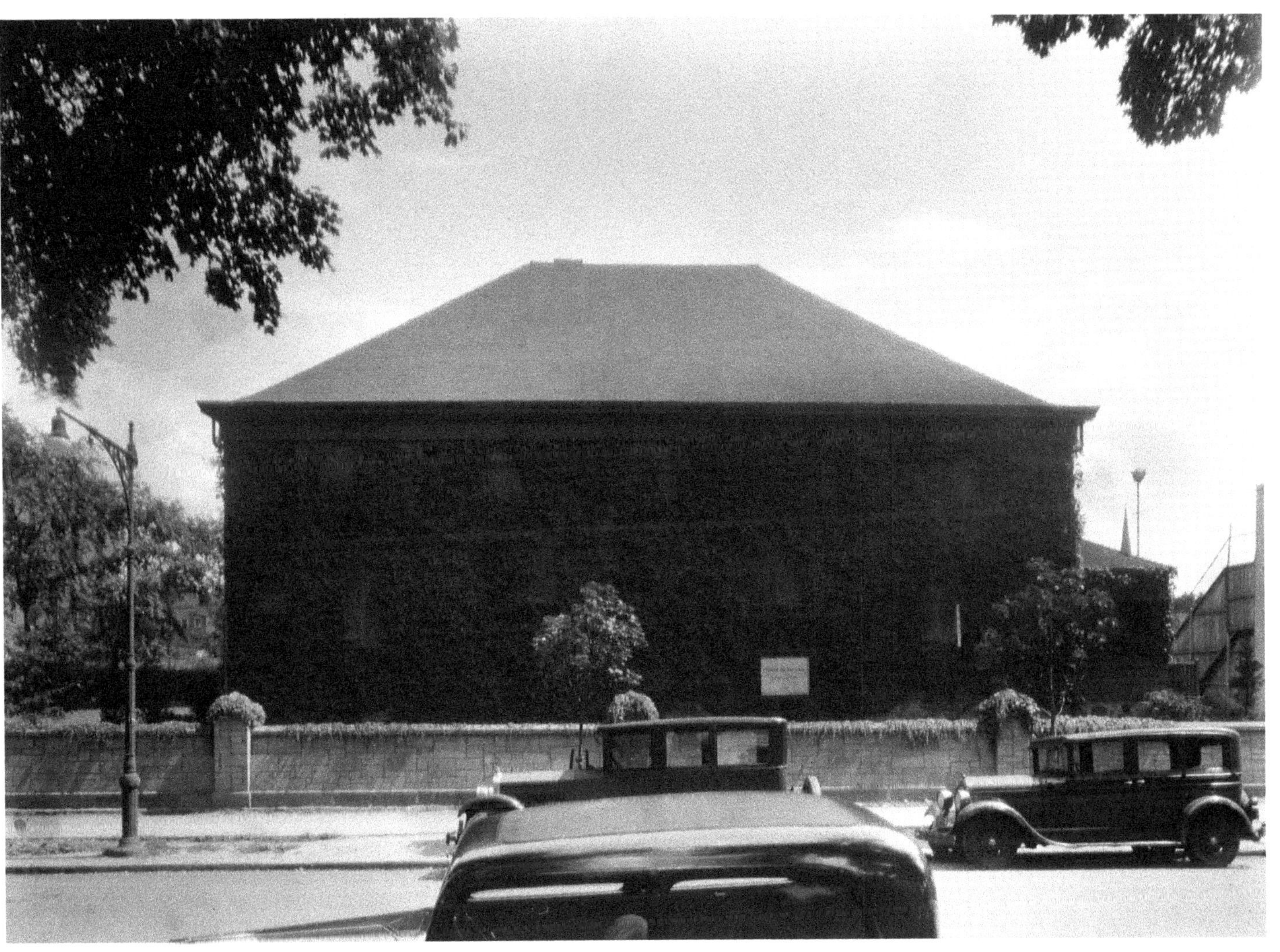

The Society of Friends Meetinghouse on Northern Boulevard in Flushing was built in 1694 and is the second-oldest Quaker meetinghouse in continuous use in the United States. It is supposedly modeled on the home of John Bowne, the leader of the Flushing Remonstrance in 1657 who fought for religious freedom with the West India Trading Company and the Director-General of New Netherland, Peter Stuyvesant.

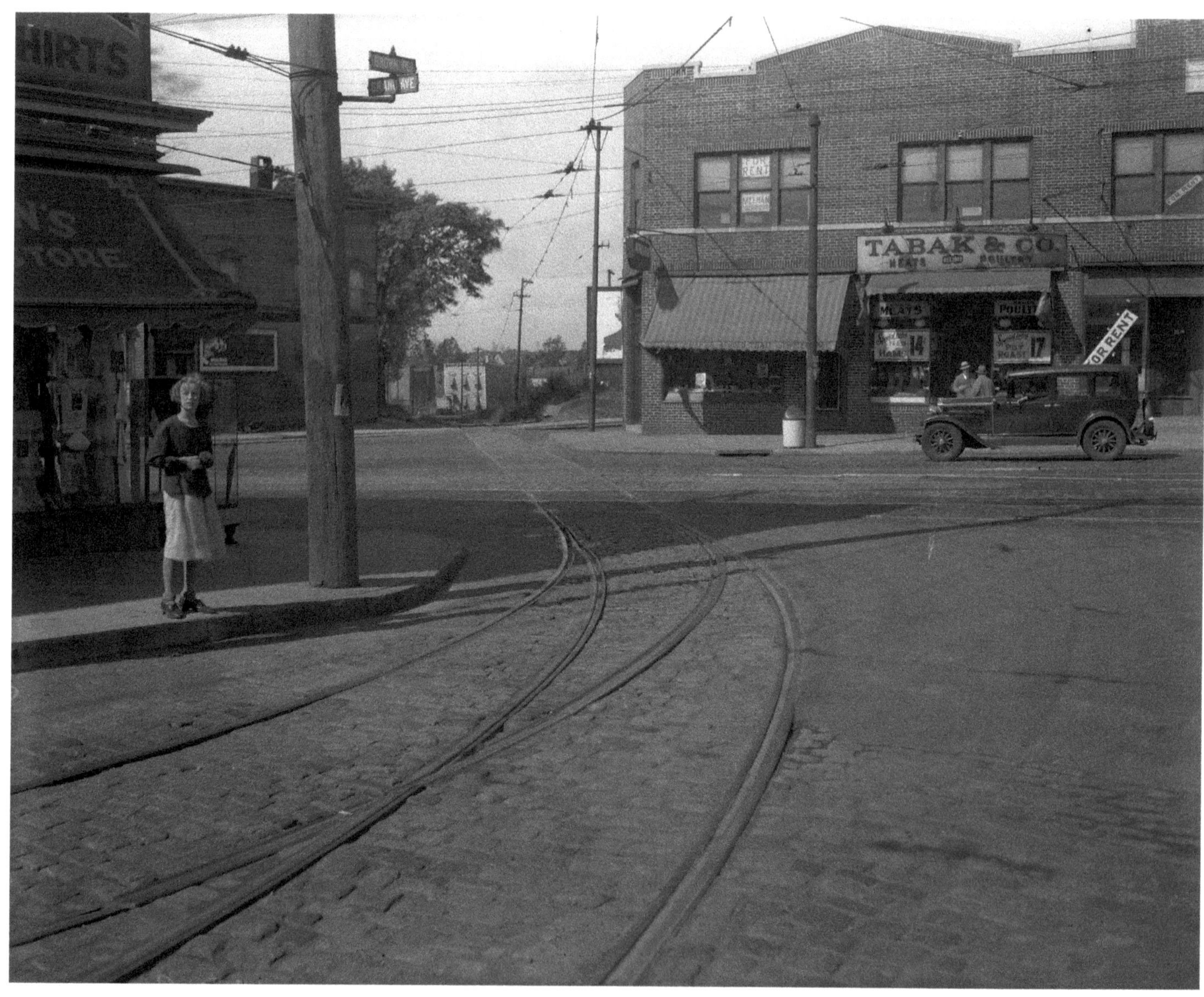

Brown Place in Maspeth in 1934, with tracks from the New York & Queens Railway Company leading to the northwest, across Grand Avenue, to a private right-of-way owned by the railroad. Within three years, the last trolley rolled down a Queens street, replaced by buses and made obsolete by the efficiency of the expanded subway lines across the borough.

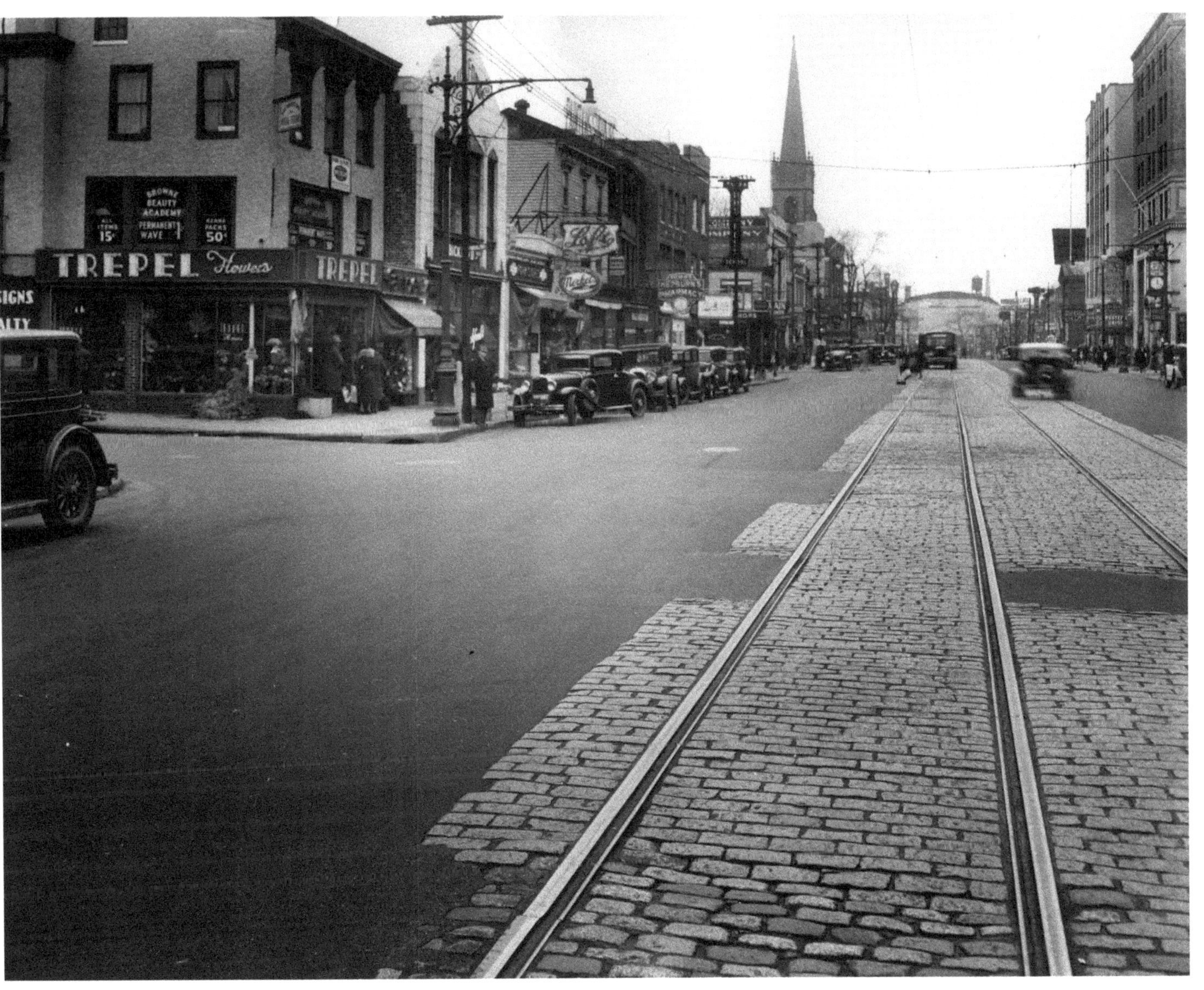

Main Street at 40th Road in Flushing. The large steeple and bell tower in the distance on the left adorns St. George's Episcopal Church, which has served Flushing residents for more than 300 years. In 1854, this Neo-Gothic building replaced the original structure built in 1746.

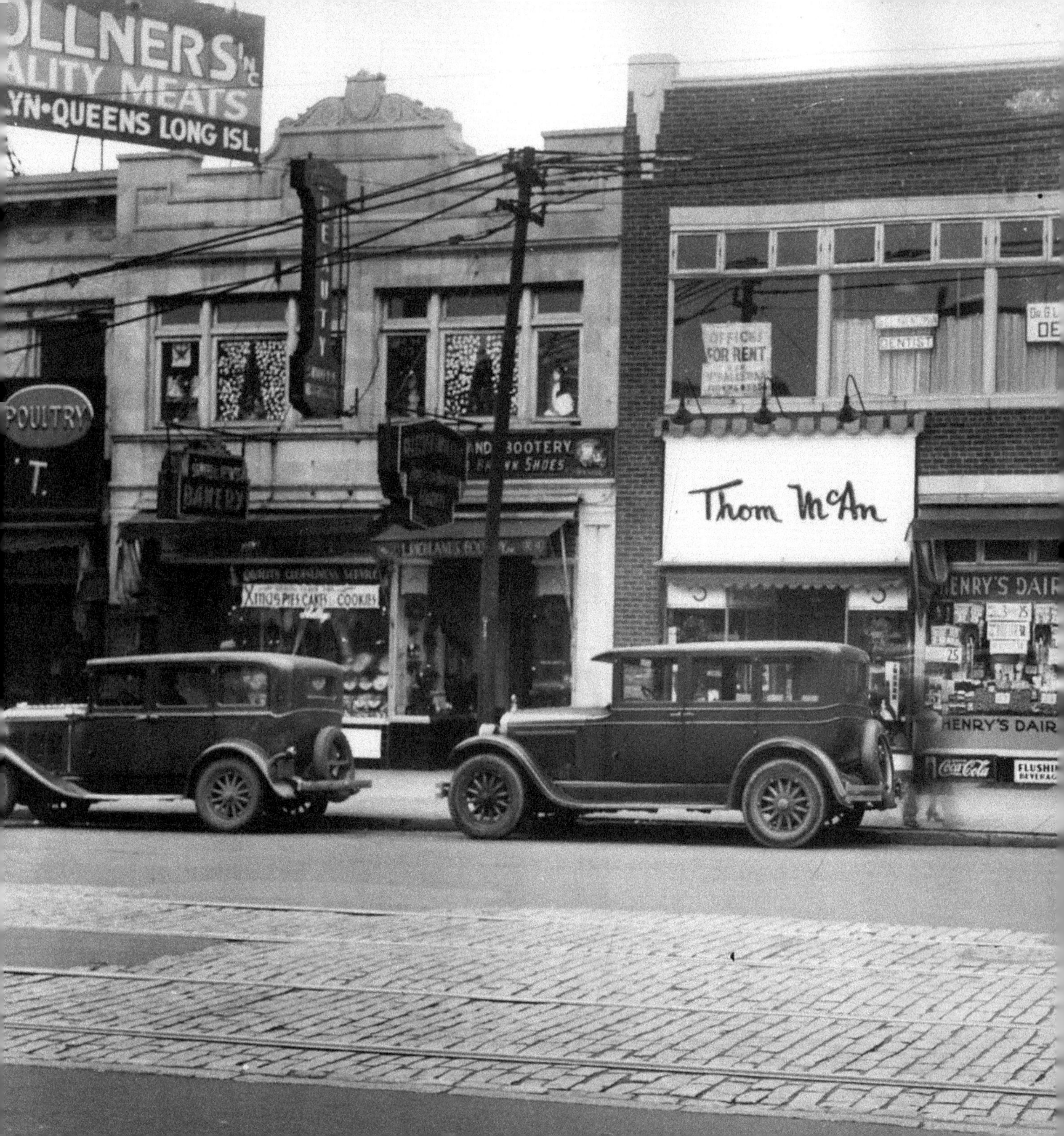
OLLNERS INC
ALITY MEATS
LYN-QUEENS LONG ISL.
POULTRY
BAKERY
XMAS PIES CAKES COOKIES
BOOTERY
SHOES
OFFICES FOR RENT
DENTIST
Thom McAn
HENRY'S DAIR
HENRY'S DAIR
Coca-Cola
FLUSHIN

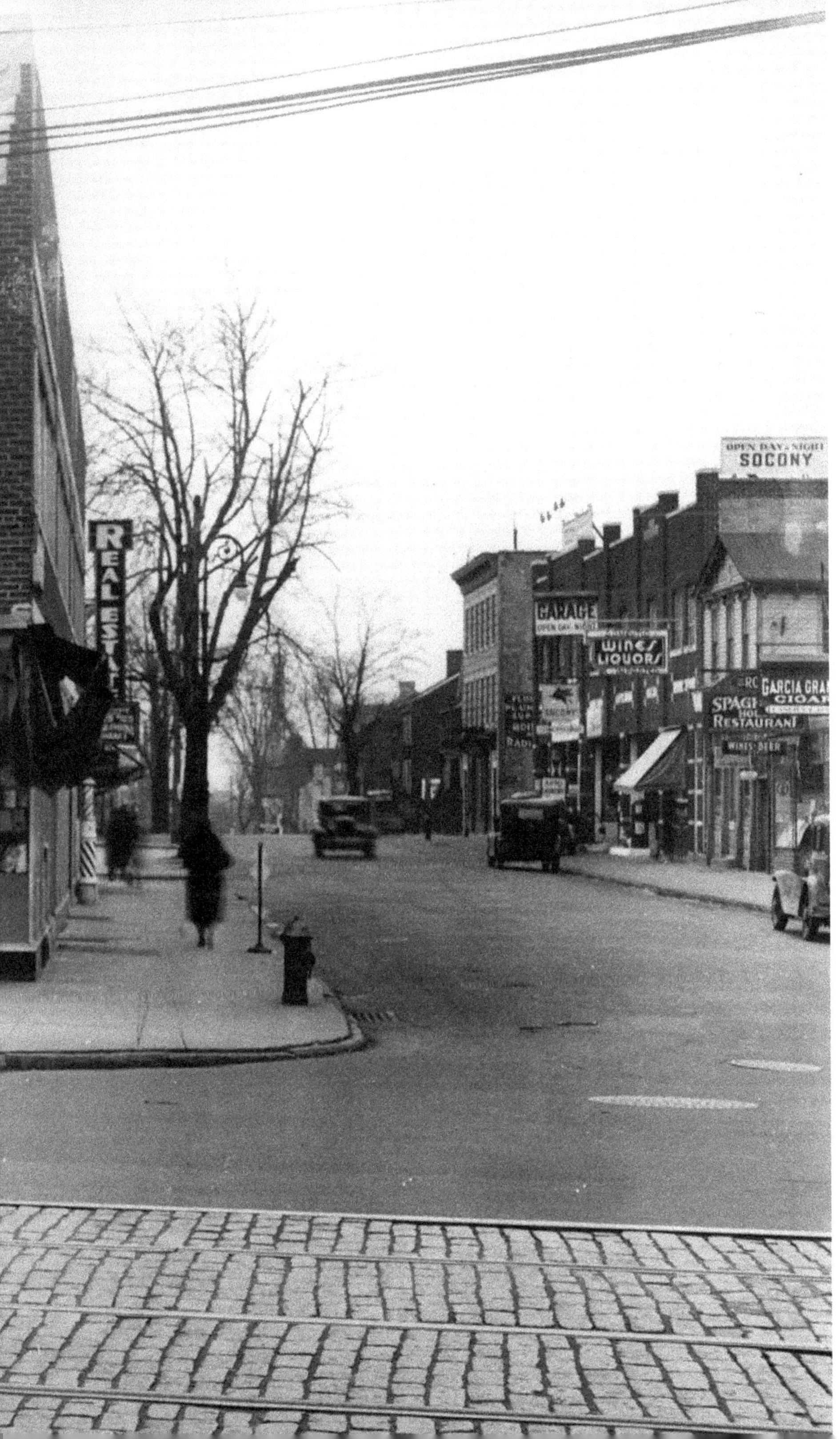

Facing west on 40th Road, from Main Street in Flushing. The Thom McAn shoe store in the center of the frame was one of hundreds of outlets across the nation, run by Ward Melville's Melville Corporation. Melville once had a broad slate of brands under his umbrella, but today the corporation shepherds only one company, CVS Pharmacies.

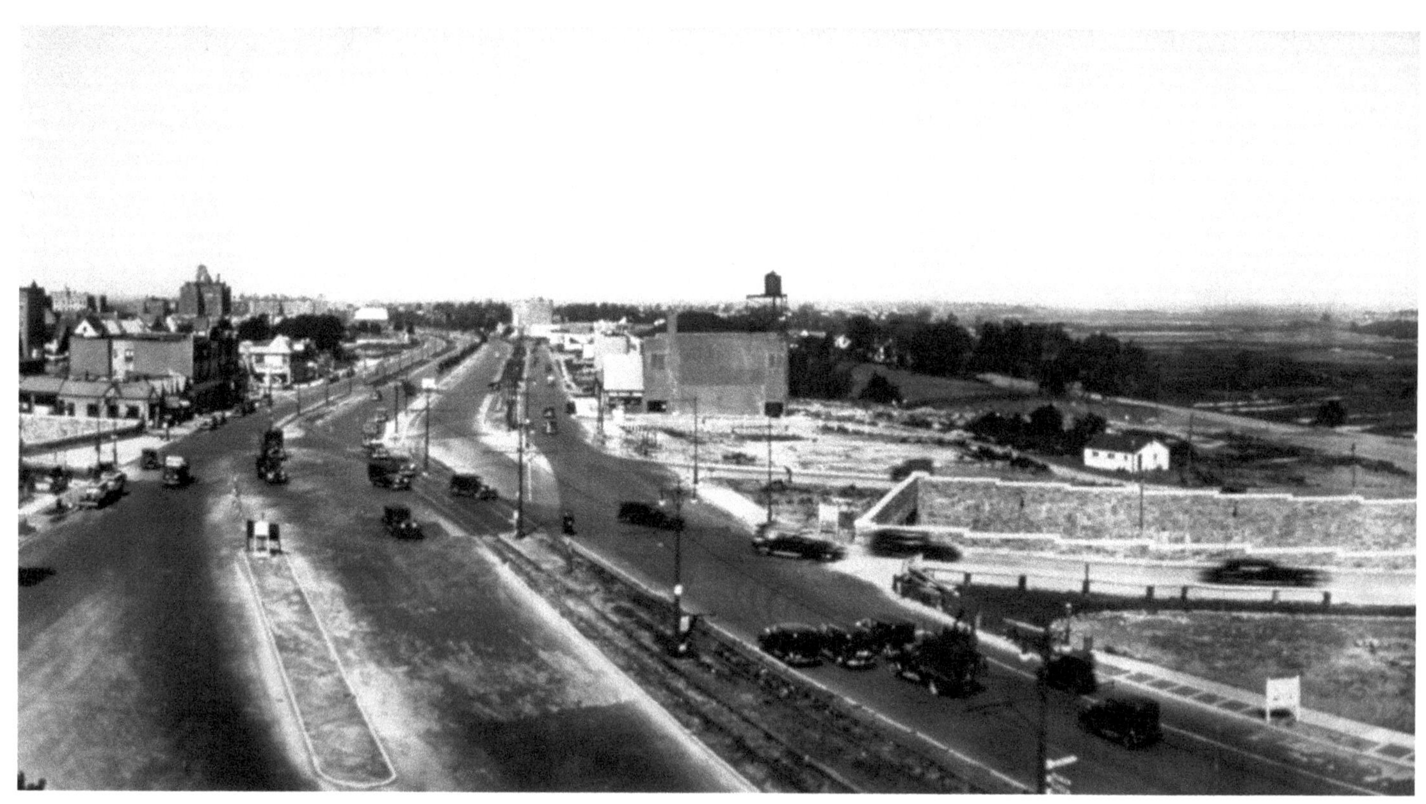

A bird's-eye view of the Kew Gardens Interchange, where Queens Boulevard (the road on top of the underpass, which is visible at right) met the Grand Central Parkway, and Union Turnpike runs along the side, seemingly the service road for the GCP. This 1936 photograph shows the parkway soon after it was completed.

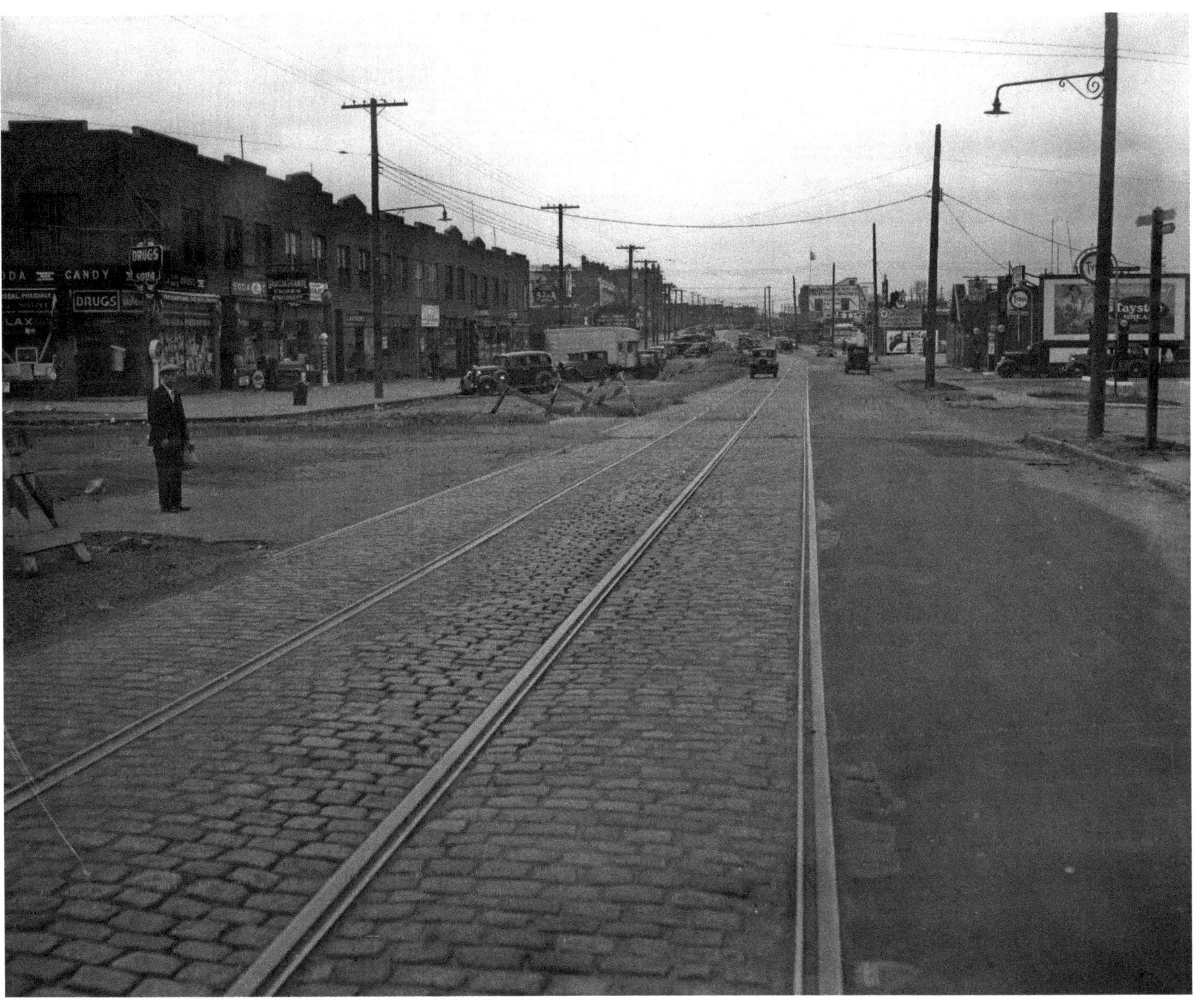

Jamaica Avenue at the intersection of Francis Lewis Boulevard in Hollis. The area was developed beginning in the late nineteenth century and experienced the same kind of boom in single-family housing as its eastern neighbor, Queens Village, in the early years of the twentieth century.

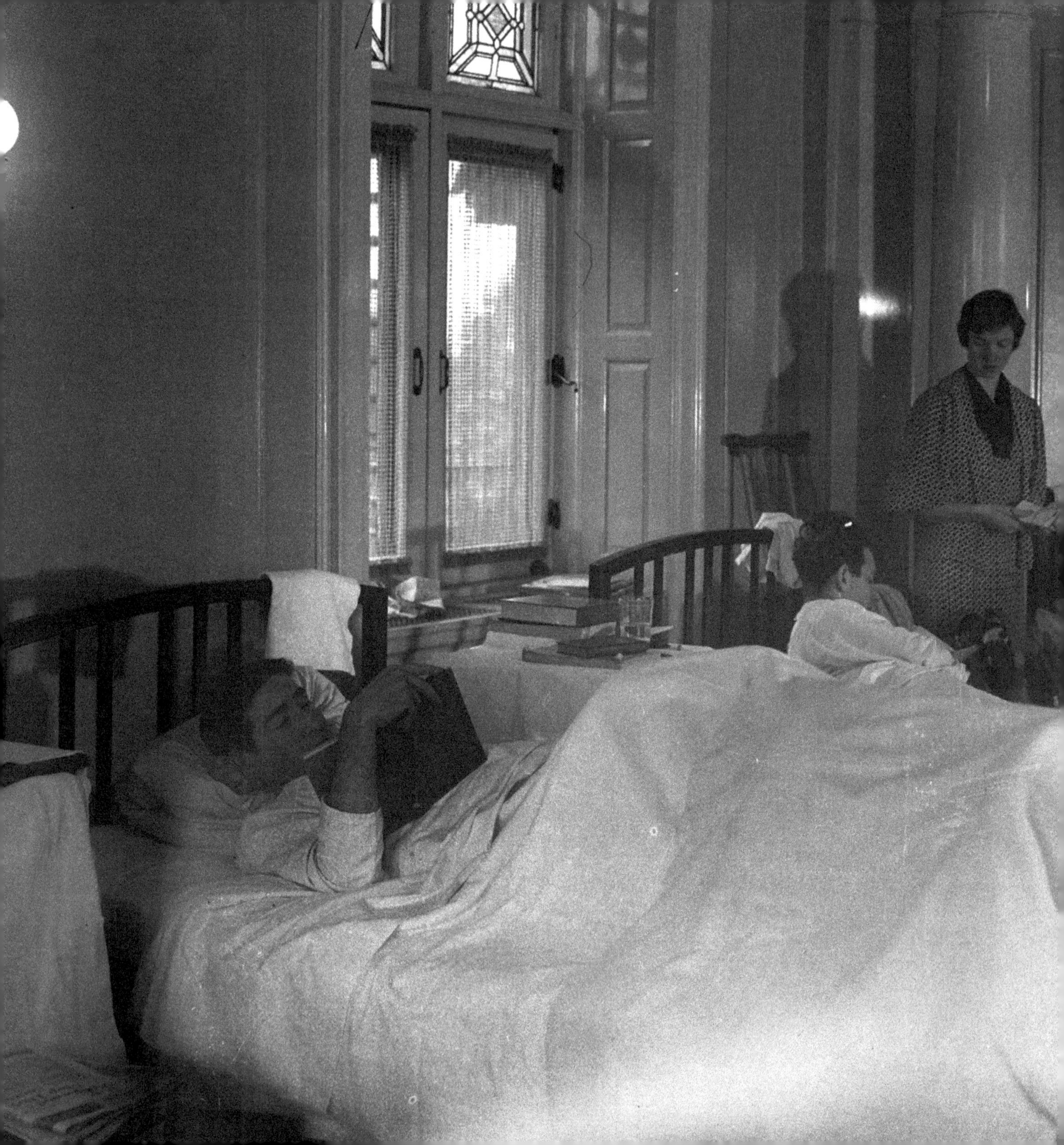

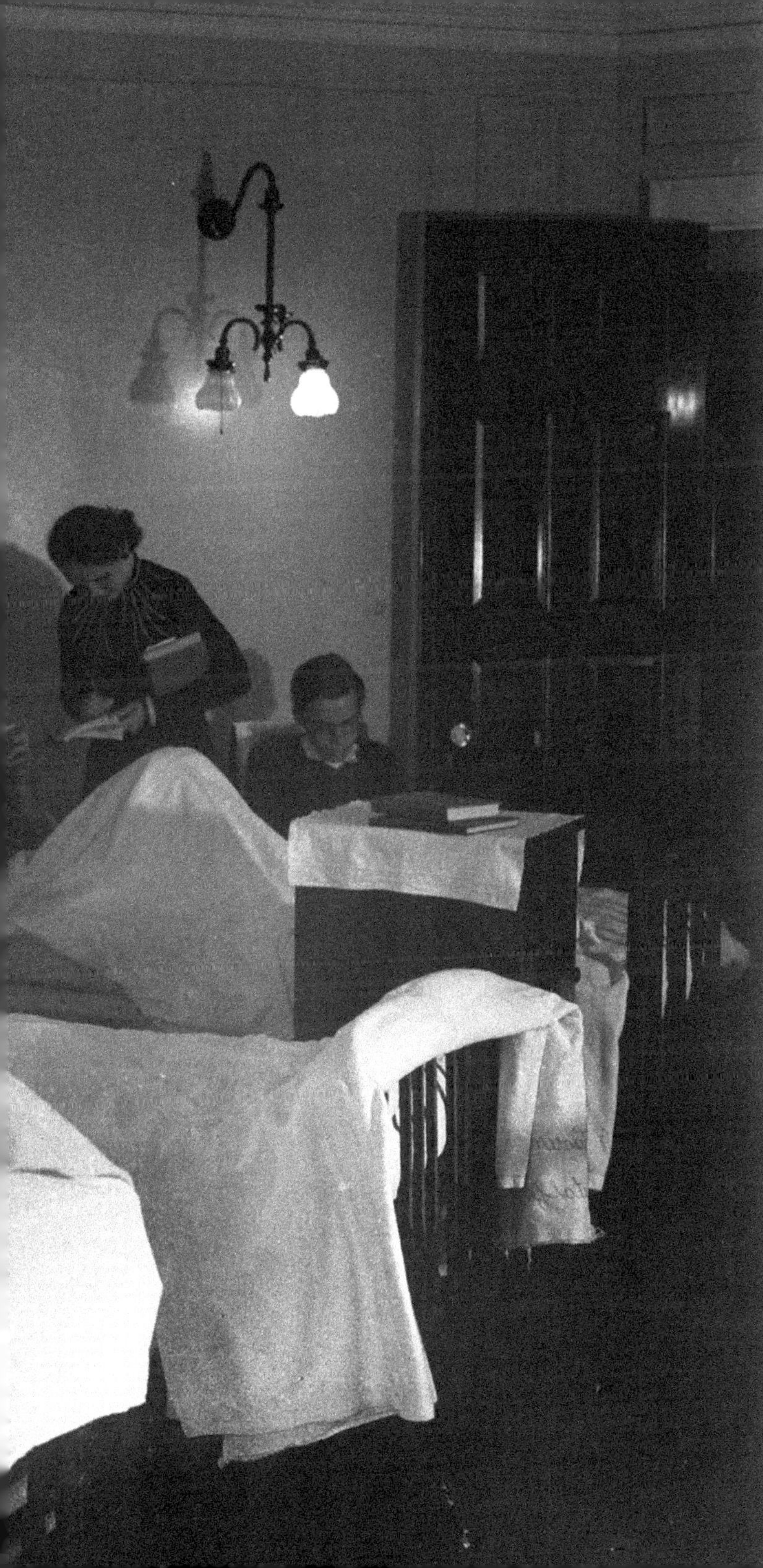

The Queens Borough Public Library provides reading material for these hospital patients, demonstrating that its traveling library served a full range of institutions across the borough.

In 1936, the progression of St. Joachim and Anne Church and the surrounding area is truly apparent, with sidewalks laid and streets paved. The church still stands on this trapezoidal block on Hollis Avenue near 218 Street in Queens Village.

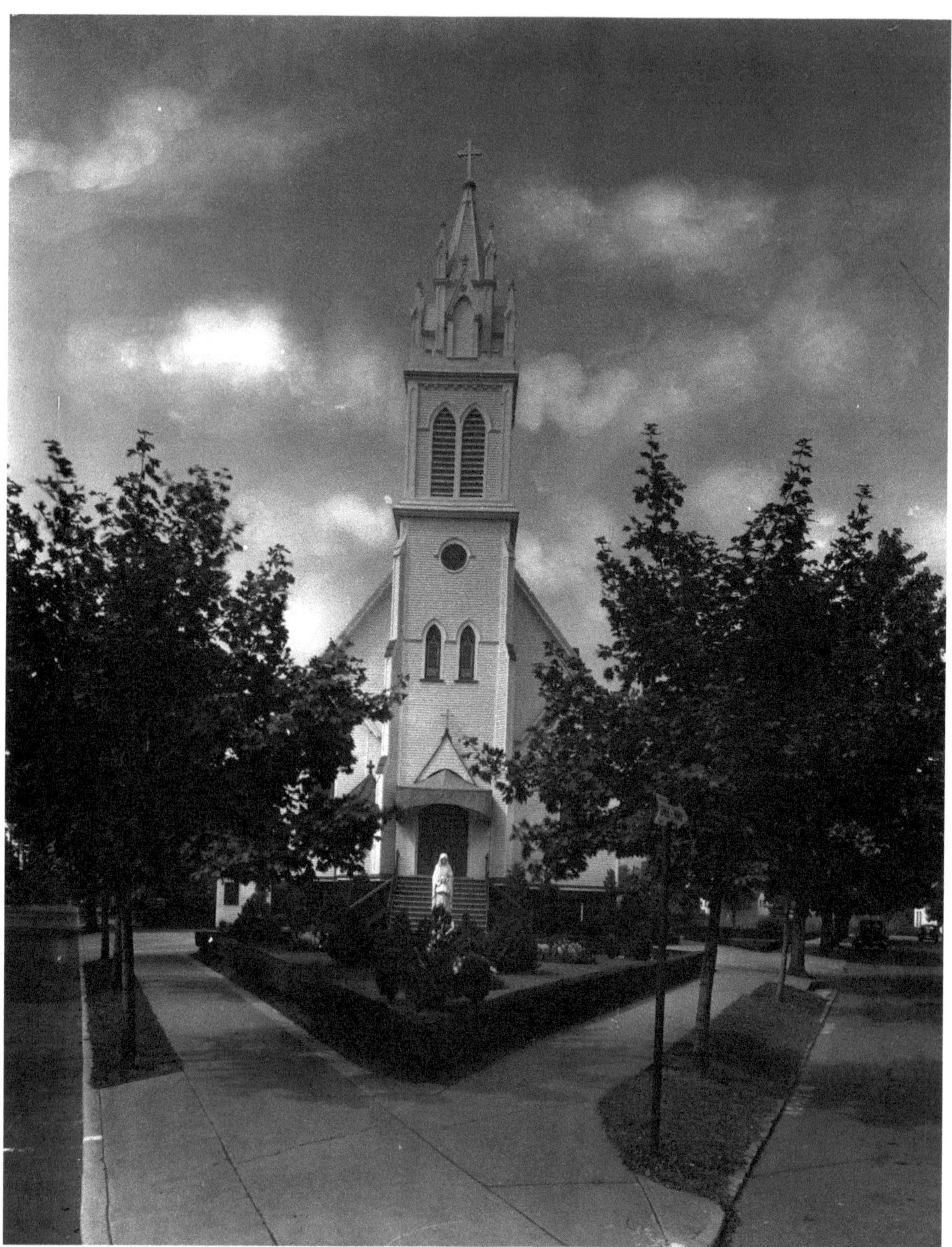

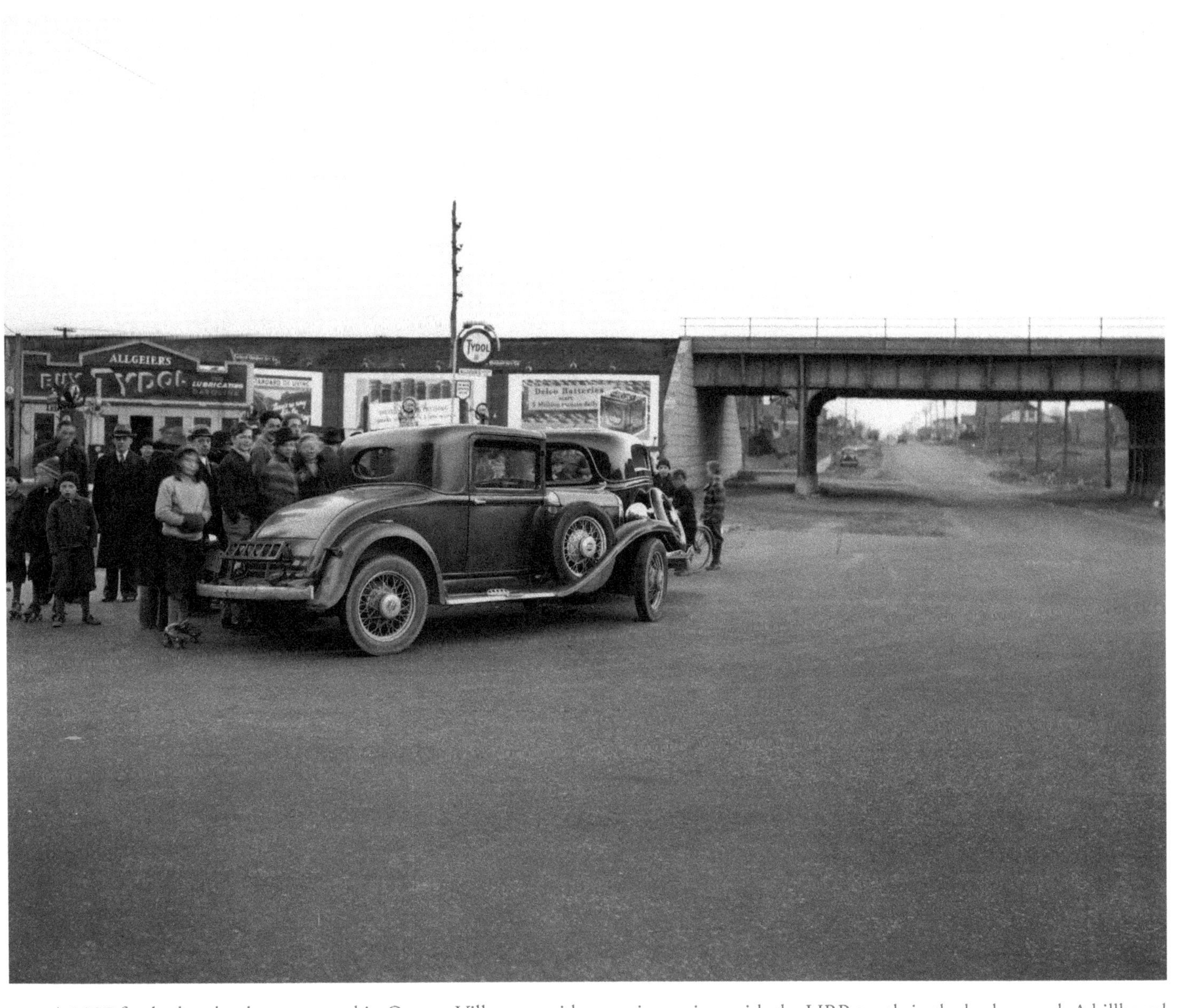

A 1937 fender bender draws a crowd in Queens Village, outside a service station, with the LIRR trestle in the background. A billboard beside the trestle proclaims, "Delco Batteries start 5 Million motors daily," but these two automobiles may need more than a start.

With greater automobile travel came greater opportunities for drivers to patronize roadside eateries like the Deer's Head Diner, one of the classic train dining-car-style diners popular around the nation in the 1930s. This one was located at 235-20 Hillside Avenue, in Bellerose.

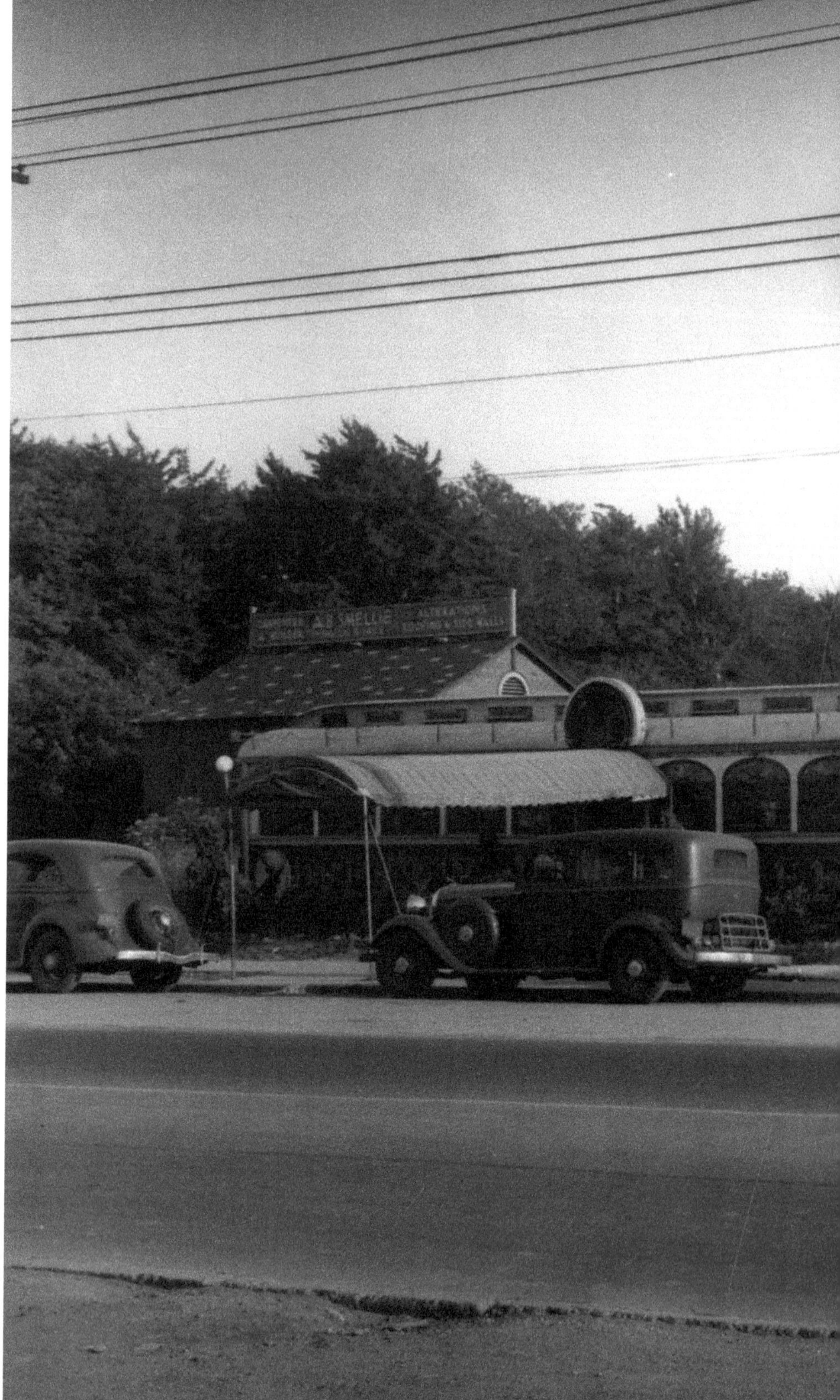

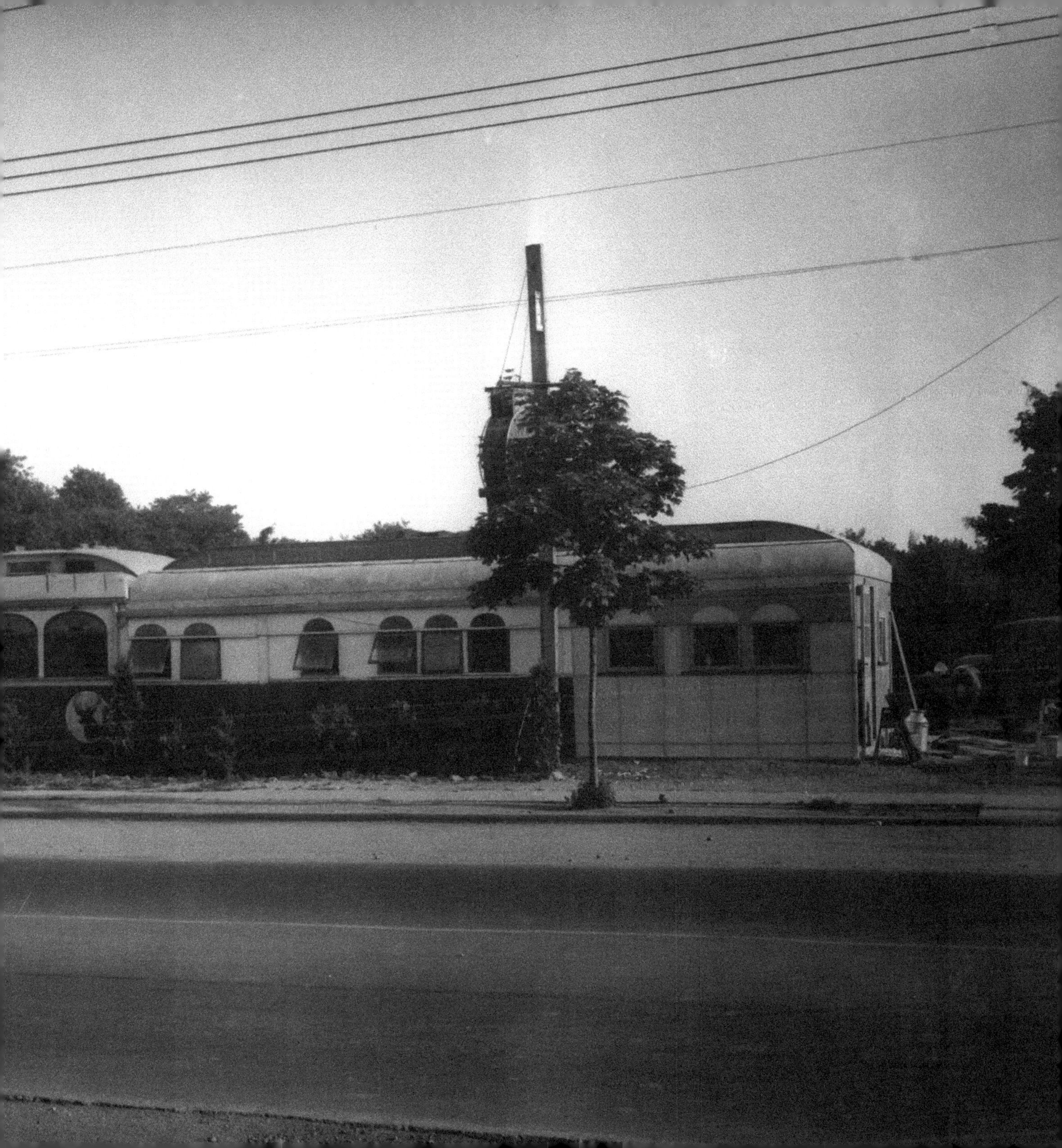

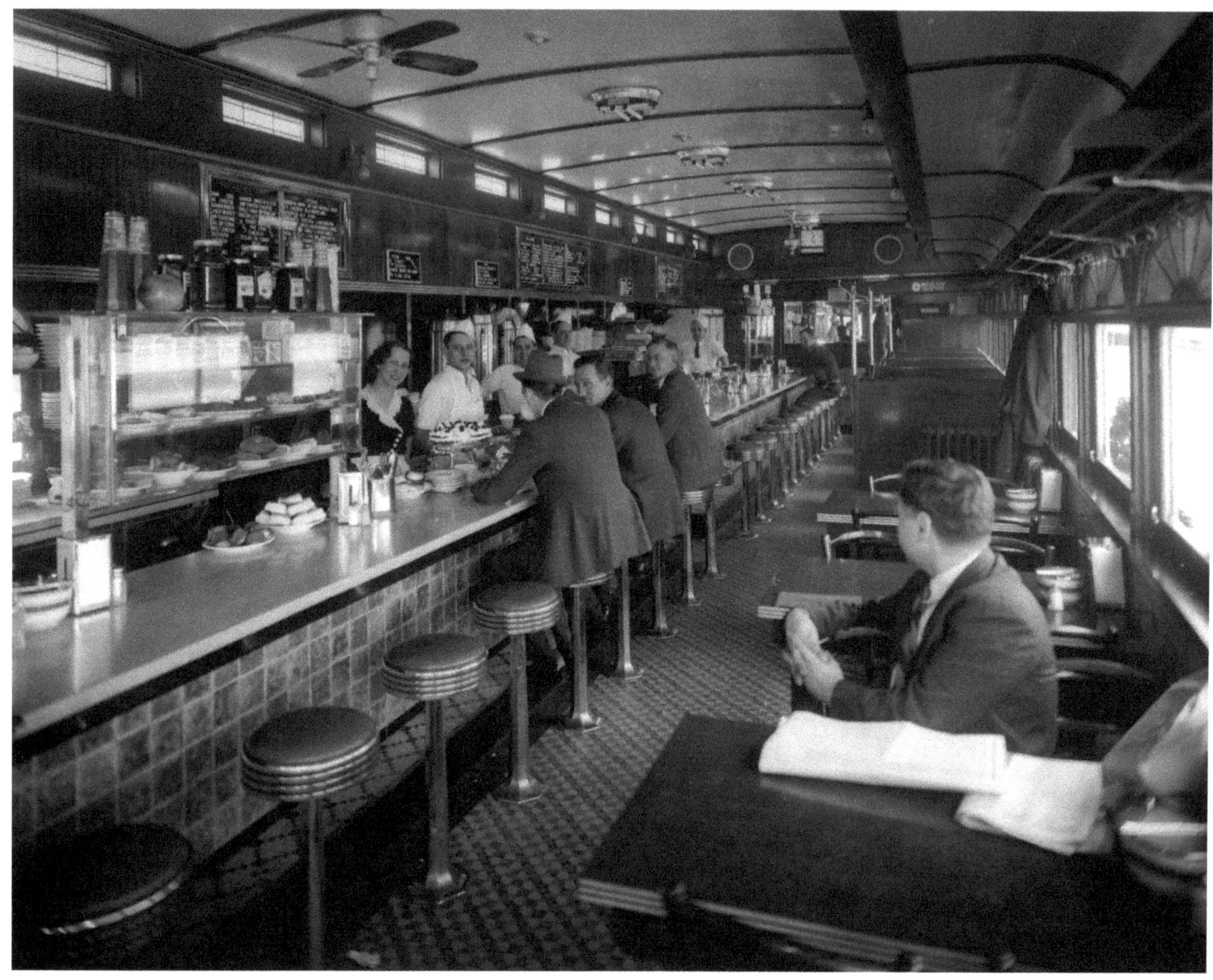

Inside at the Deer's Head diner in 1938, the long counter with round stools, tile work, and stainless steel trim completes the look, a design that still dominates at most diners in New York today.

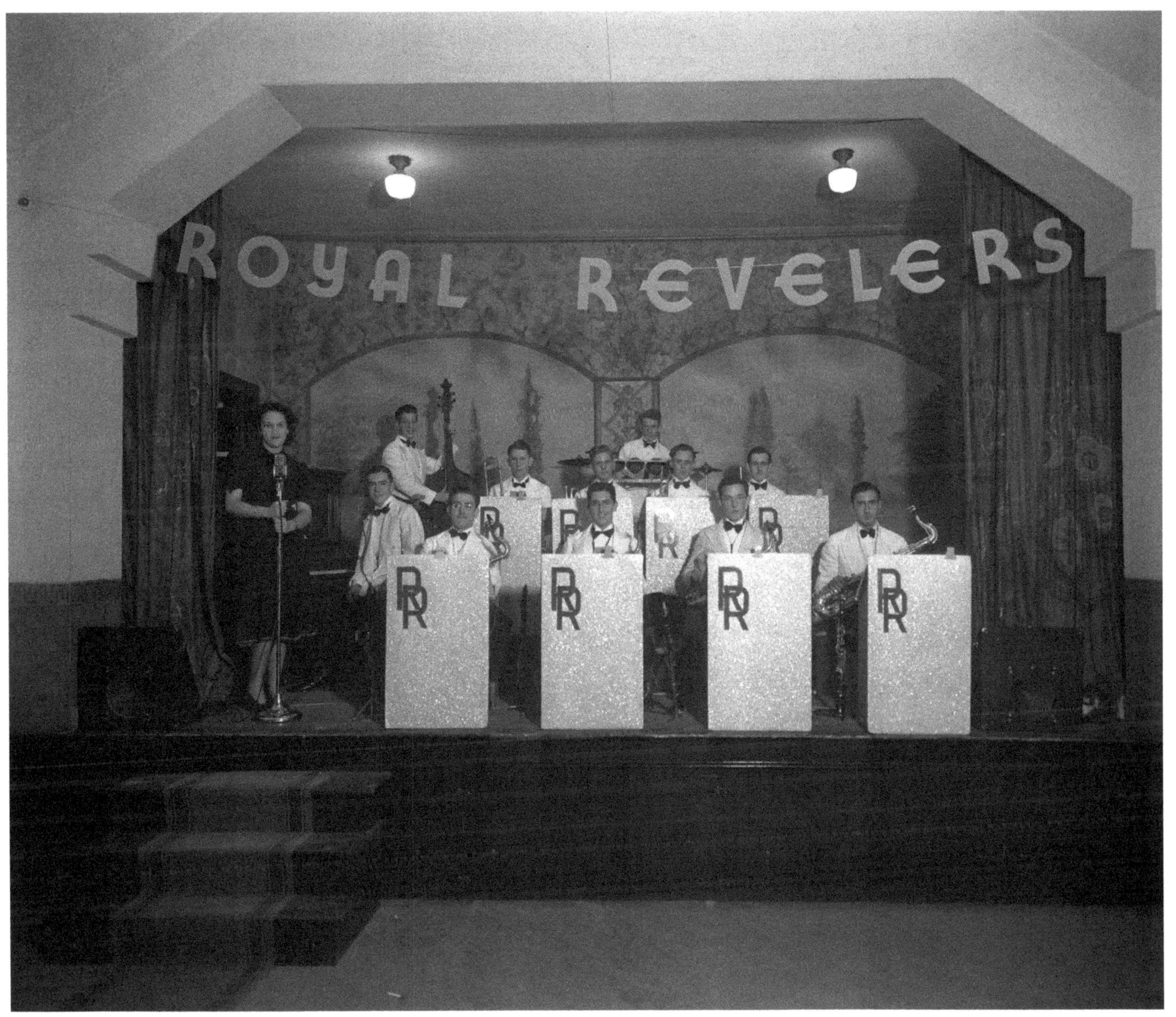

The Royal Revelers band poses during a performance in 1938. Queens was home to many famous names in jazz and big band, including Count Basie, Ella Fitzgerald, Billie Holiday, Louis Armstrong, Tony Bennett, and Lena Horne, to name just a few.

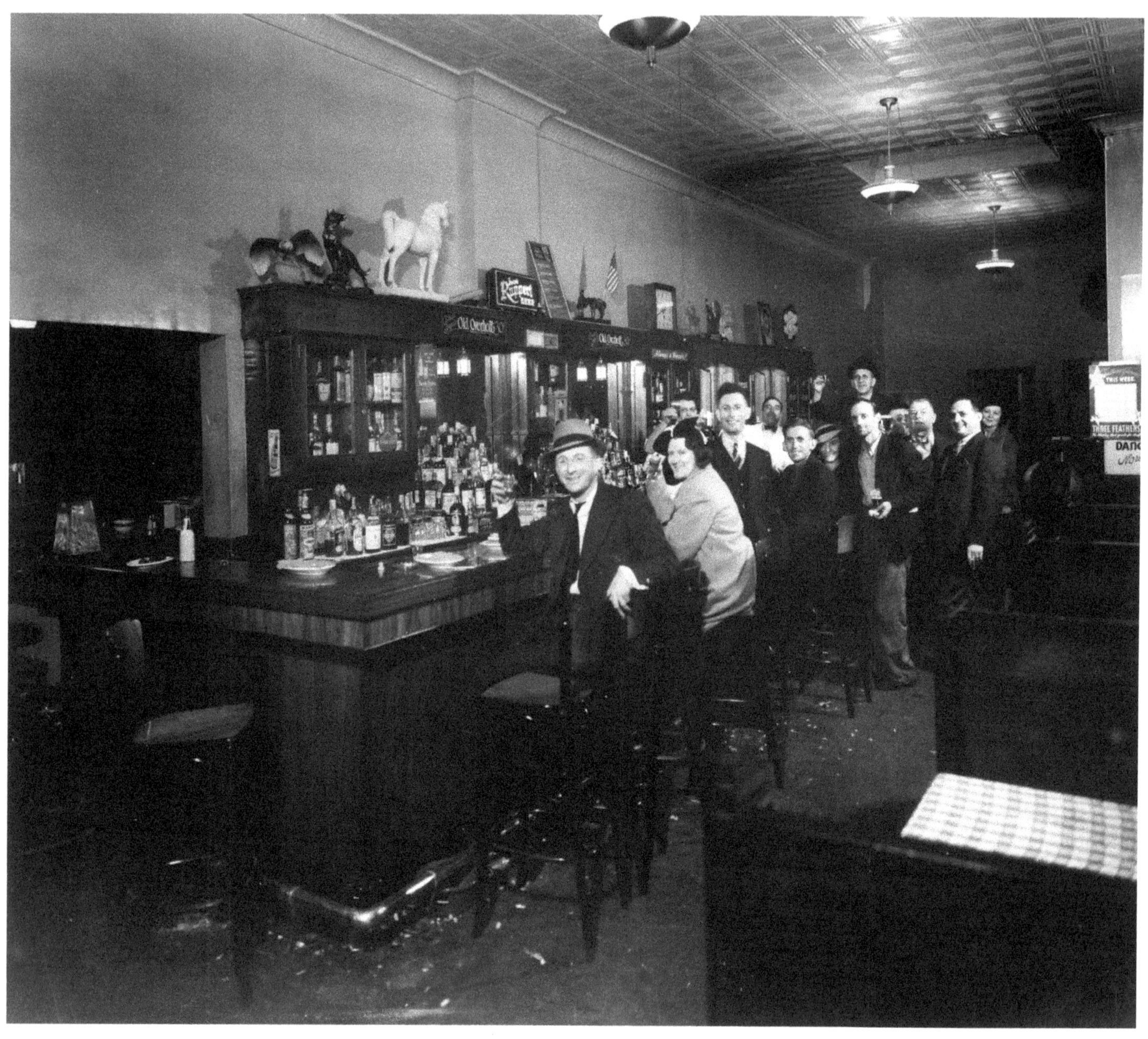

Patrons at V. Caruso's Bar and Grill, located at 35th Street and Vernon Boulevard in Astoria, happily pose for the camera in 1938. The bar would have been located across from Rainey Park, on the edge of the East River, named for Dr. Thomas Rainey who lobbied for a bridge connecting Queens to Manhattan. The Queensboro Bridge was eventually built, about a mile to the south.

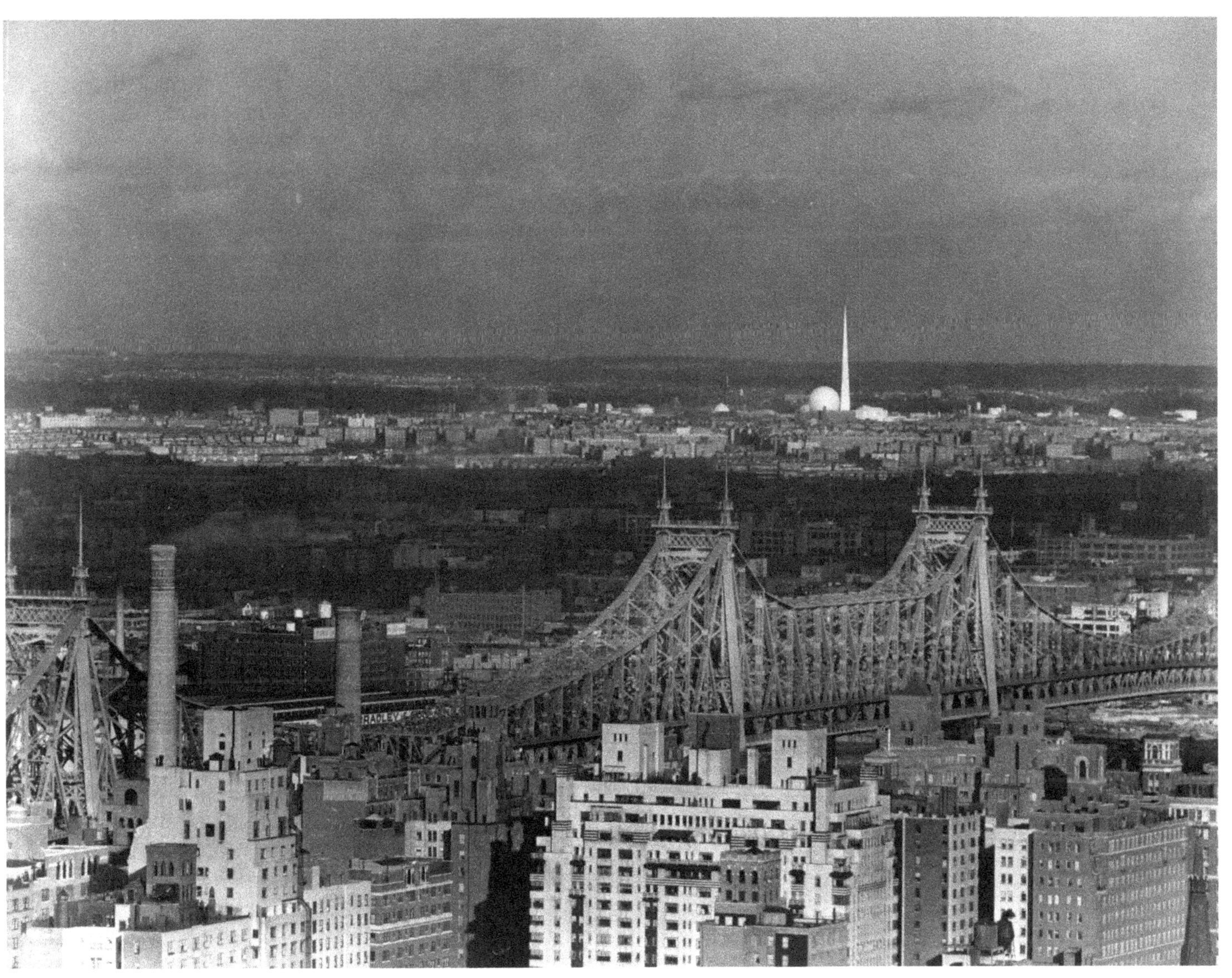

The futuristic 1939 World's Fair was the largest world's fair ever held and covered more than 1,200 acres of former marshland in Flushing. Over 200,000 people were on hand at the opening, when President Franklin D. Roosevelt gave an address. Seen here from Manhattan, with the Queensboro Bridge in the middle foreground, the Trylon spire and Perisphere in what is now Flushing Meadows–Corona Park gleam white in the distance.

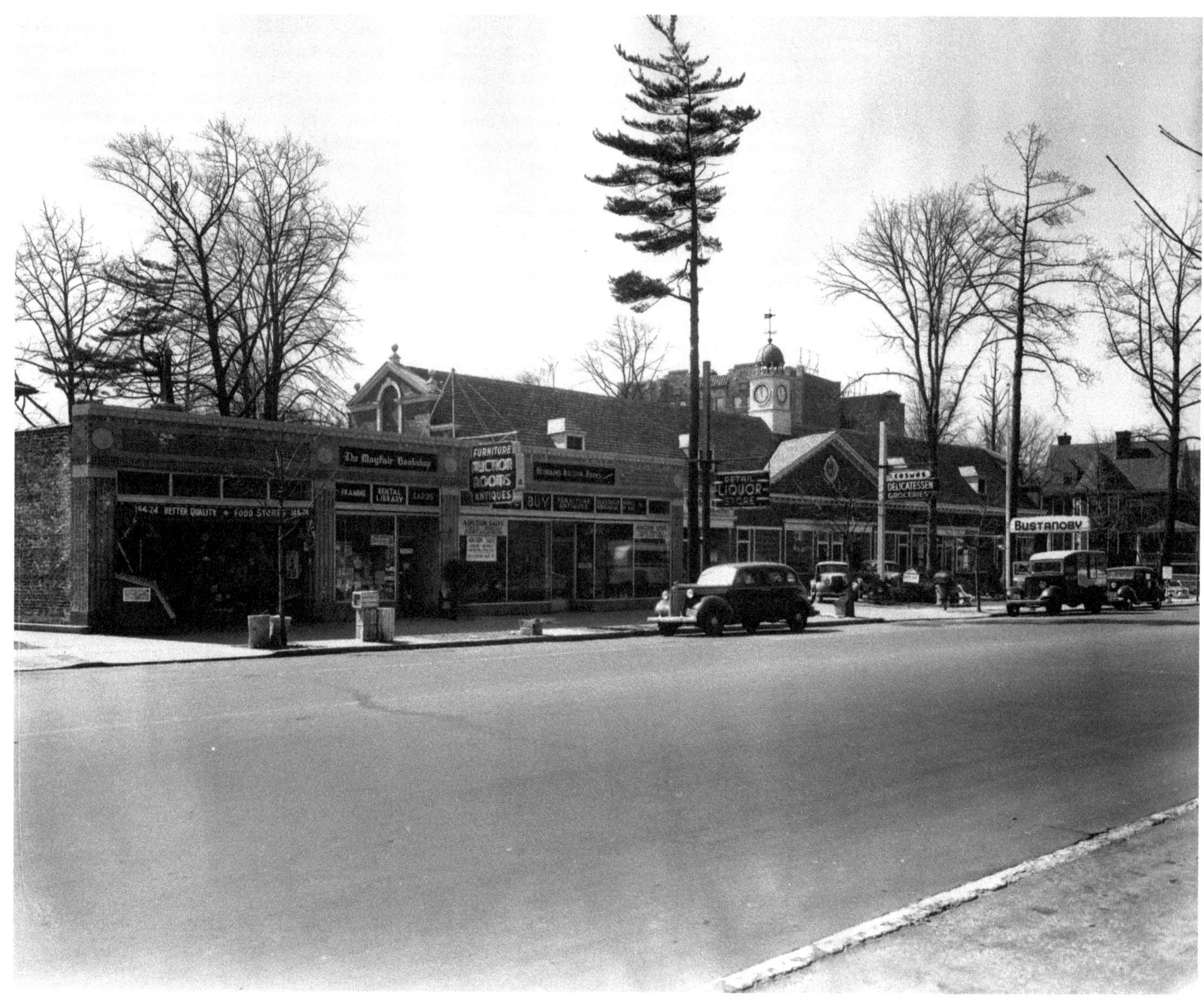

Shops along Northern Boulevard, in Flushing, looking toward the corner of Parsons Boulevard. A large section of the shopping center to the left still exists, juxtaposed against newer chain stores and restaurants.

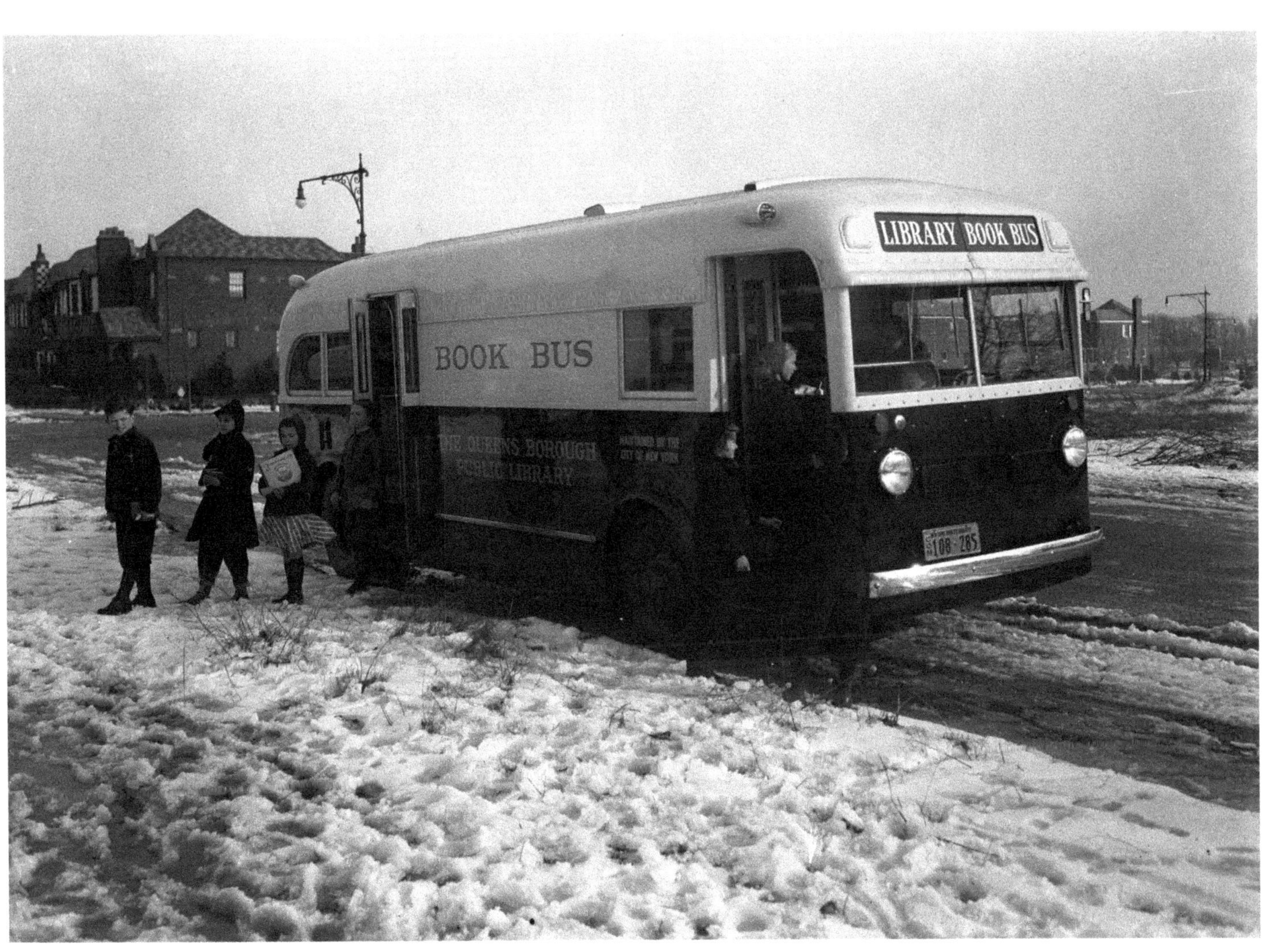

The ever-popular Queens Borough Public Library changed with the times to include this Book Bus, seen here in operation on a snowy day in 1939. The bus is shown serving patrons in Flushing's Queensboro Hill neighborhood.

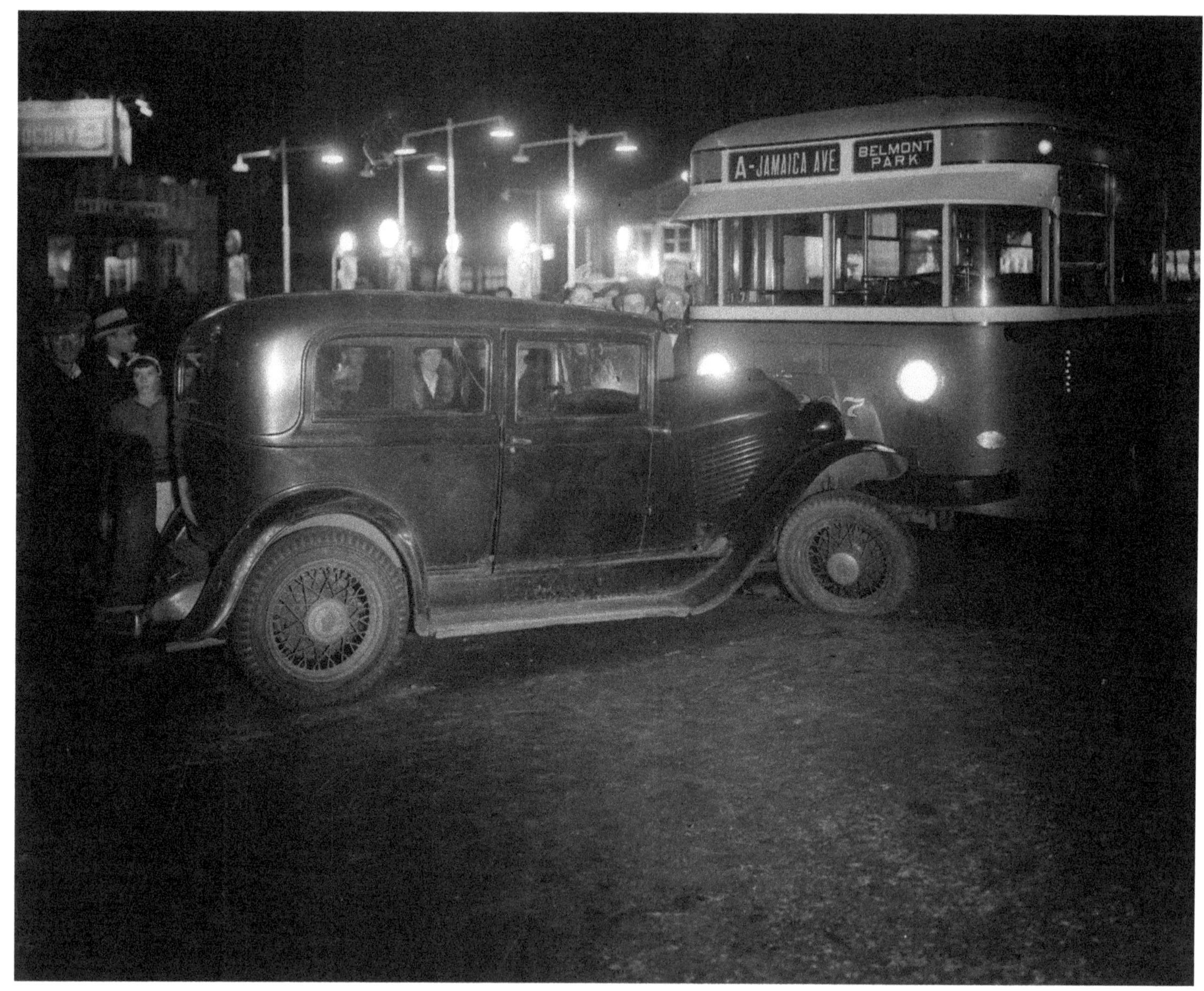

A Belmont Park–bound Jamaica Avenue streetcar delivers the knock-out punch in this 1939 collision with an automobile. Although this stretch of Jamaica Avenue had streetlights, nighttime driving was dangerous in the late 1930s.

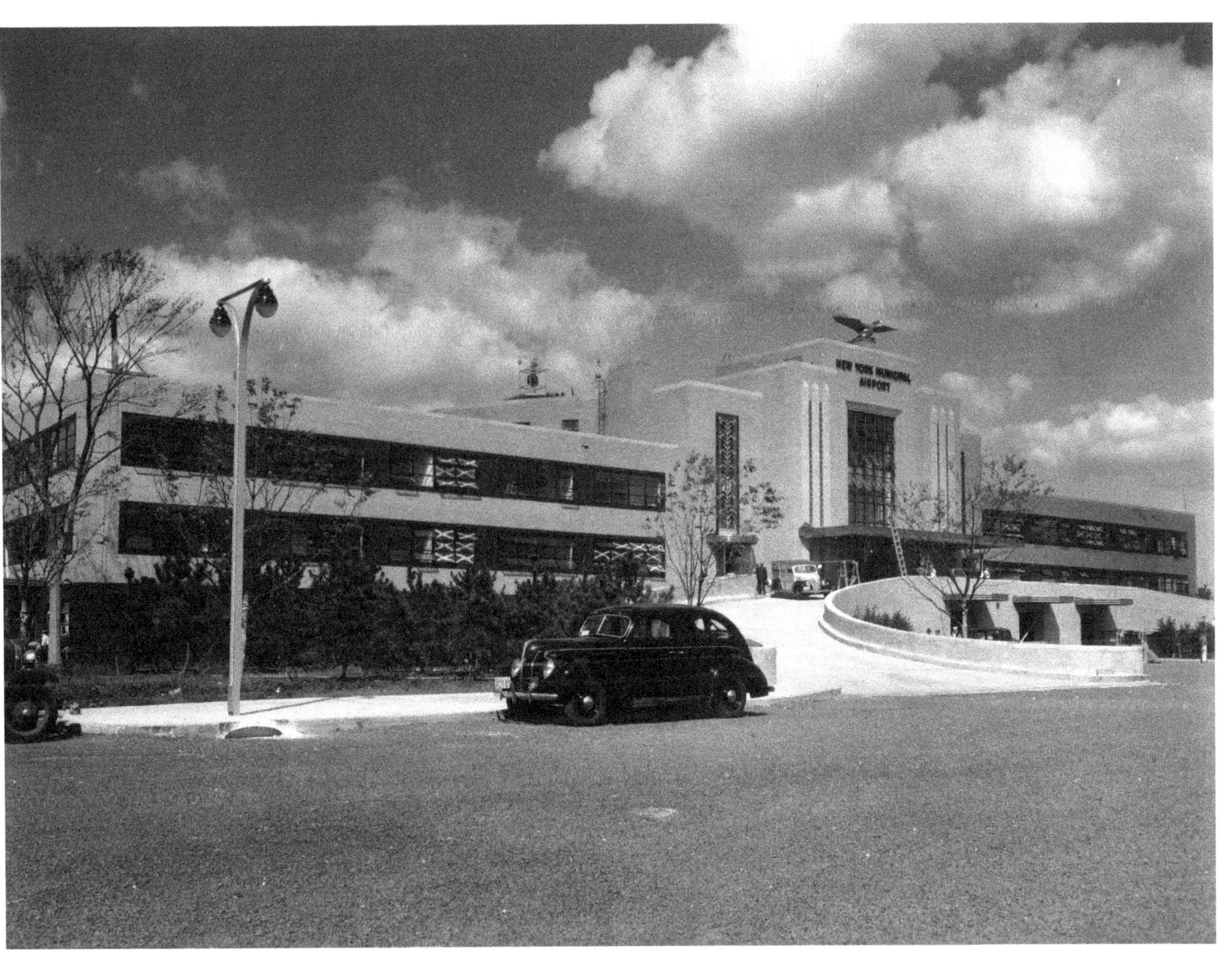

This is the new administration building for the New York Municipal Airport, later rechristened LaGuardia International Airport after Mayor Fiorello LaGuardia, who had pushed for an airport closer to New York City. The airport had previously been known as the small Glenn H. Curtiss airport for private planes and was called the North Beach airport—since it was built on the site of the Steinway family's North Beach amusement park.

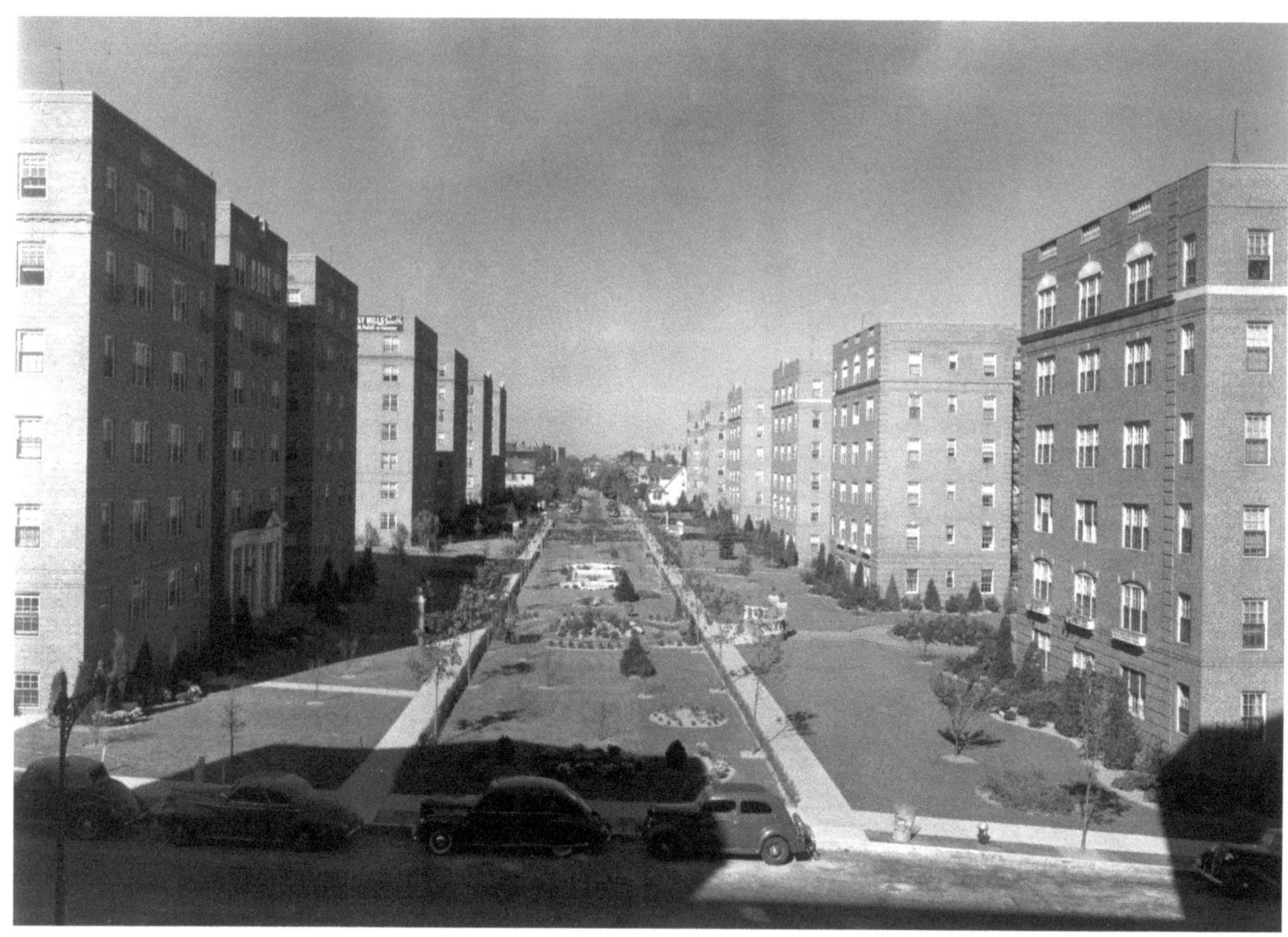

An apartment complex in Forest Hills in 1941. With an abundance of land available on Long Island, industry found expansion room in the borough. Americans seeking jobs followed, bringing their families with them to live in neighborhoods like this one.

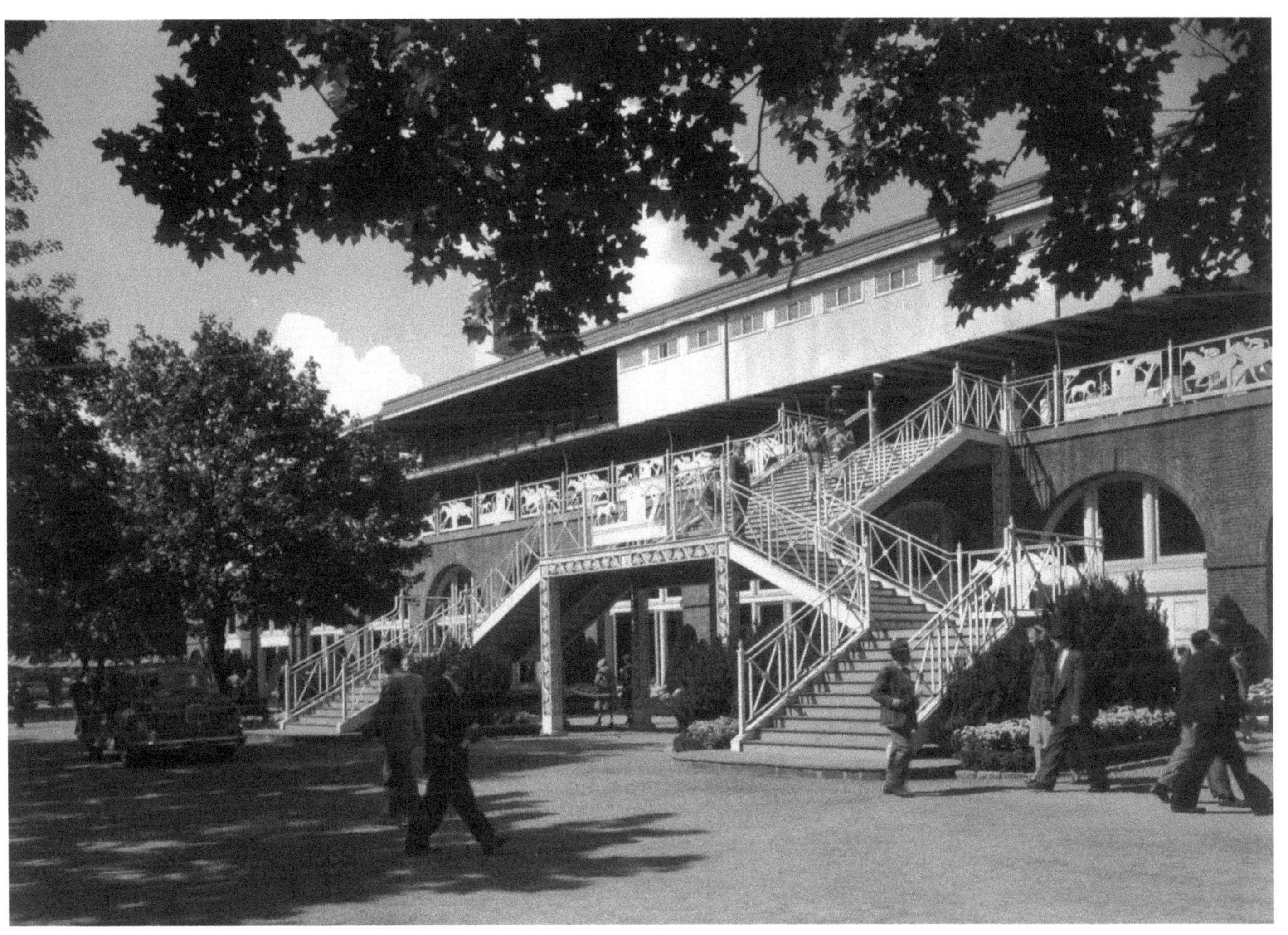

Belmont Park opened in Queens in May 1905 to the delight of horse-racing enthusiasts. Each year, the track hosts the third leg of the Triple Crown of thoroughbred racing. Nearly every champion racehorse has run the one-and-a-half-mile track, among them Secretariat, who set the Belmont Stakes record of two minutes, twenty-four seconds in 1973.

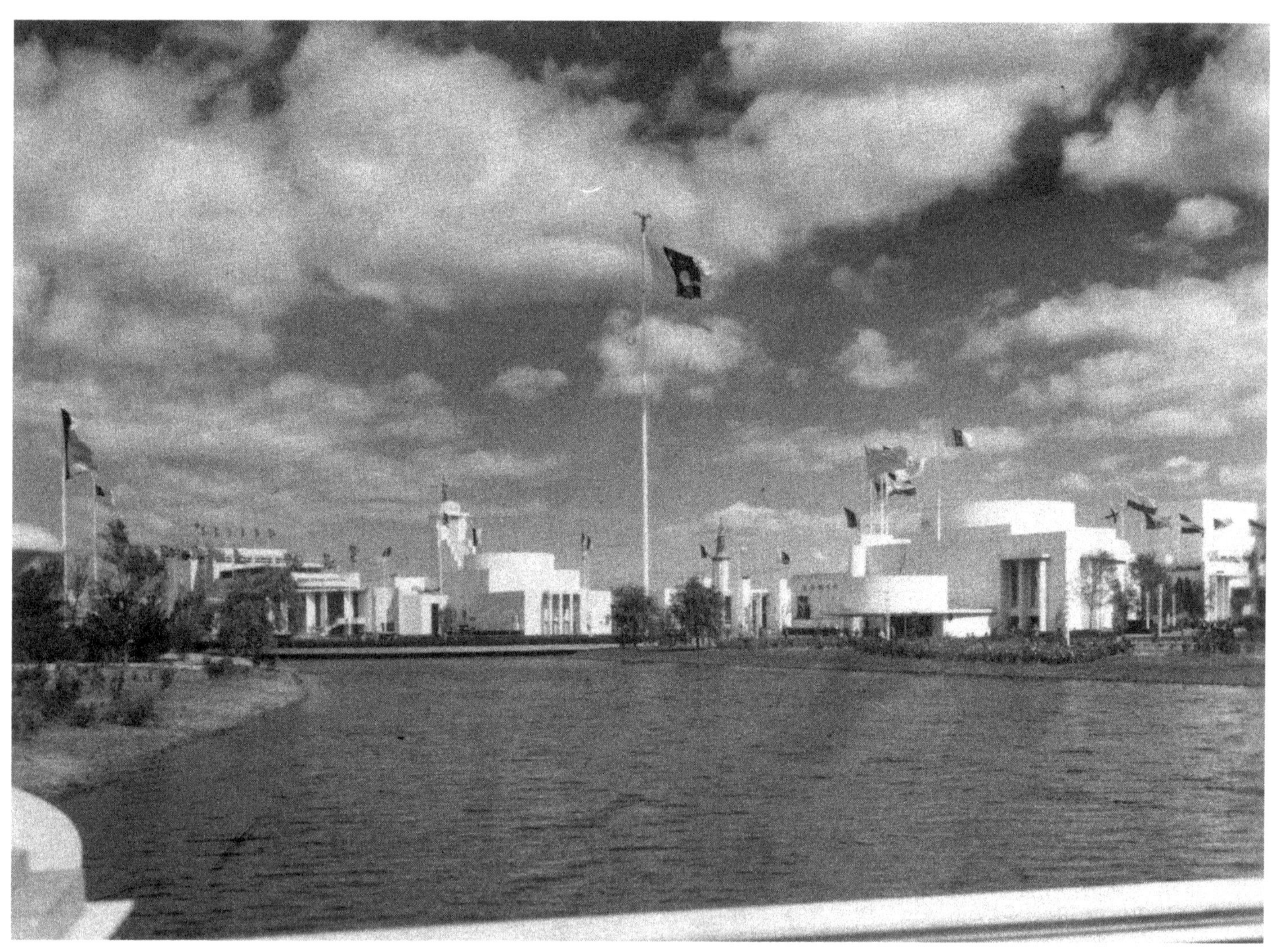

The Government and Nations Zone at the 1939 World's Fair, as seen from the Flushing River, with flags flying in the unusual winds that have plagued aircraft over the decades. More than 60 nations represented their culture at the World's Fair, which ran for two seasons, until 1940.

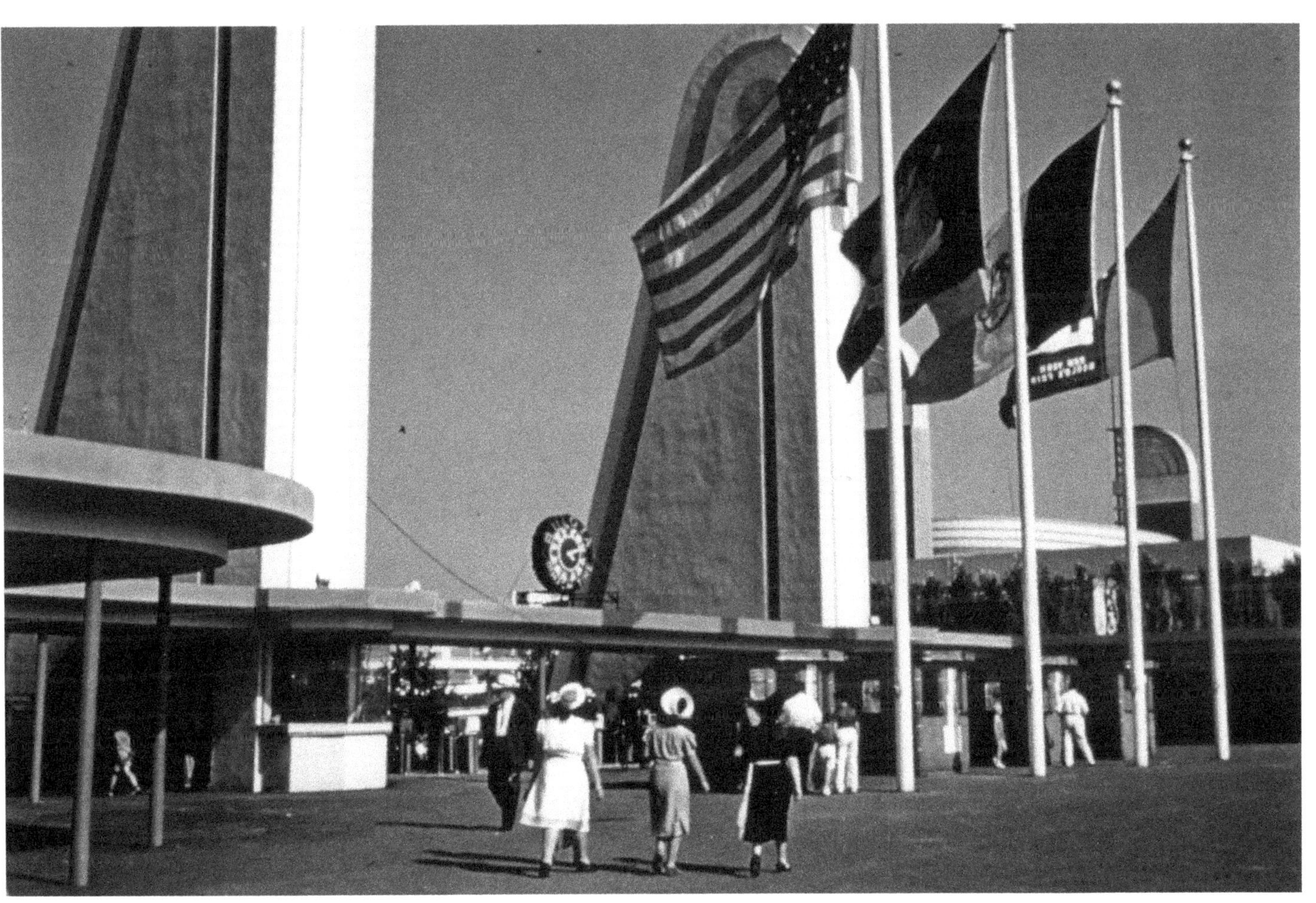

The gate to the fair on the Corona side featured a clock from Bulova, located to this day in East Elmhurst, near the Marine Air Terminal at LaGuardia Airport.

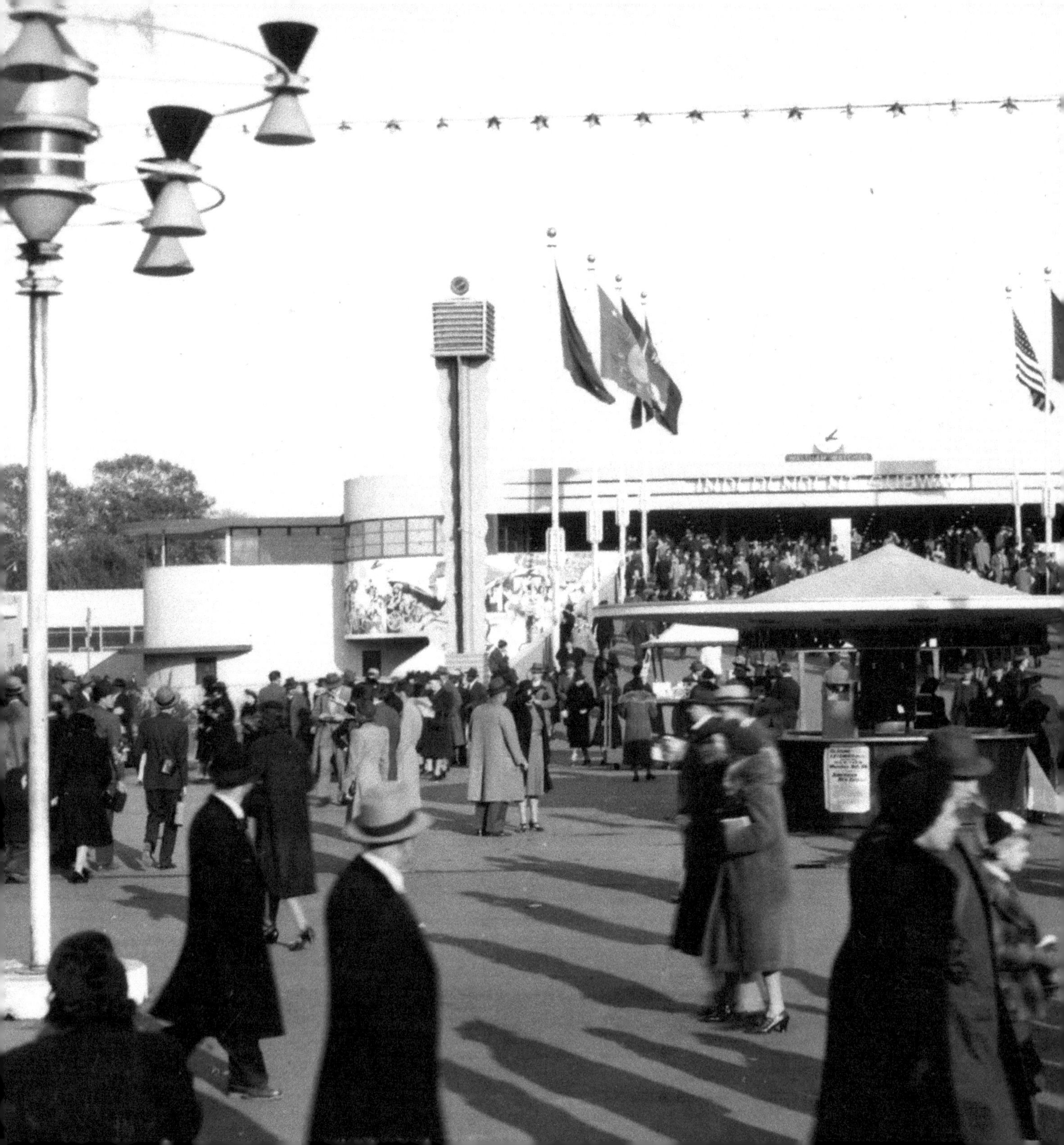

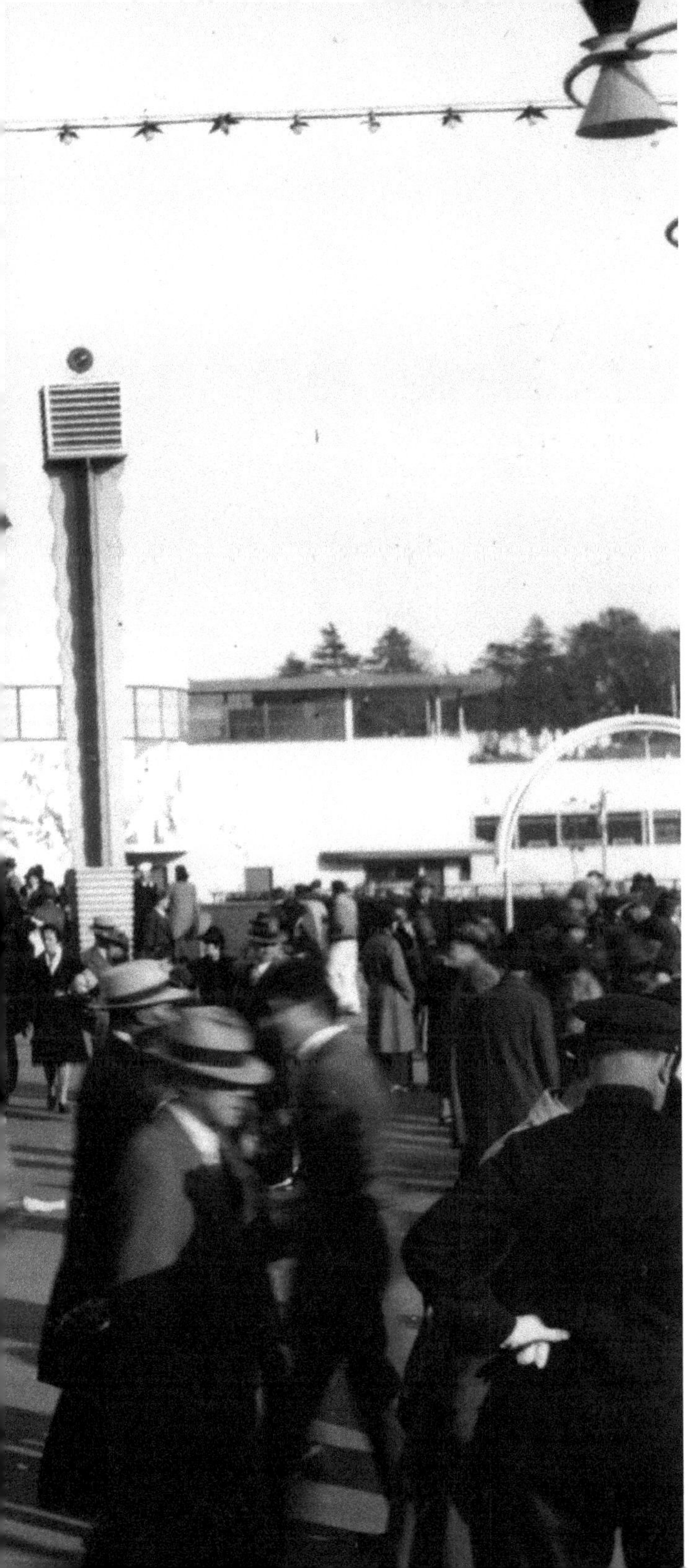

The World's Fair was served by all three subway companies in New York. In the background is the World's Fair Station (now Mets-Willets Point), which had Brooklyn-Manhattan Transit and IRT train service. There was also service from the World's Fair Railroad station, an extension of the Queens Boulevard Independent Subway Line.

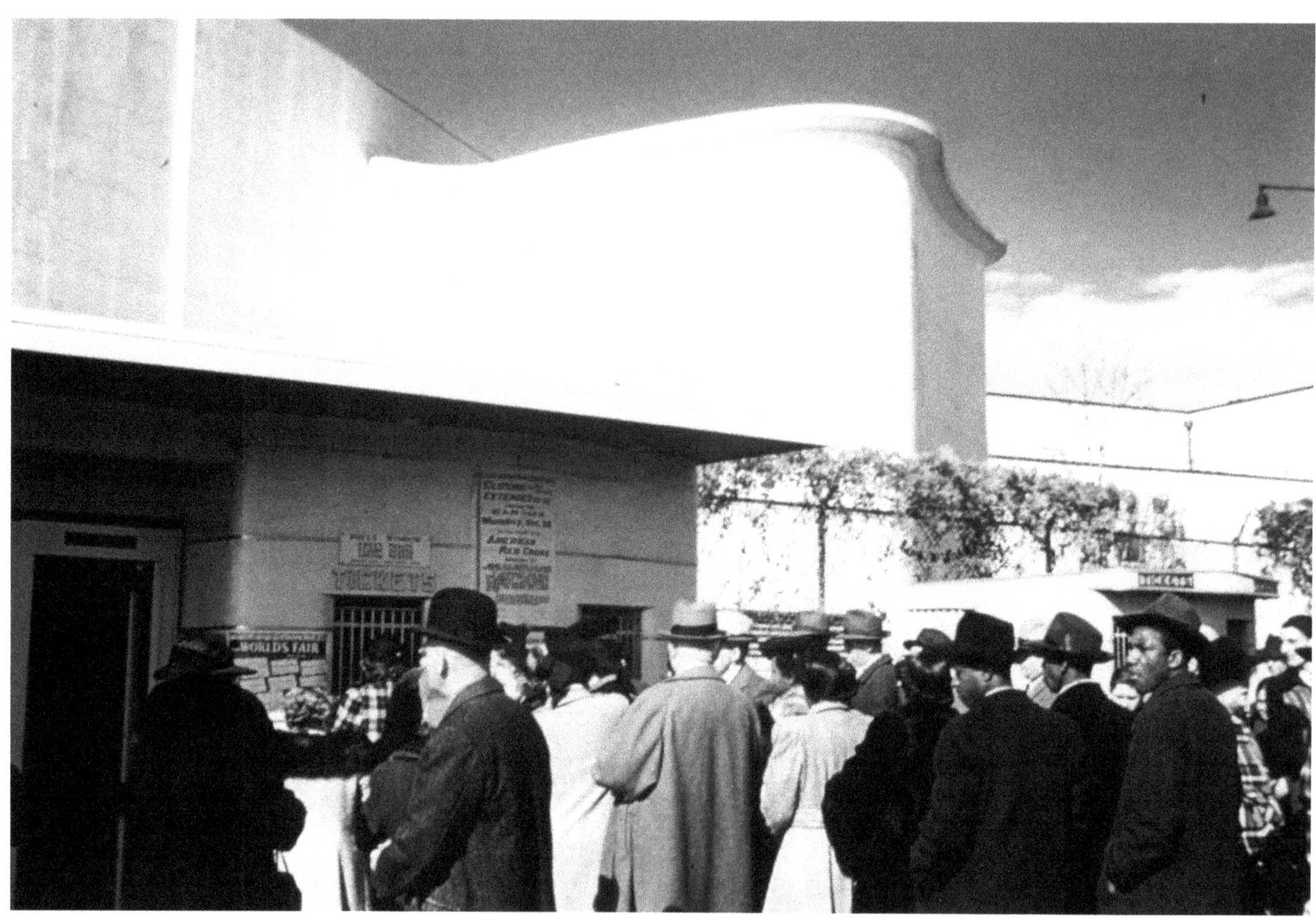

The gate for the World's Fair on the Flushing side as crowds flock to see the "Dawn of a New Day" through the exhibits looking toward the world of tomorrow. The crowds got looks for the first time at color photography, new automotive technology, and various consumer products (some of which would become everyday household goods in the years ahead).

The World War II and Postwar World (1940–1970s)

The borough contributed to the war effort at home through its industries and overseas as hometown boys went abroad to defend the nation. The wastelands of ash once commented on in F. Scott Fitzgerald's *The Great Gatsby* were gone by the end of World War II. Veterans returned and settled all over Queens, with new opportunities exploding—new construction, new jobs, and of course, new residents. Queens had found its identity—like the individuality prized in New York City, it had its own look, its own feel, and its own energy—and those who didn't like it could find the nearest train, bridge, highway, boat, or airplane out.

In the postwar era, Queens continued to evolve. A second airport, named for a president mourned by many of the borough's residents, opened on Jamaica Bay. The New York Mets arrived in Flushing, wearing Dodgers Blue and Giants Orange—something of a palliative for those in Queens who couldn't stomach the Yankees, but could handle the cold Flushing breezes and growling engines of LaGuardia planes overhead at Shea Stadium. In the Mets' off-season, the New York Jets played football amid those fierce winds and swirling currents for a time, before departing for greener pastures. St. John's University in Jamaica continued to develop a reputation for academic and athletic excellence, by recruiting the sons and daughters of the borough and the city. The City University of New York purchased a former academy and established what would become its "jewel in the crown," Queens College in Flushing. Even more bridges were built to provide even greater access into and out of the borough. Modern problems affecting the rest of the city crept east, but the borough persevered.

Today, Queens is perhaps the most diverse place on Earth, and it continues to grow. High rises dot the countryside from Floral Park to Flushing, to Forest Hills to Long Island City. Queens will always change; Queens will always be the same. Long live Queens.

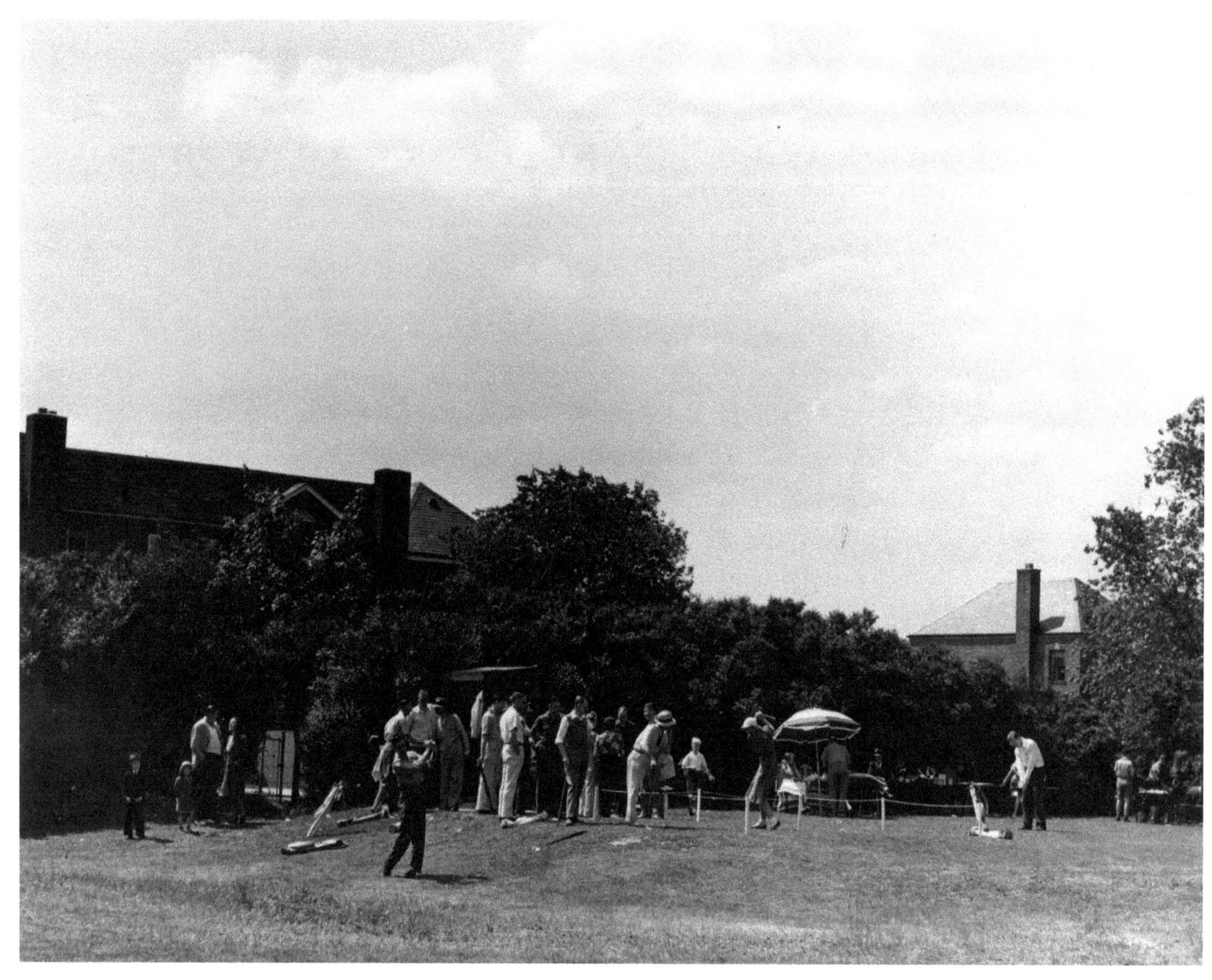

A tournament at the Jackson Heights Golf Club—a place made even more unusual because it was acres of land surrounded by the large apartment buildings the neighborhood was known for. After World War II, the golf course was paved over to make way for a new influx of residents.

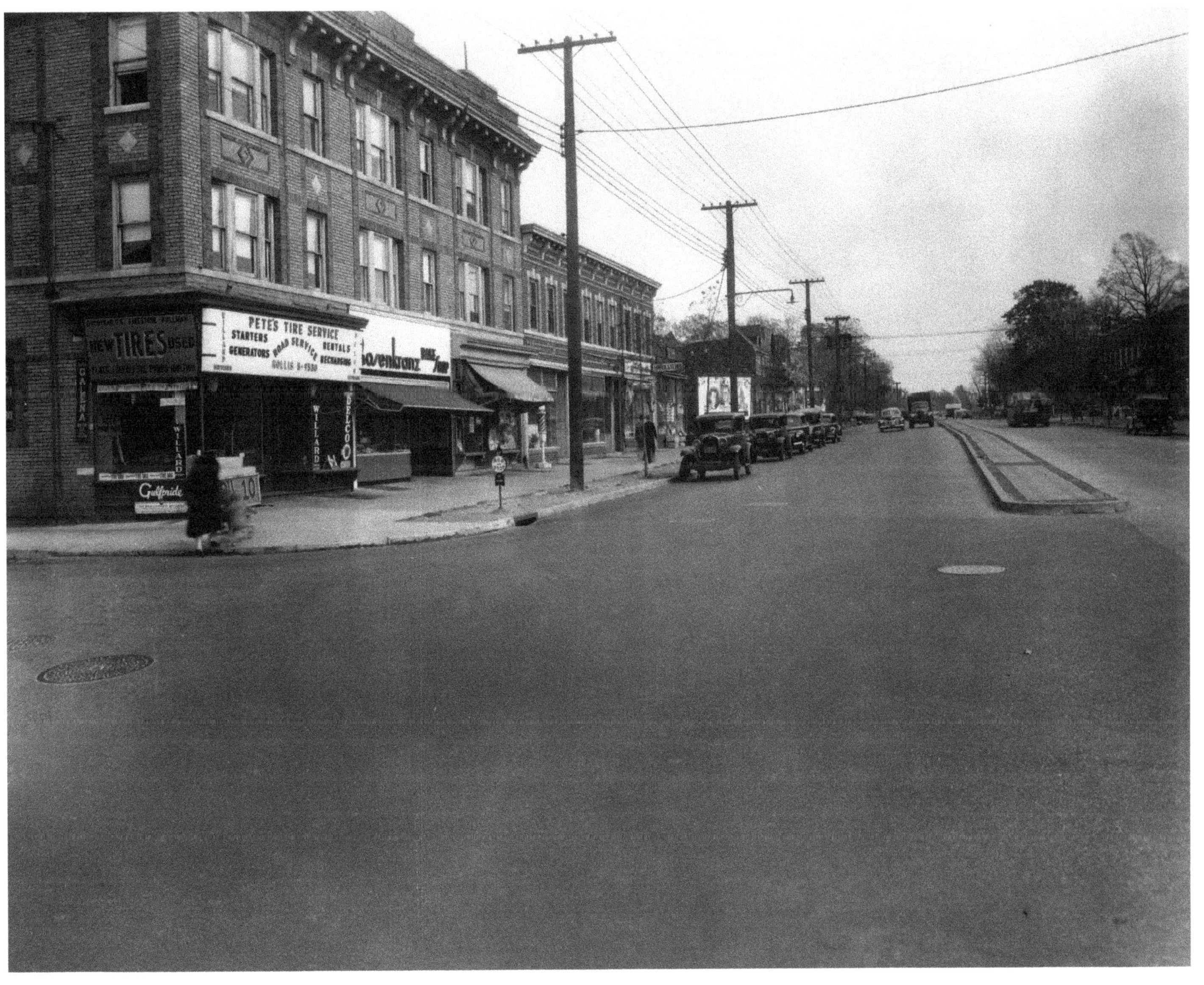

Hempstead Avenue (Turnpike) at Springfield Boulevard in Queens Village in 1940 was a thoroughfare with a median befitting the heavy traffic the densely packed neighborhood now experienced.

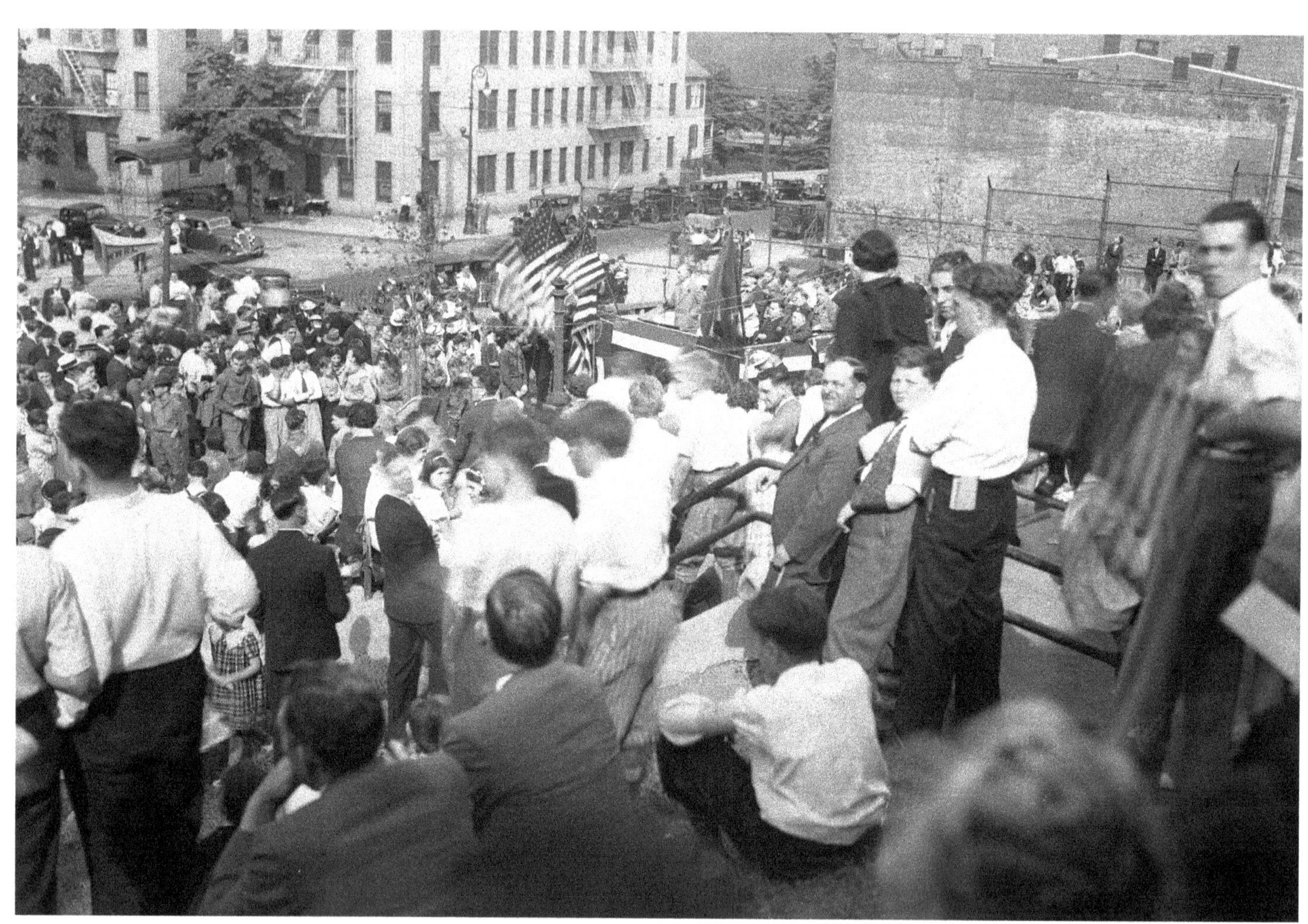

Crowds gather for an event at the Queens Borough Public Library in 1940.

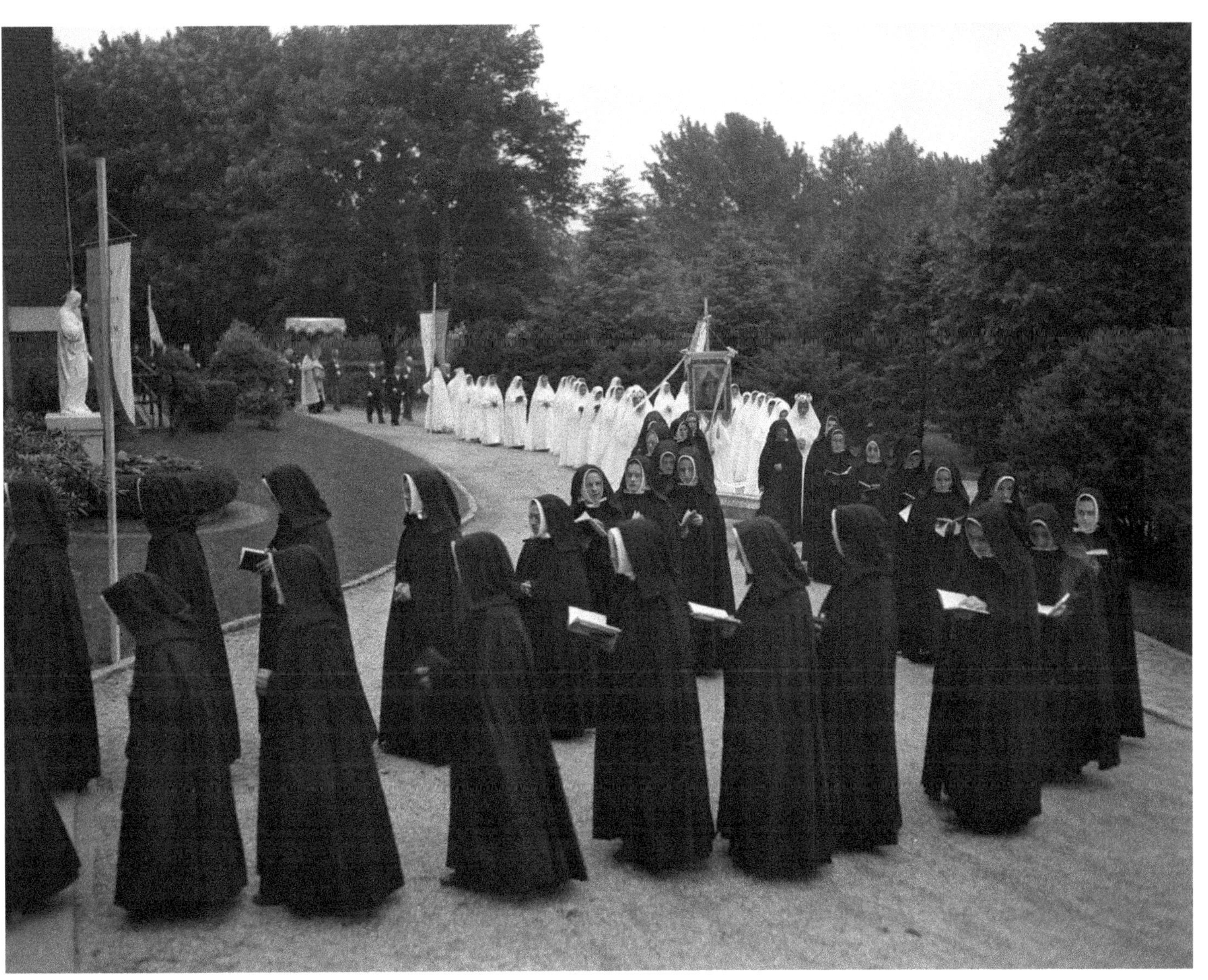

Sisters in procession, likely from the Little Sisters-Poor Convent, St. Ann's Novitiate, at 110th Avenue and Springfield Boulevard in Queens Village.

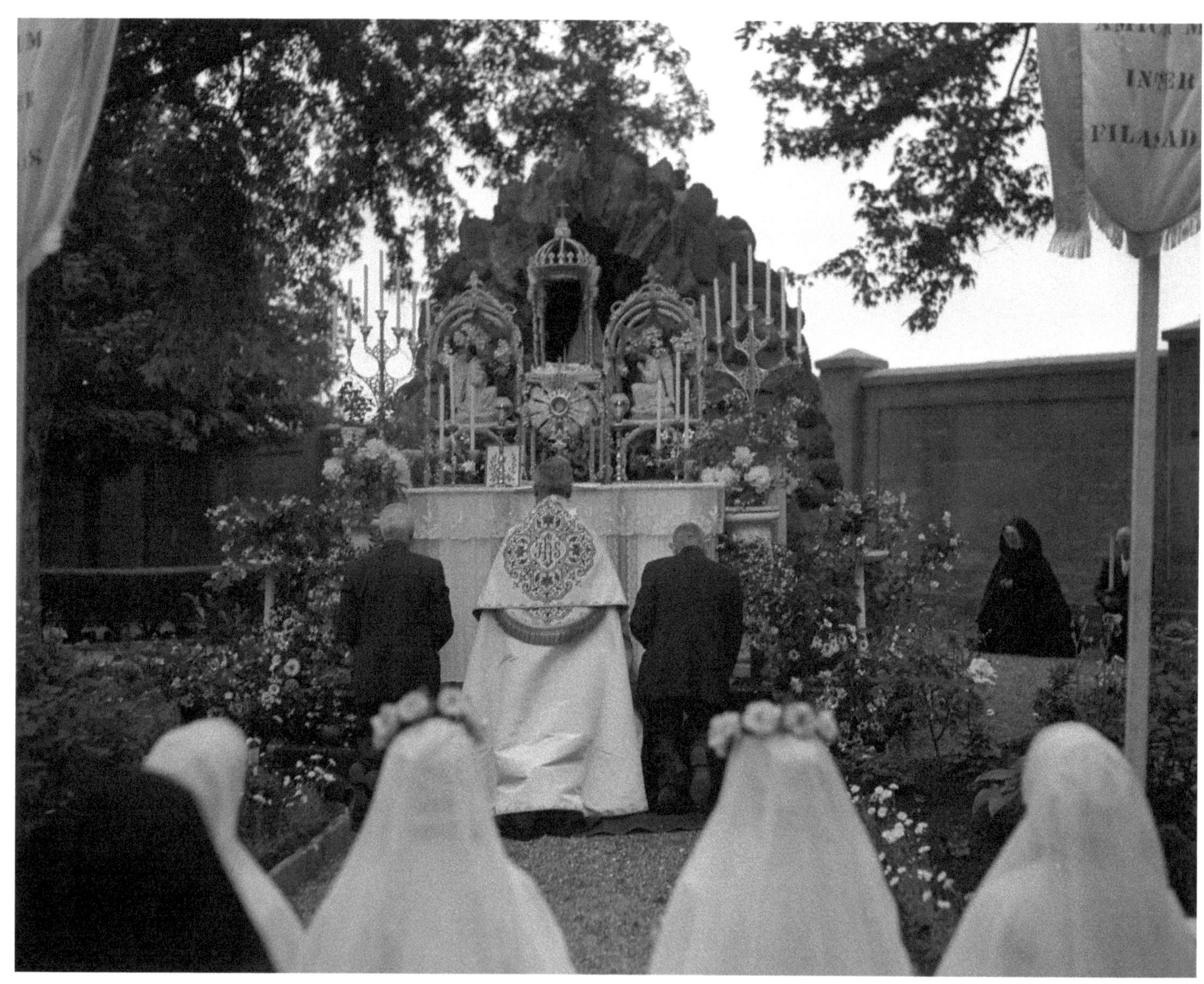

An outdoor mass at an altar set up in a grotto, with priests in the center of the frame, and sisters in the foreground.

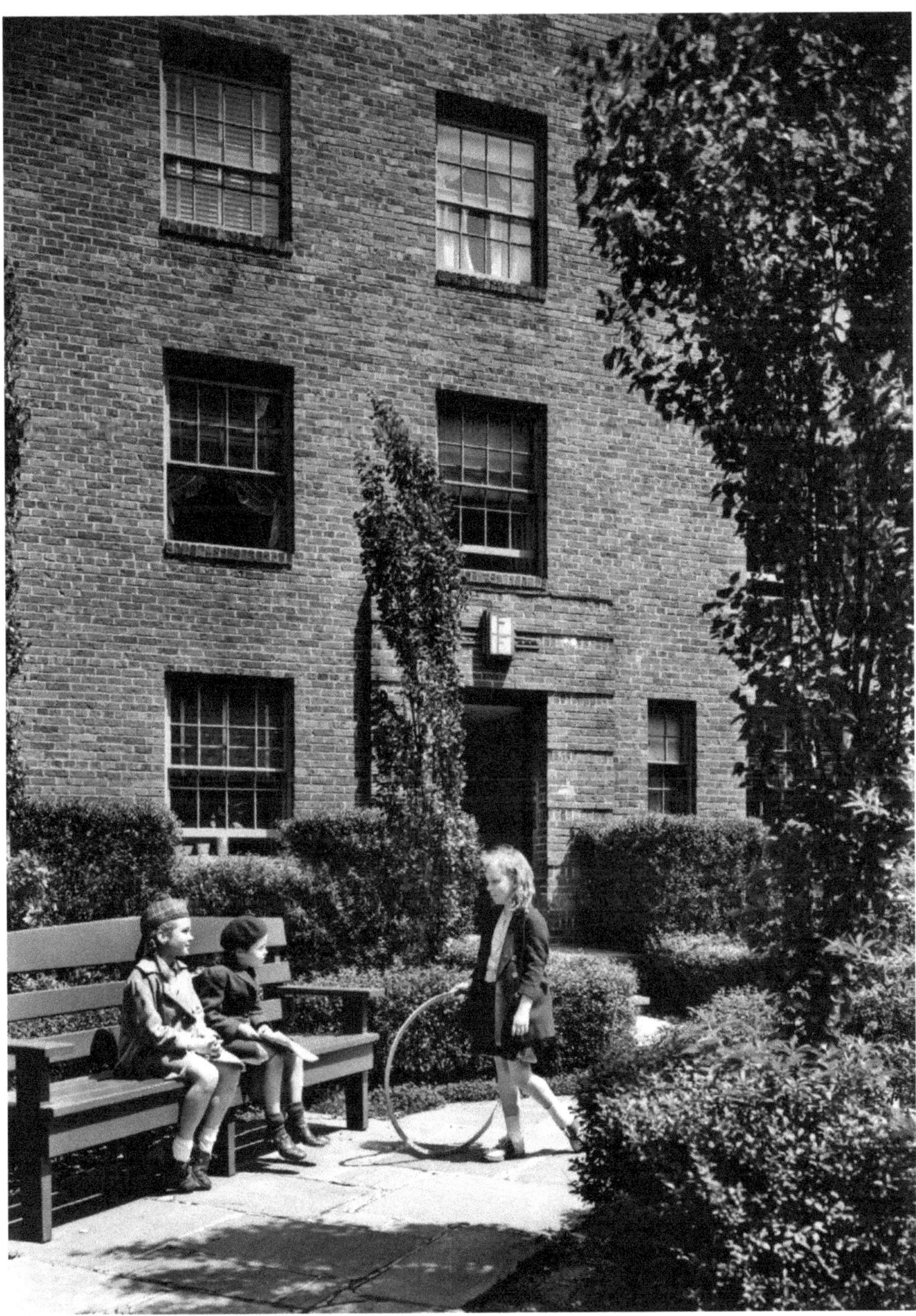

One of the garden courtyards at the Phipps Garden Apartments on 39th Avenue in Sunnyside. The development was started in 1905 with a $1 million investment by philanthropist Henry Phipps, a partner in Andrew Carnegie's steel business, and has consistently provided affordable housing to low-income and moderate-income families from that day forward.

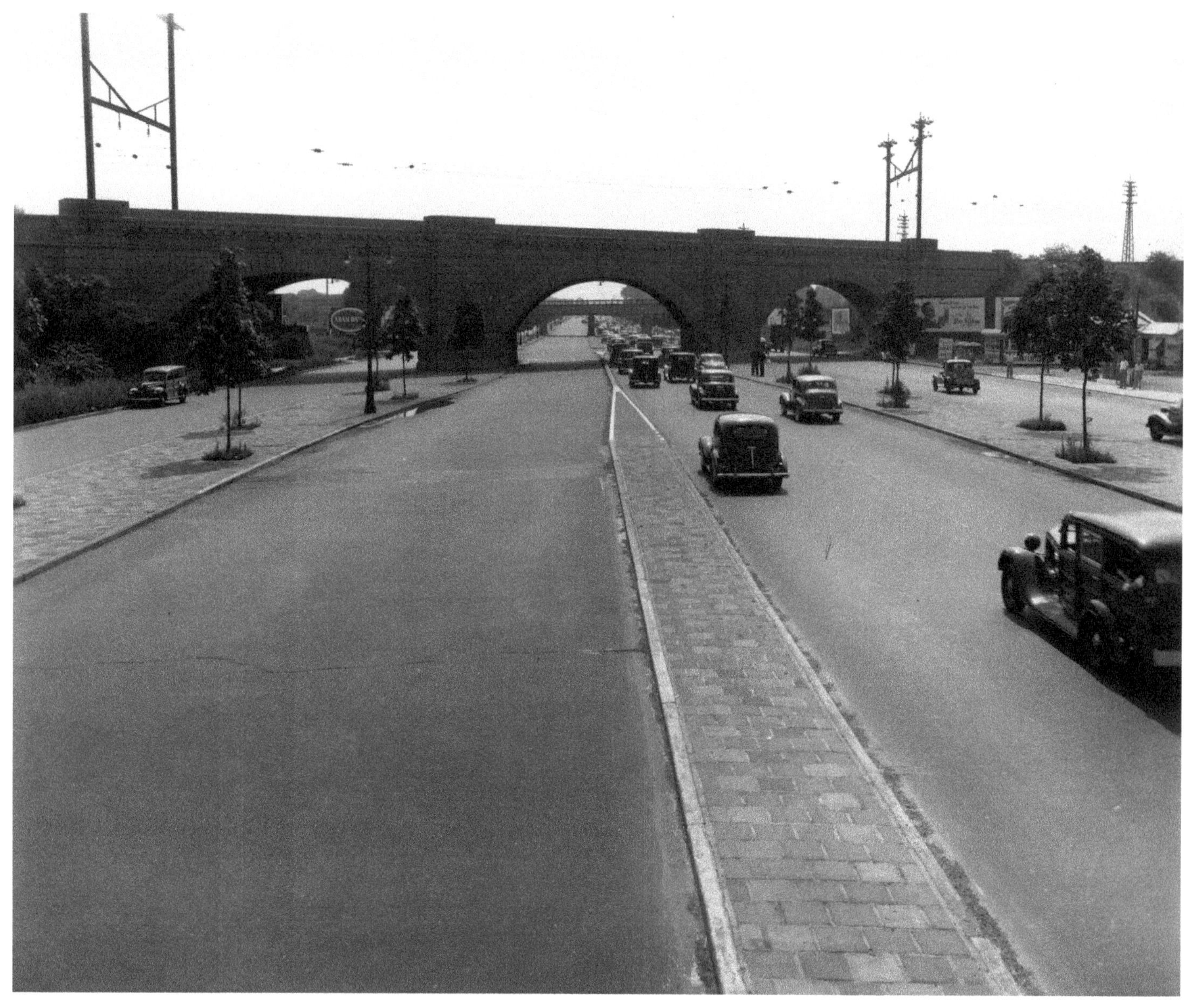

A view east in 1940 on the multi-lane Queens Boulevard, with the express lanes in the center and the local lanes on the outside, in Elmhurst. The overpass was for the New York Connecting Railroad, which is now ConRail.

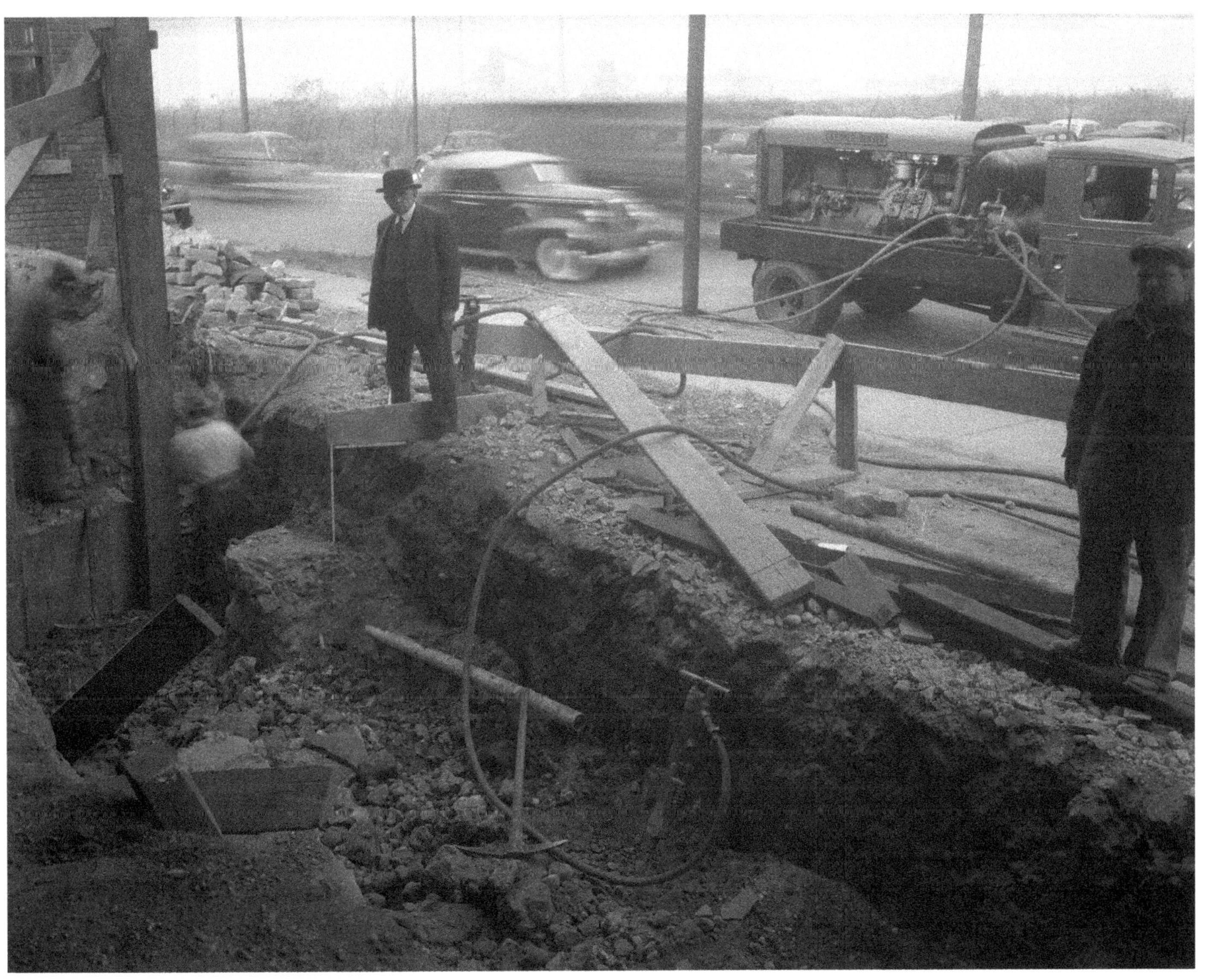

Along with construction as the twentieth century moved forward, demolition was also required, as seen here. The traffic in the background suggests the heavy volume of automobiles traveling this road.

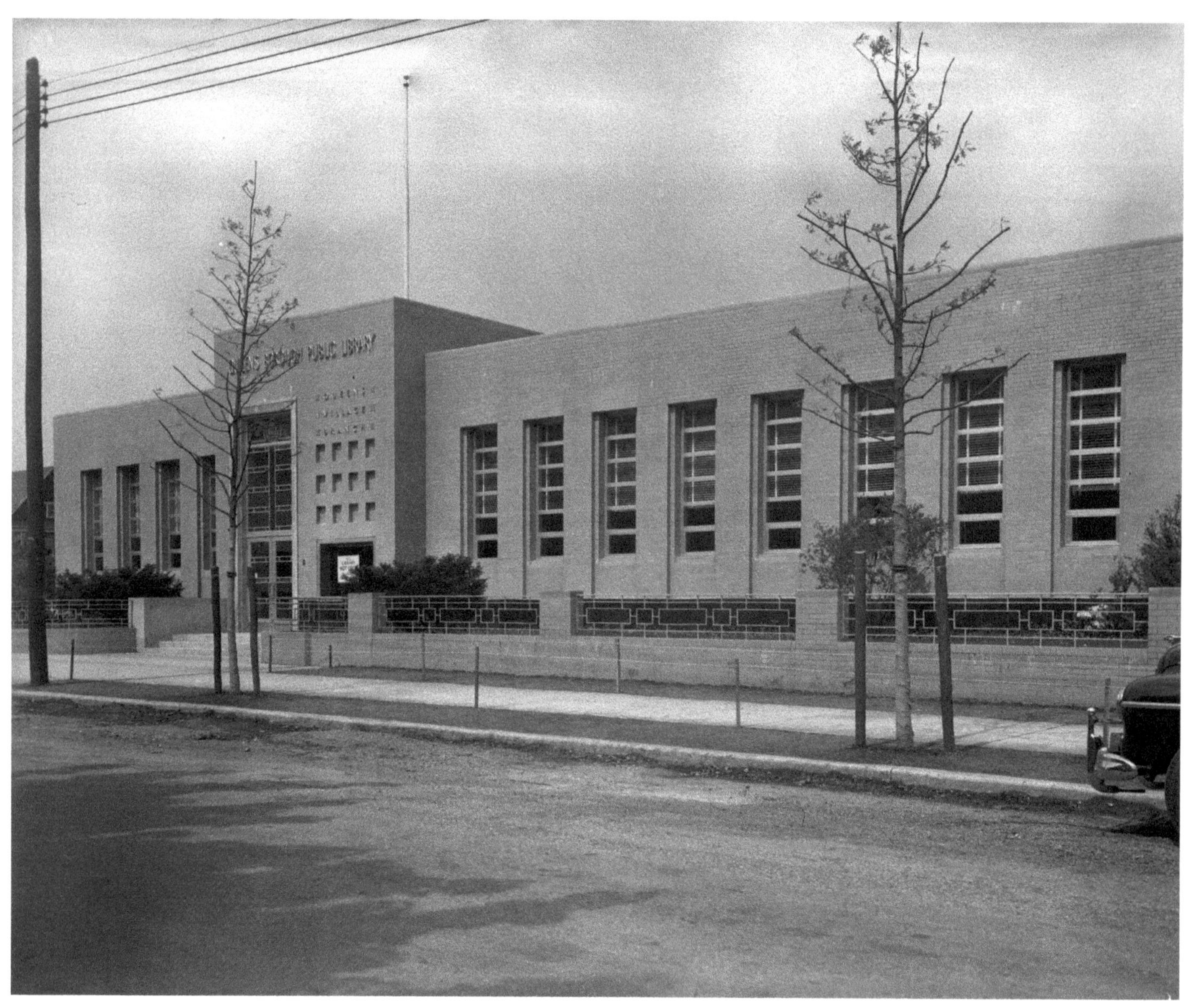

The large Queens Village branch of the Queens Borough Public Library was located on 217th Street near 94th Avenue.

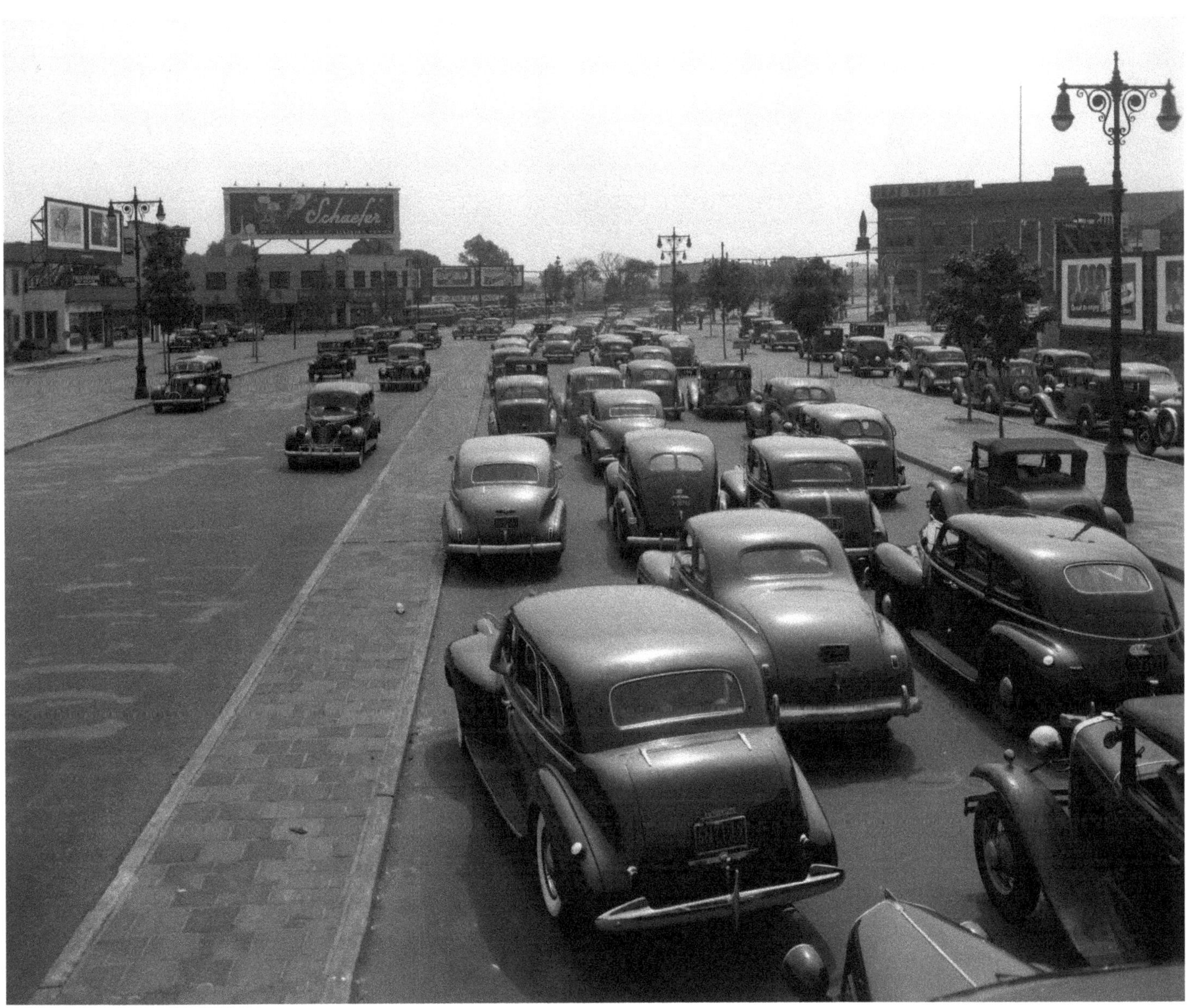

Sunday morning traffic on Queens Boulevard is heavy heading east past Grand Avenue in Elmhurst. The large Schaefer Beer ad on the billboard at upper-left advertises the brew that was one of the top beers in the world at midcentury.

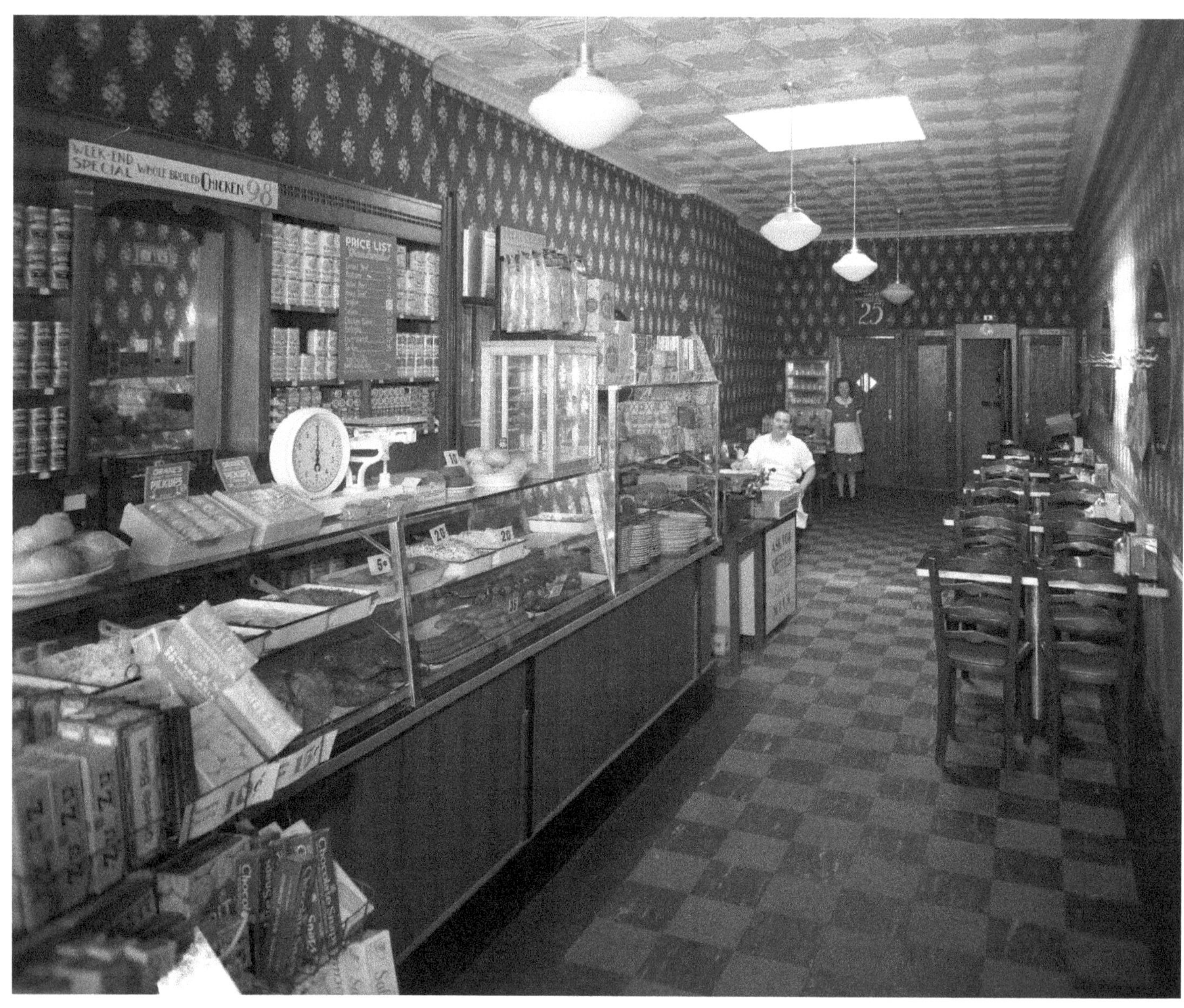

The grand opening of a Fresh Meadows delicatessen on 178th Street and Union Turnpike in 1940.

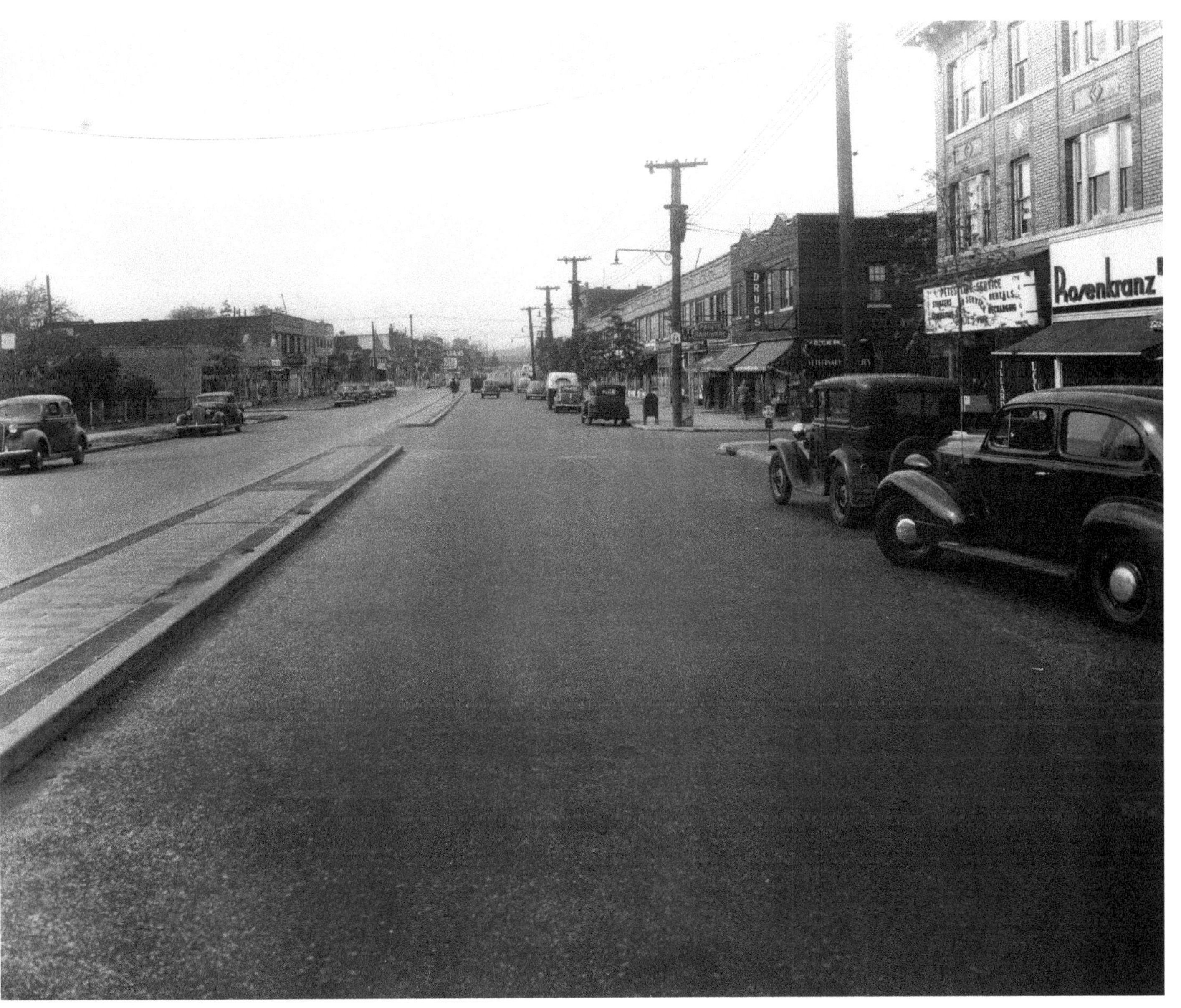

A view to the west along Hempstead Avenue (Turnpike), near 220th Street in 1941 shows how the commercial strip had grown up by the middle of the century, with automobiles defining the wide, paved streets and multi-story brick buildings, a mix of shops, and small apartments.

Crowds of both skaters and spectators enjoy the day at the New York City building's ice-skating rink, the first such facility in New York City. The massive rink was built for shows and spectator use at the 1939 World's Fair and was later used as the temporary home of the United Nations, until the U.N. building in Manhattan was completed in 1952. It regained fame during the "Ice-Travaganza" shows during the 1964-65 World's Fair. With the departure of ambassadors and fairs, skaters returned and the rink was used year-round until 2008.

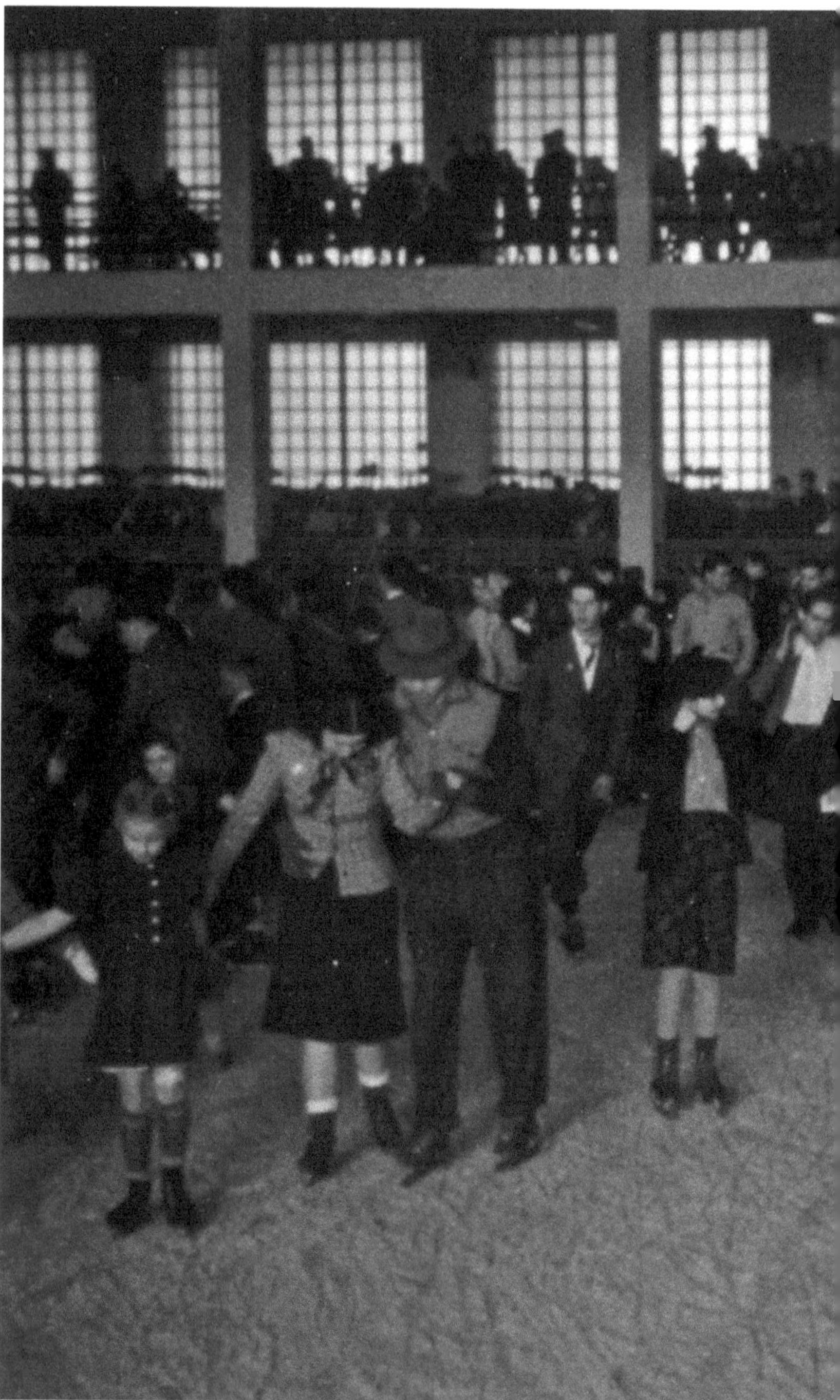

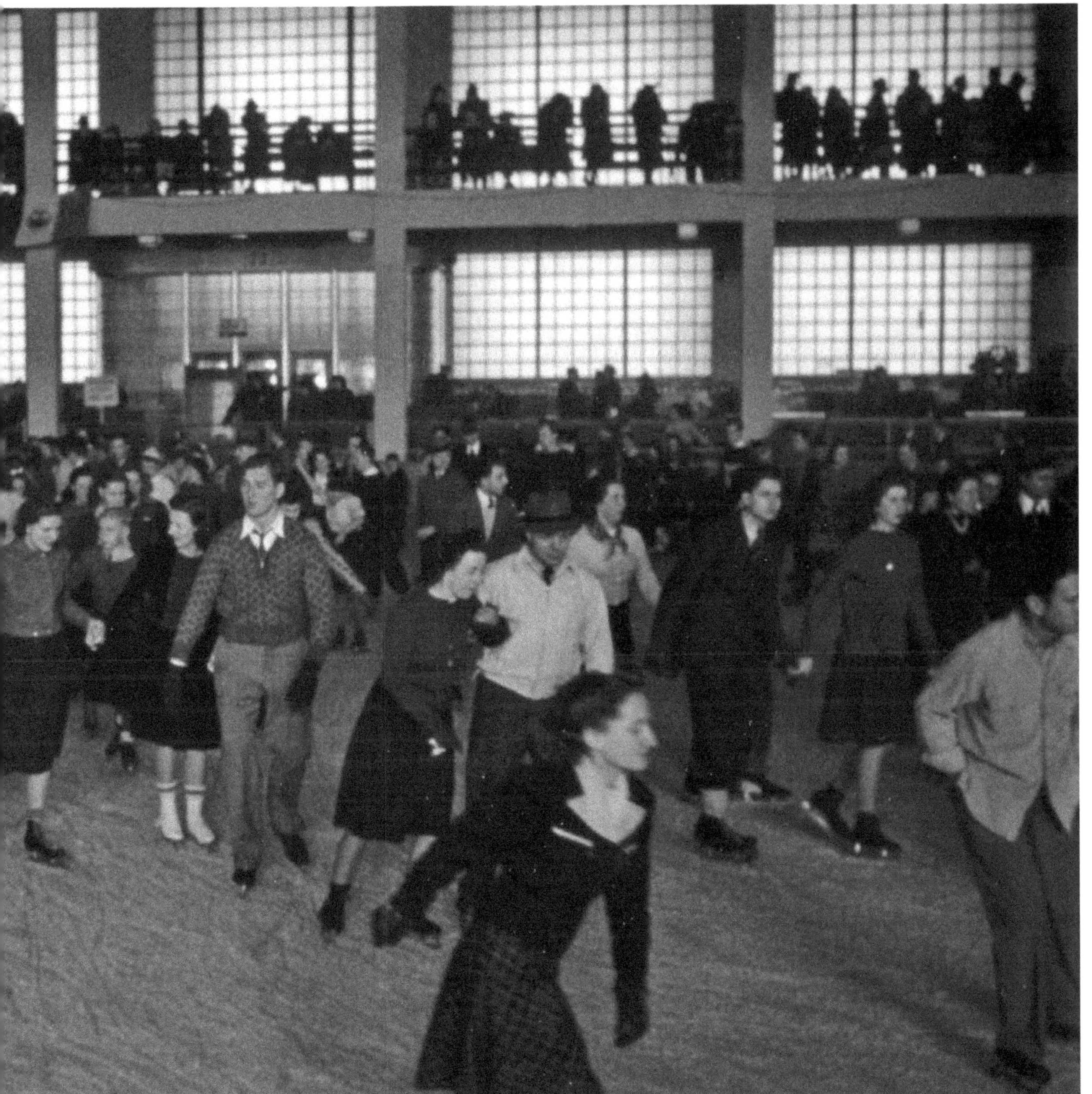

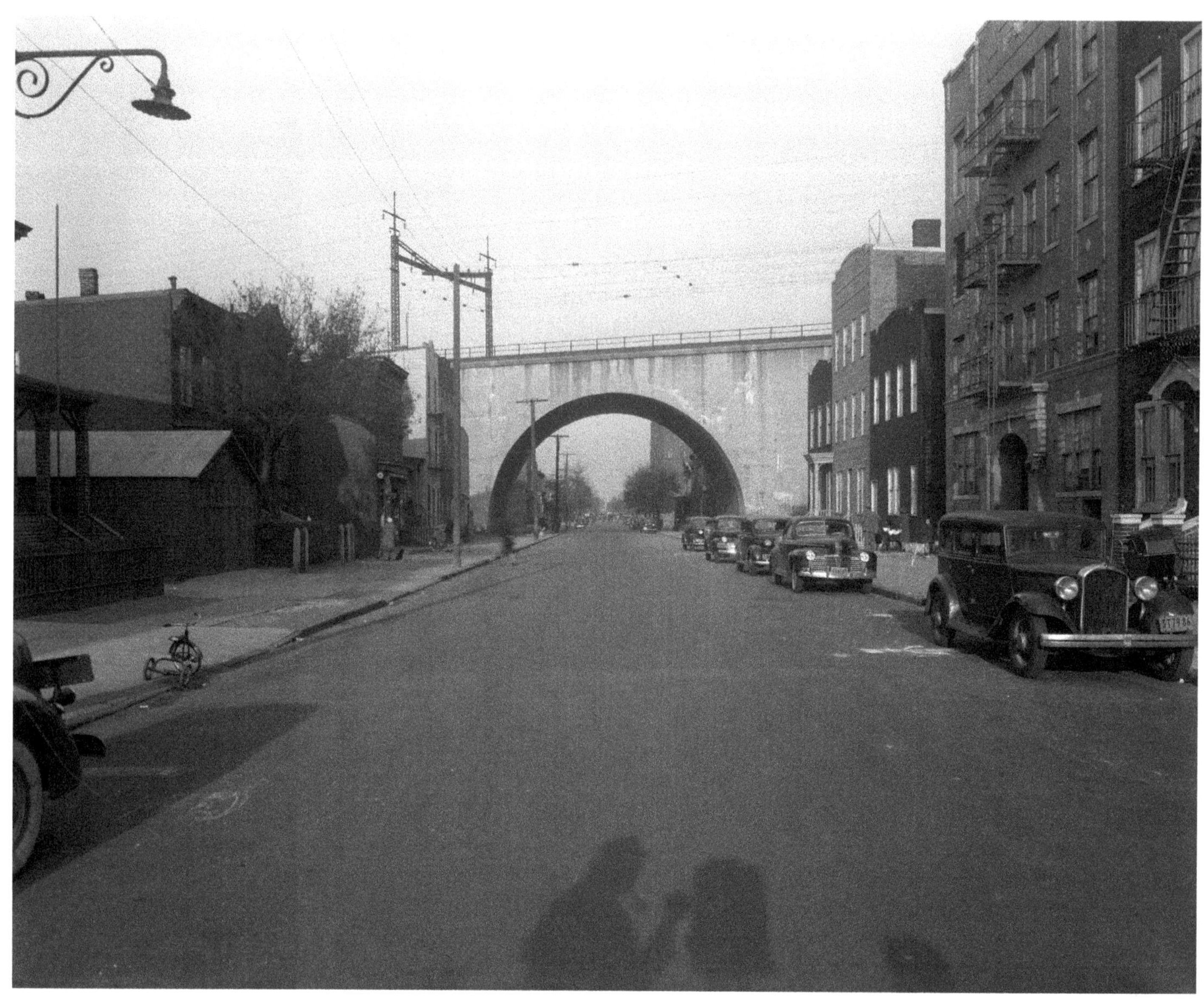

The New York Connecting Railroad (ConRail) freight line overpass on 38th Street in Astoria frames the blocks to the south with its large archway. As seen on this block, Astoria was built up with a great variety of architecture and housing options, from the one-family and two-family homes (and garage) on the left, to the tenement-style buildings on the right.

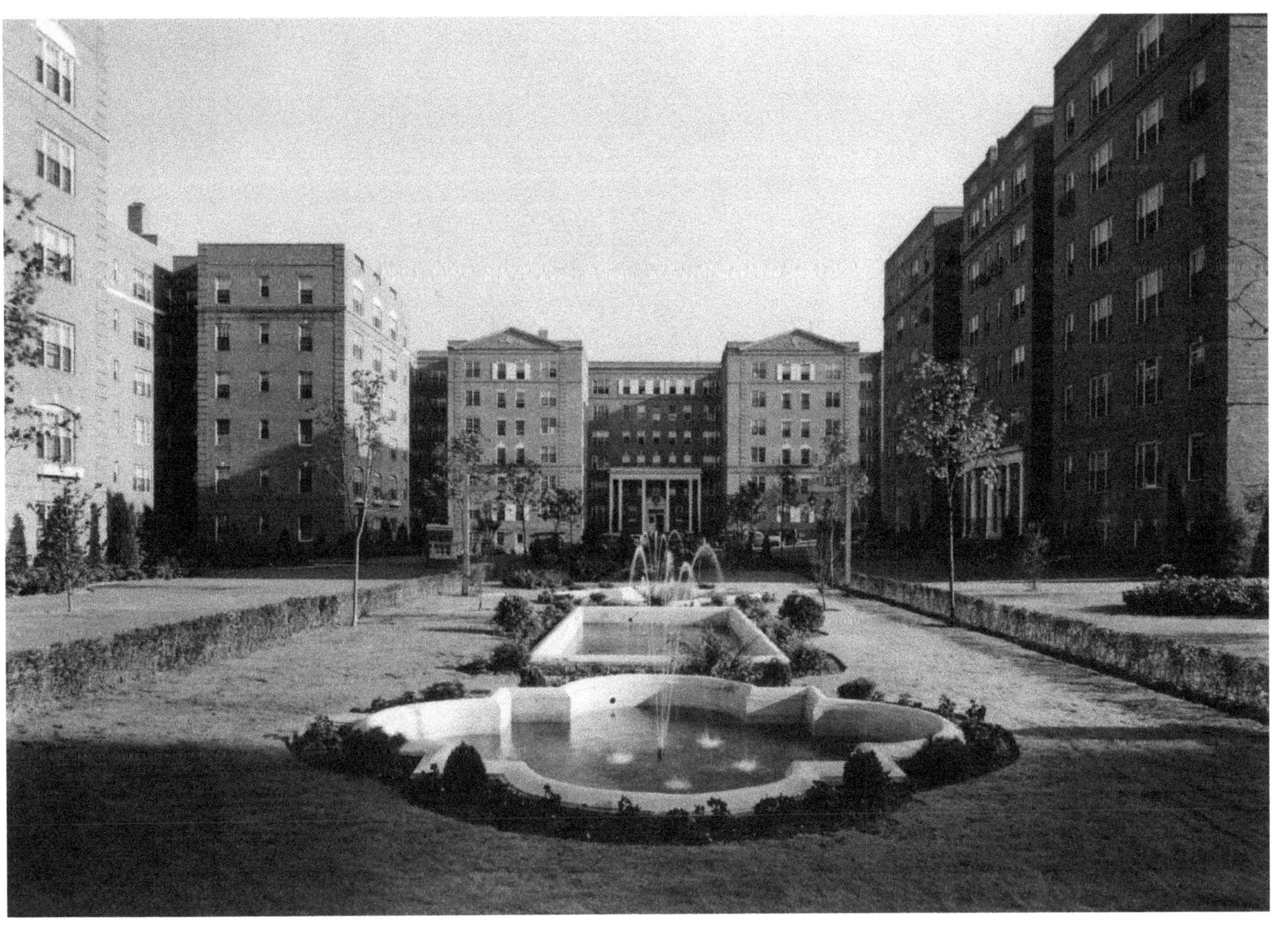

A collection of buildings around the fountains in Forest Hills South, which like Jackson Heights exhibits significant influences from the British "Garden City" movement. The area has many beautiful styles of buildings, with attention clearly paid to form as well as function, as seen here in 1941.

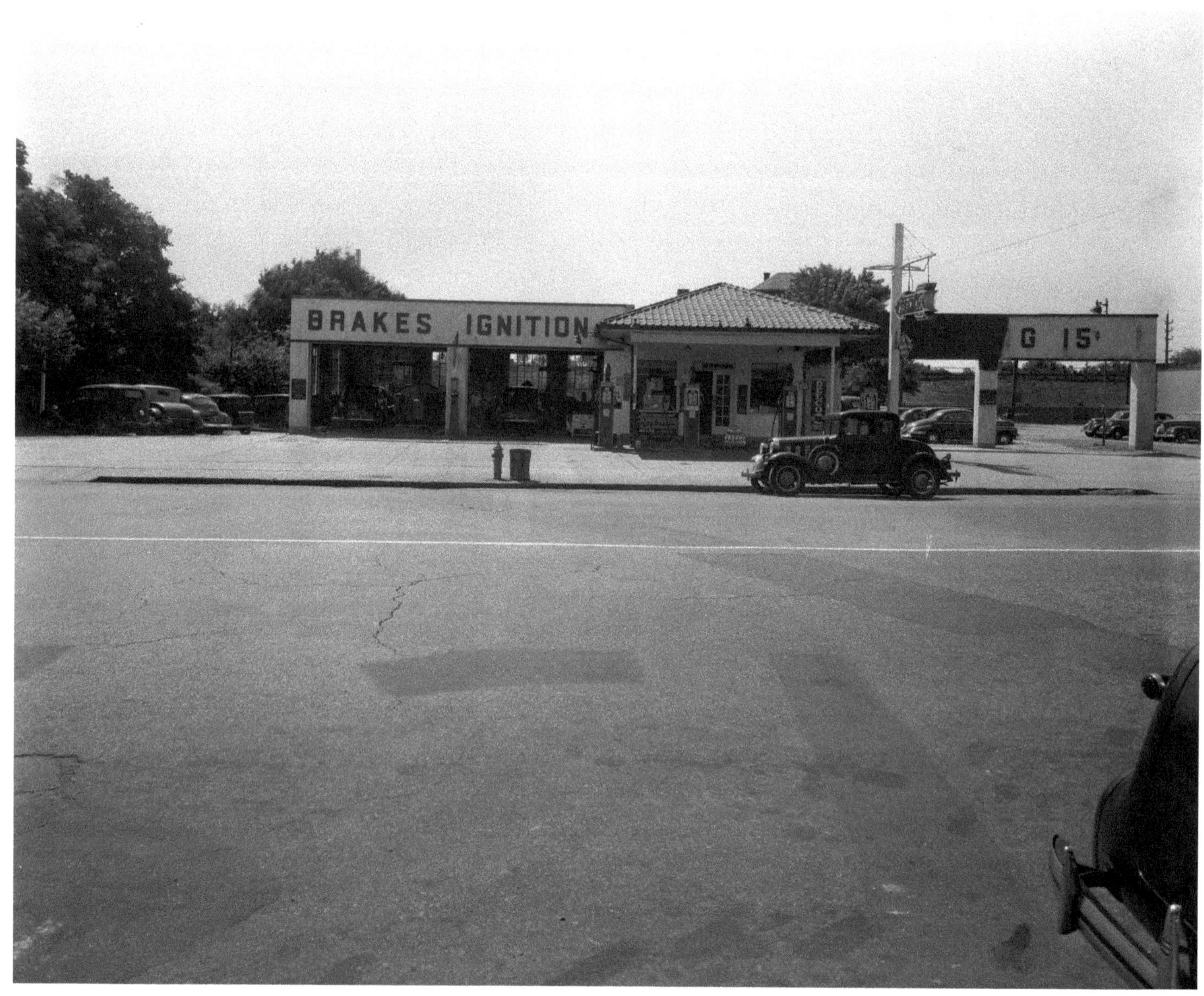

A large Mobil service station on the south side of Jamaica Avenue, near Springfield Boulevard. With the growing ranks of drivers drawn farther out into the borough as roads continued to be improved, such stations proliferated along main streets, offering gasoline and service for the hundreds of thousands of new drivers across Queens.

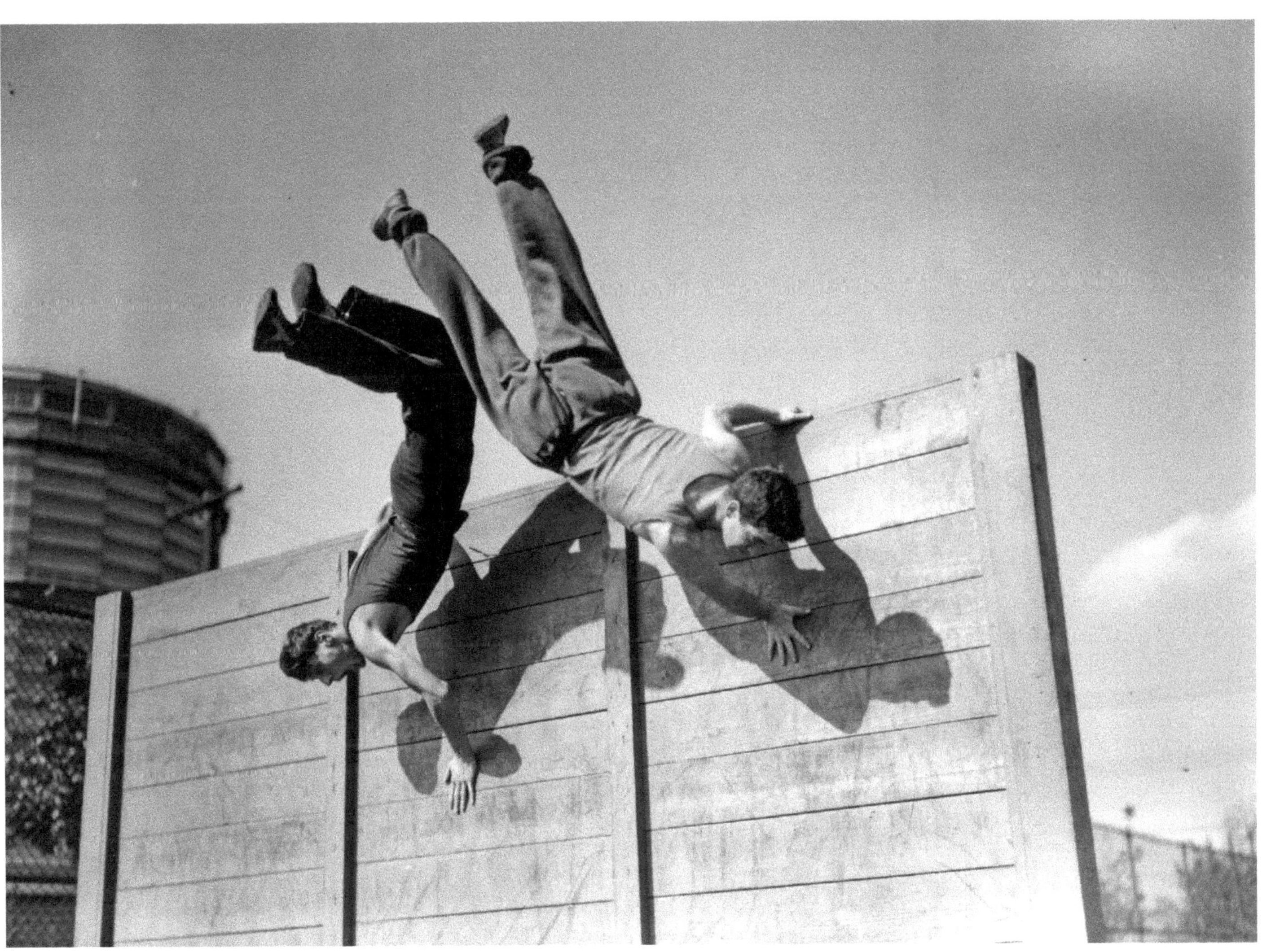

Flushing High School's Victory Corps during a commando training course in 1942. The course was offered by the physical education department and featured basic training drills, such as the wall scaling seen here, intended to keep the boys in top shape in case they were called to serve in World War II.

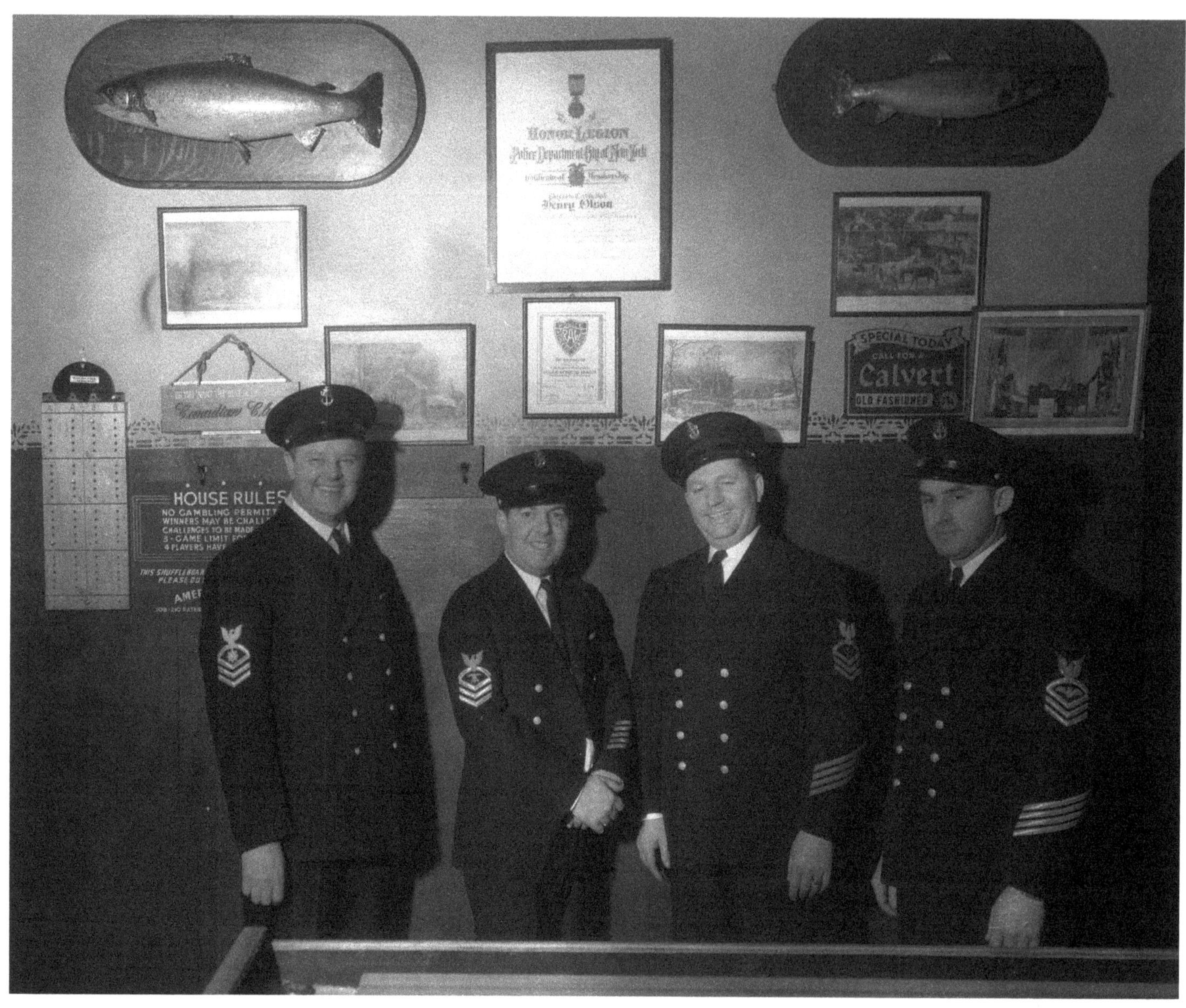

With the Japanese attack on Pearl Harbor in December the year before, the nation was now at war. This group of off-duty officers pose in full Navy blues for a bit of shuffleboard at a tavern in 1942.

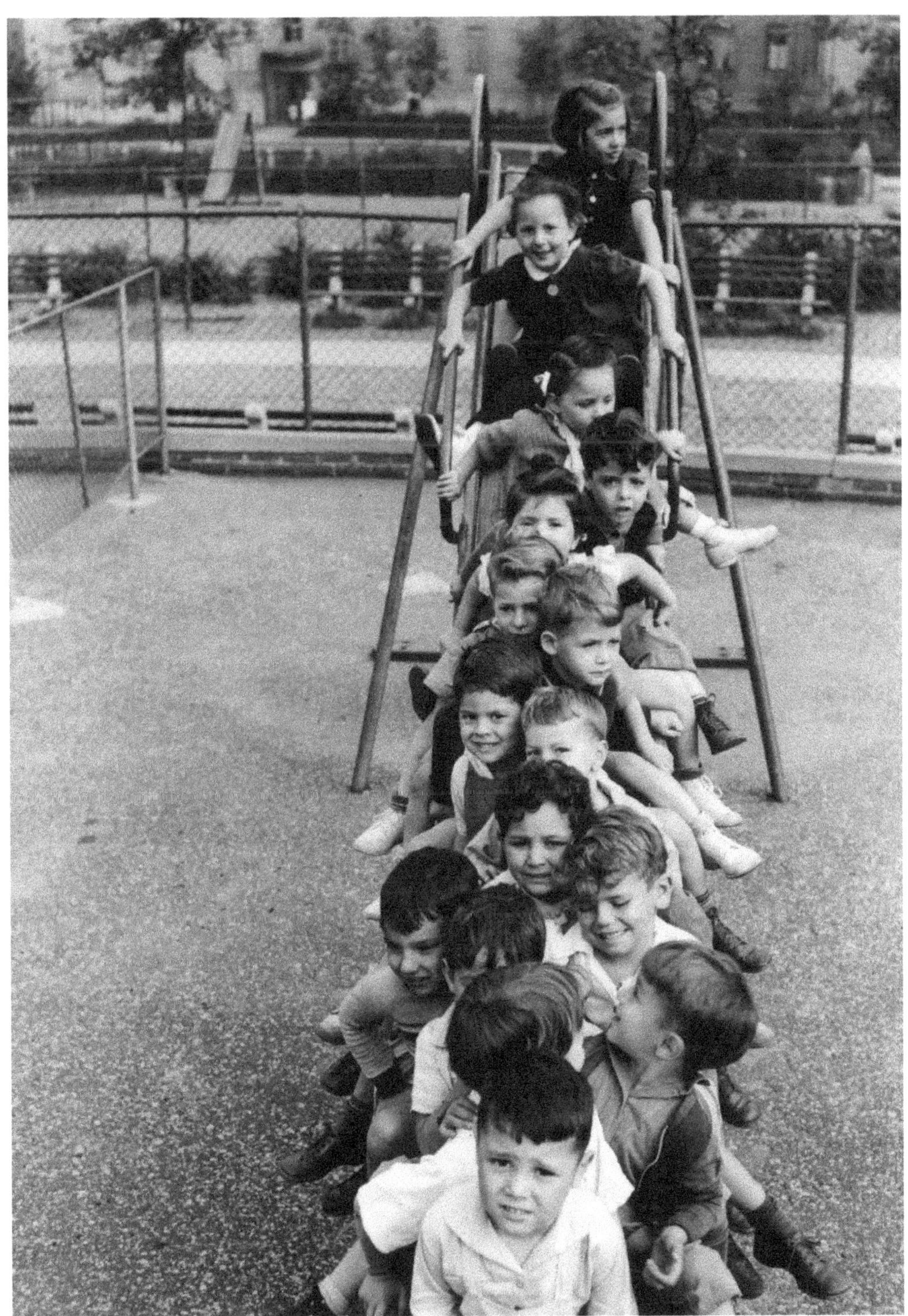

More than a dozen children at the Queensbridge Housing Project are perhaps trying to set a record on this slide at the playground on the grounds of the complex, which is directly adjacent the Queensboro Bridge landing in Long Island City. The project is the largest in the nation, with nearly 7,000 residents in more than 3,100 units, built in a nontraditional "Y" shape, which was thought to be more economical. The buildings were completed in 1939.

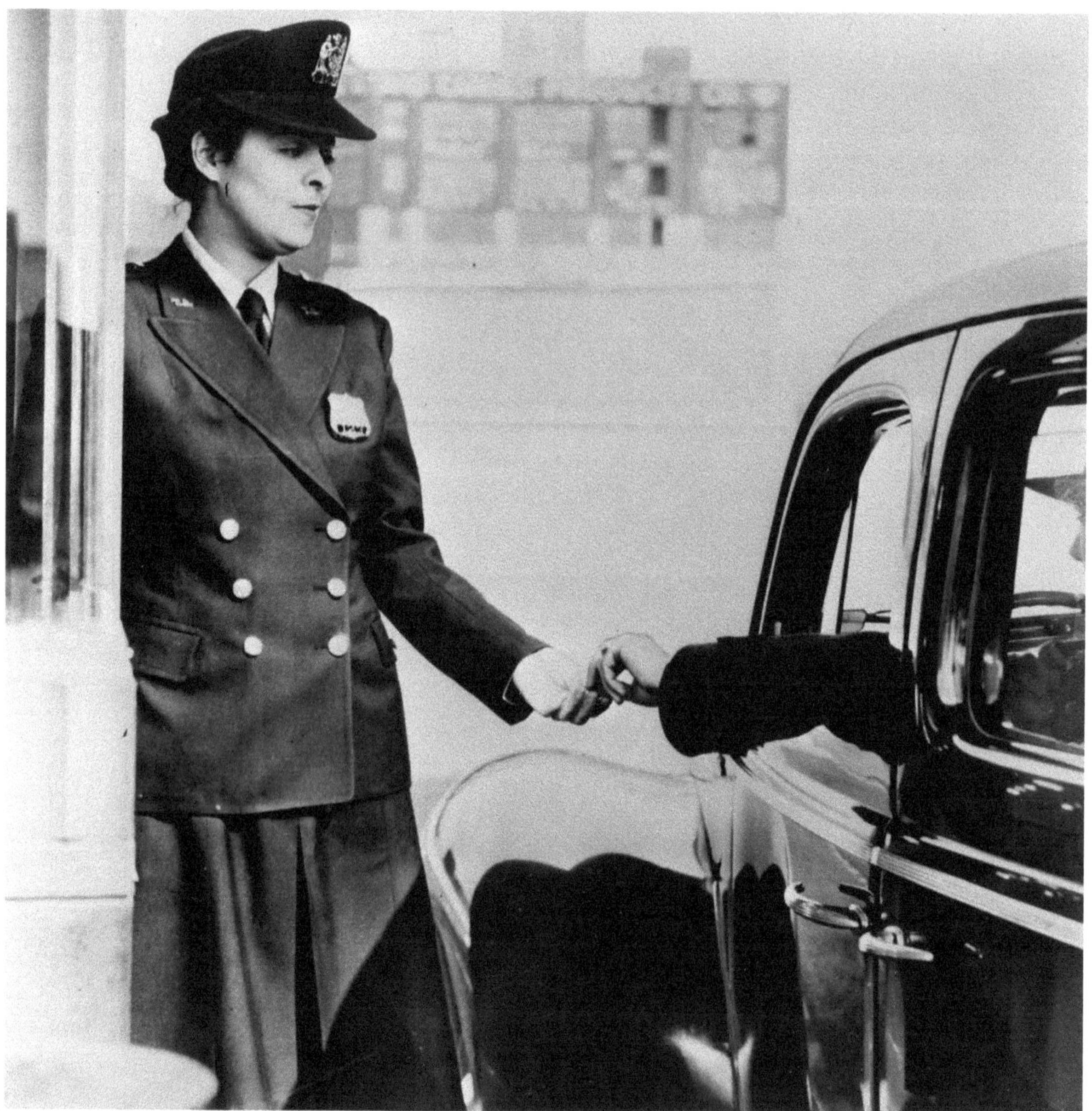

Mrs. Joliet Jones works as a toll collector at the Queens-Midtown Tunnel, apparently hired to replace a man who joined the armed forces to defend the nation in World War II. Mrs. Jones is seen here on her first day as a collector on special duty.

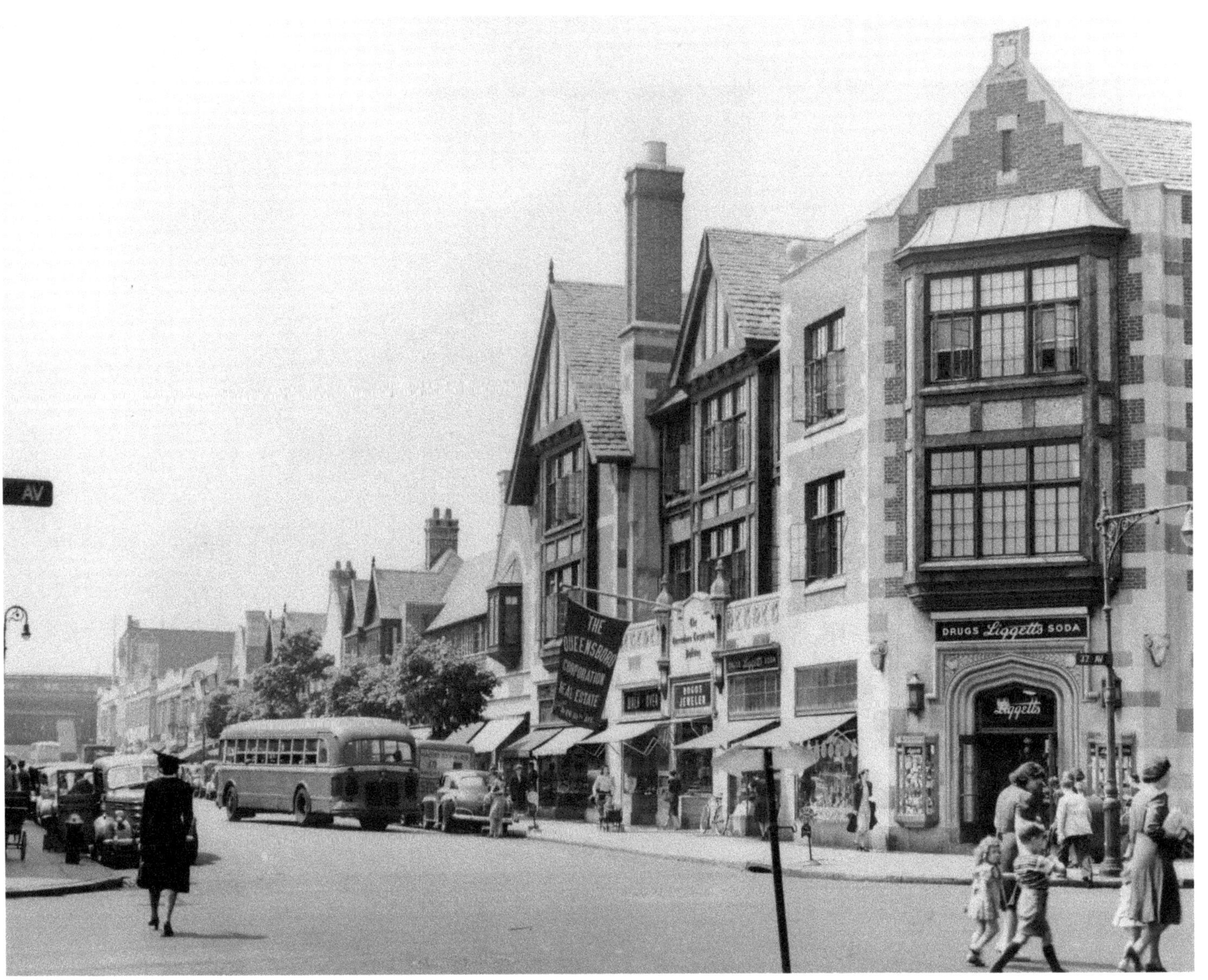

Seen here is the English Gables of the Jackson Heights shopping district on 82nd Street near Roosevelt Avenue, where the IRT elevated subway station is visible in the left distance. The building on the corner was Liggett's drugstore, with the offices of the Queensboro Corporation to the left.

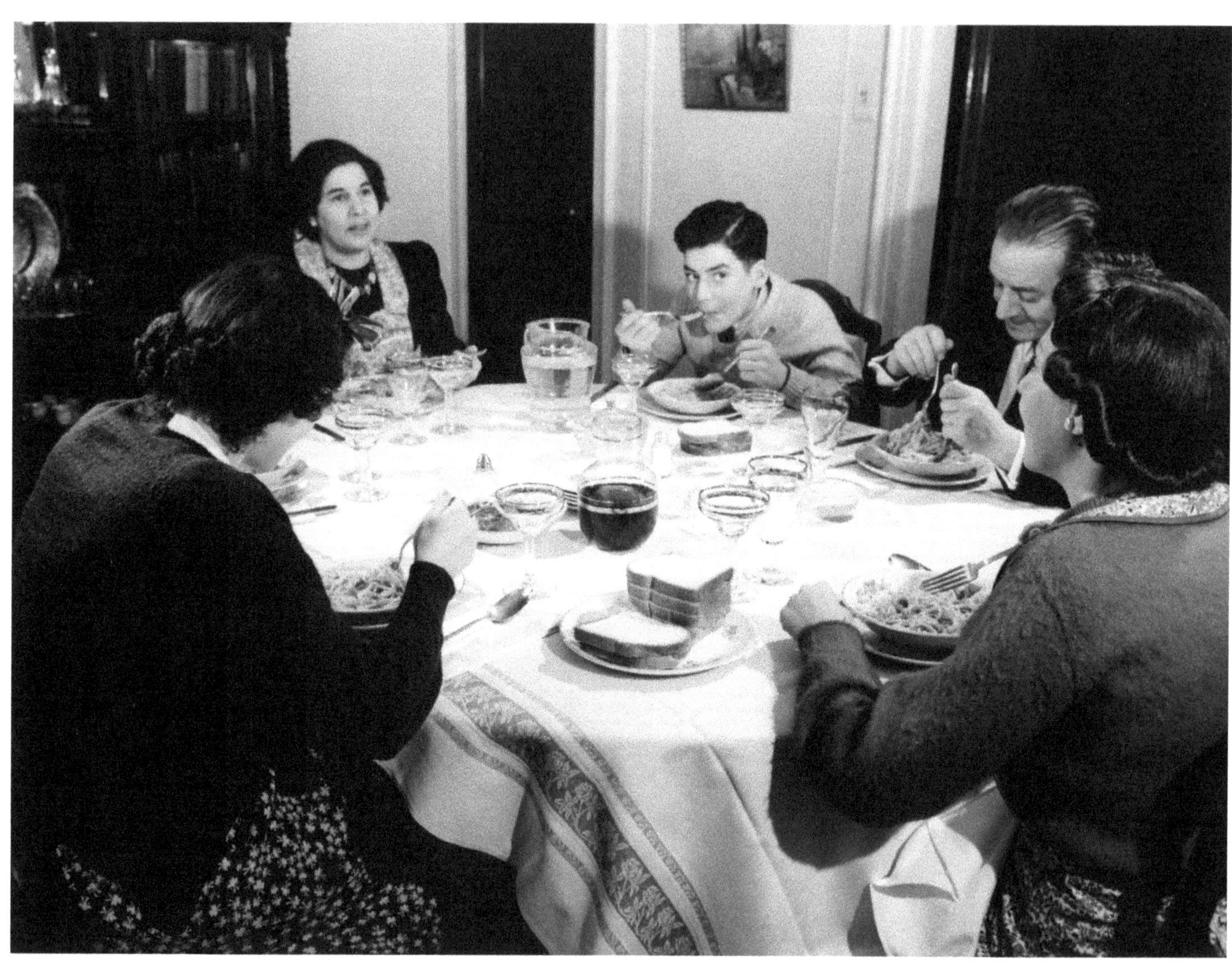

An intimate portrait of life in Corona in January 1942. Enjoying a meal with family members at home in the dining room are Raymond Fazio, a garment worker, and his wife, also in the garment business.

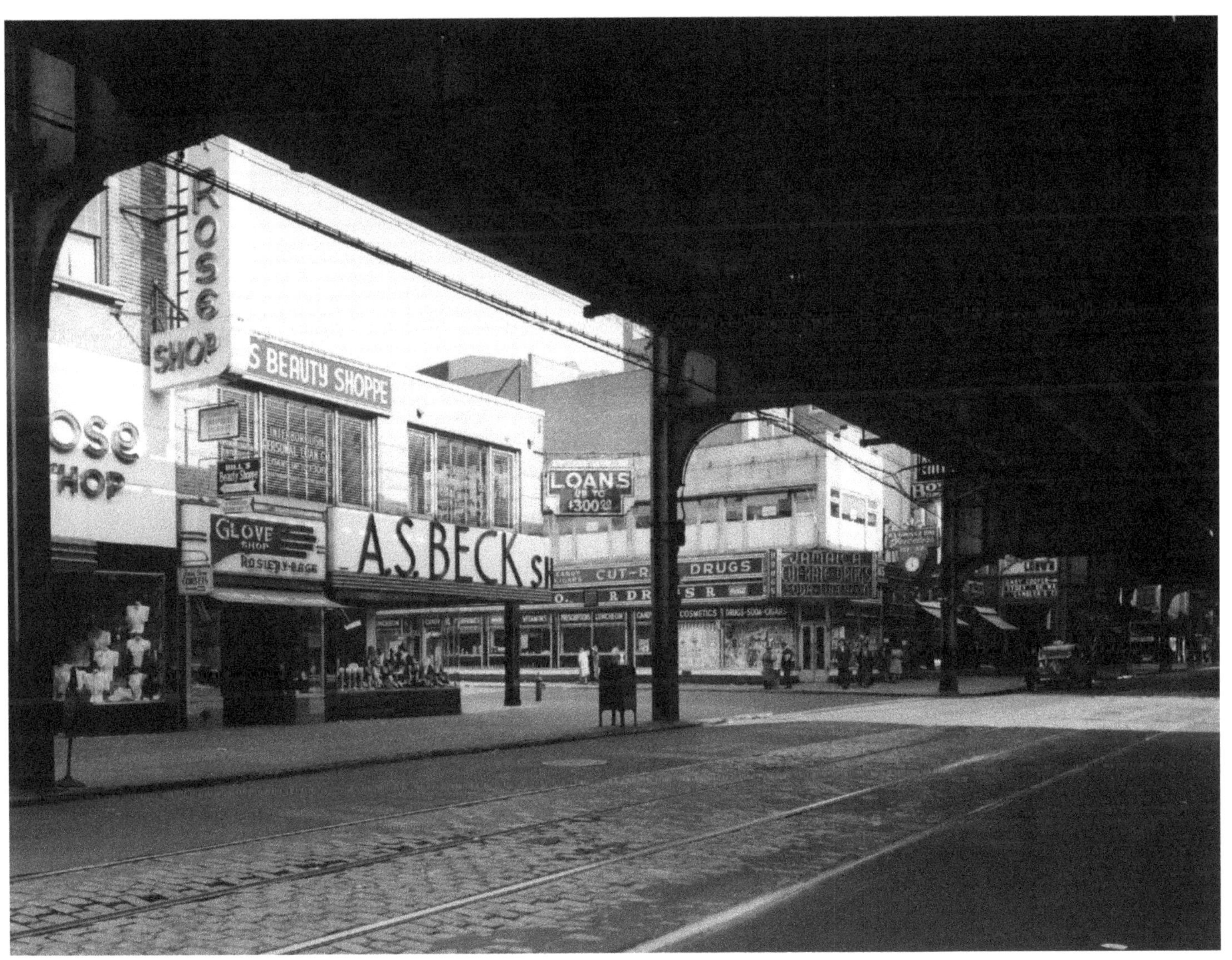

The elevated tracks on Jamaica Avenue dominate the sky and frame the largest shopping area in Queens during the war era, with retail establishments large and small stretching for miles. Parts of Jamaica Avenue still have elevated tracks today, although the area in Jamaica now has underground tunnels. Jamaica was also the main hub of the Long Island Railroad in Queens, where transfers to nearly every line took place at the station on Sutphin Boulevard—which now gives access to John F. Kennedy Airport.

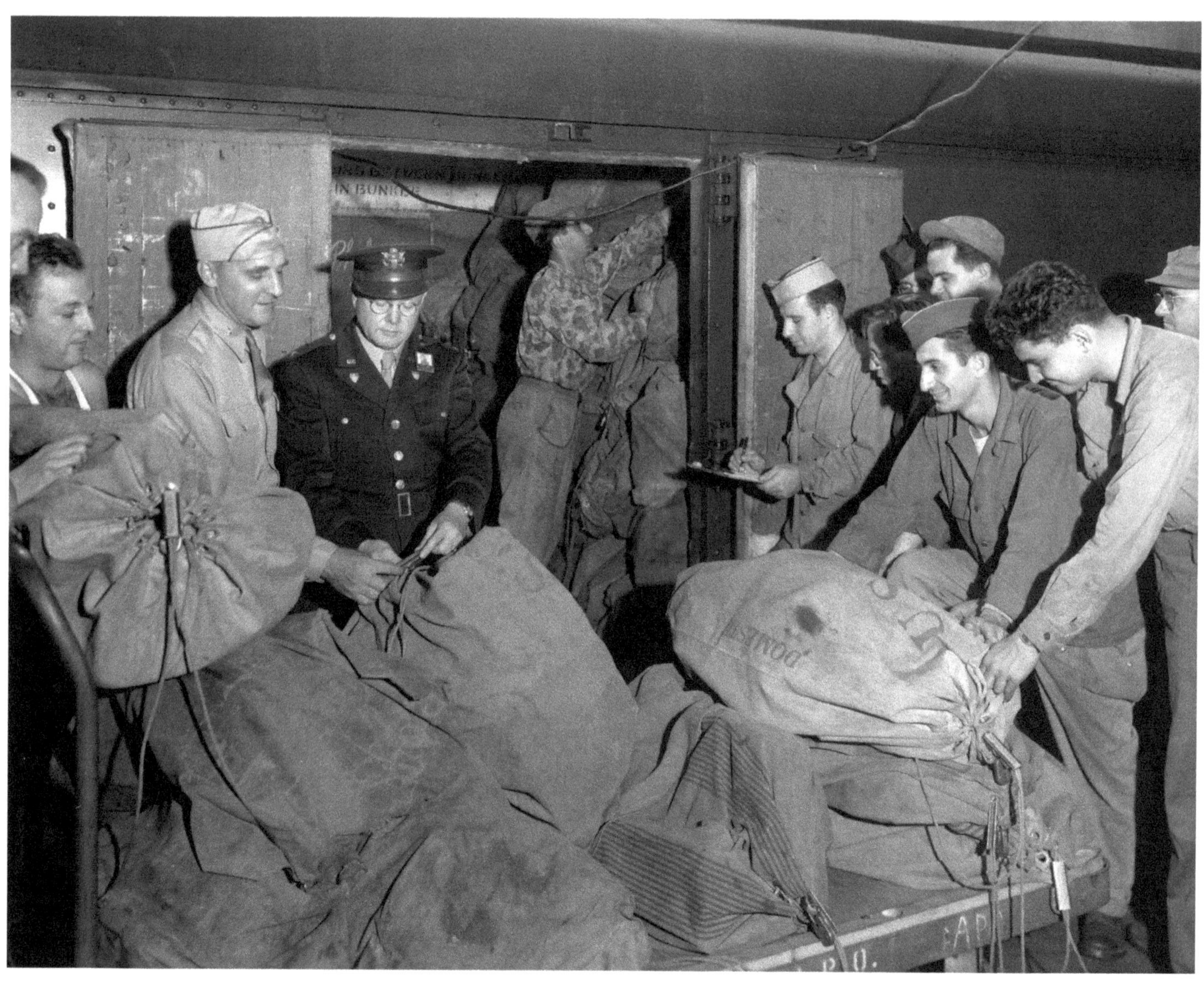

An Army Post Office mail and package inspection takes place at the Long Island City port of embarkation in 1944. Fourth from the left is Colonel Richard E. Eggleton, the port's postal officer conducting the inspection with Colonel Edgard W. Garbisch, the district engineer. The APO was located on Northern Boulevard, near 42nd Street.

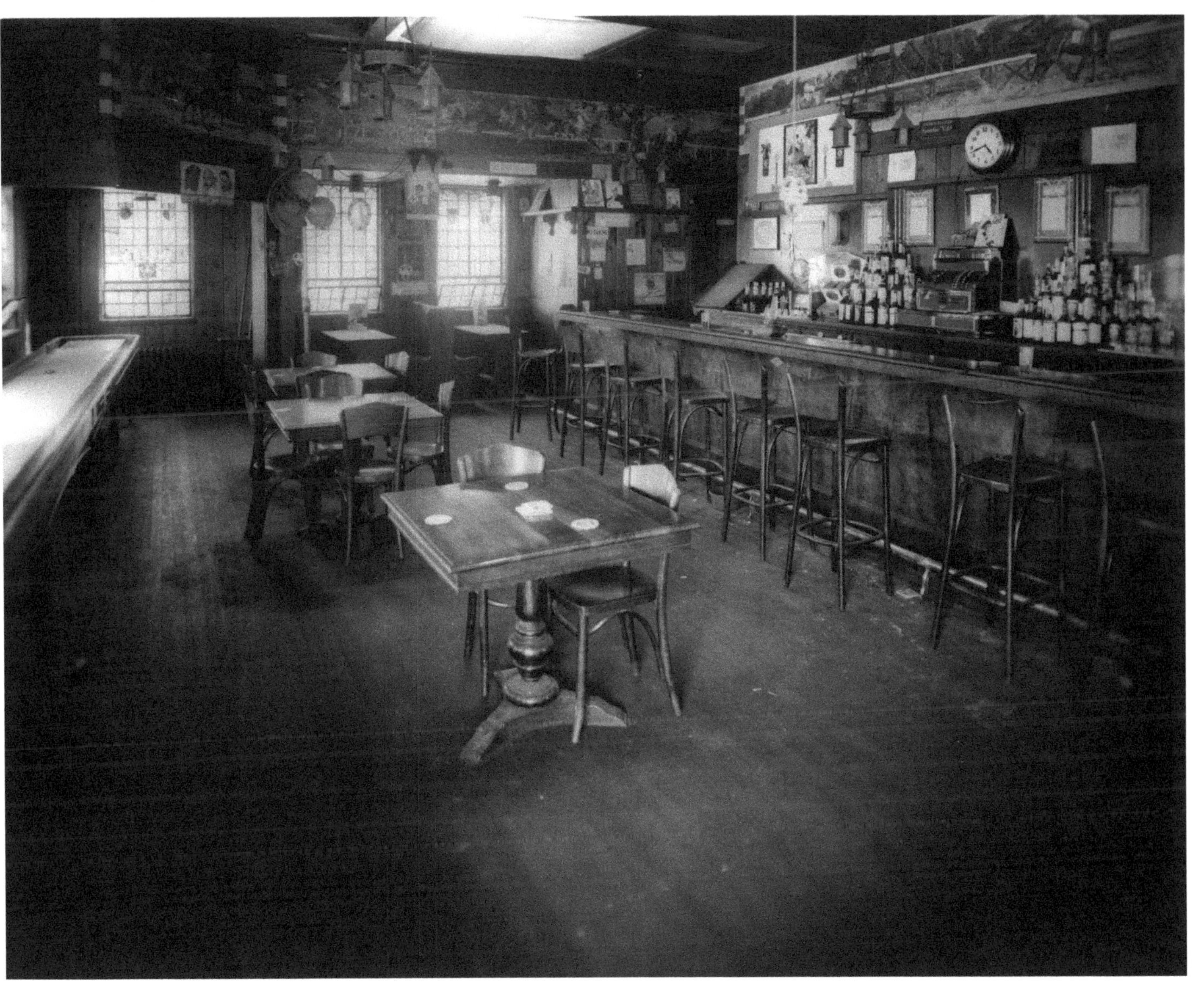

An interior view of a finely appointed Queens Village watering hole, Percy J. Flint's Bar and Grill, located at Springfield Boulevard and Hempstead Turnpike. Captioned "Enemy Ears Are Listening," a poster on the back wall depicts Hitler and other Axis dictators, cautioning patrons with access to war-related information to guard their tongues. Spies sympathetic to the enemy were considered a threat as the war ground forward.

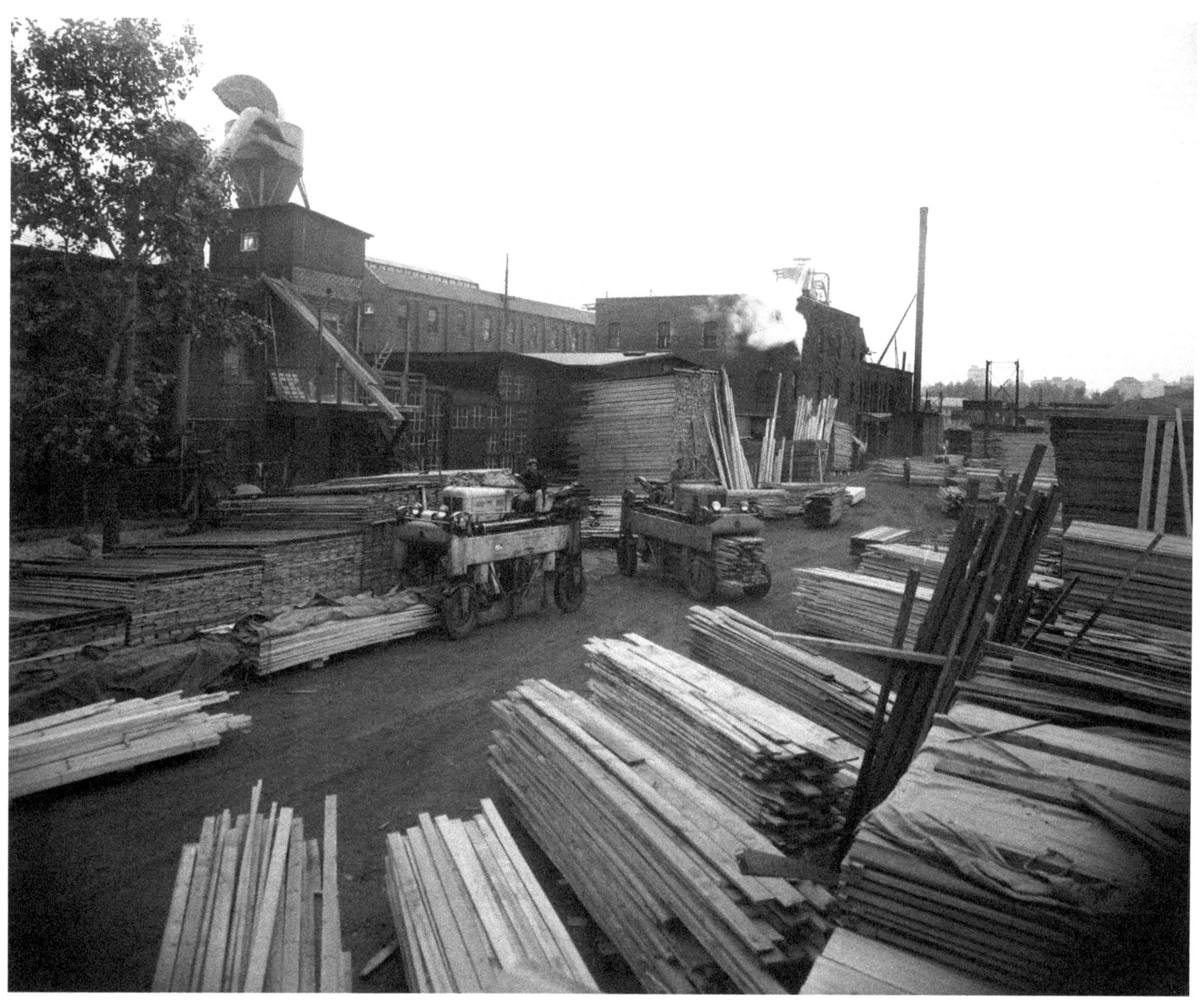

In 1945, this lumberyard and mill remained very busy contributing to the war effort.

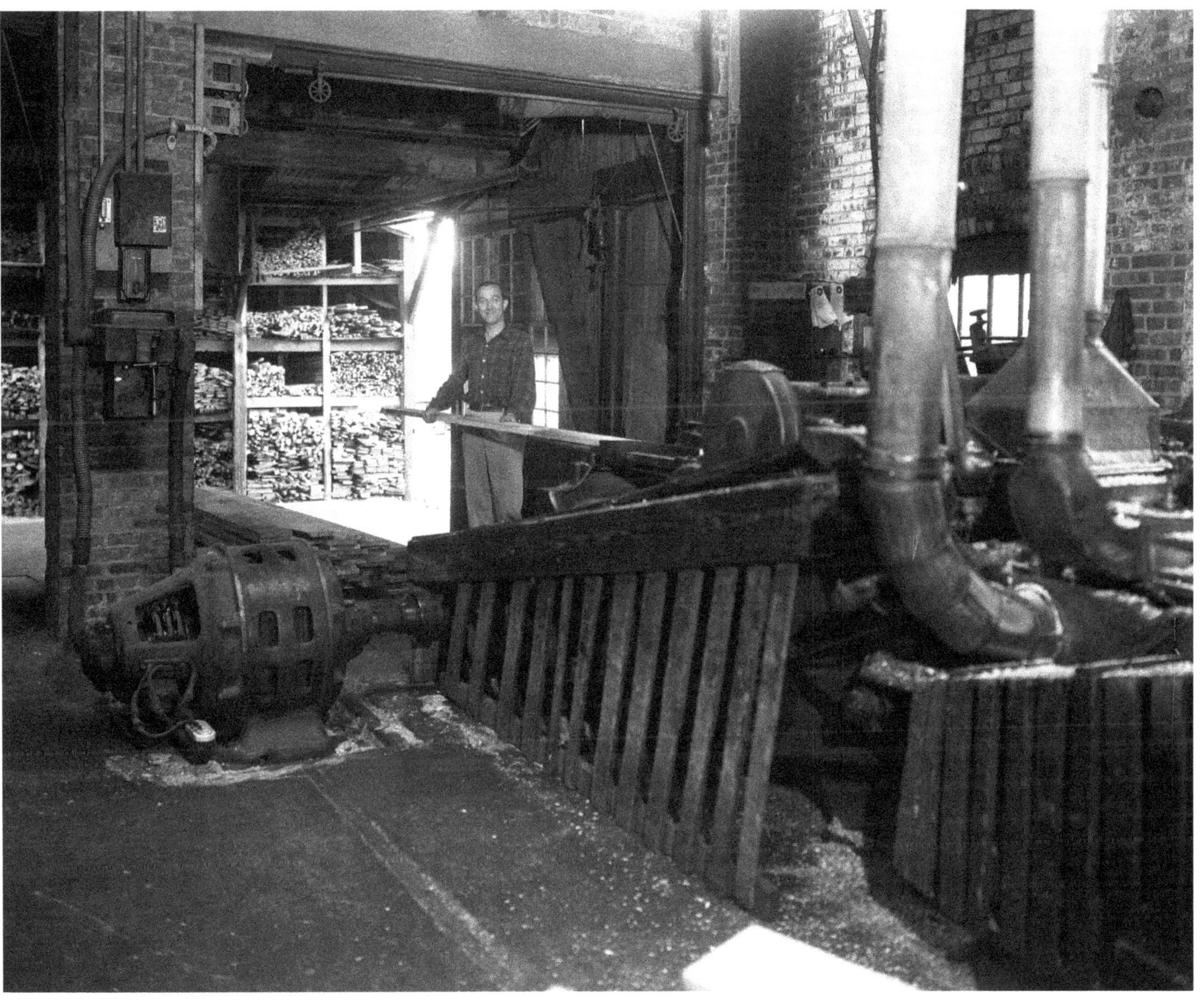

A look at machinery used to make lumber—in high demand for the building boom that would follow the end of the war—although much of that building would be for homes in Nassau and Suffolk counties, as Queens faced its share of departures for points east.

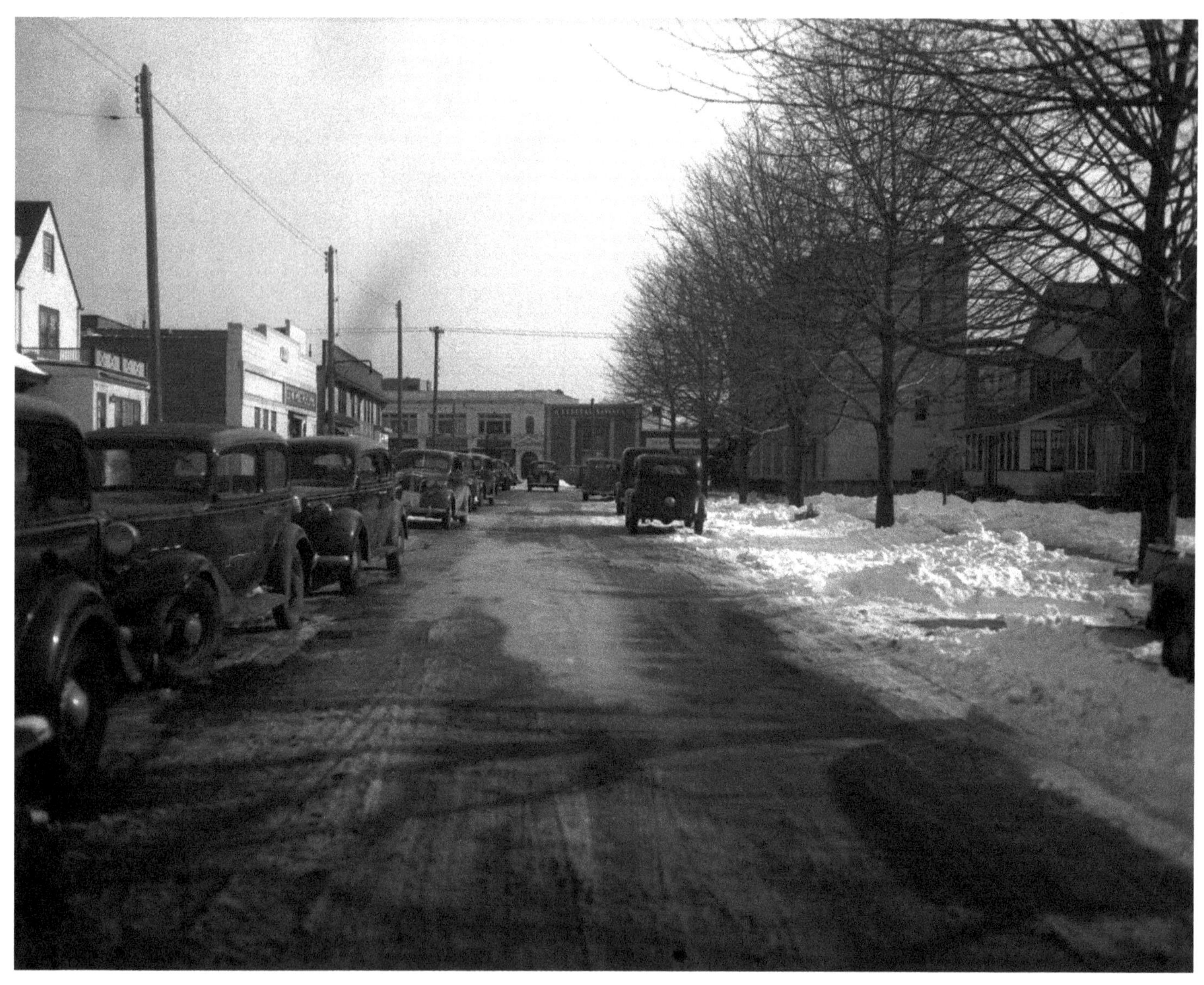

Looking toward Jamaica Avenue from 217 Street in Queens Village in 1947, after a snowstorm has blanketed the city.

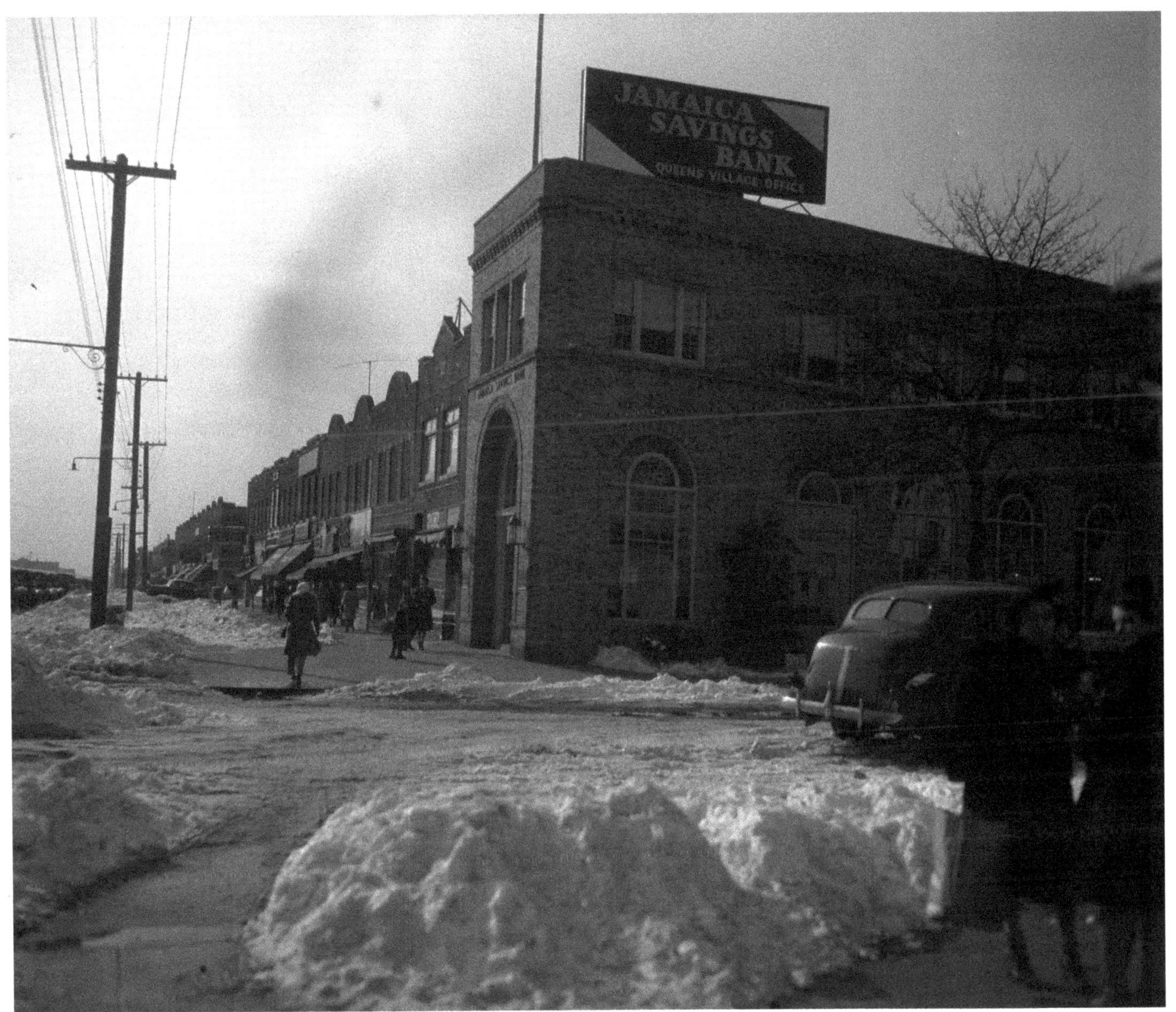

The Queens Village branch of the Jamaica Savings Bank, located on Jamaica Avenue at 217 Street. The bank was in existence for well over a century and was known for its beautifully designed buildings, particularly its Beaux-Arts Jamaica headquarters.

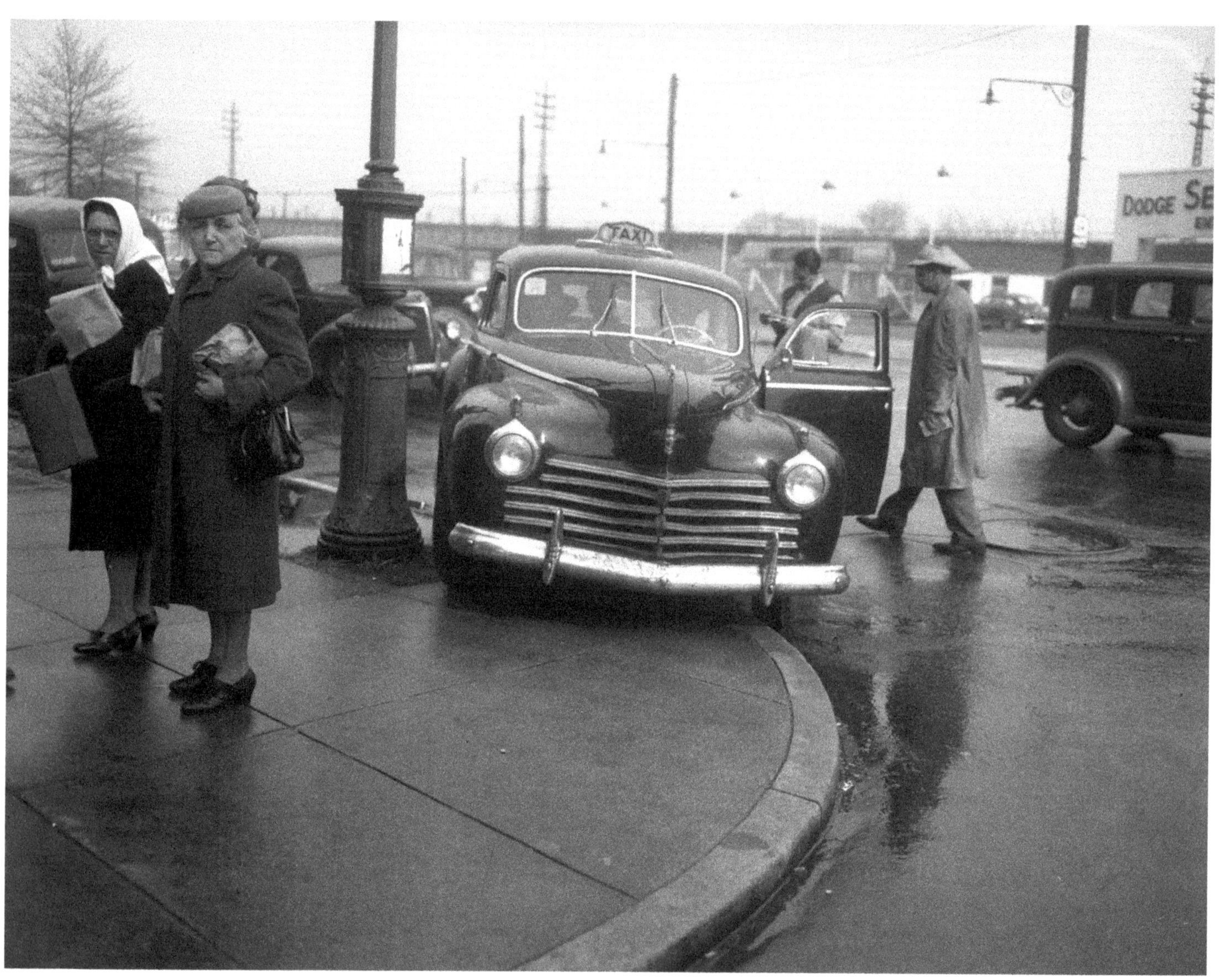

These ladies look more annoyed by having their photograph taken than by the large taxi that has jumped the curb at 212th and Jamaica Avenue in Hollis, in a 1947 accident.

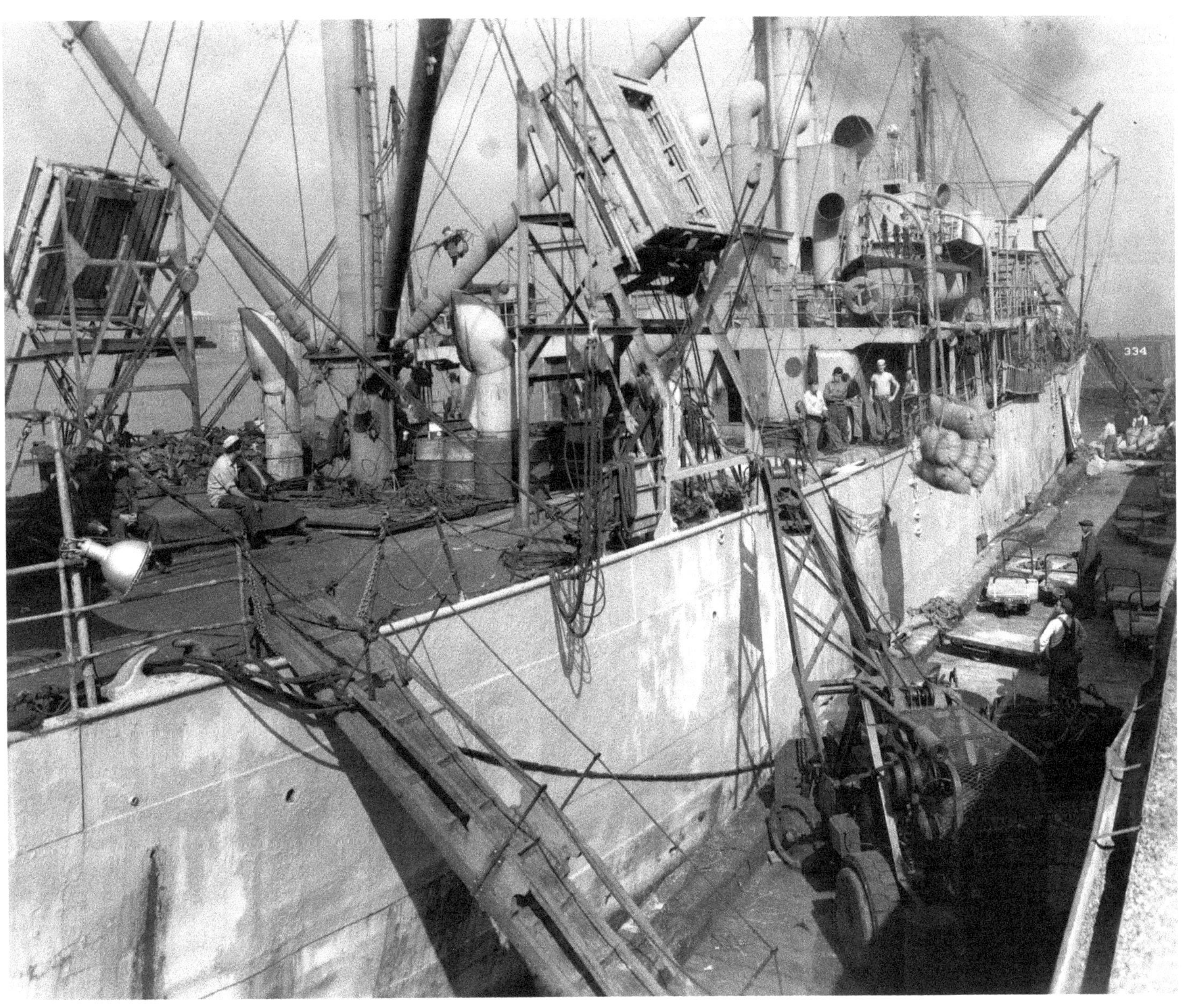

Not to be outdone by the docks of the Brooklyn Navy Yard and Red Hook, Queens did its part during the war. Seen here, a cargo ship is being unloaded at the East River dock at a Queens manufacturing plant a few years after the war ended.

The massive Long Island City headquarters of E. R. Squibb & Sons was located on Northern Boulevard. Squibb later joined with another New York–based pharmaceutical giant, Bristol-Myers, in a larger merger. E. R. Squibb died in 1900, but his sons Dr. Edward H. Squibb and Charles F. Squibb carried on the family business.

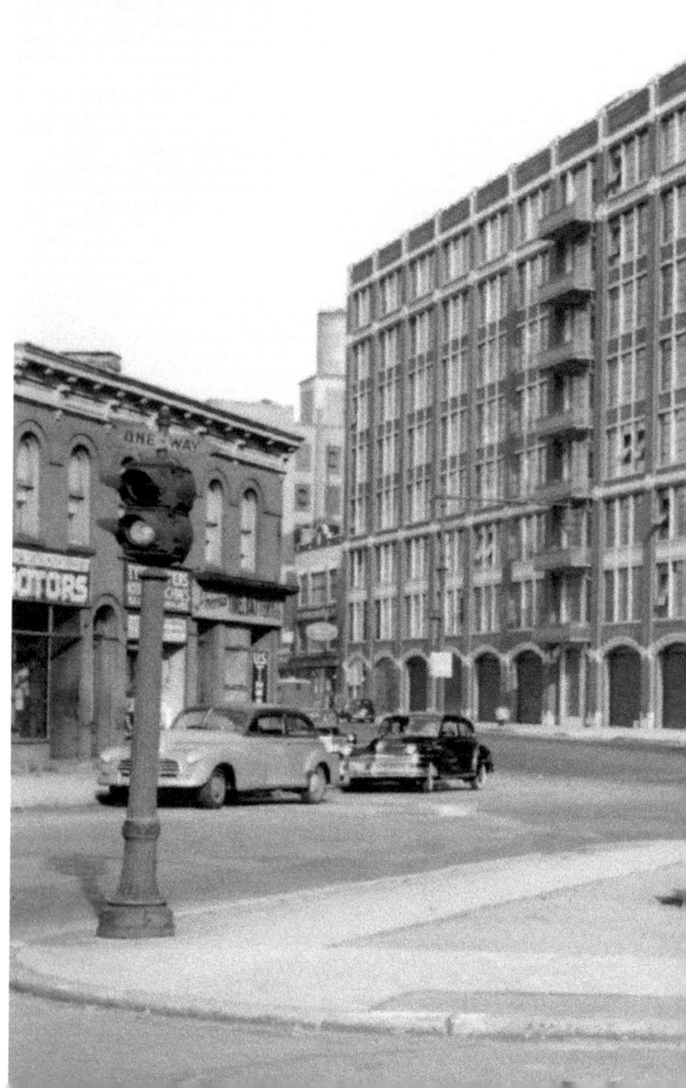

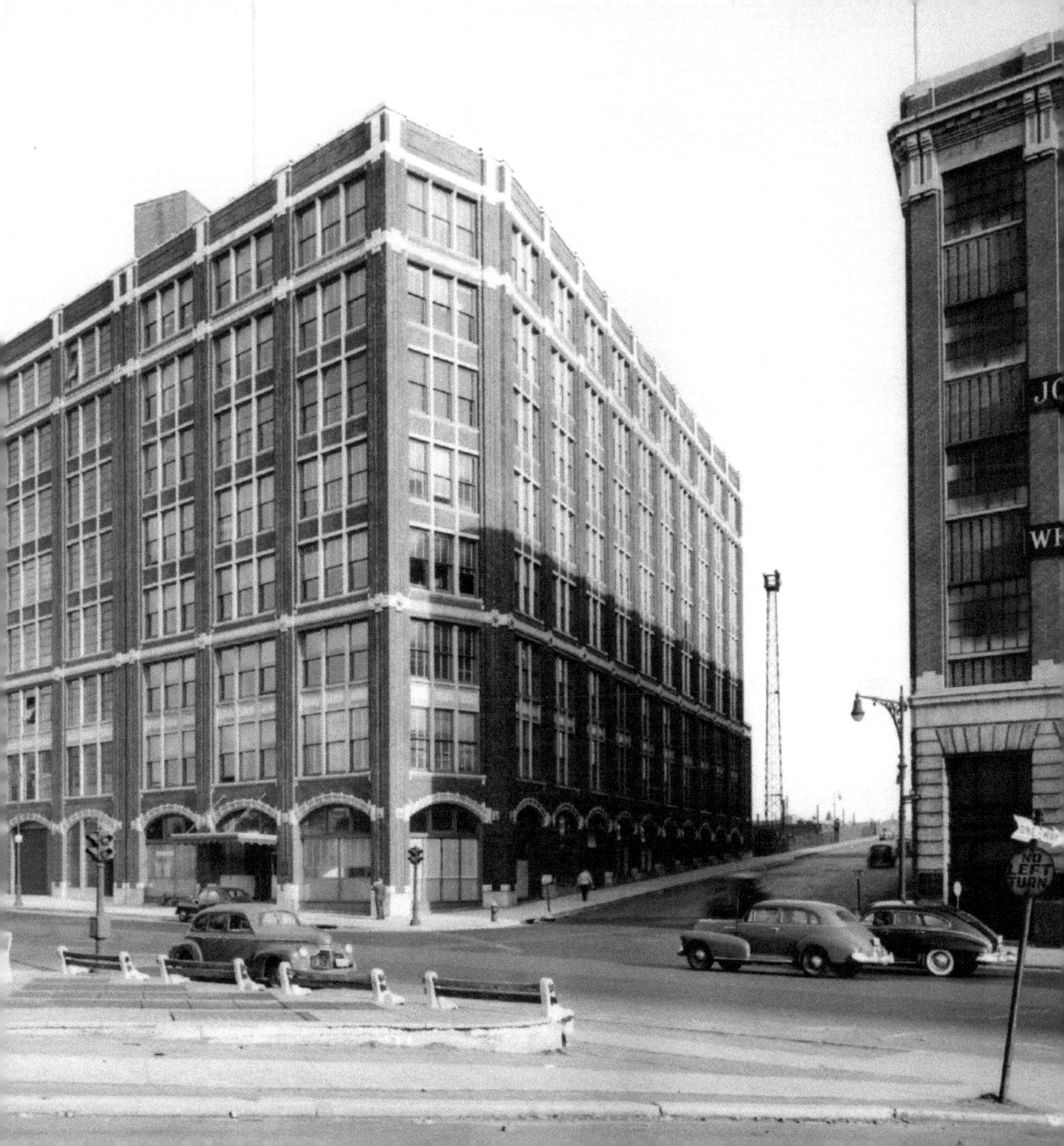
NO
LEFT
TURN

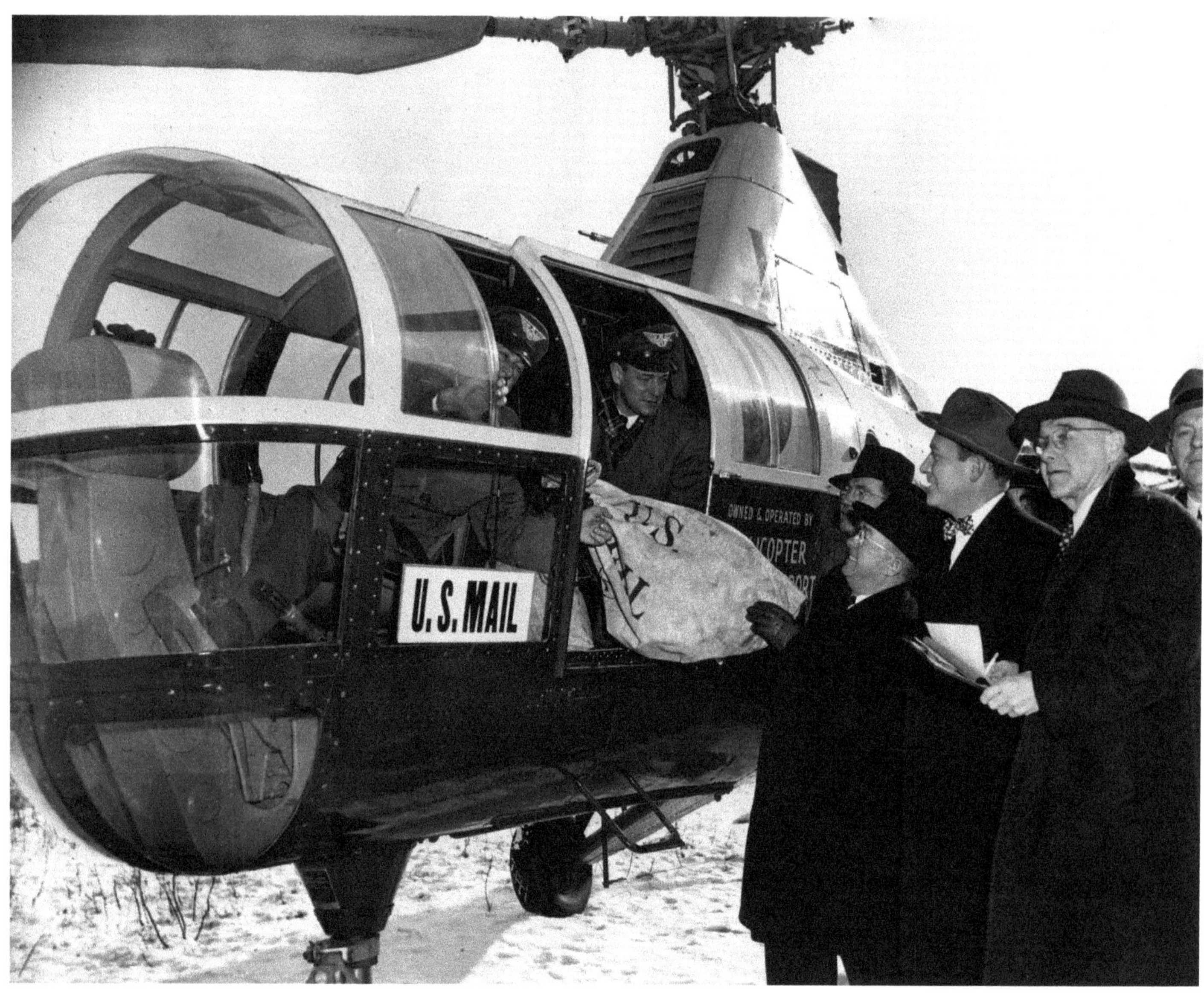

With LaGuardia's airport in Elmhurst getting into full swing, here is the first helicopter mail service flight by the United States Postal Service, an experiment with the new technology. Pictured (left to right) are Pierce H. Power, the Queens Chamber of Commerce vice-president, along with Long Island City postmaster Moses Symington, borough president James Lundy, and Francis X. Hussey, Superintendent of the Mails.

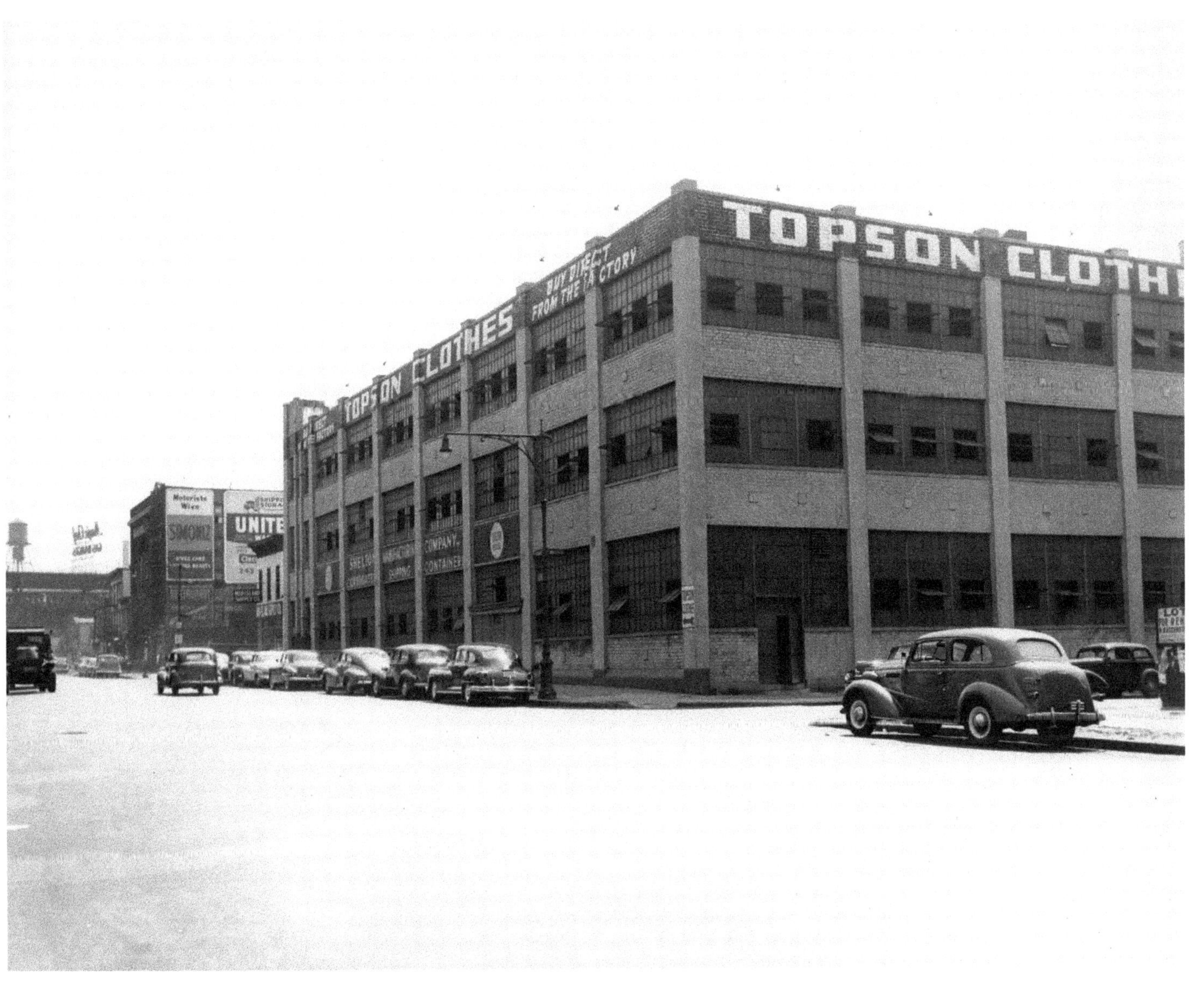

Long Island City was home to a variety of industries in 1948. Here is a view looking north along Jackson Avenue at some of the businesses, including the Topson clothing factory, which as the sign advertises also did some of its own discount retailing.

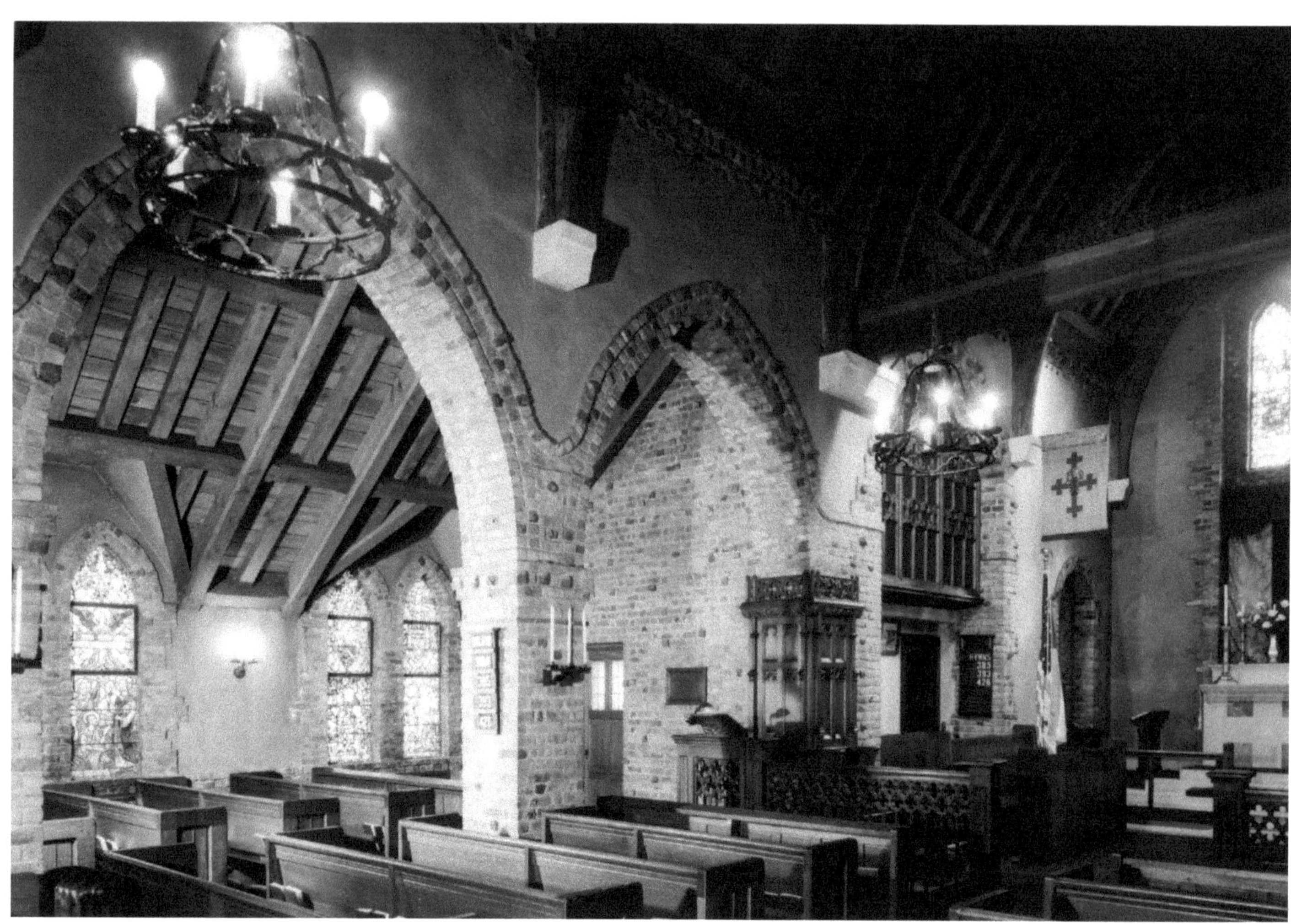

The English Gothic arches of St. Luke's Church, in Forest Hills. The church was designed by Robert Tappen, an architect who was a member of the Episcopal congregation. Tappen was overseeing construction of the Cathedral of St. John the Divine in Manhattan (one of the city's greatest houses of worship) by day and devoted his spare time to this smaller project, which features soaring ceilings and a shape much like an upturned ship from the inside, with high stained-glass windows allowing ample light to fill the nave.

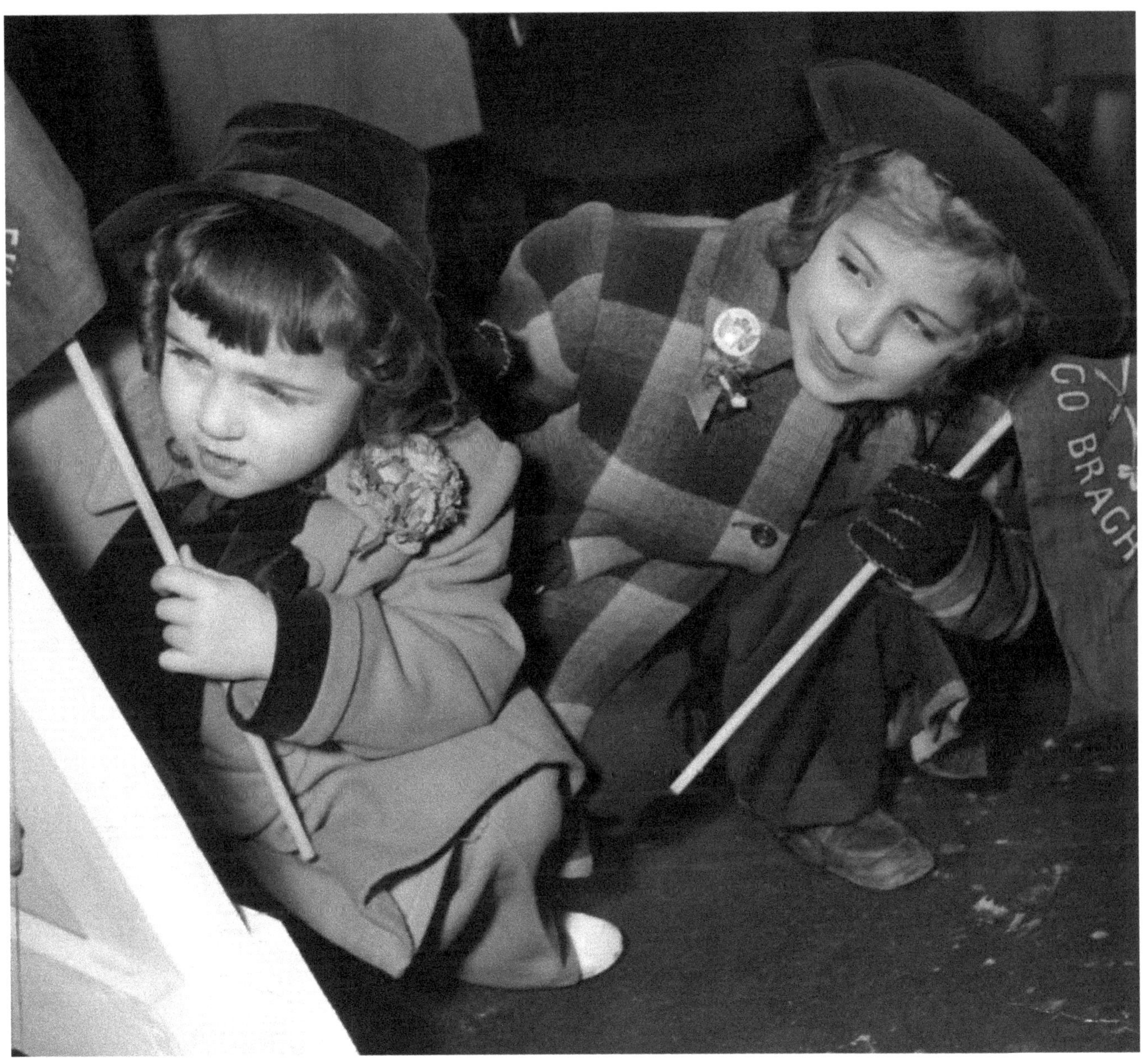

Two young girls crane their necks to get a look at the marchers participating in the oldest, largest, and greatest St. Patrick's Day parade in the world. Queens has always had a large concentration of Americans of Irish descent—from Woodside to Bayside to the Rockaways—and the annual event not only includes many Irish-American marchers from schools, the NYPD, FDNY, and other organizations, but also draws large crowds from the borough.

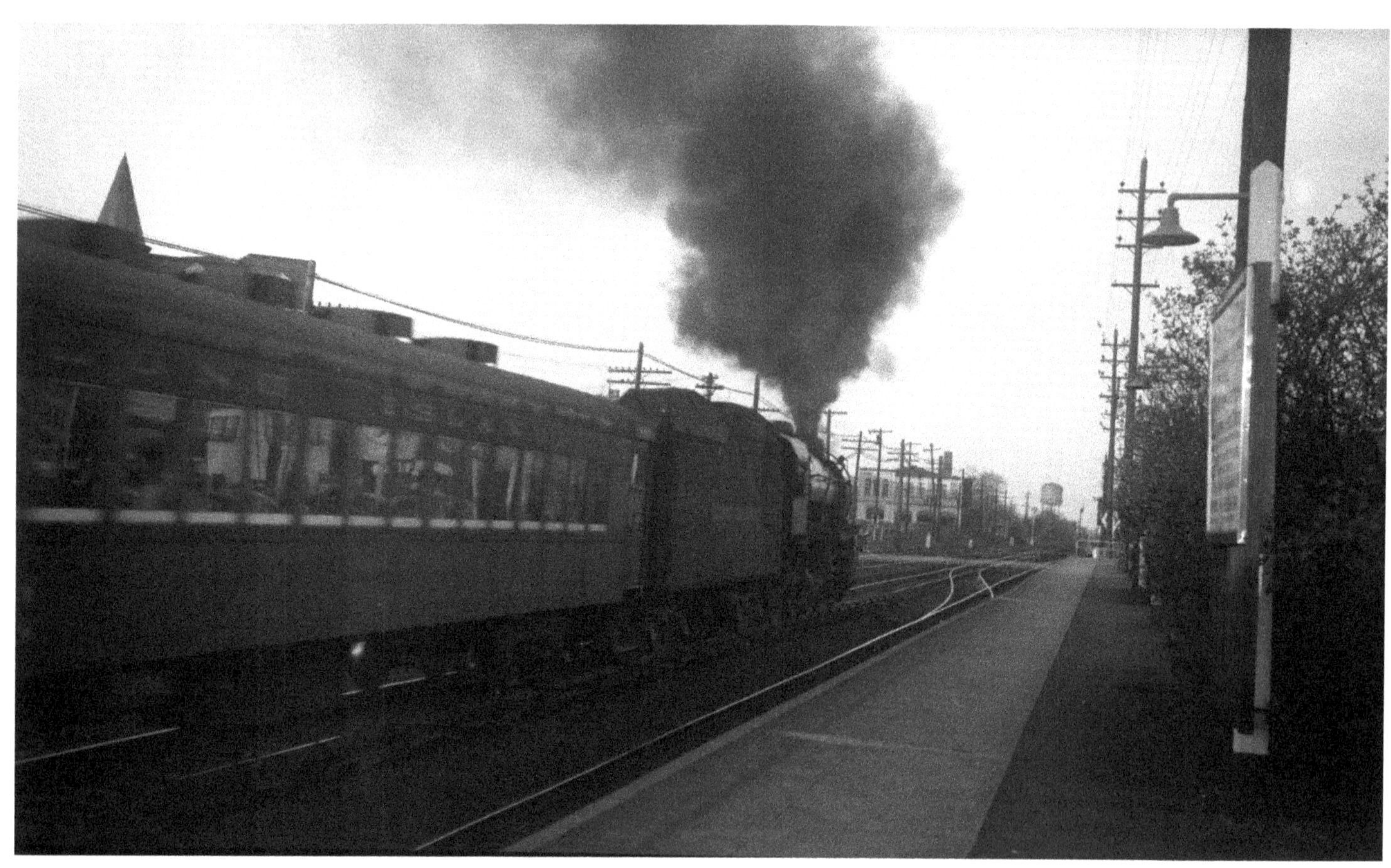

A view of the Long Island Railroad's G-55 engine belching out thick, black smoke as it pulls a passenger car west toward Manhattan. Today the trains are powered by electricity and are nearly silent as they roll through the various neighborhoods of the borough.

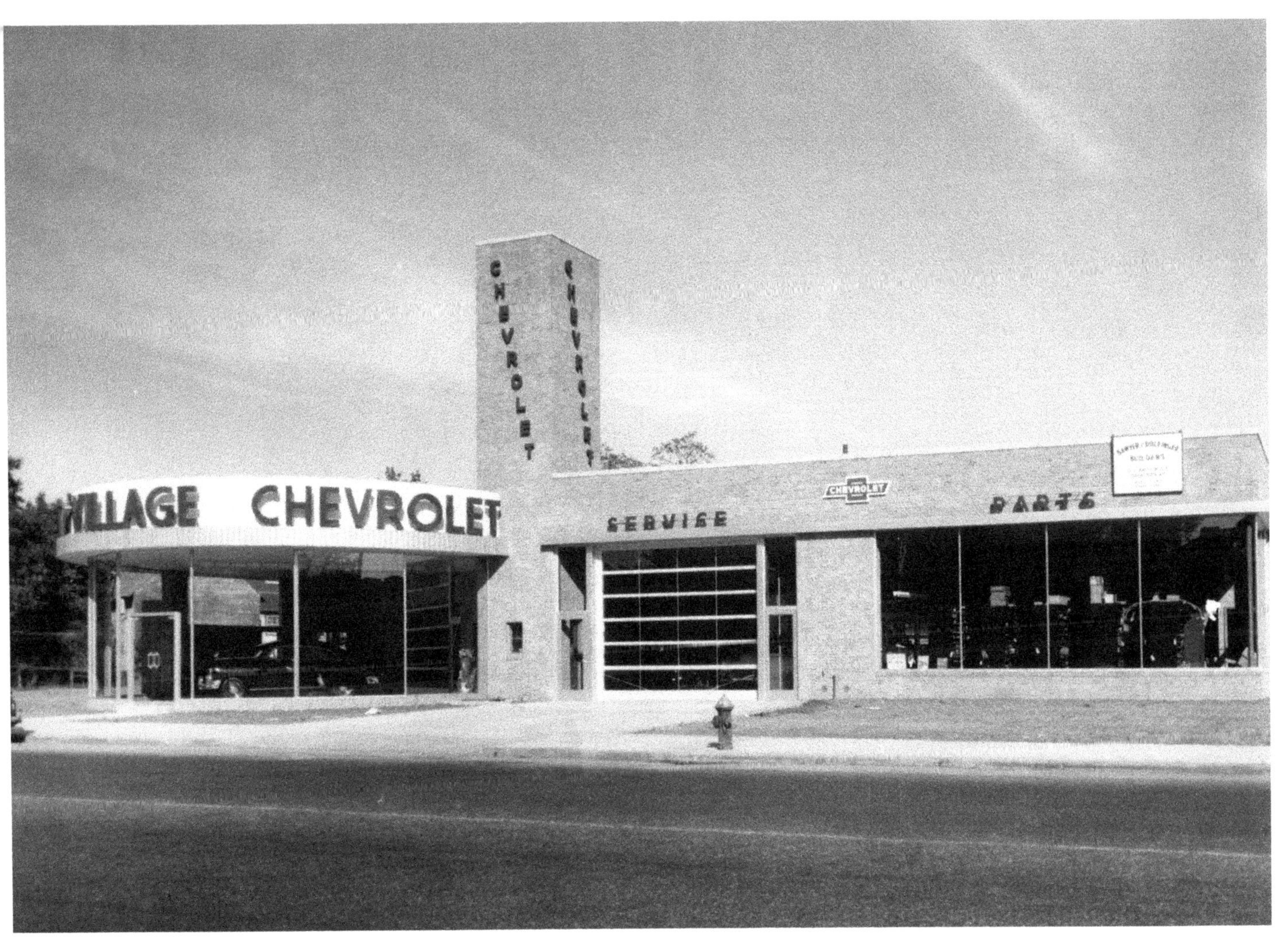

Village Chevrolet received a Best Building award in 1951 for "Excellence in Design and Civic Value" for its dealership, located in Queens Village at 222nd Street and Jamaica Avenue.

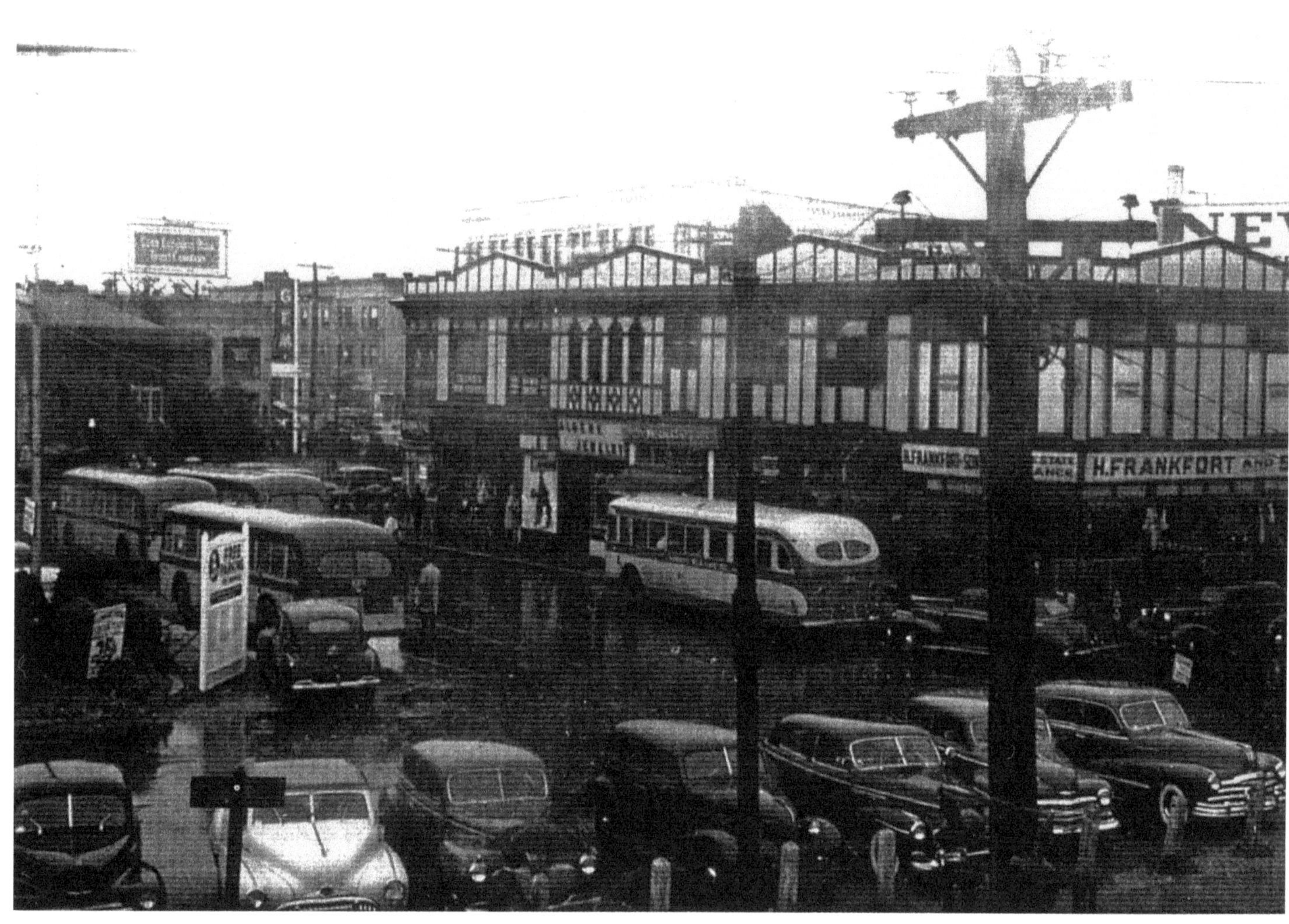

In Queens as across the nation, city leaders came to view streetcars as an outdated mode of transportation, replacing them with buses in the 1930s and 1940s. Buses ferried railroad commuters to and from stations, as parking was not always available. Seen here in 1953 is the Far Rockaway Bus Terminal located outside the railroad station that keeps the isolated community connected to the rest of the city.

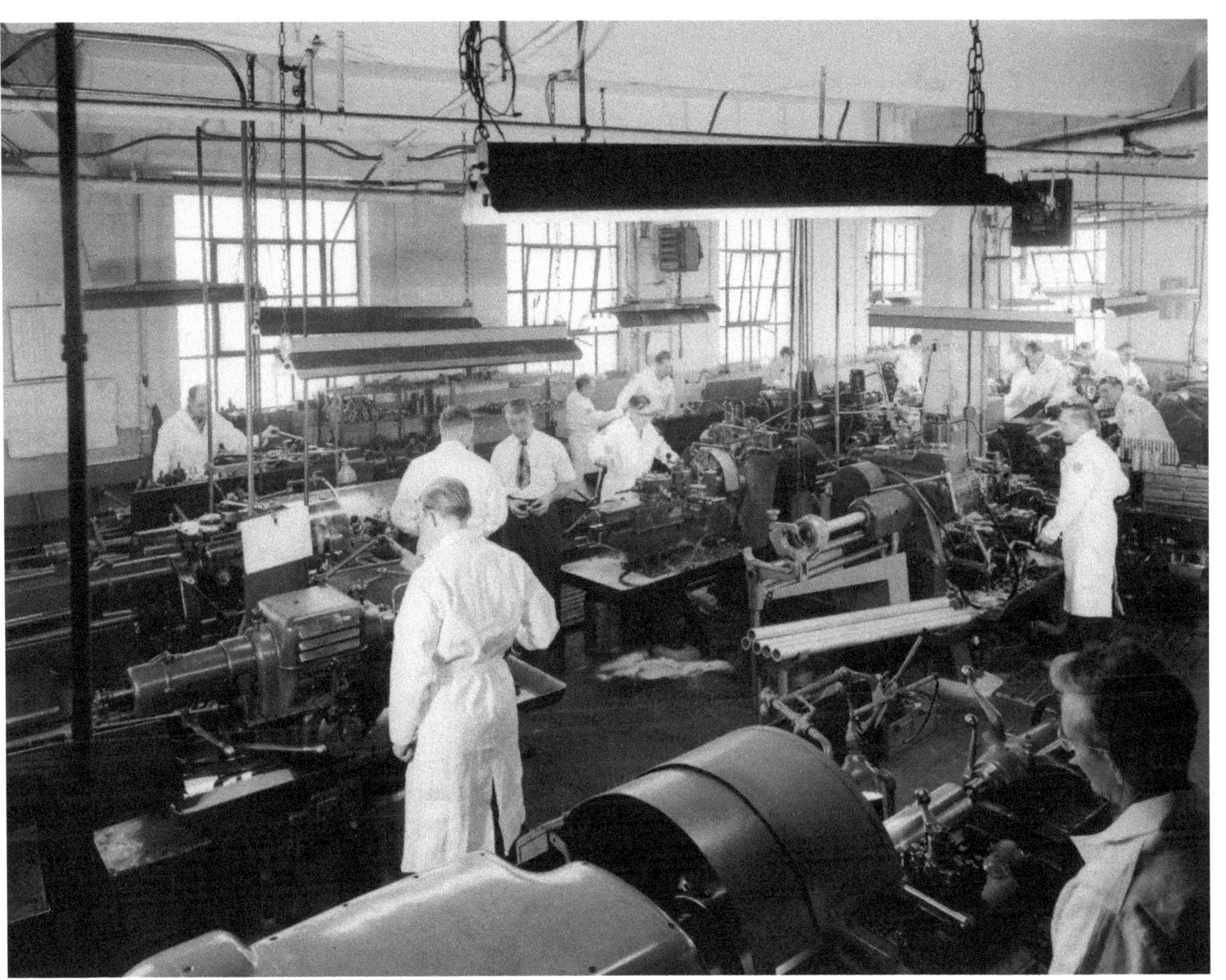

A view from the balcony of the F & R Machine Works factory located at 44th Street and Astoria Boulevard, in full swing in 1953.

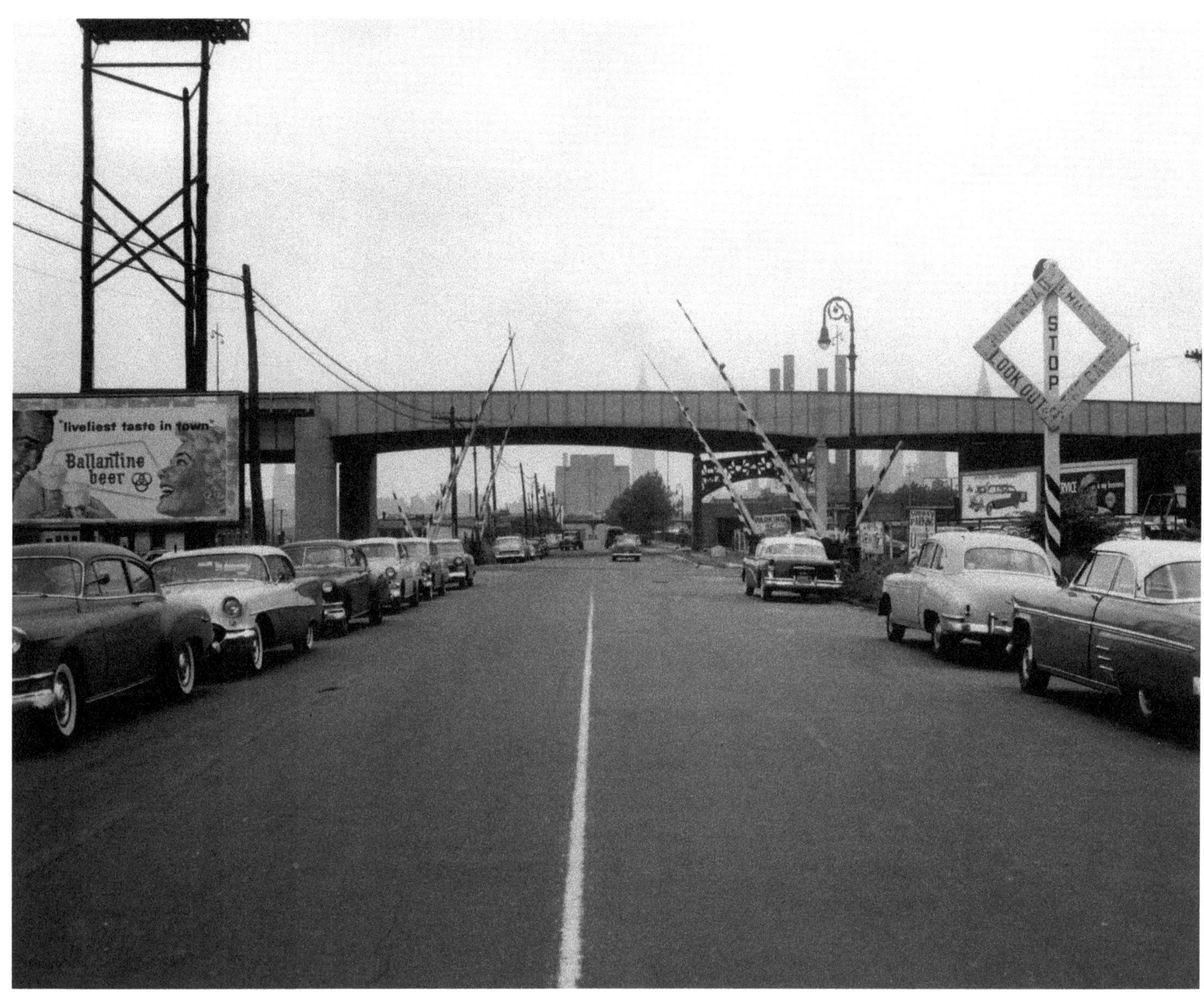

The Borden Avenue train crossing in 1956, looking west toward Manhattan, whose tall buildings can be seen in the far distance. Such crossings were eventually moved to overpasses or underpasses, or traffic was diverted, as cars became more popular and impatient New Yorkers could not stand to wait.

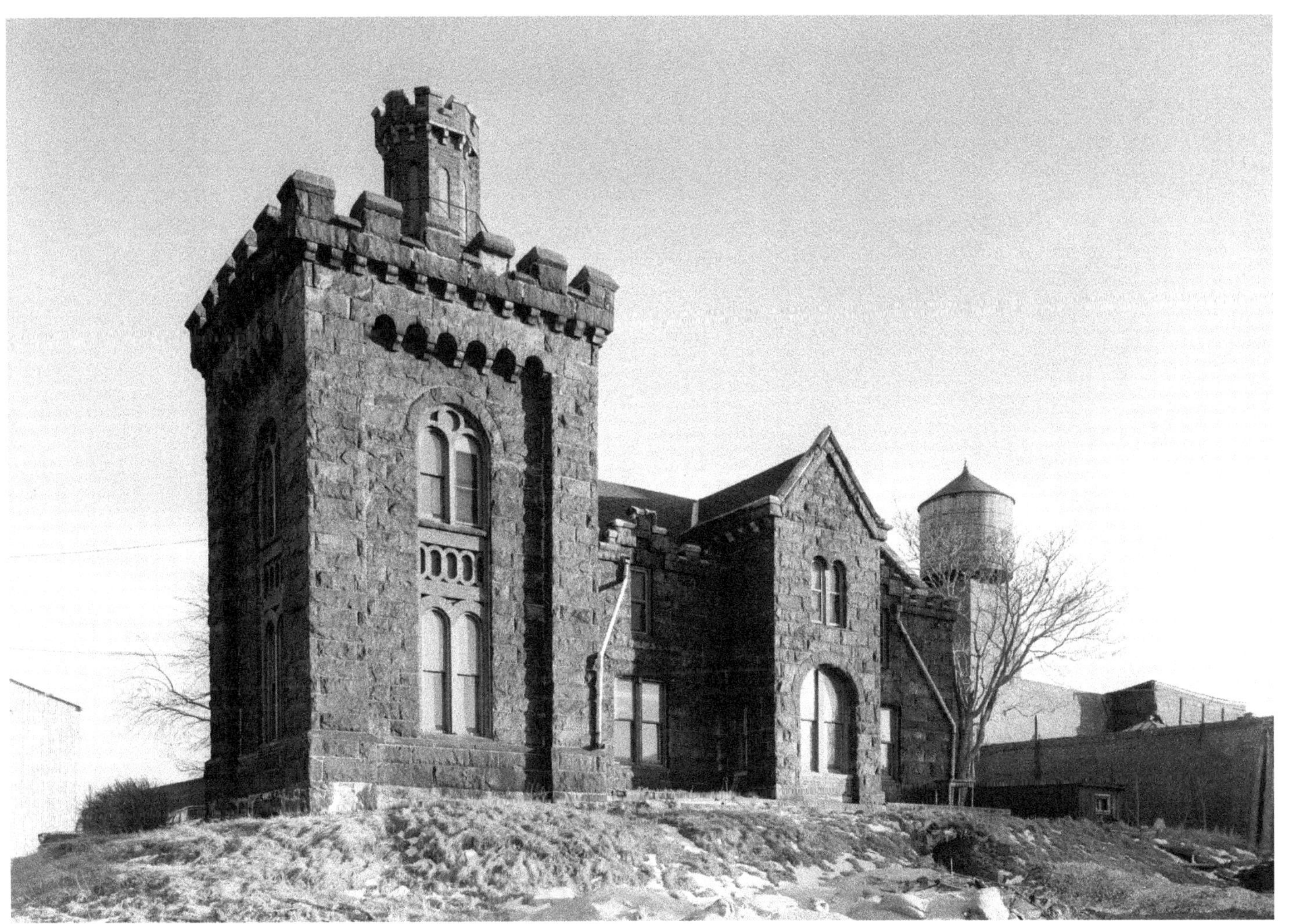

Seen here in 1960, a few years before its demolition, Bodine Castle was long a Ravenswood landmark.

Following Spread: Bathers enjoy the sunshine in August 1959 at Linden Woods Swim Club in Howard Beach, named for the vast woodlands that once covered the peninsula, just north of Rockaway, before it was developed. Clearly, attitudes toward swimwear had relaxed significantly by the middle of the century as seen by the bathing suits worn by club members.

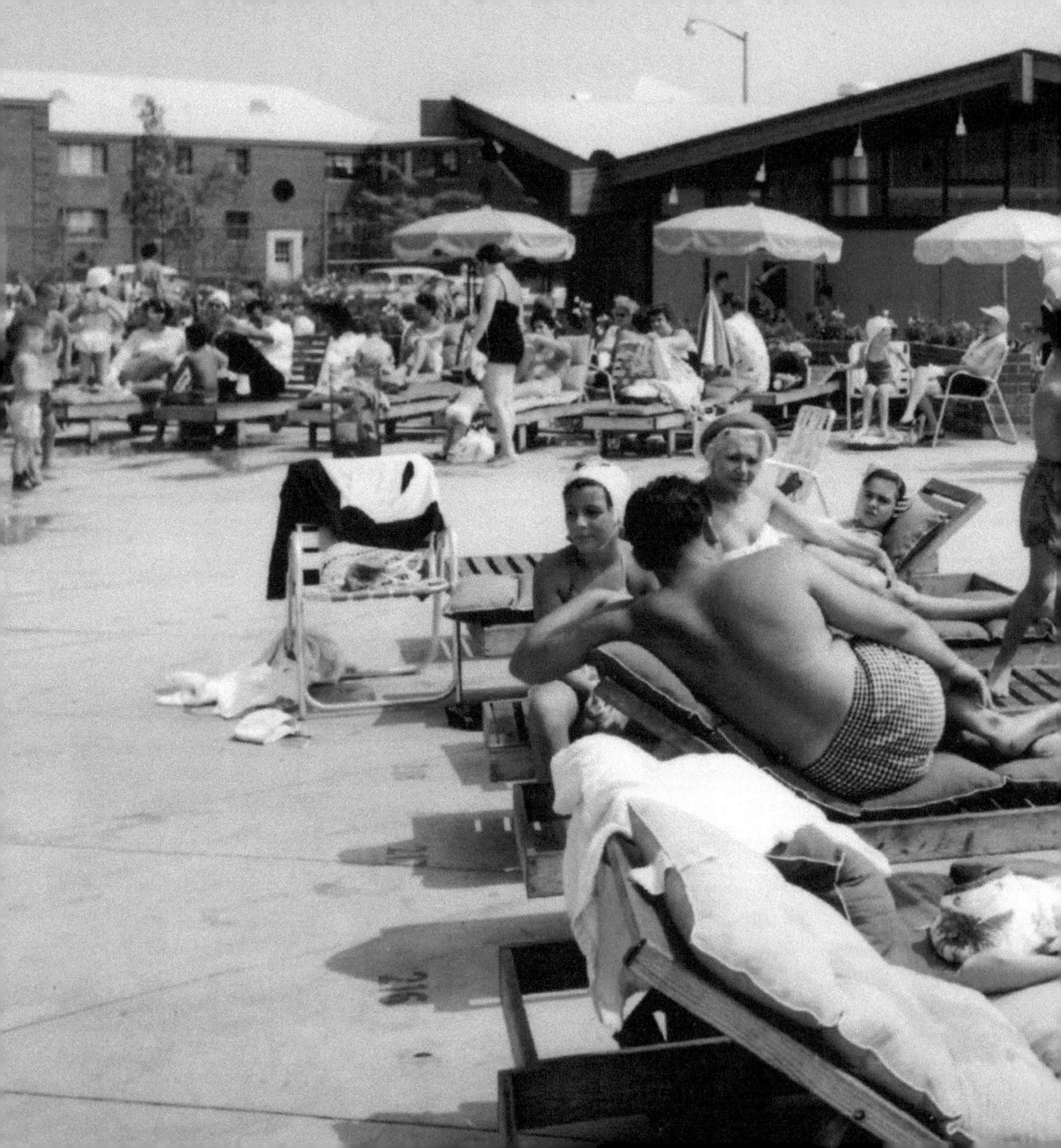

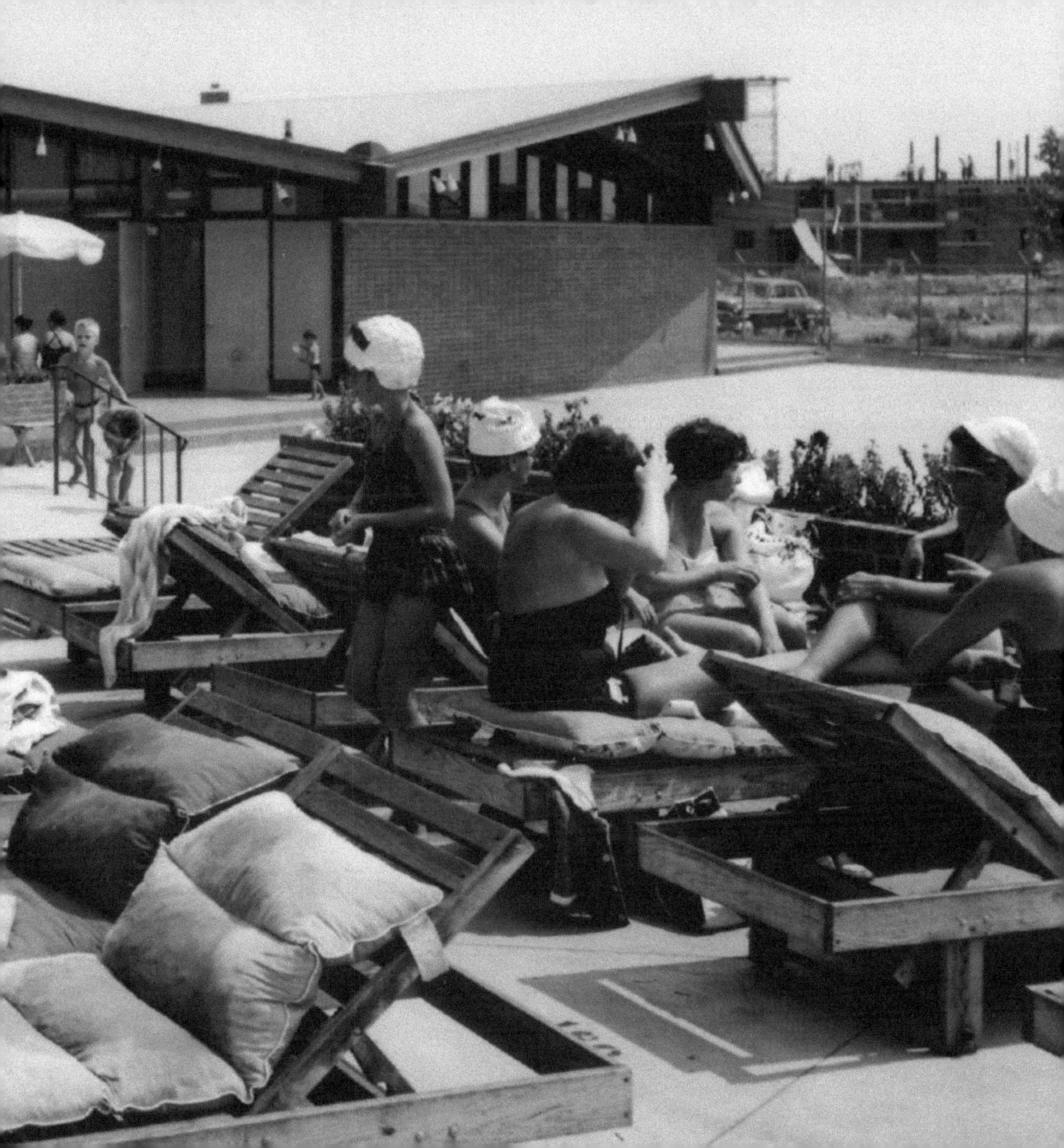

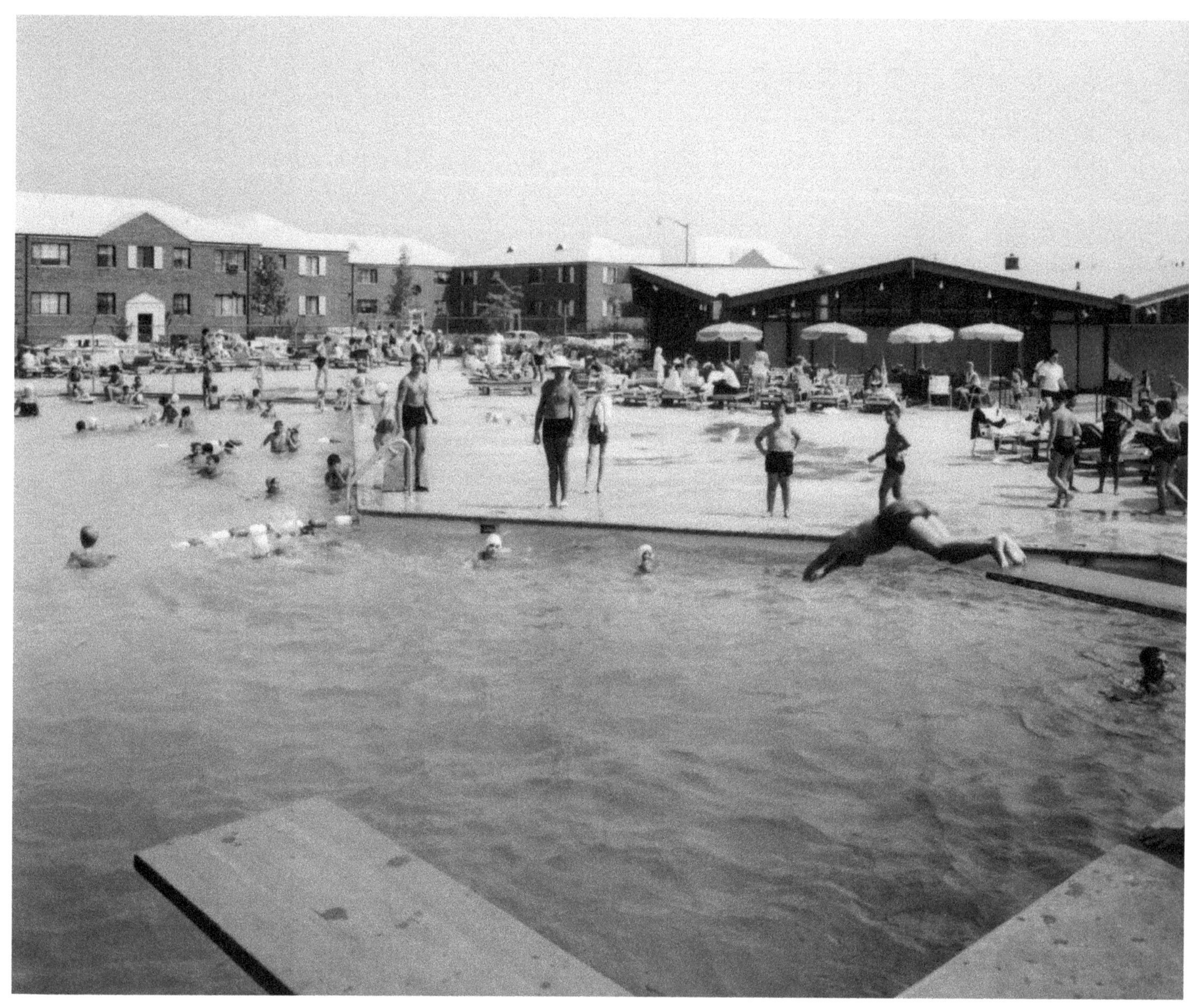

Time for a dip in the pool at the Linden Woods Swim Club, in this view from the diving board of the clubhouse.

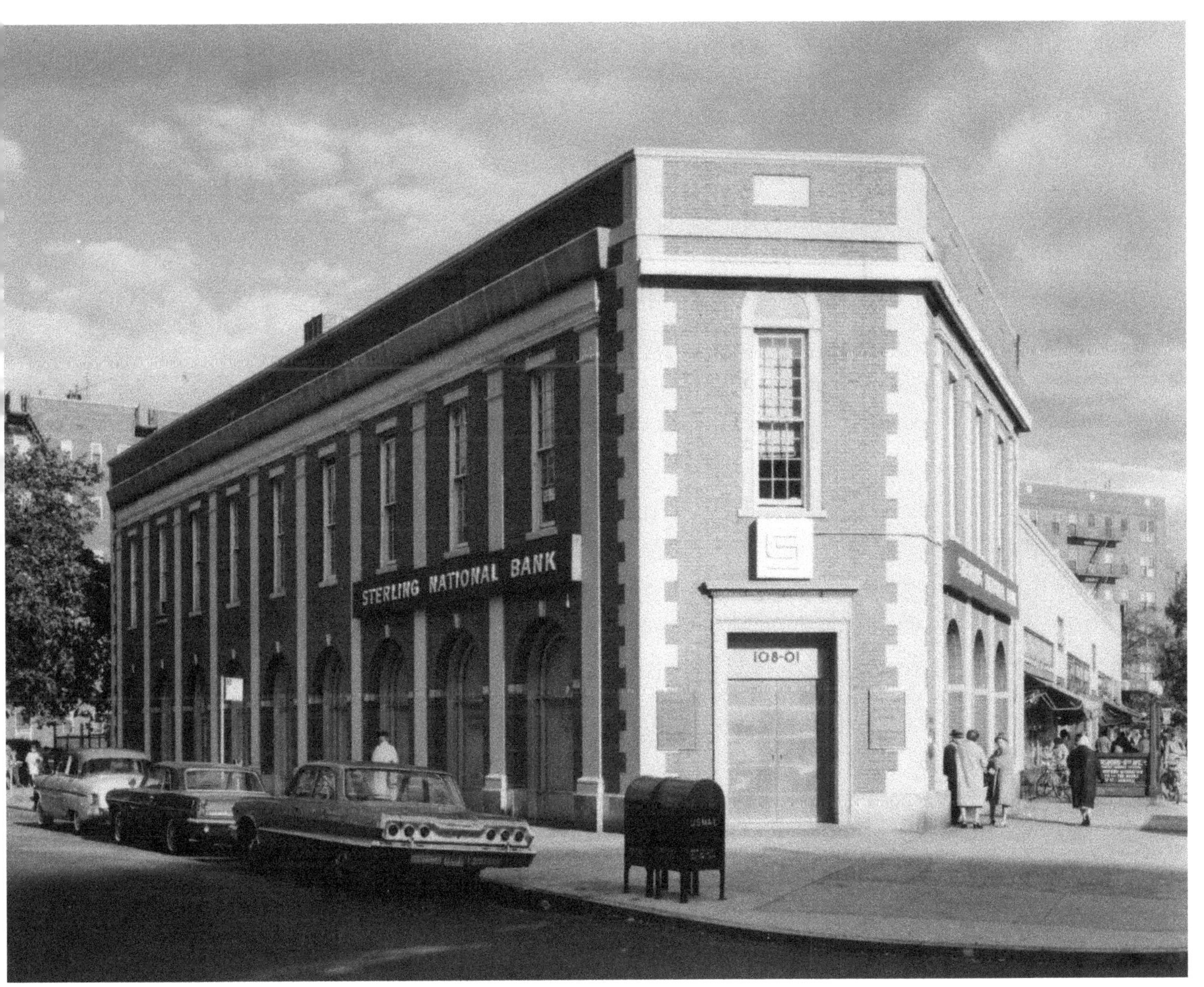

The Sterling National Bank on Queens Boulevard in Forest Hills, around 1963. At one time, the building was used as a Masonic Temple. This unusual bank is still operating near the center of Forest Hills, just steps from the 71st-Continental Avenue subway station, which is just to the right of the bank.

The Marine Air Terminal at LaGuardia Airport seen here in 1968, complete with its "flying frieze" around the top, was built as part of a WPA project and is a shining example of Art Deco architecture. In addition to the frieze is a mural on the round ceiling of the waiting room titled *Flight,* which was created under the Federal Arts Project, a federal program that funneled tax dollars into jobs for artists during the Great Depression. The terminal was built on the bay for seaplanes that made transatlantic flights. It remains in use today.

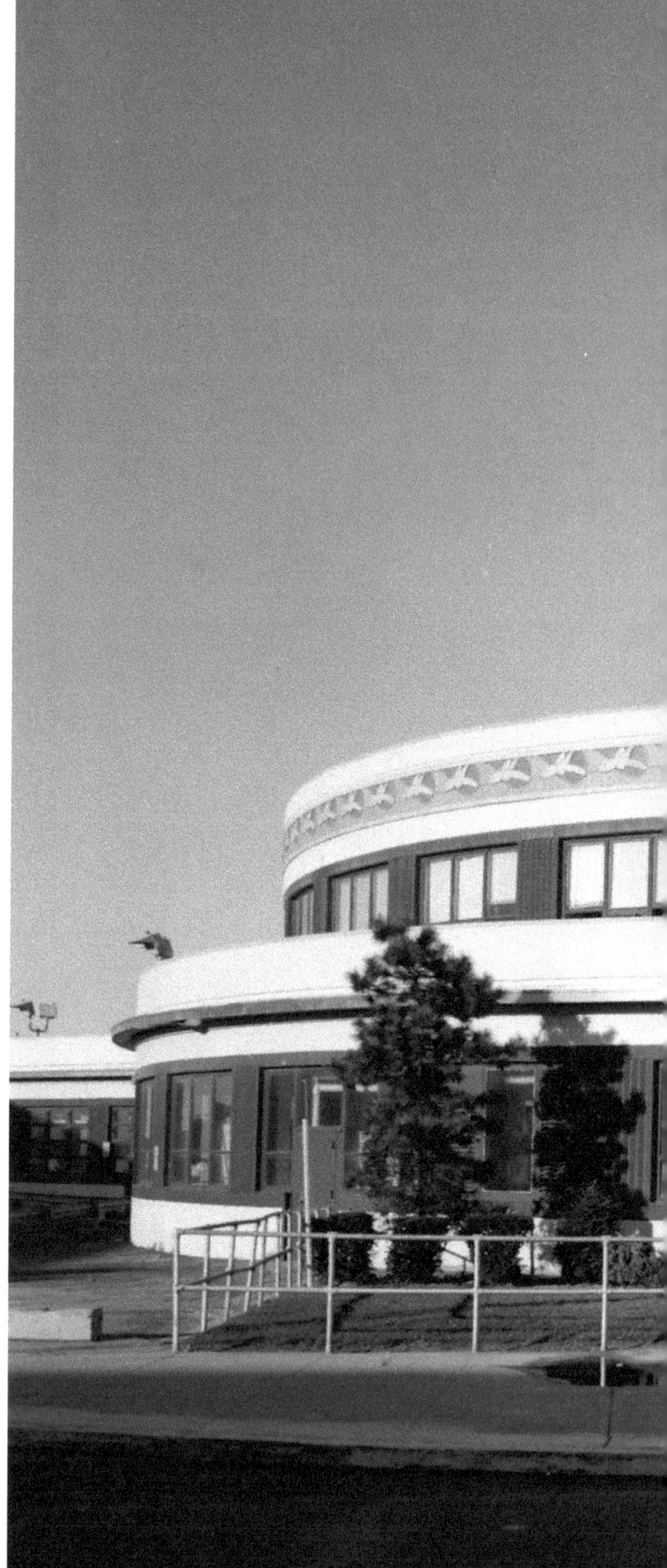

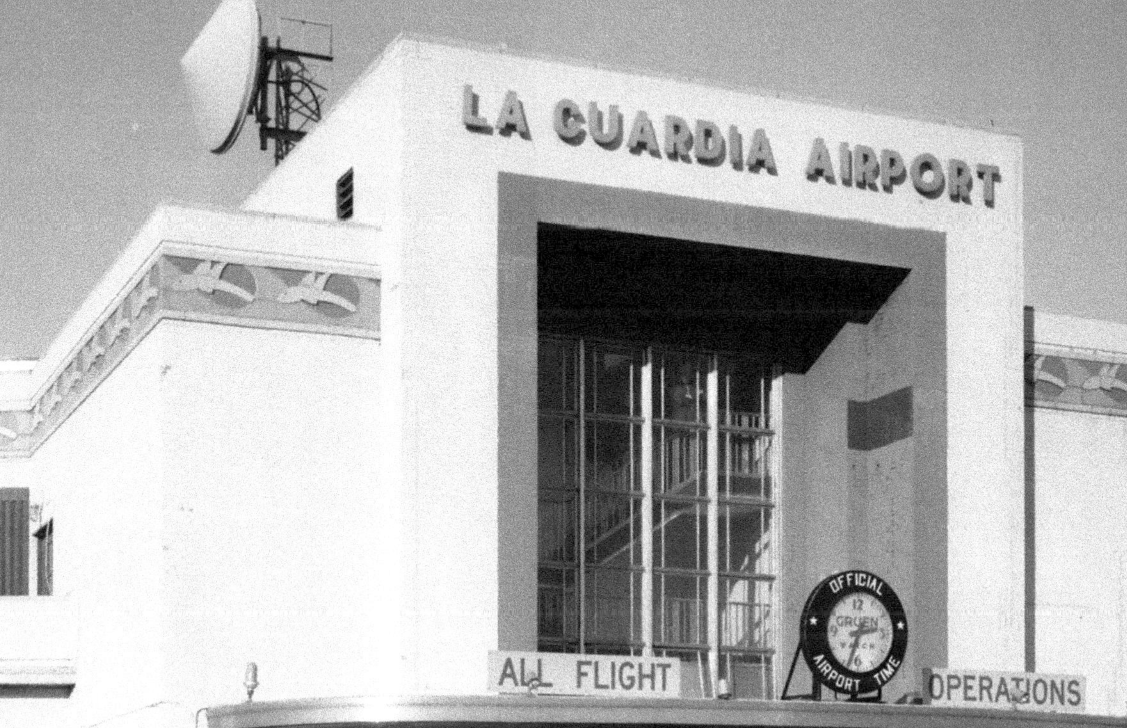
LA GUARDIA AIRPORT
ALL FLIGHT
OFFICIAL
GRUEN
AIRPORT TIME
OPERATIONS

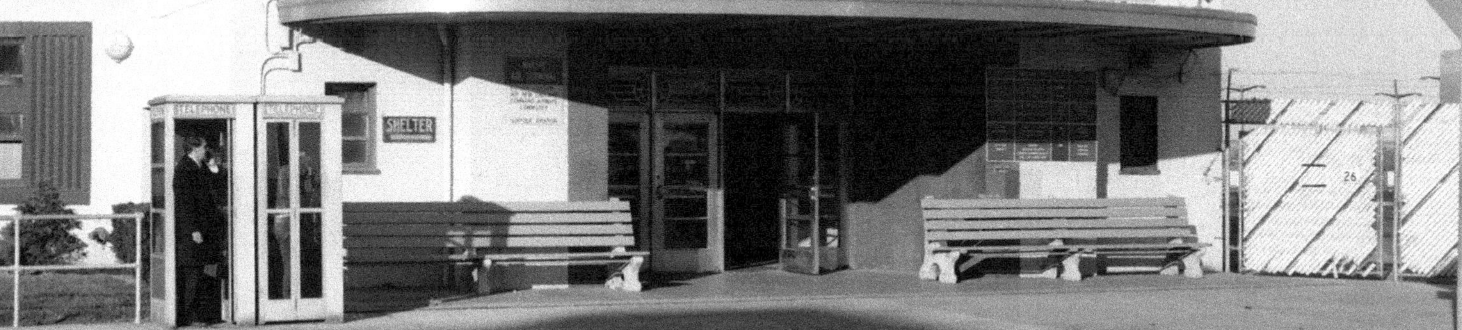
TELEPHONE
TELEPHONE
SHELTER

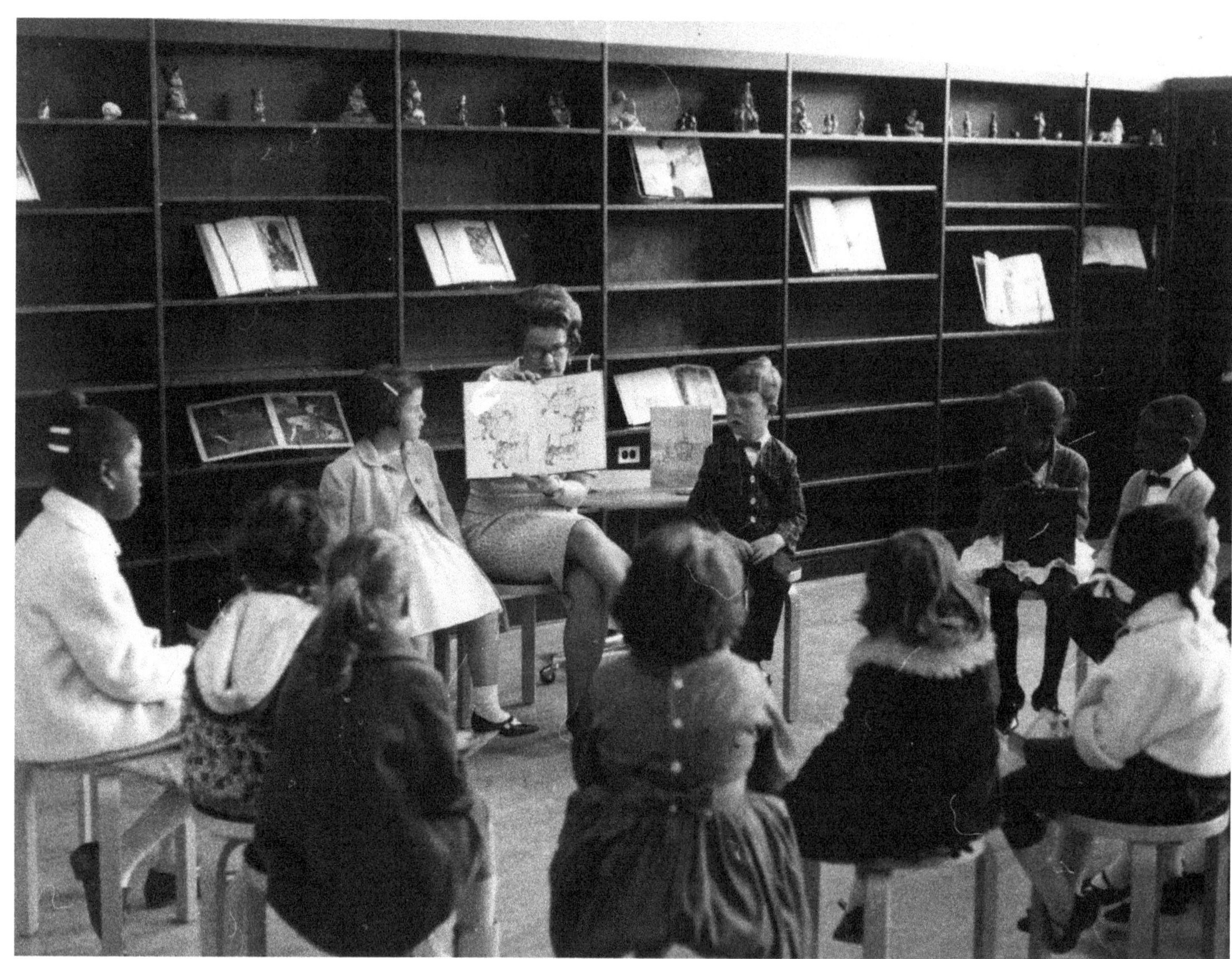

The Queens Borough Public Library has not lost its allure for this multi-ethnic group of youngsters, gathered for story time at a library branch in the 1960s. At a time when issues of segregation rocked the nation, there seems to be no problem in this story room beyond getting a closer look at the pictures.

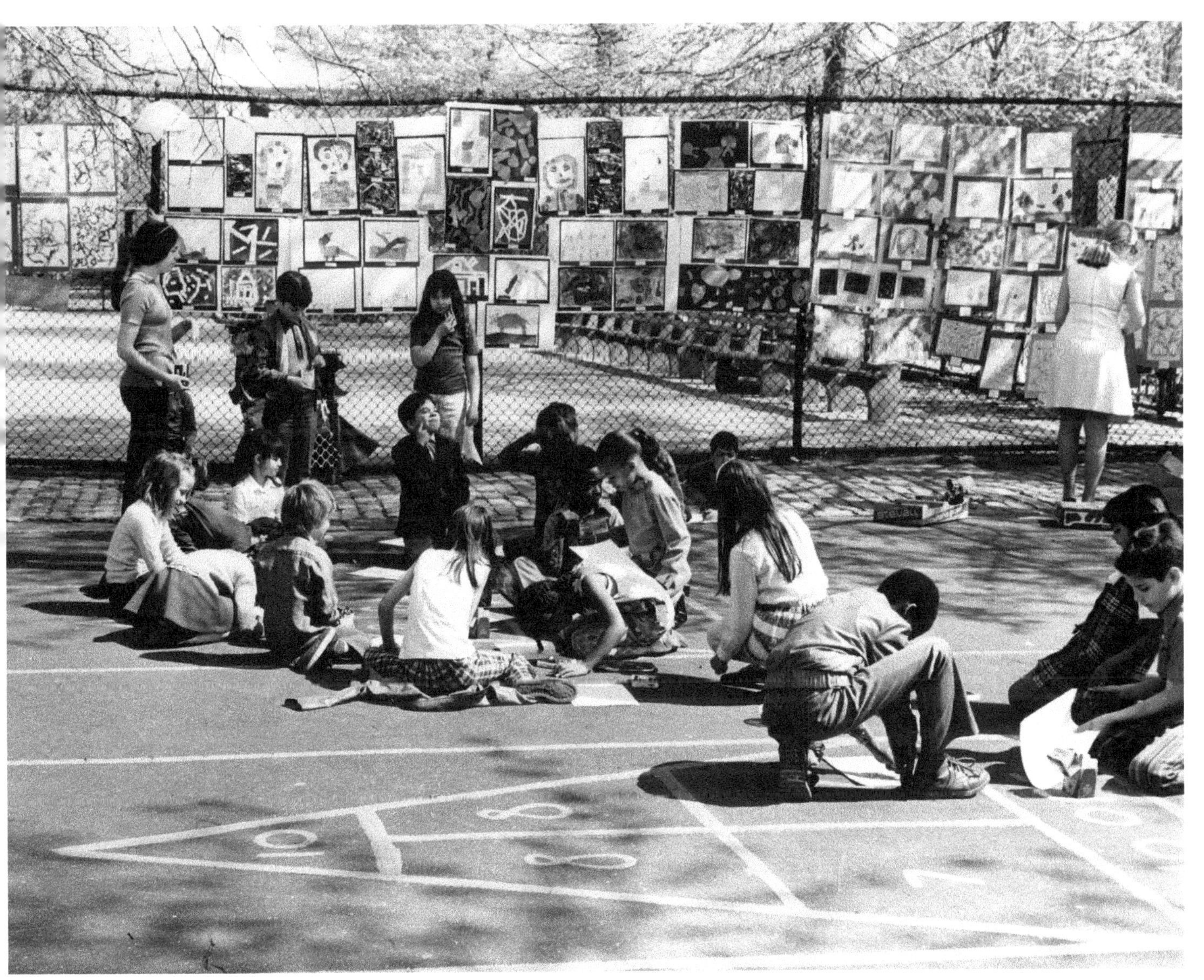

Students at public school 201 in Flushing create art work for an outdoor art show in May 1971

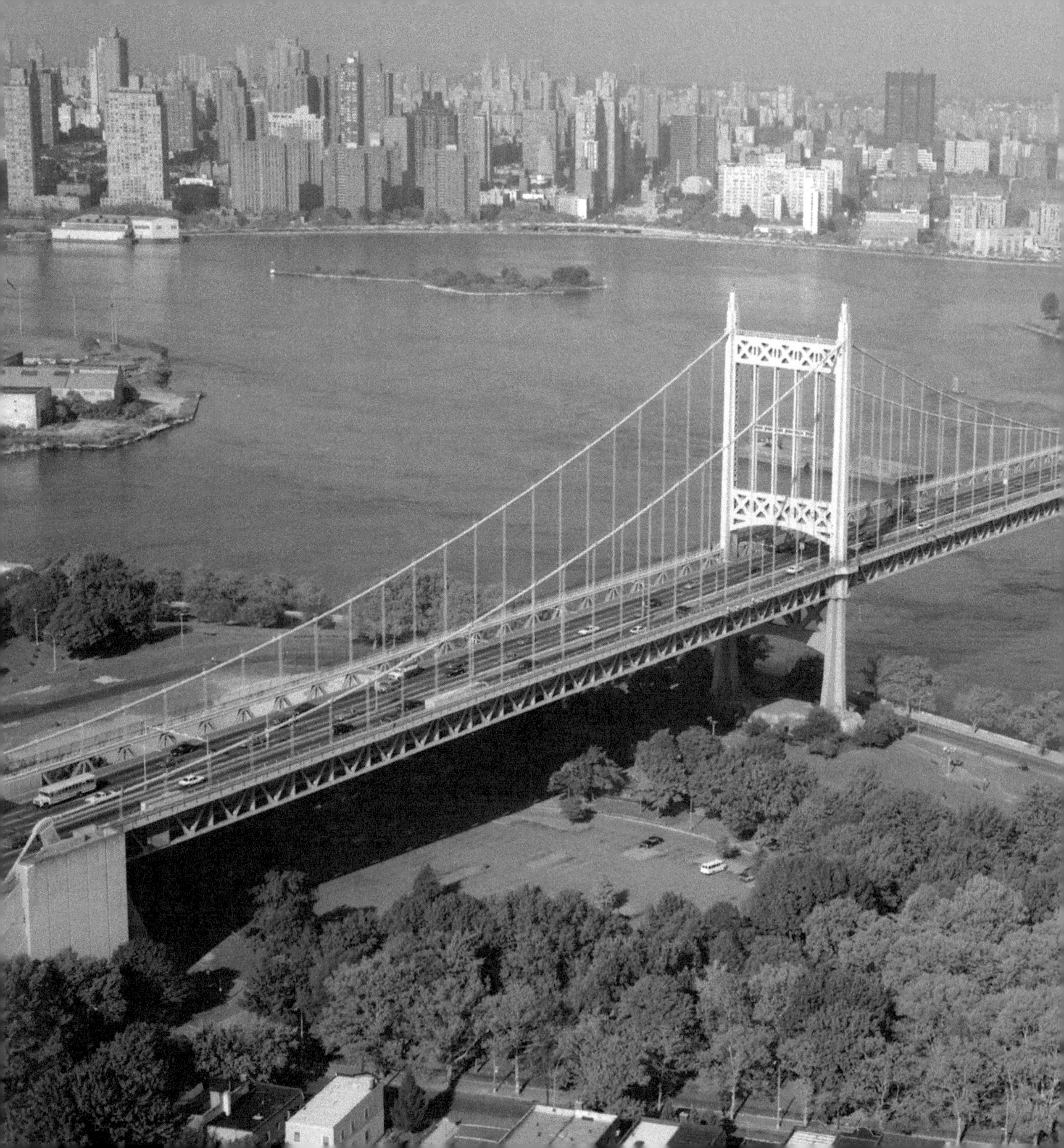

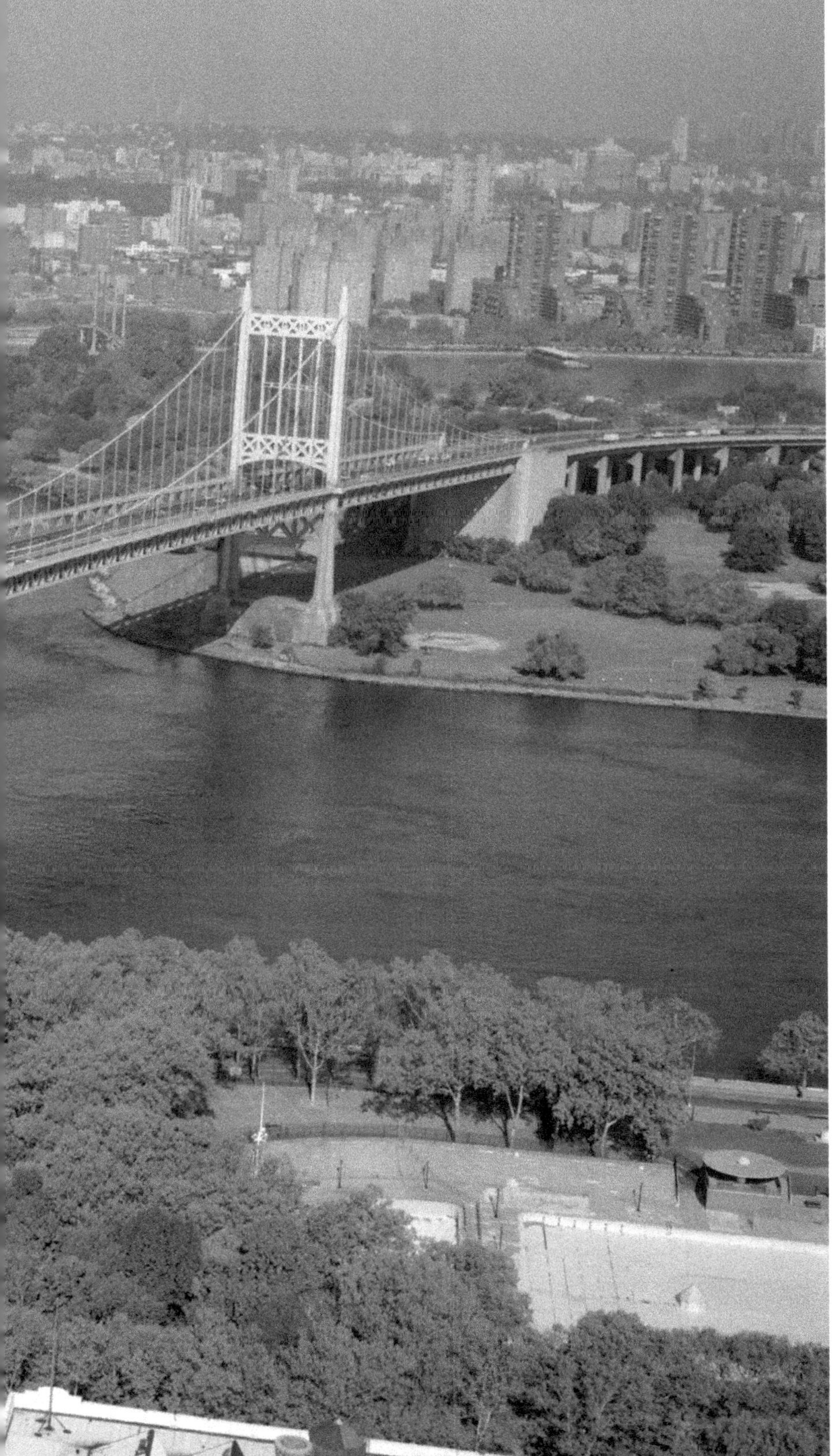

The Robert F. Kennedy (Triborough Bridge), with Astoria in the foreground, upper Manhattan in the background, and Randall's Island in the center, around 1968. Randall's Island has multiple ball fields and today is a popular site for large outdoor concerts.

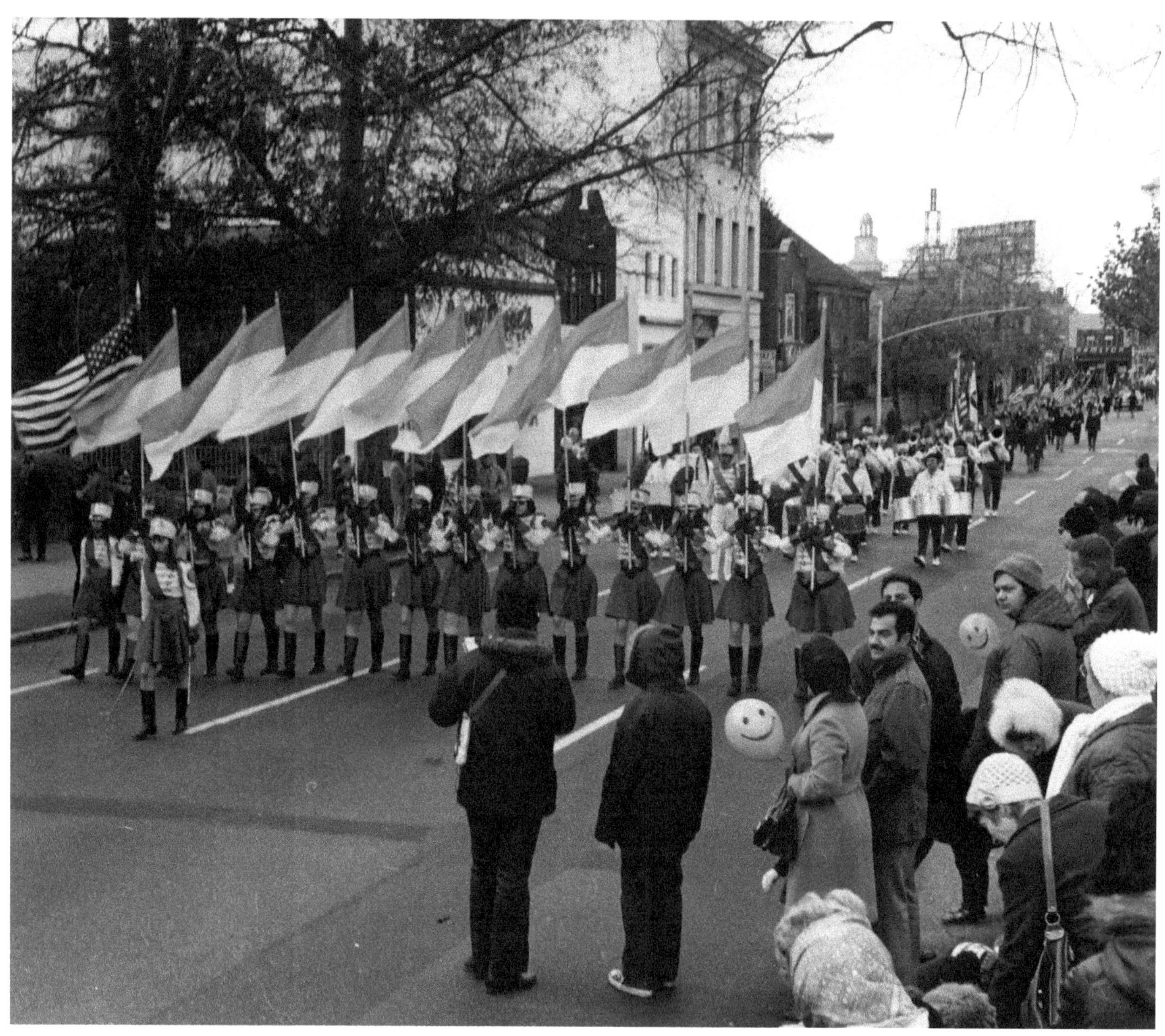

Marchers and spectators enjoy the 15th Annual Flushing Community holiday parade in 1973.

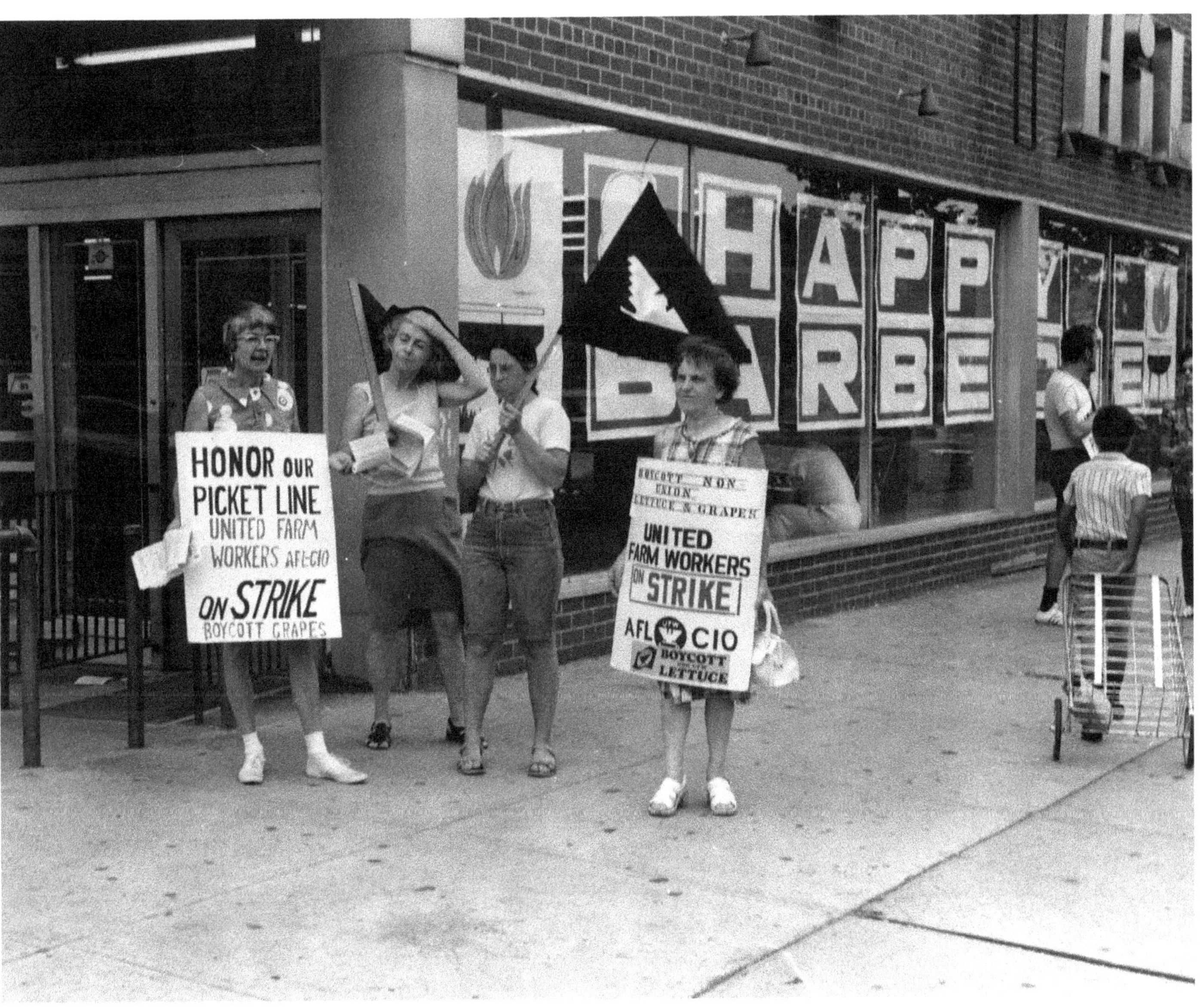

A 1974 demonstration by union members of the United Farm Workers AFL-CIO. They are picketing the Hills Supermarket at Franklin Avenue and Main Street, in Flushing, for selling non-union picked grapes and lettuce.

Notes on the Photographs

These notes, listed by page number, attempt to include all aspects known of the photographs. Each of the photographs is identified by the page number, photograph's title or description, photographer and collection, archive, and call or box number when applicable. Although every attempt was made to collect all data, in some cases complete data may have been unavailable due to the age and condition of some of the photographs and records.

ii **Playland, 1906**
Library of Congress
LC-USZ62-048242

vi **The Throgs Neck Bridge**
Library of Congress
351436pu

x **Trylon and Fountains at 1939 World's Fair**
Library of Congress
LC-G613-T01-35354

2 **Southern Railroad Ticket Office**
Courtesy of the QBPL, Long Island Division, Ron Ziel Collection
rz-unk-233

3 **Shinnecock Indians**
Library of Congress
3c19203u

4 **Albert Moritz Tavern**
Courtesy of the QBPL, Long Island Division, Illustrations Collection—Astoria
illustration-34488

5 **Early L.I.R.R. Steam Engine**
Courtesy of the QBPL, Long Island Division, Ron Ziel Collection
rz-unk-431

6 **Wilson's Mill in Astoria**
Courtesy of the QBPL, Long Island Division, Illustrations Collection—Astoria
illustration-52005

7 **Queens Village Hose Company**
QBPL, Long Island Division, Frederick J. Weber Photographs
w-8-31

8 **Long Island Express Delivery Service**
Courtesy of the QBPL, Long Island Division, William J. Rugen Collection
rugen-63

9 **Civil War Veterans at Newtown Hotel, 1891**
Courtesy of the QBPL, Long Island Division, Borough President of Queens Collection
bpq-372

10 **Grand Pier in North Beach**
Courtesy of the QBPL, Long Island Division, Borough President of Queens Collection
bpq-1773

11 **Ports at Long Island City**
Courtesy of the QBPL, Long Island Division, Queens Chamber of Commerce Collection
qcc-814

12 **Railroad Mishap at Queens Village, 1898**
Courtesy of the QBPL, Long Island Division, Hal B. Fullerton Photographs
hbf-9942

13 **Crowd at Burning Wreckage**
Courtesy of the QBPL, Long Island Division, Hal B. Fullerton Photographs
hbf-9920a

14 **Wreckage of the Russell Wedge Plow**
Courtesy of the QBPL, Long Island Division, Ron Ziel Collection
rz-unk-713

15 **Long Island City Courthouse**
Courtesy of the QBPL, Long Island Division, William J. Murray Photographs
wjm-21

16 **The Rockaway Boardwalk in 1900**
Library of Congress
4a09118u

17 **Dressed for the Beach**
Library of Congress
4a05580u

18 **Long Island Railroad Train En Route**
Courtesy of the QBPL, Long Island Division, Ron Ziel Collection
rz-unk-438

20 **Broadway in Flushing Facing West**
Courtesy of the QBPL, Long Island Division, William J. Murray Photographs
wjm-155 2

21 **Promoting the Rockaway Boardwalk**
Courtesy of the QBPL, Long Island Division, Emil R. Lucev Collection
erl-462

22 **Bodine Castle**
Library of Congress
122410pu

24 **Rockaway Pier and Bowling Alley, 1902**
Library of Congress
LC-USZ62-083219

25 **Boarding the Steamship Mobjack**
Library of Congress
4a11258u

26 **The Bowery at Rockaway Beach**
Library of Congress
4a11259u

27 **Tent City at the Beach**
Library of Congress
3b46513u

28 **Gravity Highway at the Playground**
Library of Congress
3b05370u

29 **Interstate Park Casino**
QBPL, Long Island Division, Frederick J. Weber Photographs
w-4-1

30 **Public School 34 in Queens Village**
QBPL, Long Island Division, Frederick J. Weber Photographs
w-1-9-8

31 **Maspeth Fire Fighters with Steam Engine**
QBPL, Long Island Division, Frederick J. Weber Photographs
w-8-30

32 **Fire Aftermath at Long Island City Terminal**
Courtesy of the QBPL, Long Island Division, Hal B. Fullerton Photographs
hbf-9917b

33 **LIRR Station, 1909**
QBPL, Long Island Division, Frederick J. Weber Photographs
w-13-596

34 **Construction of the Queensboro Bridge**
Courtesy of the QBPL, Long Island Division, Queens Chamber of Commerce Collection
qcc-269

35 **Construction of the Bridge, no. 2**
Courtesy of the QBPL, Long Island Division, Queens Chamber of Commerce Collection
qcc-272

36 **The Span Nearing Completion**
Courtesy of the QBPL, Long Island Division, Queens Chamber of Commerce Collection
qcc-275

37 **Opening Day Ceremonies, 1909**
Courtesy of the QBPL, Long Island Division, Queens Chamber of Commerce Collection
qcc-283

38 **Queens Public Library, 1910**
QBPL, Long Island Division, Queens Borough Public Library Photographs
qbpl-324

39 **Preparing Books for the Stacks**
QBPL, Long Island Division, Queens Borough Public Library Photographs
qbpl-338

40 **Fire Fighters Reading Books**
QBPL, Long Island Division, Queens Borough Public Library Photographs
qbpl-2

42 **Police Department Main Desk**
QBPL, Long Island Division, Queens Borough Public Library Photographs
qbpl-873

43 **Sub-Precinct Building at North Beach**
Courtesy of the QBPL, Long Island Division, Borough President of Queens Collection
bpq-1772-b

44 **Tent City Boardwalk**
Library of Congress
01985u

45 **Campers in Tent at Rockaway Beach**
Library of Congress
01987u

46 **Concert at Forest Park**
Library of Congress
LC-USZ62-45754

47 **Trolley Cars on Borden Avenue**
QBPL, Long Island Division, Frederick J. Weber Photographs
w12-288

49 **Crosstown Streetcar at Queens Plaza**
Courtesy of the QBPL, Long Island Division, Queens Chamber of Commerce Collection
qcc-1787

50 **The Sunnyside Yards**
Courtesy of the QBPL, Long Island Division, Eugene L. Armbruster Photographs
ea-qc-lic-9116

51 **Bavarian Band at Hofbrauhaus**
Library of Congress
LC-USZ62-44477

52 **Crossing at Main Street in Flushing**
Courtesy of the QBPL, Long Island Division, William J. Rugen Collection
rugen-407

53 **View of the Queensboro Bridge Plaza**
QBPL, Long Island Division, Frederick J. Weber Photographs
w-12-35

54 **Vernon Boulevard near 47th, 1915**
QBPL, Long Island Division, Frederick J. Weber Photographs
w-12-12a

55 **Jamaica Bay Neighborhood**
Library of Congress
3b06712u

56 **Busy Day Along Mott Avenue, 1916**
Courtesy of the QBPL, Long Island Division, Emil R. Lucev Collection
erl-468

57 **Farmers with Cabbages and Potatoes**
New York State Archives
NYSA_A3045-78_Dn_LpX7

58 **Rescue Device for Ice Skaters**
Library of Congress
3c11103u

59 **The Hell Gate Bridge**
Library of Congress
4a28410u

60 **Steinway Street in Astoria**
QBPL, Long Island Division, Frederick J. Weber Photographs
w-2-40

61 **Early Open-air Automobile**
QBPL, Long Island Division, Frederick J. Weber Photographs
w-5-7

62 **Aftermath of Rockaway Storm, 1920**
Library of Congress
3b25391u

63 **Broadway Avenue Subway Platform**
Courtesy of the QBPL, Long Island Division, Queens Chamber of Commerce Collection
qcc-1410

64 **The Van Siclen House on Springfield**
Courtesy of the QBPL, Long Island Division, Eugene L. Armbruster Photographs
ea-qc-ja-464

65 **Factory at Bushwick and Ridgewood**
Courtesy of the QBPL, Long Island Division, Eugene L. Armbruster Photographs
ea-kc-bu-314

66 **American Chicle Company Building**
Library of Congress
LC-USZ62-077888

67 **Interior of Our Lady of Grace Church**
Library of Congress
LC-USZ62-099379

68 **Ward Avenue Toward Steeplechase Park**
Courtesy of the QBPL, Long Island Division, Public Service Commission Photographs
psc-140-lirr

69 **Practicing a Putt**
Library of Congress
cph-3c16767

70 **Automobile on Jacks**
Library of Congress
LC-USZ62-087741

71 **Dutch Reformed Church, 1922**
Courtesy of the QBPL, Long Island Division, Eugene L. Armbruster Photographs
ea-qc-ja-186

72 **Dealership at Jamaica Avenue and Hempstead**
Courtesy of the QBPL, Long Island Division, Eugene L. Armbruster Photographs
ea-qc-ja-182a

73 **Long Island City Rail Yards**
New York State Archives
NYSA_A3045-78_Dn_LqX

74 **Hotel on Jamaica Avenue**
Courtesy of the QBPL, Long Island Division, Eugene L. Armbruster Photographs
ea-qc-ja-182

75 **H. C. Poppenhusen House**
Courtesy of the QBPL, Long Island Division, Eugene L. Armbruster Photographs
ea-qc-fl-307

76 **East Elmhurst Frame House**
Courtesy of the QBPL, Long Island Division, Eugene L. Armbruster Photographs
ea-unk-191

77 **Housing Boom Home in the Borough, 1920s**
Courtesy of the QBPL, Long Island Division, Eugene L. Armbruster Photographs
ea-unk-201

79 **Sledders at Jackson Heights**
Courtesy of the QBPL, Long Island Division, Illustrations Collection—Jackson Heights
illustrations-35772

80 **Eastern Queens LIRR Station**
Courtesy of the QBPL, Long Island Division, Queens Chamber of Commerce Collection
qcc-910

81 **Y.M.C.A. Basketball Champions for 1925**
QBPL, Long Island Division, Frederick J. Weber Photographs
w-17-44a

82 **The Neighborhood of Corona**
Courtesy of the QBPL, Long Island Division, Public Service Commission Photographs
psc-4-21-10-5

84 **Queens Village Row Houses**
Courtesy of the QBPL, Long Island Division, Eugene L. Armbruster Photographs
ea-qc-ja-9076

85 **Catholic Church in Queens Village, 1927**
Courtesy of the QBPL, Long Island Division, Eugene L. Armbruster Photographs
ea-qc-ja-9035

86 **Train Trestle at Springfield**
Courtesy of the QBPL, Long Island Division, Public Service Commission Photographs
psc-19-lirr

87 **Pony Cart on Braddock Avenue**
Courtesy of the QBPL, Long Island Division, Eugene L. Armbruster Photographs
ea-qc-ja-9084

88 **Clearing Trees for Roads**
Courtesy of the QBPL, Long Island Division, Eugene L. Armbruster Photographs
ea-qc-ja-9071

89 **Mayor Walker's Trip**
QBPL, Long Island Division, Frederick J. Weber Photographs
w-16-3-102a

90 **Hempstead Turnpike Paved**
QBPL, Long Island Division, Frederick J. Weber Photographs
w-2-90

91 **Floral Park, 1928**
QBPL, Long Island Division, Joseph Burt Photographs
jb001820

92 **Main Street in Flushing**
QBPL, Long Island Division, Frederick J. Weber Photographs
w-2-302

93 **Queens-Bellaire Bank**
QBPL, Long Island Division, Frederick J. Weber Photographs
w-1-7-30

94 **Book Bus Pioneer**
QBPL, Long Island Division, Queens Borough Public Library Photographs
qbpl-23

95 **Tennis Tournament Courts, 1928**
Courtesy of the QBPL, Long Island Division, Illustrations Collection—Jackson Heights
illustrations-35873

96 **The English Gables in Jackson Heights**
Courtesy of the QBPL, Long Island Division, Illustrations Collection—Jackson Heights
illustrations-35925

97 **Stars and Stripes Steamroller**
Courtesy of the QBPL, Long Island Division, Borough President of Queens Collection
bpq-842-a

98 **H. C. Bohack Grocery**
Courtesy of the QBPL, Long Island Division, Flushing Avenue Improvement Collection
flushing-ave-dp-18

100 **Bohack Headquarters**
Courtesy of the QBPL, Long Island Division, Flushing Avenue Improvement Collection
flushing-ave-dp-39

101 **Miniature Golf at Riker's Island, 1931**
Courtesy of the QBPL, Long Island Division, Eugene L. Armbruster Photographs
ea-ri-6

102 **Scene at Bookmobile**
QBPL, Long Island Division, Queens Borough Public Library Photographs
qbpl-947

103 **Jackson Heights Tennis Courts**
Courtesy of the QBPL, Long Island Division, Queens Chamber of Commerce Collection
qcc-212

104 **Northern Boulevard in Corona, 1930**
QBPL, Long Island Division, Frederick J. Weber Photographs
w-12-152a

105 **Pure Oil Purol Pep**
Courtesy of the QBPL, Long Island Division
rutter_dp25

106 **Dignitaries at Triborough Bridge**
Courtesy of the QBPL, Long Island Division, Borough President of Queens Collection
bpq-1498-a

107 **Streetcar at Vernon and 50th**
Courtesy of the QBPL, Long Island Division, Borough President of Queens Collection
bpq-1252-b4

108 **Sideswiped Streetcar at Hempstead**
QBPL, Long Island Division, Frederick J. Weber Photographs
w-12-207a

109 **Survey of Damaged Streetcar**
QBPL, Long Island Division, Frederick J. Weber Photographs
w-12-207b

110 **LIRR Station in Queens Village**
QBPL, Long Island Division, Frederick J. Weber Photographs
w-13-597b

111 **Ceremony for Queens Boulevard Underpass**
Courtesy of the QBPL, Long Island Division, Borough President of Queens Collection
bpq-1224-mb2

112 **Ceremony for New Subway Line**
Courtesy of the QBPL, Long Island Division, Borough President of Queens Collection
bpq-1493-j

113 **Intersection of Jackson and 82nd**
QBPL, Long Island Division, Frederick J. Weber Photographs
w-2-334b

114 **Cigar Shop in Queens Village**
QBPL, Long Island Division, Frederick J. Weber Photographs
w-2-95

116 **Flooded Street in Elmhurst**
Courtesy of the QBPL, Long Island Division, Borough President of Queens Collection
bpq-1646-a

117 **Quaker Meetinghouse on Northern**
Library of Congress
122350pu

118 **Brown Place in Maspeth**
QBPL, Long Island Division, Frederick J. Weber Photographs
w-12-123b

119 **Main Street at 40th in Flushing**
QBPL, Long Island Division, Frederick J. Weber Photographs
w-2-277a

121 **Melville's Thom McAn Shoe Store**
QBPL, Long Island Division, Frederick J. Weber Photographs
w-2-277b

122 **Kew Gardens Interchange**
Library of Congress
6a36480u

123 **Jamaica at Francis Lewis in Hollis**
QBPL, Long Island Division, Frederick J. Weber Photographs
w-2-296b

125 **Reading Material for the Infirm**
QBPL, Long Island Division, Queens Borough Public Library Photographs
qbpl-1471

126 **Catholic Church in Queens Village, 1936**
QBPL, Long Island Division, Frederick J. Weber Photographs
w-1-11-29c

127 **A 1937 Fender Bender**
QBPL, Long Island Division, Frederick J. Weber Photographs
w-5-6-a

128 **Deer's Head Diner in Bellerose**
QBPL, Long Island Division, Frederick J. Weber Photographs
w-1-2-27c

130 **Inside at the Deer's Head, 1938**
QBPL, Long Island Division, Frederick J. Weber Photographs
w-1-2-27b

131 **Royal Revelers Performance**
QBPL, Long Island Division, Frederick J. Weber Photographs
w-16-3-99a

132 **V. Caruso's Bar in Astoria**
QBPL, Long Island Division, Frederick J. Weber Photographs
w-1-2-73b

133 **Bird's-eye View of 1939 World's Fair**
Courtesy of the QBPL, Long Island Division, World's Fair Collection
wf001083

134 **Shops Along Northern Boulevard**
QBPL, Long Island Division, Frederick J. Weber Photographs
w-2-253

135 **Book Bus on Snowy Day, 1939**
QBPL, Long Island Division, Queens Borough Public Library Photographs
qbpl-1188

136 **Streetcar Collision on Jamaica Avenue**
QBPL, Long Island Division, Frederick J. Weber Photographs
w-5-15

137 **New York Municipal Airport**
Courtesy of the QBPL, Long Island Division, Queens Chamber of Commerce Collection
qcc-122

138 **Forest Hills Apartment Complex, 1941**
Library of Congress
LC-G12T-41289

139 **Belmont Park**
Library of Congress
LC-G612-T-53903

140 **New York World's Fair from the Flushing River**
Courtesy of the QBPL, Long Island Division, World's Fair Collection
wf000458

141 **Gates to the Fair on the Corona Side**
Library of Congress
LC-USZ62--2

142 **The World's Fair Station**
Courtesy of the QBPL, Long Island Division, William J. Rugen Collection
rugen-734

144 **Gates to the Fair on the Flushing Side**
Library of Congress
LC-USZ62--1

146 **Jackson Heights Golf Club Tournament**
Courtesy of the QBPL, Long Island Division, Tom Langan Collection
tl-4-illustration

147 **Hempstead Avenue at Springfield, 1940**
QBPL, Long Island Division, Frederick J. Weber Photographs
w-2-236

148 **Crowds at Library Event**
QBPL, Long Island Division, Queens Borough Public Library Photographs
qbpl-2142

149 **Sisters in Procession**
QBPL, Long Island Division, Frederick J. Weber Photographs
w-6-17b

150 **Outdoor Mass**
QBPL, Long Island Division, Frederick J. Weber Photographs
w-6-17q

151 **Courtyard Scene at Phipps Garden Apartments**
Library of Congress
LC-G612-T-37624

152 **Queens Boulevard in Elmhurst, 1940**
Courtesy of the QBPL, Long Island Division, Borough President of Queens Collection
bpq-7113-c2

153 **Scene of Demolition**
QBPL, Long Island Division, Frederick J. Weber Photographs
w-1-13-41b

154 **Queens Village Branch of QBPL**
QBPL, Long Island Division, Queens Borough Public Library Photographs
qbpl-2677

155 **Sunday Morning Traffic on Queens Past Grand**
Courtesy of the QBPL, Long Island Division, Borough President of Queens Collection
bpq-7113-d1

156 **Fresh Meadows Delicatessen Opening**
QBPL, Long Island Division, Frederick J. Weber Photographs
w-1-2-38b

157 **View to the West Along Hempstead**
QBPL, Long Island Division, Frederick J. Weber Photographs
w-2-230

158 **Skaters at World's Fair Ice-skating Rink**
Library of Congress
LC-G623-T-39258

160 **Railroad Overpass in Astoria**
QBPL, Long Island Division, Frederick J. Weber Photographs
w-2-232d

161 **Fountains at Forest Hills South**
Library of Congress
LC-G612-T-41291

162 **Service Station on Jamaica Avenue**
QBPL, Long Island Division, Frederick J. Weber Photographs
w-1-6-43a

163 **Flushing High School's Victory Corps**
Library of Congress
LC-USE6-D-007142

164 **Officers in Full Navy Blues**
QBPL, Long Island Division, Frederick J. Weber Photographs
w-16-3-83a

165 **Children at Queensbridge Housing Project**
Library of Congress
LC-USW3-04767-D

166 **First Day of Duty at Midtown Tunnel Office**
Library of Congress
8e01094u

167 **English Gables at 82nd near Roosevelt**
Courtesy of the QBPL, Long Island Division, Tom Langan Collection
tl-16-illustration

168 **Life in Corona, 1942**
Library of Congress
LC-USW3-013946-D

169 **The Elevated Tracks on Jamaica**
Library of Congress
LC-G613-T-46467

170 **Army Post Office Mail Inspection**
Courtesy of the QBPL, Long Island Division, Queens Chamber of Commerce Collection
qcc-794

171 **Percy J. Flint's Bar and Grill**
QBPL, Long Island Division, Frederick J. Weber Photographs
w-1-2-58b

172 **Scene at Lumberyard, 1945**
QBPL, Long Island Division, Frederick J. Weber Photographs
w-1-6-50c

173 **Lumber-making Machinery**
QBPL, Long Island Division, Frederick J. Weber Photographs
w-1-6-50e

174 **Blanket of Snow in Queens Village, 1947**
QBPL, Long Island Division, Frederick J. Weber Photographs
w-2-415h

175 **Jamaica Savings Bank**
QBPL, Long Island Division, Frederick J. Weber Photographs
w-2-415b

176 **Jumping the Curb in Hollis**
QBPL, Long Island Division, Frederick J. Weber Photographs
w-2-391c

177 **Stevedores Unloading Cargo Ship**
Courtesy of the QBPL, Long Island Division, Queens Chamber of Commerce Collection
qcc-939

178 **Squibb and Sons Headquarters**
Library of Congress
LC-G612-T-52819

180 **First Mail Service Flight by Helicopter**
Courtesy of the QBPL, Long Island Division, Queens Chamber of Commerce Collection
qcc-116a

181 **Topson Clothing at Long Island City**
Courtesy of the QBPL, Long Island Division, Queens Chamber of Commerce Collection
qcc-1432

182 **St. Luke's Church Interior**
Library of Congress
LC-G612-T-55215

183 **Girls at St. Patrick's Day Parade**
Library of Congress
01204u

184 **LIRR Steam Train Heading to Manhattan**
Courtesy of the QBPL, Long Island Division, Ron Ziel Collection, Jeffreay Winslow Photographs
rz-wsw-6

185 **Best Building Award for 1951**
Courtesy of the QBPL, Long Island Division, Queens Chamber of Commerce Collection
qcc-316

186 **Far Rockaway Bus Terminal, 1953**
Courtesy of the QBPL, Long Island Division, Emil R. Lucev Collection
erl-314

187 **F & R Machine Works**
Library of Congress
LC-G613-T-6461

188 **Borden Avenue Train Crossing**
QBPL, Long Island Division, Frederick J. Weber Photographs
w-13-761f

189 **Bodine Castle, 1960**
Library of Congress
122405pu

190 **Sunbathers at Linden Woods Swim Club**
Library of Congress
LC-G613-74401

192 **Sunbathers at Linden Woods no. 2**
Library of Congress
LC-G613-74403

193 **Sterling National Bank, 1963**
Library of Congress
LC-5a-28888

194 **Art Deco Terminal at LaGuardia, 1968**
Library of Congress
122389pu

196 **Story Time at the Library**
QBPL, Long Island Division, Queens Borough Public Library Photographs
qbpl-340

197 **School Art Show**
Courtesy of the QBPL, Long Island Division, Joseph A. Ullman Photographs
ullman-57-2

199 **The Triborough Bridge**
Library of Congress
351351pu

200 **Flushing Community Holiday Parade, 1973**
Courtesy of the QBPL, Long Island Division, Joseph A. Ullman Photographs
ullman-441-1

201 **Union Members Demonstration in Flushing**
Courtesy of the QBPL, Long Island Division, Joseph A. Ullman Photographs
ullman-598-1

HISTORIC PHOTOS OF QUEENS

The borough of Queens has been many things—a playground for wealthy Manhattanites, a recreation area for pleasure seekers, a highly industrialized pocket of New York City, and one of the most beautiful and residential sections of which the city can boast.

Queens is home to the Mets, airports LaGuardia in the north and JFK in the south, and a steady force behind New York City, sheltering its laborers, builders, taxi drivers, teachers, fire fighters, police officers, lawyers, businesspeople, and everyone else for more than a century.

From the borough's rural origins to its multiethnic, metropolitan character of recent times, *Historic Photos of Queens* celebrates the legacy of those who dared to head east, who settled the countryside, and who tempted the Atlantic when they built lives on the Rockaway peninsula. Nearly 200 images reproduced in vivid black-and-white, with captions and introductions, tell the story.

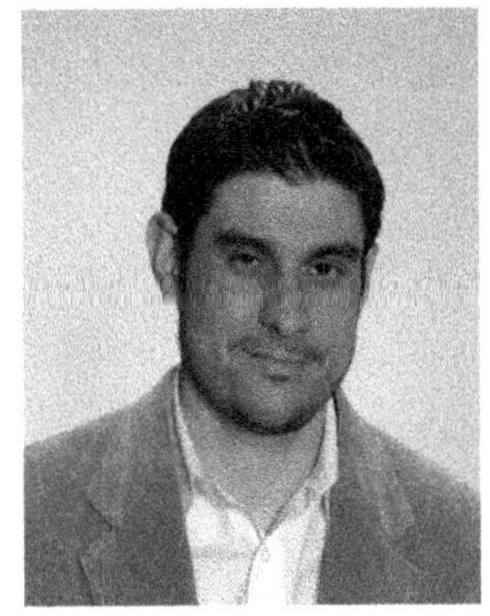

Kevin Sean O'Donoghue is a fourth-generation resident of Queens and has lived there for most of the past 30 years—having left and returned both by choice and by necessity. He grew up and currently resides in Bayside with his wife, Kate, where they have personally added to the borough's growth with children Desmond Jane, Deirdre, and Declan.

In addition to being a writer, Mr. O'Donoghue has taught English and writing at New York universities and is a practicing attorney before the courts of the State of New York. While he enjoys the beaches of Rockaway, rooting for the home team at Citi Field, and life in the borough generally, he most enjoys getting on a train in hectic Penn Station and pulling into serene Queens just 25 minutes later.

WWW.TURNERPUBLISHING.COM

www.ingramcontent.com/pod-product-compliance
Lightning Source LLC
LaVergne TN
LVHW060613110826
845154LV00003B/77

9781684420513